FORM AND FEELING

FORM AND FEELING

THE MAKING OF CONCRETISM IN BRAZIL

Antonio Sergio Bessa, Editor

BRONXMUSEUM FORDHAM UNIVERSITY PRESS

New York 2021

Visit us online at www.fordhampress.com.

Library of Congress Control Number: 2020922741

Printed in the United States of America

23 22 21 5 4 3 2 1

First edition

CONTENTS

FORM AND FEELING

POSTEVERYTHING—AN INTRODUCTION

Antonio Sergio Bessa

On May 27, 1971, six months after moving to New York on a Guggenheim Fellowship, neoconcrete artist Hélio Oiticica had the opportunity to meet with concrete poet Haroldo de Campos, who was in town following a brief stay in Austin, Texas. The two men met in the lobby of the Chelsea Hotel where Campos was staying, and there they recorded an interview published shortly after in the weekly *Flor do Mal*, a broadside that for a short period was the voice of the Brazilian counterculture. Their meeting was of particular relevance, as it seemed to put to rest the decade-old diatribe that pitched concrete artists and poets against their neoconcrete counterparts. A particularly important moment happened toward the end of the interview, as Oiticica suddenly seemed to realize that pivotal moments in European culture had happened as the "culmination of an intellectual refinement, differently of much that happens in Brazil, which appears as if discovered for the first time." Oiticica's intuition of a discrepancy between how modernism evolved in Europe and Brazil predates the more informed thesis that sociologist Roberto Schwarz would put forth merely five years later in *Ao vencedor as batatas* (The potatoes go to the winner), his startling charge that Brazil was condemned by the "machinery of colonialism" to embrace liberal ideas impossible to put in practice in a country still relying on slave work.[1] The recording captures Oiticica in a genuine moment of discovery, as if wondering about the forces that caused the emergence of concretism and neoconcretism in Brazil; or, what exactly was the cultural process that led to the flourishing of geometric art in the country during that period?

Half a century later, Oiticica's disquiet echoes in academic circles as historians and critics look back at the postwar era in Brazil attempting to piece together disparate elements into a cohesive narrative. For starters, how to account for the fact that the "constructive project in Brazilian art," to paraphrase Aracy Amaral,[2] coincided with a brief democratic interlude folded in between two brutal dictatorial phases?[3] Although Ferreira Gullar—in his 1969 collection of essays, *Vanguarda e subdesenvolvimento: Ensaios sobre arte* (The avant-garde and underdevelopment: Essays on art)[4]—has already polemically approached the challenges in putting forward a rigorous formalist program in a country still grappling with the colonial machinery, the topic is still worth exploring. For despite the many lacunae and contradictions, Brazil's brief but intense constructivist period stands as an intriguing episode in art history that conveys a more complex image of our global village, particularly in regard to the reliance of European modernism on the colonialist structure. With the benefit of hindsight, recent studies approaching the aesthetics of concretism have attempted to break away from the polemics as a way to establish a more productive narrative of the era. In *The Object of the Atlantic: Concrete Aesthetics in Cuba, Brazil and Spain, 1868–1968*, for instance, Rachel Price commended Gullar for his "keen" critique of concrete poetry. She noted, however, that "in a populist turn, he opposed 'realism'—understood as 'committed' and appropriate to a nationalist project—to 'formalism,' which he claimed turned its back on Brazilian reality and sought an irresponsible universalism." Summing up her argument, Price suggested that those early writings by Gullar (and Ronaldo Brito) "missed the extent to which form was a theme of 1960s Brazil."[5]

Form was not merely a theme but rather a developmental program that aimed to correct in five years the erratic course set forth by an incipient republic. This developmental zest was shared quasi unanimously among architects, artists, writers, and intellectuals intent on restructuring the country (socially, culturally, and politically) based on the exploration of new forms. In that context, the creation of new forms also entailed the formation of a new individual. Not unlike the European countries that inspired it, Brazil's "constructive project" also carried with it an educational component that, to paraphrase Mário Pedrosa, would prepare children "to think correctly and to act with reason."[6] Considered in this context, one could argue that the campaign inveighed against concretism in the late 1960s and its critique of reason and technology strikes as a misunderstanding of that pivotal moment in the aftermath of World War II when the outline of a global village was being delineated. Indeed, with the proliferation of new media such as portable typewriters, tape recorders, and photographic cameras, the means of artistic production was bound to sacrifice regional characteristics as the price for participating in the global dialogue.

In his introduction to *Vanguarda e subdesenvolvimento*, Gullar pointedly asks whether a European or North American concept of the avant-garde could be valid in an underdeveloped country like Brazil.[7] Aware of the economic and political pressures exerted by international powers bent on controlling underdeveloped countries, Gullar articulated the mechanics of cultural subjugation thus: "The old is the domination, among us, of the past and also of the present, because our present is dominated by those who bring the new. While we need industry and knowhow, which they possess, with this industry and knowhow comes domination. Hence, the new for us is, contradictorily, our freedom and our submission."[8] In face of such daunting predicament in which the system seemed rigged from the start, navigating between "the new" and "the old" was not merely a matter of aesthetics but tantamount to crossing a cultural, political, and social minefield. The failure of our republic to provide a sense of identity to the country weighs heavily in this equation. Founded in 1889 and constituted for the most part as a succession of military governments, the Republic of Brazil came into being precisely at the same time when the main powers in Europe were turning to design and art as tools for asserting national identity and autonomy in a new landscape transformed by the industrial revolution. One need only to consider the proliferation of new movements such as Arts and Crafts in the England, Art Nouveau in Belgium and France, and later the German Werkbund—movements that paved the way to modernist models such as the Bauhaus—to realize that notions related to industry, knowhow, and market were aligned with national politics and ideology. Indeed, the international modernist movement of the early twentieth century was the product of the heated style wars in the late nineteenth century among industrialized European countries—what Oiticica would call "the culmination of an intellectual refinement." As it happened, given the lack of a strong visual arts tradition in Brazil, a productive dialogue with European models of modernity could not be taken for granted, and our romance with the avant-garde materialized rather through literature in the work of great precursors such as Joaquim de Sousândrade. Nonetheless, mistrust of the avant-garde in Brazil was deep-rooted regardless of one's political affiliation, as can be attested in Roberto Schwarz's 1987 analysis of Augusto de Campos's "Póstudo" (Posteverything, 1985), in which he mocked the poem's conclusion (the word *mudo*, "mute") as something futile and inconsequent that registered "the failure and irrelevance of the cultural avant-garde movements in our century that were nevertheless remarkable."[9]

Playing with the militaristic origin of the expression *avant-garde*, literary scholar Marjorie Perloff has suggested that Brazilian concrete poetry ought rather be seen as part of the *arrière-garde*, the troops that in battles finish the job initiated by the frontlines: "When an *avant-garde* movement is no longer a novelty, it is the role of the *arrière-garde* to complete its mission, to ensure its success."[10] In sum, Perloff's analogy allows us to analyze the outcomes of a specific cultural moment in relation to the broader historical continuum to which it relates. If we are to agree with Perloff, the emergence of concretism in Brazil in the early 1950s did not represent "the new" but rather the culmination of a process initiated half a century earlier in Europe. Of course, the idea of an arrière-garde is not unique to the so-called avant-garde in underdeveloped environs; the same argument can be used to explain Max Bill's role as an artist, architect, and educator. Having studied at the Bauhaus for one year, Bill was keen on hiring key Bauhaus instructors such as Josef Albers and Walter Peterhans during his tenure as the director of the Hochschule für Gestaltung in Ulm, Germany. We can also cite as branches of this arrière-garde the Illinois Institute of Technology, led by Mies van der Rohe, and the Black Mountain College under Albers. Considered in its broadest scope, the work proposed by the avant- and arrière-gardes entailed first and foremost a restructuring of the educational system, a project pioneered in the early nineteenth century by educators such as Johan Heinrich Pestalozzi and Friedrich Froebel who proposed new models focused on how sense perception leads to thinking. Their ideas, particularly Froebel's work on the role of play in early childhood, would eventually be reflected in some of the most advanced educational experiments of the early twentieth century.

In Brazil, the search for continuity with the European modernist program, as Perloff suggested, is best exemplified by the Noigandres poets' systematic engagement with the poetics of Ezra Pound, starting in the late 1940s (when they took their name from a neologism found in Pound's Canto 20) and culminating with the translation of *ABC of Reading* in 1975. More importantly, they clearly outlined the pedagogical drive of their enterprise in early theoretical texts that cited Guillaume Apollinaire, Sergei Eisenstein, and Stéphane Mallarmé as precursors of a new mode of reading.[11] Indeed, for the pioneers of concretism in Brazil, whether from São Paulo or from Rio, the main concern relied on understanding how one's mind operates in a new environment transformed by industry. But the aspiration to form new individuals through education reform—Pedrosa's ideal citizen who will not "applaud hysterical dictators"— collapsed as the 1964 coup brought to a halt programs such as Paulo Freire's Plano Nacional de Alfabetização (National Literacy Plan).

Half a century after the demise of its constructivist project, Brazil still grapples with issues related to nationalism and art as evidenced in the recent episodes related to government support for culture. Early in the morning on January 17, 2020, a Twitter post by Secretary of Culture Roberto Alvim announcing a $4.8 million investment in arts programs sent out chills throughout the Internet. Widely disseminated through social media, Alvim's cultural vision for the country paraphrased an infamous speech by Adolf Goebbels from 1933, calling for a new art free of sentimentalism to better serve the state aims: "a culture that doesn't destroy, but one that will save our youth."

Augusto de Campos, "Póstudo," 1984.

QUIS

MUDAR TUDO

MUDEI TUDO

AGORAPÓSTUDO

EXTUDO

MUDO

Alvim's appalling delivery prompted a widespread outcry and he was demoted from his position by the day's end. More importantly, his bizarre, dangerous flirt with Nazi ideology laid bare the stakes culture play in society.

The fourteen essays that comprise *Form and Feeling: The Making of Concretism in Brazil* tackle a number of key topics related to that unprecedented era in cultural production in Brazil—from the emergence of concrete art in Brazil and the groundbreaking art education initiatives that began in the late 1940s to the Brazilian counterculture of the 1960s and early 1970s. The collection opens with an essay by José T. Lira who takes a close look at the paradoxes in the work of the architect-artist Flávio de Carvalho whose controversial career was launched following the upheavals related to the Semana de Arte Moderna in the 1922. A larger-than-life figure who experimented with different disciplines and media, Carvalho provides an important link between the wave of experimentation that characterized Brazilian art in the 1960s and 1970s and the strategies of early modernism. Michael Asbury (essay no. 2) offers a thoroughly researched and pointed overview of the main events that helped solidify the constructivist aesthetics in Brazil. Departing from a consideration on the "rift" between São Paulo artists and their counterparts in Rio de Janeiro, Asbury offers insight on foundational texts by Mário Pedrosa and Ferreira Gullar and identifies common traits with ideas proposed by Herbert Read, Alfred North Whitehead, and Susanne Langer. Adele Nelson (essay no. 3) probes the contradictions of importing the Bauhaus model to Brazil and highlights the role of the first two museum-sponsored art schools in negotiating claims on the German school and its pedagogy for the emerging Brazilian postwar avant-garde. Martin Mäntele (essay no. 4) provides an overview of how the Ulm School of Design came into being with support from the Marshall Plan as an effort to promote reconstruction in post–World War II Germany. Mäntele offers a vivid account of Max Bill's tenure as the school's first director and his efforts to put together a faculty based on his experience as a student at Bauhaus. Luisa Valle (essay no. 5) approaches the work of the elusive artist Mary Vieira, who, like Almir Mavignier, opted early in her career to further her training at the Ulm School of Design under Max Bill. Valle's essay focuses for the most part on Vieira's most iconic work, the interactive sculpture *Polyvolume*, while also astutely situating the artist's practice within the context of post–World War II Brazilian art. Claudia Saldanha (essay no. 6) offers a brief overview of Lina Bo Bardi's effort to create an art school in Rio de Janeiro in the early 1960s. Given Bo Bardi's extensive list of accomplishments in the area of architecture and museology, it is not entirely surprising that her efforts in the pedagogical area would be obscured over the years. The fact that Rubens Gerchman asked Bo Bardi a decade later to participate in the nucleus tasked with restructuring the school in the early 1970s indicates that arts education played an important role in her holistic vision.

Part II spotlights some key figures and moments of the Brazilian counterculture of the late 1960s and early 1970s. Frederico Coelho (essay no. 7) considers the dénouement of the heroic phase of the constructive project in Brazil at the end of the 1960s as it gradually gives way to a counterculture movement driven for the most part through several publications that allowed young artists to follow from afar the significant cultural changes fueled by sociopolitical unrest. Besides the appearance of new voices and tendencies, the 1970s are also notable for how artists that emerged under the constructivist paradigm responded to a new sociopolitical landscape fostered by the military regime. Claudia Calirman (essay no. 8) examines a series of works by Lygia Pape and Anna Maria Maiolino that reflect on the constructed identity of women in Brazilian society. My "Word-Drool" (essay no. 9) explores a series of texts produced by Lygia Clark in the early 1970s while undergoing psychoanalysis in Paris. Curator Fernanda Lopes (essay no. 10) offers an insightful overview of the brief career of Emil Forman, while also revealing the complex cultural landscape following the heydays of the concrete/neoconcrete diatribe. Having studied under Ivan Serpa at the Ipanema Research Center in the early 1970s, Forman was recognized at a young age for works that dealt with his personal life as the son of Czech immigrants. Marcos Augusto Gonçalves (essay no. 11) takes a fresh look at Glauber Rocha's infamous short documentary on the memorial for early modernist painter Emiliano di Cavalcanti. A dazzling, anarchic tour de force, Rocha's film is an unforgiving critique of Brazil's modernist ambition and a fitting closure to this group of essays.

The three essays in part III consider the resurgence of the Romantic poet Joaquim de Sousândrade (1833–1902), half a century after his death, through the critical work of concrete poets Augusto de Campos and Haroldo de Campos. Eduardo Jorge de Oliveira (essay no. 12), focuses on the already mentioned encounter between Hélio Oiticica and Haroldo de Campos in New York. Brazilian poet Simone Homem de Mello (essay no. 13) provides a comparative analysis of German poet Arno Holz and Sousândrade, whose productions had been dismissed by mainstream historiography and reassessed by the Noigandres poets in the 1960s. And Eduardo Sterzi (essay no. 14) explores Sousândrade's epic poem *O Guesa* in all its Pan-American breadth, vis-à-vis the global spread of capitalism and the displacement of indigenous people.

While it might seem harsh to suggest that Brazil did not have a visual arts tradition strong enough to account for the constructivist impetus of the 1950s, it is undeniable that our experimental tradition is rooted in literature, as these essays on Sousândrade indicate. Oiticica, who in his meeting with Campos at the Chelsea Hotel seems eager to discuss Sousândrade's period in New York, would dedicate a great part of his years in New York to a kind of experimental writing that taps into this tradition. His copious output, which has been approached insightfully by Frederico Coelho, challenges us to reconsider the complex legacy of Brazil's constructivist project.

Notes

1 / Schwarz's study approaches the nineteenth-century bourgeois romance novel in Brazil as a "system of ambiguities" that he also detects in the Russian romance: "In Russia also, modernity got lost in the vastness of the territory and the social inertia." In an aside he noted that it might have been easier for the visual arts through the "adoring, citing, parroting, sacking, adapting or devouring of manners and modes that reflected, in their failure, the kind of stiff neck in which we recognize ourselves." Roberto Schwarz, *Ao vencedor as batatas: Forma literária e processo social nos inicios do romance brasileiro* (São Paulo: Livraria Duas Cidades, 1977), 26–28; my translation.

2 / Aracy A. Amaral, ed., *Projeto construtivo brasileiro na arte* (São Paulo: Pinacoteca do Estado, 1977).

3 / Brazil's short democratic period starts after the suicide of Gétulio Vargas, who ruled the country almost intermittently from 1930 to 1954, and ends in 1964, when democratically elected João Gulart is ousted by a military coup.

4 / Ferreira Gullar, *Vanguarda e subdesenvolvimento: Ensaios sobre arte*, 2nd ed. (Rio de Janeiro: Editora Civilização Brasileira, 1978).

5 / Rachel Price, *The Object of the Atlantic: Concrete Aesthetics in Cuba, Brazil and Spain, 1868–1968* (Evanston, IL: Northwestern University Press, 2014), 185.

6 / Mario Pedrosa, "Crescimento e criação," in *Forma e percepção estética: Textos escolhidos II*, ed. Otília Arantes (São Paulo: Editora da Universidade de São Paulo, 1996), 71–79.

7 / Gullar, *Vanguarda e subdesenvolvimento*, 19; my translation. In the original: "Um conceito de 'vanguarda' estética, válido na Europa ou nos Estados Unidos, terá igual validez num país subdesenvolvido como o Brasil?"

8 / Gullar, 24; my translation. In the original: "O velho é a dominação, sobre nós, do passado e também do presente, porque o nosso presente é dominado por aqueles mesmos que nos trazem o novo. Precisamos da indústria e do *know-how*, que eles têm, mas com essa indústria e esse know-how, de que necessitamos para nos libertar, vem a dominação. Assim, o novo é, para nós, contraditoriamente, a liberdade e a submissão."

9 / Roberto Schwarz, "Marco histórico" [Historic milestone], in *Que horas são* (São Paulo: Companhia das Letras, 1987), 61.

10 / Marjorie Perloff, *Unoriginal Genius: Poetry by Other Means in the New Century* (Chicago: University of Chicago Press, 2010), 53.

11 / See "Pilot Plan for Concrete Poetry," in *Novas: Selected Writings of Haroldo de Campos*, ed. Antonio Sergio Bessa and Odile Cisneros (Evanston, IL: Northwestern University Press, 2007), 217.

1

ARCHITECTURAL MECHANISMS AND BODY TECHNIQUES
The *Experiências* of Flávio de Carvalho

José T. Lira

From Madrid to Istanbul, from New York to Berlin, some of the works and ideas of Flávio de Carvalho (1899–1973) have recently emerged on the international art scene.[1] A restless protagonist in the history of Brazilian modernism, he has been the subject of a fair amount of studies over the years in Brazil.[2] Whereas some earlier studies tended to look closely at key aspects of his extensive work, most seem to have fallen into the biographical trap of the "total artist," the "romantic revolutionary," the "emotive cannibal," and so on. More recent monographs have proposed new approaches to Carvalho's complex activity. Yet they too fail to look beyond this or that specific field of interest: architecture, the visual arts, theater, fashion, performance, design, and so on.[3] None of the existing approaches, however, seem to grasp the major paradoxes his work addresses.

Some of the most exciting readings of Carvalho's work have focused on his pioneering experiments in performance, namely, *Experiência no. 2* (1931) and *Experiência no. 3* (1956). In *Experiência no. 2*, Carvalho marched in the opposite direction to a Corpus-Christi procession in downtown São Paulo, wearing a hat and challenging the emotional limits of the Catholic mass of worshipers around him. In *Experiência no. 3*, he paraded through the streets of the city's center wearing a very unusual male costume, which he called a "new look for the summer." Both *experiências* received wide media coverage.[4] The first performance thrilled the local press and led, three months later, to the publication of the book *Experiência no. 2, realizada sobre uma procissão de Corpus-Christi; uma possível teoria e uma experiência* (*Experience no. 2*, undertaken across a Corpus-Christi procession; a possible theory and an experience/experiment),[5] which he illustrated with a series of narrative caricatures. *Experiência no. 3* entailed careful preparation as Carvalho arranged for interviews and press releases; produced descriptive sketches, pamphlets, and photographs to be published on prestigious magazines; rehearsed a fully dressed public outing; and garnered the support of intellectuals, journalists, and actresses as well as wide news coverage for the event, including the new medium of television.

With respect to those two *experiências*, the Brazilian concrete poets Haroldo de Campos and Décio Pignatari hailed Carvalho as the inventor of happenings in Brazil,[6] and several critics have recently stressed the anticipatory role of his work to neoconcrete experimental exercises on freedom, rupture, and appearance of the late 1950s and the 1960s, as well as to nonobjective art, that aimed to synthesize mental and sensorial experiences. Taking a closer look at Carvalho's two *experiências* might indeed offer a great opportunity to grasp a rather anticipatory discursive strategy that Carvalho was to employ throughout his career—not only in these two performances and within the performative arts (in dance, theater, scenography, and costume design) but also as a procedure that was intrinsic to his approach to architecture, urban planning, drawing, painting, sculpture, journalism, literature, and theory, as well as in the development of his private life, body, and sense of self.

In this regard, the image on the front cover of the small personal portfolio documenting his architectural projects between 1927 and 1929 is quite suggestive. The image depicts a yellow steel beam in perspective supporting a thin white concrete slab. The slab seems to be worked by two green mechanical hands, a sort of a screwdriver, and a classical bust. The screwdriver seems to twist the iron grid inside the slab, the bust is holding a compass and stands on top of a book: tradition on one hand, workforce and the building site on the other. The ensemble sits on a pile of drawing sheets, and we can read at its side the inscription: "Matter follows reasoning." In other words, if the preeminence of logic is seen as a pathway to progress, progress itself refers to a rational or a spiritual force rather than to material progress, thus requiring readiness for change and the exercise of new meanings and domains of life.

RESHAPING PRIVACY

Indeed, Carvalho's country home—Fazenda Capuava, which he designed and built in the outskirts of São Paulo in the 1930s—is quite revealing in this regard.[7]

Often described as a site free of moral and social conventions, as a region of excesses and devious behavior, the dwelling of this stubborn forty-year-old bachelor might indeed be understood as a perfect arena for certain unusual kinds of domesticity—contrary to nuclear, monogamous, stable, and moralized family and marriage—or a sort of laboratory, if not a totemic machine, designed to bring eroticism back to social life. In fact, his notoriety as *enfant terrible* in life, sex, and art, diving headlong into a roaring sociocultural and emotional life was by no means accidental but the result of a psychosocial self-elaboration. It was not by chance that in the early 1930s he devoted himself to writing an unpublished manuscript, "Mechanism of loving emotion,"[8] in which he focused on the tumultuous world of human desires, base instincts and emotions, sexual and love anxieties, the cyclical struggles between men and women, and the ethical, psychic, and anthropological basis of matriarchy, patriarchy, monogamy, adultery, and incest.

Finished in 1938, the house soon became his first residence and throughout his life a private platform for socioerotic staging: "sumptuous, lubricious, and dramatic," "a mix of a temple and an aircraft," and although rural, in no way could it be described as a haven where to lament for "the loss of simplicity and ingenuity."[9] Conceived, inhabited, and animated by an avant-garde artist whose activity had been informed by a strong modernist and anthropophagic sensibility and a high awareness of the "principle of pleasure," Carvalho's house was entirely devoted to the art of living: sensual life, feast, and festivity. The architect himself has emphasized the project's poetic tenor thus: "The conception of the whole house is a pure product of imagination, trying to create an ideal way of living."[10]

The house stands out in the landscape with the imposing trapezoidal silhouette of its double-height main hall, almost hermetic, intercepted by the long reinforced concrete pergola structures, covering two long lateral terraces. Sitting on a small elevation, the property does not show itself in its entirety, lacking references to human scale such as windows, parapets, or doors. Its basic design, albeit strongly iconographic and perfectly symmetrical as often is the case in his projects, does not easily conform to available classifications, such as modernism, classicism, expressionism, or other *-isms*—not because of its references to different epochs and cultures, but because of the way it appeals to them without embracing any eclecticism of style. The design combines archaic allusions with current, unusual, or exotic solutions, like the reference to a domestic program or the use of modern technics and materials, the combination of machine aesthetics and primitivism, the majestic scale of the main door, the profusion of indigenous hammocks, and so on.

Indeed the house is characterized by its generous living and hosting spaces: in addition to the main hall and the large terraces and side patios in the front and the six bedrooms placed in the opposite wing, there are three other rooms also

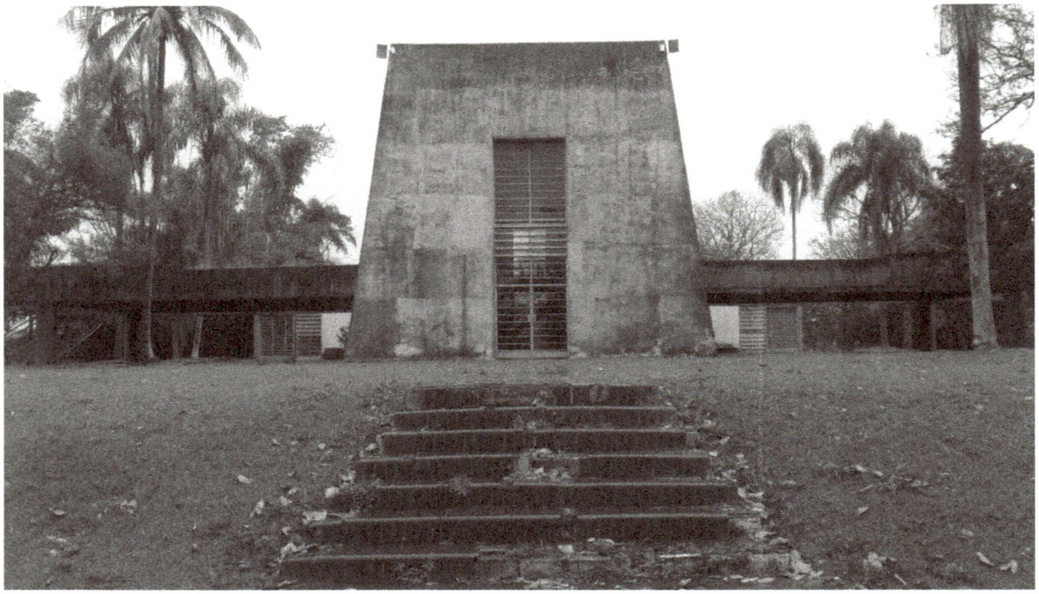

Flávio de Carvalho, *Fazenda Capuava*, ca. 1930s. Photograph by José T. Lira.

opened to the back, including a library that would soon become his main studio and an idiosyncratic "ancestral room," a sort of Oedipal chapel, scenically set with the family's gloomy furniture, crocheted table cloths, worn-out pillows, velvet curtains, his mother's objects, and family portraits hanging on the walls. Rooms and bedrooms are connected by a succession of halls and aisles that limit inner circulation as in a labyrinthine itinerary, typical of libertine interiors,[11] which provide autonomy to each one of the rooms and direct escape to the outside.

The largest and liveliest part of the house—the huge trapezoidal main room, which had no interior partitions and was informally decorated[12]—is both a living and dining room, as well as a space for performances and recitals on the mezzanine protruding on top of the dining table. On the ceiling, a vertical aluminum plate was illuminated by colored lamps that ascended in clusters, also reflecting the cloth bands curtain that covered the monumental main door (according to Carvalho, dancing "in and out with the wind and the eventual rhythm of the music").[13] The use of the inner space evidently changed over the years, but it seems to have always been heavily invested of symbolism and emotional values. Be it from the point of view of the subversion of Victorian domesticity or of the aseptic modernist interiors, every element in Carvalho's house exudes a lust for ornament. In the kitchen and bathrooms, the walls and cabinets are lined with gleaming aluminum plates and their windows protected by shutters of the same material, as if to accentuate its connotations to machines. In the main hall, in turn, the walls are covered with slats of wood at half a height and dark colors on top as opposed to the vivid colors of curtains and upholsteries that brightened the room. One of its most notable elements is the main fireplace, ingeniously planned to bring together the four elements of nature. Located in the middle of the room, the wood burns in the semicircular cast-iron basket hanging from the wall. Over the flames, a bright aluminum dome is connected to a small water fountain lit by lamps of various colors. With the heating of the aluminum, the water poured over the dome vaporizes the whole room with colored steam. Also in that hall, the dining table could be mistaken for an altar: designed by Carvalho in chrome-plated metal and a one-inch-thick Belgian crystal top, it was able to accommodate fourteen people in comfortable armchairs of the same material. Spotlights beneath the table produced unusual reflections of porcelain, cutlery, and crystals over the surfaces and diners' bodies, often obscuring the food they ate but allowing perfect view of their legs and torsos. The strategy flirted with surrealistic investments in trompe l'oeil techniques in domestic interiors. In fact, the visual treatment of the place of repast—a first-rate cannibal theme, by the way—evokes Louis Aragon's manifesto for the *réforme des habitations*, with their "radiant tables for love."[14]

Over the furniture and on the walls, there was a small, but carefully installed, imaginary museum: a bric-a-brac of amulets, weapons, and other Indigenous artifacts; ceramics from the Andes, the Amazonian, and the Brazilian Northeast regions; sacred images and fine porcelain sets; a carved figurehead from a São Francisco river boat; a Chinese mask; and a stuffed alligator head. Mixing up different provenances, epochs, forms, materials, and social strata, combining the popular, the modern, the bizarre, and the ritual, densely accumulated in space, the objects seemed to interact with one another to create an atmosphere of displacement, sensuality, buzz, and detachment. Everything staged as if those objects were the "bones of the world," as he referred to in the title of his 1936 book: some of them were inherited, others were entirely new or found in the course of life, and arranged in a sort of collection "as if to suggest comparisons and contrasts," or to sustain, as fetishes, spiritual bonds with individuals, as if belonging to the "morphology of the waste of lost worlds."[15]

Carefully planned to accommodate a reasonable amount of people—as well as conflicting imaginaries and more or less informal, ritualized activities—from beginning to end one finds clear psychological, ethical, aesthetic, and political statements in the house's role to resist the bourgeois family life model: pacified, inviolable, austere, civilized. Far from being a place of seclusion, Carvalho's house would indeed be marked by an enormous social activity. It is significant that he kept a guest's album, which over the years accumulated autographs and messages from visitors, and the photographs he took from his guests in and around the house with his Rolleiflex camera. In his guest book, poet Murilo Mendes wrote: "Flavio's house was built under the sign of reason and imagination. I think it would please both

Flávio de Carvalho, *Experiência no. 3*, 1956. Photo by Norberto Esteves and Jack Pires for *Tribuna da Imprensa*. Collection of Hugo Segawa.

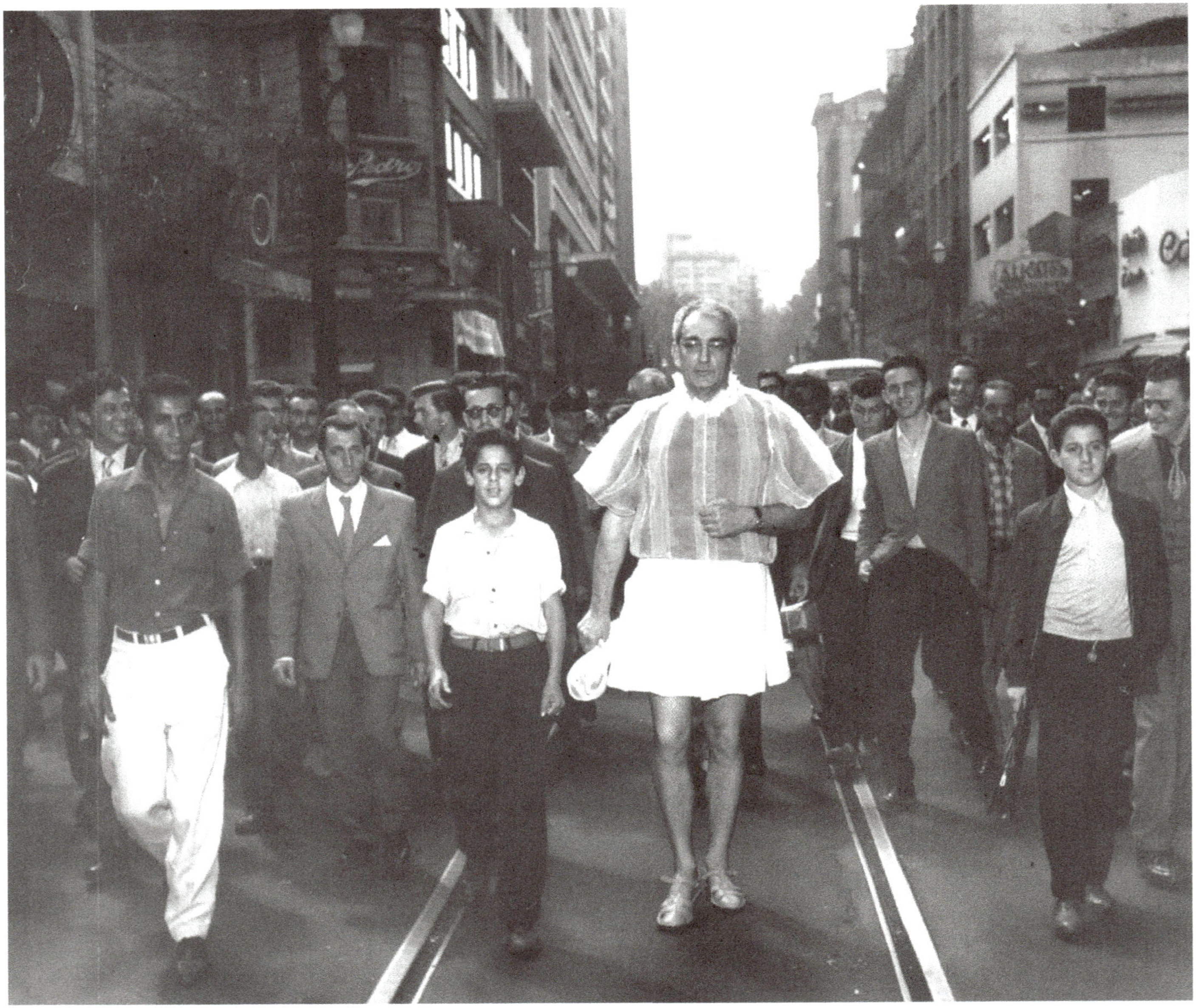

Flávio de Carvalho, *Experiência no. 3*, 1956. Photo by Norberto Esteves and Jack Pires for *Tribuna da Imprensa*. Collection of Hugo Segawa.

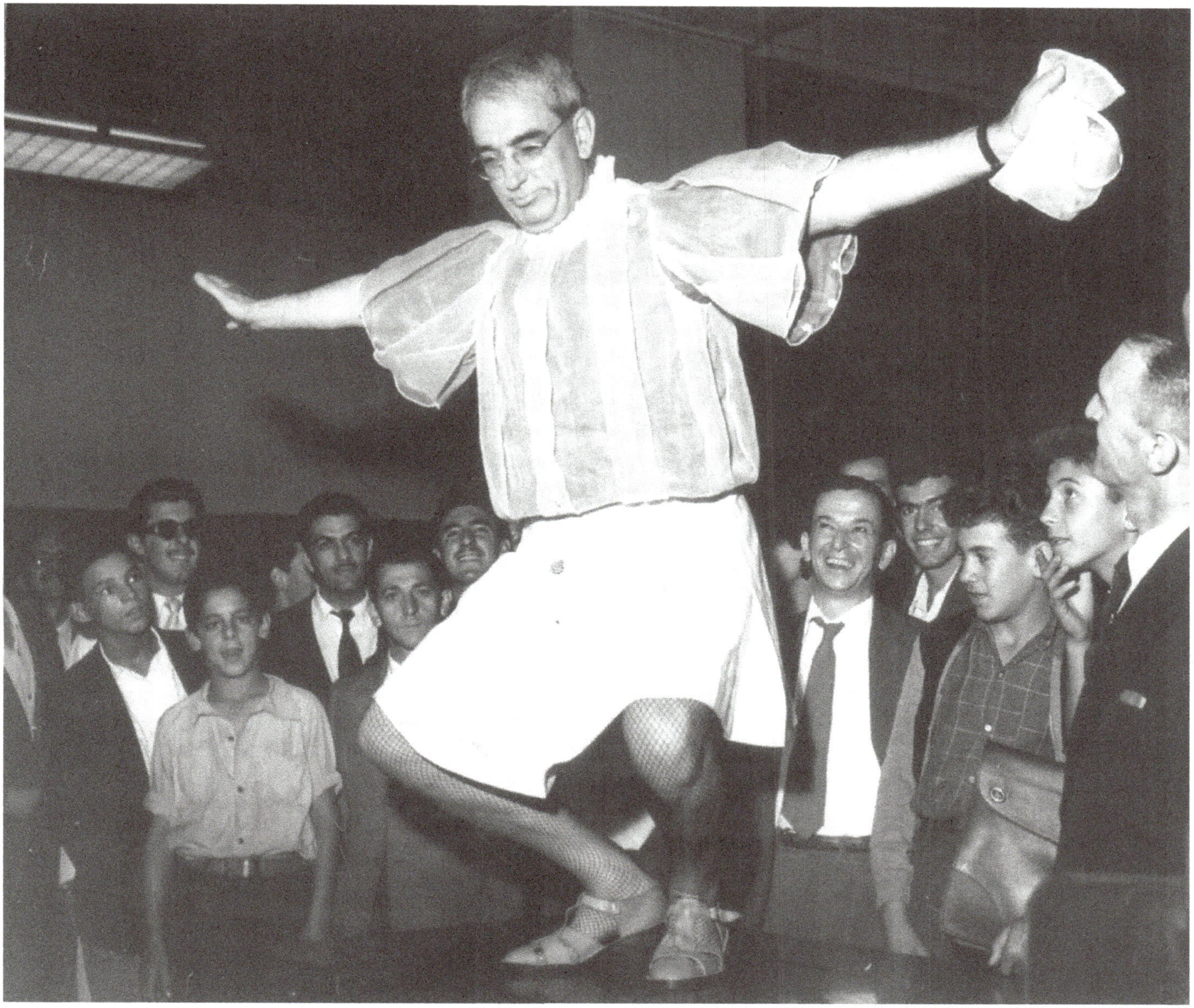

Descartes and Lautréamont." From Oswald de Andrade: "Without glasses, I can only see with the eyes of the soul—and I have always turned the eyes of my soul to the cannibal Flávio de Carvalho." Both men were there on September 4, 1949. Haitian poet René Depestre noted shortly after: "A warm tribute to his talent for light. A memory of a day in his house, where the taste for life, the delicious taste of being in the world . . . animates the thrill of a long, mind-blowing kiss."[16] French ethnologist Paul Rivet noted to have passed there "hours in the company of men and women who love art and beauty. Thank you."[17] The house often welcomed reasonably sized groups and small crowds of visitors, including fashion models, artists, poets, intellectuals, actresses, politicians, architects, composers, singers, students and many anonymous men and women, young and old, Brazilians and foreigners: Jean Lurçat, Philip Goodwin, Aran Khachaturian, Henry Moore, Bruno Giorgi, Nicolás Guillén, Giuseppe Ungaretti, Vinicius de Moraes, Roger Caillois, Gregori Warchavchik, Lasar Segall, Gilberto Freyre, Alberto Cavalcanti, André Chamson, Sérgio Buarque de Holanda, Caio Prado Jr., Georgia Gomide, Ruth de Souza, Maria Della Costa, Noêmia Mourão, Maria Leontina, Darcy Penteado, Yara Bernette, Anselmo Duarte, Paulo Mendes de Almeida, Geraldo Ferraz, Paulo Duarte, among hundreds of other guests along the years.[18] They came for cheerful wine receptions and lush feasts or longer periods of stay and intense weekends featuring topless women and nudity parades. It was not exactly a private Oikema—although his plan, like Ledoux's, alluded to the phallic form—nor an avant-garde Playboy Mansion, like Hugh Hefner's (although naked women would take a major role in the local atmosphere and décor).[19] Indeed, it was not a regular space for conviviality or for the regular standards of sociability. There were days when, near the large swimming pool in front of the house, a red flag would stand high on a metal mast to warn the farm workers not to allow anyone in because of a special party with everyone naked. Nudism was actually a sort of ritual, and the pool, where they eventually swam naked, would become the greatest temple for these sensual practices. After all, the experience of the body in space was at stake all throughout his career, in his theater, dance, and costume work, as well as in his public performances. As I have pointed out, such a performative dimension provides a privileged entry into one of the most intriguing aspects of Carvalho's work and thought process, which wavered constantly between constructive principles and disruptive imaginaries; practical and delusional values; objectivity and fetishism; logic-scientific persuasions and a radical investment on the unconscious; techno-social convictions and an emotional, derisive, obscene, or, even, a perverse bias.

EXPERIMENTING ON THE URBAN HORDE

There are no records about an *Experiência no. 1*, but he eventually referred to an "*Experiência* Number Zero."[20] One must not forget that Flávio de Carvalho was trained as an engineer and first appeared in the Brazilian cultural landscape as perhaps the most visionary of all Brazilian architects. Indeed, in 1922, soon after his return from a ten-year period of study in France and England, he began to work at Ramos de Azevedo's office, the most prestigious architecture and construction company in São Paulo between the end of the nineteenth century and the early twentieth century. It is true that he didn't seem at ease with the prevailing academic canon there, but even after his break with the office in 1926, it was still through architecture that he was identified as one of the most outstanding individual artists in São Paulo's growing liberal talent market. His rather unique entries to major architectural competitions between 1927 and 1931 gave him enormous visibility and a prominent role both within the architectural field and the arts and literary avant-garde scene as a whole. He never won a single one of these design competitions, but a few aspects of his proposals seem quite revealing in respect to a performative attitude. Firstly, all his projects suggest a close tie to the early avant-gardes, drawing upon architectural imageries based on futurism, expressionism, anthropophagia, or even surrealism. Secondly, most of his projects, including the last, contain a strong symbolic appeal either recurring to primary iconographies (of abstract, figurative, contemporary, or archaic bonds) or launching into analogical or parody exercises on programs, functions, customs, values, and norms. As such, they are often combined to proposals on human moods, bodies, complexions, gestures, and behaviors. Thirdly, all of his projects seem to aim at some kind of public amazement, shock, admiration, or even scandal, not by accident activating and motivating significant public debate and media strategies. Such emphasis on media as a proper arena for public action has been highlighted as an artistic strategy he would often employ everywhere as a performative device.[21]

We could perhaps think of his proposal for the São Paulo Governor's Palace competition, in 1927, as his undocumented *Experiência no. 1*. As customary, he named the project *Eficácia* (Effectiveness), and it received extensive media coverage because of its dazzling renderings and extravagant detailing with suspended forests, huge elevators, civic halls designed as ballrooms, war paraphernalia such as cannons, catapults, spotlights, and airstrips on the rooftop. But that first *experiência* could also refer to the speech he delivered at the 4th Pan-American Conference of Architects, held in Rio de Janeiro in 1930, titled "The City of the Naked Man," where a new urban model was outlined as a center for the "natural sublimation of human desires" and their liberation from repetitive routines and mechanisms, scholastic philosophy, Christian and classical dogmas, and other so-called taboos. Even before his presentation, the press was trumpeting the speech as carrying a defiant theme. In advance of the event, Carvalho himself visited newspapers in Rio to spread his ideas. On the day of the speech, the auditorium was packed and, according to contemporary records, there was a mood of outrage and disgust in the air. When he started reading, the audience burst into protest and disruption. Entire groups left the space. In face of threats, the police was called. After all, the speech aimed at the "exaltation of the Nietzschean biological man" as he appeared in nature, wild, with all his desires and intact curiosity, calling upon those present to withdraw "their civilized masks" and admit and endorse their cannibal tendencies, repressed by their colonial and academic background.[22]

There is no doubt that both the Governor's Palace project and the "Naked Man" speech in their own ways confronted the hegemonic architectural and civilizing values, deliberately bumping the audience's aesthetic, epistemic and cosmological impermeability. Oscillating between the spatial and the symbolical, the rational and the erotic, the functional and the critical, the fact is that both the project and the speech somehow operate on the limits of the discipline. More than that, as they reinforce the links between design practice, social life, and emotional effects (of surprise, displacement, disturbance, or rupture), they anticipate the idea of performance as an artistic genre.[23]

By that time Flávio de Carvalho was aware of a whole set of avant-garde ideas in art and thought. Since the period in England he seems to have read Nietzsche's *Zarathustra*, James Frazer's *Golden Bough*, a tremendous bestseller after its abridgment, and he was also familiar with some of Sigmund Freud's books, including *Totem and Taboo* and *Mass Psychology*, which one could find full of notes in his personal library.[24] Through his engagement starting in 1922 with the São Paulo–based modernism and, after 1928, with the anthropophagia movement, he got in contact with the most recent European art movements, particularly with expressionism, Dadaism, cannibalism and surrealism. As a matter of fact, since 1929, when the French writer, artist, and activist Benjamin Péret fled to Brazil to found Rio de Janeiro's chapter of the International Communist League, Carvalho reached out to the French-based surrealists and a few years later published in São Paulo interviews he had conducted with Tristan Tzara, André Breton, Man Ray, and Roger Caillois in Paris in 1934, clearly collaborating on the effort to spread out their ideas in Brazil.[25]

The approach to the avant-gardes gained an institutional ally in São Paulo with the establishment, in 1932, of the Modern Artists' Club (Clube de Arte Moderna, CAM). Flávio himself was elected its first president and opened up the club to a whole range of avant-garde soirées, lectures, exhibitions, banquets, parties, concerts, performances, and public readings, always marked by a clear sense of engagement, irreverence, gaiety, and informality. The program included Käthe

Kollwitz's first show in Brazil; exhibitions of Russian posters and of art of children and the mentally ill; conferences by Osorio Cesar around psychiatry and art, by Tarsila do Amaral on proletarian art, by David Siqueiros on politics and muralism in Mexico, by Mário Pedrosa on art and Marxism, by Caio Prado Junior on the Soviet Union, and by Oswald de Andrade on his play *O homem e o cavalo* (The man and the horse)—all were very well attended. In 1933, the CAM became the seat of the Teatro da Experiência, conceived and directed by Flávio de Carvalho himself, where he premiered his *Bailado do deus morto* (Ballet of the dead god), a sort of Dadaist musical, weaving Afro-Brazilian rites and interpreted by amateur black artists. The play focused on human emotions related to god, from its mythical figures toward monotheism and, finally, to its assassination by men. Not surprisingly, the play was censored, and the venue was permanently closed by the police three days later.[26] CAM wouldn't survive much longer to the reactionary state of mind that took hold of São Paulo's cultural scene by 1934.[27]

There is a clear avant-garde commitment in *Experiência no. 2*. Recall the postwar Barres Process performance of 1921 in Paris, in which the young Péret took part as the "unknown German soldier." The large and virulent Dadaist and Surrealist public performances in Paris in the 1920s were clearly aimed at promoting public turmoil and inciting outbursts of rage within the popular crowds. Many of them indeed addressed politically relevant topics such as patriotism, Christian morality, bourgeois society, and social taboos, among others. Their main support was also the artists' bodies themselves, motionless or moving, alone or collectively mobilized, silent or vocally active, dressed or undressed, disguised, masked, travestied, or ordinarily performed; in sum, just like Carvalho's procession intervention in 1931: "It was Corpus-Christi Day. The sun bathed the city. There was a festive mood everywhere. Women, men and children were moving in brightly colored clothing; old black women were wearing glasses and robes or something similar; black men's fraternities were holding banners and candles."[28] It is striking how focused he was on the ways people dressed during the procession, his attention to colors, fabrics, accessories, as well as the ritual objects they carried with them: crucifixes, candles, rosaries, ribbons, torches, and flags which he would characterize in a heretic (or "symmetrical") point of view, as "fetish-objects." After all, as Bruno Latour has observed, being modern has a lot to do with the obsession with finding those *objets-fées/objets-faits* everywhere but not in its own world of references.[29] The whole scene is depicted through the human bodies and their attributes—costumes, Christian emblems, and insignia, human physical characteristics, faces, gestures, groupings, either ritual or social, of race, sex, and age.

Carvalho probably wore a coat and tie like any other upper-class adult male in Brazil at the time. But a missing piece would encourage him to go back home as soon as he met the procession in order to perfect his outfit: a green velvet cap. He thus dressed in an ordinarily respectful way except for the impious attitude of keeping his hat on while following the pious procession. He didn't much refer to the surrounding urban landscape, except that the whole thing took place on the streets of the old São Paulo city center, which he characterized as an extremely dense built environment. By all means he was mostly interested in the psycho-anthropological landscape, starting with the picturesque human scenery he described. In his own words, his experiment meant: "To unveil the soul of worshipers through some kind of reagent that would allow me to study the reactions on the faces, the gestures, the pace, and the eyes, to finally feel the pulse of the environment, to psychically touch the tempestuous emotion of the collective soul, to register the flow of that emotion, to provoke a rebellion in order to watch something of the unconscious."[30]

Against the religious cortege there emerges a scientific attitude, his own *experiência* which he refers to as a sort of chemical experiment within a previous social performance; thus, halfway between artistic practice and a political act, a new dramatic form emerges as well as an intellectual one. This appeal to science is not at all at odds with the kind of psychology and anthropology he had in mind—nor with the anthropophagic ideal he held high. As a matter of fact, as he had pointed out a year before: "[It] responds to the cry of the unconscious. It offers man a fantastic mechanism, through which he may progress freely, with no embarrassment at all. Anthropophagy intends to scientifically study the human soul and get to know its biological inclinations. It intends to create to such inclinations a mechanism of maximum performance, of maximum efficiency."[31]

Following Freud's belief that becoming a member of a crowd served to displace the super-ego and unlock the unconscious mind, he would challenge the crowd's investment on the body of Christ—the Corpus Christi—as a charismatic holder. Accordingly, the architect/performer inserted his body in the public flow of bodies, or else, against the flow of the event, assuming the temptations and risks of it for the sake of a desired empirical knowledge. He declares his action to aim for the "pulsation" of the environment and of collective emotions, and that marching against the procession could offer him the possibility to amaze and exasperate the masses and at the same time to better watch their reactions. The *experiência* is carefully depicted in its whole process, step by step, scene by scene, through the attitudes performed by Carvalho (the march itself, his body gestures, visual connections, flirting and "vamping" attitudes, some verbal exchanges and affront at the end) and through the different effects (indifference, desire, repulsion, hesitation, anger) produced over the procession and its side audience, male and female, young and old, religious and secular. He was clearly in search of some sort of violent connection with the crowd that would supposedly allow him access to the collective unconscious.

It is true that he didn't succeed at first, but at some point, in face of a "mass of people pushed to the extreme of hatred and wishing to devour" him, the *experiência* became extremely dangerous, eventually growing into an attempt to lynch him: "An immense rumor filled the space; a multitude of threatening arms with clenched fists were shaking in the air; huge mouths shouted angrily: Lynch! Crucifixes and colorful banners trembled in cadence according to the guidelines of hatred. There was a unanimous wish: Grab! Kill! Lynch! Priests, elders, women, young people, they were all vibrating with fury. The noise echoed everywhere. Everything was resonating. I felt an immense volume of sound invading my ears."[32] When it comes to how he managed to escape, the focus suddenly switches from his interactions with the procession to an interior landscape, the impact on himself of the crowd's attitudes and expressions, the actual risks he faced and his own emotional and physical distress finally took the foreground amid the great panic that takes hold of him. The whole thing ended in the police department, where he was escorted to and arrested for the day. His statements to the police and the press would amaze the public opinion. Having described the whole episode and declared his scientific motivations—"to approach the aggressive power of a religious crowd in face of civil laws, or to find out whether the power of faith was stronger than the power of law and the praise of human life"[33]—he would be taken as an eccentric maniac. Nonetheless, the huge media coverage he gained would rank the whole thing as an *experiência*.

A second and significantly longer part of the book proposes a totemic analysis of it: the religious mechanism of faith in an invisible leader, the worshiping of a dead god; Christ's monopoly of sex; the submissive role of women in that order and their mechanisms of psychic self-preservation; the gregarious behavior of the Christian horde; the mechanisms of fetish-objects, the narcissistic behavior in contemporary Catholicism, and its emotional mechanisms toward other totemic organizations.

Regardless of the references to Frazer and Freud in his analysis, Carvalho does not adopt a narrow concept of "totem"; rather he defines it as a vaguely symbolic object or a general structure able to host the self and thus to work as an erotic holder for narcissistic behavior.[34] Such a conceptual move seems to allow him to redefine the totem as a sort of machinery, a powerful operating object able to drive human performances and emotions through certain directions, by the exchange of energies with the environment and bodies around it.

THE NEW LOOK AS TOTEM

Twenty-five years later, in 1956, the subject matter of *Experiência no. 3* does not seem to have anything to do with religion. Or maybe it does, after all there is another social taboo to be faced in public: the secular taboo of male dress codes. Flávio de Carvalho is at the time fifty-seven years old, still very prolific, gray hair, a public figure acclaimed as a pioneer of modernism in Brazil as well as an influential chronicler, critic, and polemicist. He had personally organized, from 1937 to 1939, three important contemporary art shows, including the Salões de Maio (May Salons), widely considered the embryo of the São Paulo Biennial. The number of exhibitions of his own artwork had also increased, including individual exhibitions at the Museu de Arte de São Paulo (MASP) and the Museu de Arte de São Paulo (MAM-SP), in 1948 and 1952, as well as participations at the first two editions of the Biennial in 1951 and 1953. He was therefore an established artist by that time, engaged on a much broader scope of interests, activities, networks, and institutions.

The topic of wardrobe had become more central over the years as his engagement with theater, dance, sets, and costume design had expanded. In 1944 he started a vast research project on the history of fashion that led to the publication at *Diário de S. Paulo*, seven months before his 1956 performance, of a series of thirty-nine articles titled "A moda e o novo homem" (Fashion and the new man), which he illustrated with one-hundred-and-nine drawings. The series was not at all meant for encyclopedic use or for professional purposes. It was neither very scientific nor really pedagogical.[35] Based on a so called psycho-ethnographic method and on various sources and iconographies and drawn from art history, anthropology, mythology, literature, film, and news media, it was a clear attempt to think of fashion across different epochs and cultures as marked by constant evolution, change, and variation and referring to socially, biologically, and sexually based archetypes, dreams, conventions, and dilemmas.

In the beginning of the year he started to develop a project for a new ready-to-wear men's outfit. It was meant to better correspond to the local hot and humid weather. Several sketches clarify the effort to develop a prototype with wire frames at the waist and shoulders in order to prevent contact between the tissue and the body, thus allowing inner ventilation and perspiration. The model could even contain blowing pipes to improve its performance. Comfortable and hygienic, it should also be affordable, low maintenance (washing and drying), and available in a variety of colors. After all, according to him, the joy of colors, practicality, and the freedom of movement would positively affect the health and psyche of men and "prevent wars and flu."[36]

The project soon became a public campaign. Interviews were given and dozens of supporters would soon appear, among them renowned artists, intellectuals, journalists, architects, entrepreneurs, and politicians. By the end of March, one of Brazil's most prestigious men's magazines, *Visão* (Vision), published a basic sketch of a man wearing a puffy blouse and shorts. It was reminiscent of Flash Gordon's wardrobe but adapted to contemporary urban life, to which Visão added that the "Brazilian 'Dior'" would soon also develop other wears—for beach use, for the countryside, for formal evening dinners, and for other seasons of the year, not just summer.[37] Indeed the reference to a New Look was humorously borrowed from Christian Dior's revolutionary women's fashion of the postwar period.

Around that time, a rumor was spread about the idea of a collective parade of men wearing his new costume. In interviews, Carvalho would even refer to a certain choreography: the fashion parade would open with two vagabonds in their ragged clothes; they would recite nonsensical monologues put together by the director of an asylum.[38] After all, those street dwellers, and other groups of lowest strata, "speaking to imaginary audiences, lavishly dressed with ribbons, flowers and various cloths," had always mastered "the great imagination" as "supreme creators of fashion." For if fashion was "perfectly capable of containing, of calming and replacing the first signs of mental imbalance," men tended to "adorn their bodies" to restore themselves when running out of control. Indeed, beyond its apparent futility, ornament worked as a sort of "escape valve for regulating the pressure of the psyche."[39] In June, *Time* magazine's Latin American edition was boasting about such a "Brave New Look":

> Now Carvalho has taken to designing men's summer clothing to replace "anti-functional, anti-esthetic and anti-humane" traditional fashions, which he holds responsible for the younger generation's lack of imagination and general neurosis. . . . Carvalho's brave, bright-colored summer costumes consist of a blouse, long stockings, sandals and either shorts or a skirt. Even a man bold enough to show himself in public wearing a skirt might well balk at the Carvalho blouse, a balloon garment kept off the skin by an adjustable copper-wire frame.[40]

At some point, Carvalho hired the studio of Maria Ferrara, a renowned Italian theater and dance clothier based in São Paulo since the city's Fourth Centennial, to execute the final version. After several adjustments to the original design, choice of fabrics to be used, frame, sleeves, and collar, the prototype was finished: the new look for the summer would be composed of a pleated cotton skirt (in fact a mini-skirt), a vaporous blouse (with a pullout frilled collar, sewn on crystalized nylon, a fabric recently created in the United States), a brimmed hat of the same material, long fishnet stockings, and leather sandals. The iron frames of the blouse had been replaced by plastic flippers in order to avoid rust. The first fitting was made in the presence of MASP's founder, Assis Chateaubriand, and was publicly shown at the museum's venues in a fashion show organized by the architect Lina Bo Bardi.[41]

Dressed in the outfit, Carvalho entered the public eye on the afternoon of October 18, 1956. At the last minute, all of his supporters had disappeared, surprised—as many declared—by the fact that the joke had materialized into a real event. Accounts on what happened at the parade are quite diverse, but they all identify an enormous excitement among the press and the crowd in general, both eagerly looking forward for the New Look show. One of his biographers summarizes *Experiência no. 3*'s multiple images projected by the media:

> In the vicinity of his studio, on Barão de Itapetininga street, in the city center, TV, movie, and radio trucks were parked, and there were news reporters from almost every powerful newspaper in São Paulo, Rio, and even some correspondents from the United States, Argentina, and Italy. . . . In the lobby of the building no. 297, where his studio was located, there was virtually a chaotic situation: photographers and cameramen ran over each other hysterically, livid and untidy reporters screamed and climbed the stairs and the elevators, film and TV lighting paraphernalia were hastily assembled, and a huge audience of bystanders crowded the sidewalks looking for a spot to watch the picturesque episode about to happen.[42]

In contrast to that bustle in the city's center, the route taken by the artist was fairly common. Carvalho went down Barão de Itapetininga Street and walked to a bar, where he had a cup of coffee. Then he walked through several streets and, urged by the audience, who knew that men were not allowed to go to the movies if not dressed "properly," he entered the Marrocos movie theater where the western *Tennessee's Partner* (ironically translated in Brazil as "Audacity is my law," 1955, with John Payne, Rhonda Fleming, and Ronald Reagan) was screened. Afterward he headed to 7 de Abril Street, where the headquarters of Assis Chateubriand's newspaper *Diários Associados* as well as both MASP and MAM-SP were located. In the newspaper lobby, Carvalho stood on a table, did some pirouettes for the press, answered questions, and voiced useless philosophical considerations. Inside the building, he changed his green skirt and yellow blouse for a white skirt and a red blouse, and finally returned to the streets for a triumphal parade on top of a convertible automobile. Everywhere he went, a multitude of strangers and reporters, flashes and noise, followed the artist, who was marching solemnly, erect, apparently calm, and indifferent to any stir or mockery, looking like an ordinary man on a daily walk across the neighborhood.

On the next day, the newspapers published mixed expressions of astonishment, disgust, and support about the event, and Carvalho gave a lecture about it at the Artists' and Art Friends' Club. The club would host an "outfit of the future ball" a week later, when a few other men would improvise similar outfits. For months the experience would continue to make headlines. New exhibitions of the outfit were organized. Two years later, the São Paulo newspaper *Última Hora* noted an article recently published on *Nature* magazine by three Swedish scientists at Stockholm University's Institute of Radiophysics; the researchers maintained that wearing skirts, instead of trousers, would prevent men from certain genetic mutations and reproductive diseases.[43] Carvalho's New Look could even be endorsed by scientific authorities for the welfare of the species and testicles.

In spite of its futuristic allusions, his new costume denoted a certain aesthetic archaism. He himself didn't look much at ease in it, a trait that is probably the essence of elegance. Perhaps because of the eccentric situation, the crowd's reaction (as if facing a lunatic), or the exposure of arms and legs, his desire to craft an outfit that ensures the body stays cool in the summer season could only be attained by isolating the body from the fabric. The fact is that the new look for the summer evokes a Roman centurion's costume, in his armor, striped *pteruges* and sandals, or an Ancient Egyptian skirt, or even a traditional Scottish kilt. Its stiff and severe aspect, avoiding any modeling or compromise to the shapes and volumes of the human body is actually quite traditional.[44] Nothing could be more distant from Christian Dior's contemporary creations. But the costume's formal aspects—its axes, colors, fabrics, and mobility—and even its traditional background are only comprehensible if we take into consideration its role as a performative or even a totemic device, that is, as a system of public gestures acting socially and psychologically over highly dogmatic and provincial macho values, playing down their universal claims, combining a clear emphasis on the present to a voluntary anachronism,[45] matching action and reflection about action and thus highlighting ideas, ruptures, and infinite variations instead of the object itself. In any case, the piece itself proves to take advantage of a rather permissive technique, flexible, open, incorporating the unexpected, the paradoxical, and even the risible, like the figure of pipes to be blown while marching.

ARCHITECTURE FOR/AS PERFORMANCE

Experiência no. 3 was built around the same time Flávio de Carvalho was designing the International Music University. Set in the countryside of São Paulo, near the border with Rio, the project was commissioned by Juventude Musical Brasileira (Brazilian Music Youth), an organization founded in 1952 by his friend Eleazar de Carvalho, the chief conductor of the Orquestra Sinfônica Brasileira, who had played with samba masters Almirante, Donga, and Pixinguinha in a jazz band. Eleazar de Carvalho was the mentor of several young Brazilian musicians, including Nelson Freire, Cristina Ortiz, and Issac Karabtchevsky through the Youth Concerts (Concertos para a Juventude) series he had launched in the 1940s.[46] Inspired in Tanglewood, where the conductor had studied in 1946, Flávio's plan for the University proposed a similar infrastructure to Berkshire Music Center, including a monumental stadium theater with a revolving stage, an amphitheater for thirty thousand people, a five-thousand-seat auditorium, teaching studios, dorms for four hundred students, restaurants, and a museum among other features. Composed of eighteen different buildings, the institution was conceived to include seven different departments: music, opera, dance, theater, humanities, electronic music, and visual arts.[47] Dedicated to the performing arts, its performative dimension would also be present in its unique, dashing, ultra-modern architecture, appealing to a space age, googie styling (akin to Oscar Niemeyer, Buckminster Fuller or John Lautner) through a variety of structures,[48] parabolic arches, geodesics, porticos, cupolas, sloping roofs, suspended buildings of steel, concrete, and lots of glass.

As usual, Carvalho's plan wasn't executed; the whole idea was aborted under Juscelino Kubitschek's term as president of Brazil, while Brasilia was being built. Nevertheless, it is probably more intriguing to find such a performative dimension in a less noticeable or excessive project, to which the links between architecture and performance rise on a different level. Consider the group of seventeen middle-class houses he designed and built as a personal investment, from 1933 to 1938, at Alameda Lorena in São Paulo. The ensemble is certainly appealing to an architectural historian working with modernism in Brazil, but it is far from being an amazing design achievement, like for instance the streets Robert Mallet-Stevens and André Lurçat designed in Paris in the late 1920s. To a certain extent it is quite a conventional project. For example, the way the whole group faces the urban scale in terms of individual lots and single-family houses; its traditional brickwork, at a time when Brazil saw tremendous development with concrete and reinforced concrete among other building technologies; or its basic attitude toward the domestic program, with the typical Brazilian middle-class four-bedroom home, including one for the housekeeper. In my opinion, the most innovative aspects of the project are connected to its scenic effects.

On the one hand, Carvalho approaches the built environment as a provocative device, breaking with the functionalist asceticism—hence, the volumetric animation of the whole public vista by means of variation of planes, volumes, heights, silhouettes and openings; the inclusion of almost scenic episodes as little exterior staircases leading to roof-terraces, some of which are protected by concrete umbrellas; several kinds of plaster and texture employed on vertical surfaces; and the animistic solution of a few individual facades, like human masks or faces. The interior is no less relevant scenically with its high-ceiling living rooms, long upstairs galleries, and freakish elements, such as curtains acting as partitions.

On the other hand, the building exhibits a discursive agency, embodied in its propaganda and in the very peculiar users' manual, which should instruct their renters on "how to use" their homes. It advertises, for instance, the houses as "new models made for 1938 and 1939," like a fashion collection or a certain car model. They even take advantage of the architect's celebrity on the presentation of his "latest creations." But it is surely the "How to use" pamphlet that seems to act as releasing a system of actions. It is not only a set of instructions on practical ways of living, as usual among modern architecture advertising but a performative gesture in itself. Its content might be helpful in functional terms, even when it sounds not that useful, like when describing how to fix "colored canvas curtains" in the solarium, "sloping as a tent," employing different colors of curtains according to the weather or the tenant's mood, or when suggesting the use of railings "to hang bird cages or vases" for paper flowers. But the very fact of providing his eventual tenants with such "carefully specified 'directions for use'"[49] implies a screenplay of sorts. Everywhere, then, the architectural space is thought through "the signs of a world as theater."[50]

What is at stake, therefore, is neither a specific setting nor a given scene, not even a certain mis-en-scène in the traditional sense of representation. The center is still the body in its organic, motor, mental, and emotional functioning, in its role as a dwelling place in time and space. And in this process, thus, it is again his own body the actual battlefield; in this case for a new spatial organization which would only be complete through the development of new body techniques, that is, a new way of ritualizing certain parts of the body, certain physical provisions, reactions, and movements, certain environmental circumstances, certain everyday gestures and current sensations, feelings, and experiences. In short, then, what is at stake is another body technique, a fixation, as Mauss would say, under the conditions of contemporary urban-industrial society, of certain physio-psycho-sociological assemblies of series of acts related to dwelling, of a new tradition of making use of our own bodies at home.[51]

Flávio de Carvalho knew that one of the very values of the mechanized world was actually the possibility of emancipating man's bodies to other social gestures. Since at least 1937 he had insisted in several articles and radio lectures on the "twentieth-century man's house." Entirely permeated by the machine it should be redefined as a mere "point of passage, a resting place in the daily routine," increasingly enjoyed within the "city's premises." The house in general and the workers' housing in particular needed to be redefined in light of the legitimate achievements of "mentalism" against the ancestral powers of emotions.[52] Notwithstanding, those dirty and grotesque emotions, always in friction with each other, continued to operate and required the overtaking of scientific knowledge by the use of instinct and intuition in order to act effectively on the world. Irreducible to the functionalist concept, such a "machine for living" would thus also operate as a kind of totem. Offered to the sacred, its raison d'être passed by the celebration of tensions between constructive powers and the unconscious drives in man. This seems quite evident in a 1940 text, in which Carvalho advocated the refusal of the manorial idea of the house as a defensive space, a place of fear. For him, a new domestic cosmogony should be created in close and sensitive connection to life around it. That would be both its fragility and strength, allowing the contemporary expansion of men's "time for action," the "internationalization of their ways to perceive life," the collective enjoyment of "a new emotivity" and the occupation of streets.[53]

It is true that the group of houses at Alameda Lorena does not entirely materialize these ideas. And the numerous newspaper articles published at its inauguration, often resulting from the architect's media strategies, were surprisingly almost always completely indifferent to such issues, mainly interested in its functional proposals—indeed more appealing to its commercial purpose—and leaving aside its most experimental aspects. One exception is a short article, unassumingly titled "New Models of the Rental House," in which the author relates a conversation he had with the architect, whose project he would question if it was about "houses or voodoo; architecture or fetish." There, we find, for instance, Carvalho placing those new models into the performative vein he would keep on exploring all throughout his life: "I wish a thorough explanation of these rental homes," asks the reporter; "The idea is not mine. It's Jules Verne's. I do not adorn myself with peacock feathers," Carvalho answers; the reporter insists: "Flávio, my Flávio, why are you so modest?"; to which Carvalho replies, "It is not a matter of modesty. I don't want people to call me crazy. I also did these houses as an *experiência*. It is my fifth or sixth *experiência*. If it works, it's my idea; if not, it is Jules Verne's." He thus ascribes a broader role to architecture, much closer to invention, utopia, and scientific fiction than solely a functional mechanism. Toward the end of the interview he offers us a performative pearl: "On the day that I rent one of these houses . . . either myself or the tenant is nuts."[54]

Notes

1 / *Desvíos de la deriva: Experiencias, travesías y morfologías*, May 5 to August 23, 2010, Museo Nacional Centro de Arte Reina Sofia, Madrid; *Form and Feeling: The Making of Concretism*, February 8, 2016, Bronx Museum, New York; *Are We Human?*, October 22 to November 2016, 3rd Istanbul Design Biennial, Istanbul; *The Bones of the World*, September 7 to November 9, 2019, 11th Berlin Biennale for Contemporary Art, Berlin.

2 / Luiz Carlos Daher, *Arquitetura e expressionismo: Notas sobre a estética do projeto expressionista, o modernismo e Flávio de Carvalho* (São Paulo: FAU-USP, 1979); Daher, *Flavio de Carvalho e a volupia da forma* (São Paulo: Ed. K, 1984); Rui Moreira Leite and Walter Zanini, *Flávio de Carvalho—Exposição retrospectiva* (São Paulo: Bienal Internacional de Arte, 1983); Sangirardi, Jr., *Flávio de Carvalho, o revolucionário romantic* (Rio de Janeiro: Philobiblion, 1985); Antonio Carlos Robert Moraes, *Flavio de Carvalho* (São Paulo: Brasiliense, 1986); J. Toledo, *Flávio de Carvalho: O comedor de emoções* (São Paulo: Brasiliense/Campinas, Ed. da Unicamp, 1994); and Rui Moreira Leite, *Flávio de Carvalho (1899–1973): Entre a experiência e a experimentação* (São Paulo: PhD dissertation, Escola de Comunicação e Artes, Universidade de São Paulo, 1994).

3 / Americo Ishida, *Desenho, desejo e designio na arquitetura de Flávio de Carvalho* (master's thesis, FAU-USP, São Paulo, 1995); Valeska Freitas, *Dialética da aoda: A máquina experimental de Flavio de Carvalho* (master's thesis UFSC, Florianópolis, 1997); Luis Camilo Osório, *Flavio de Carvalho* (São Paulo: Cosac and Naify, 2000); William Golino, *História d'O bailado do deus morto: Uma radical modernização do teatro no Brasil* (master's thesis, UFMG, Belo Horizonte, 2002); Carolina Pierotti Rossetti, *Flávio de Carvalho: Questões de arquitetura e urbanismo* (master's thesis, EESC-USP, São Carlos, 2007); Simone Aparecida de Oliveira, *A poética radical no modernismo brasileiro: A "Experiência no. 2" de Flávio de Carvalho* (master's thesis, PUC-SP, São Paulo, 2008); Ana Maria Maia Antunes, *Da contemporaneidade de Flávio de Carvalho: Revisão bibliográfica dos principais estudos sobre o artista de 1979 a 2010* (master's thesis, Faculdades Santa Marcelina, São Paulo, 2012); Marco Anselmo Vasques, *Ideias e práticas teatrais de Flavio de Carvalho* (master's thesis, UFSC, Florianópolis, 2014); Veronica Stigger, "Flavio de Carvalho: Arqueologia e contemporaneidade," *Celeuma*, no. 4 (May 2014).

4 / The word *experiência* in Brazilian refers to both the ideas of an (artistic or scientific) experiment and a living, sensorial, and social experience. In that sense we have opted to keep the original word in Portuguese in this version of the essay.

5 / Flavio de Carvalho, *Experiência no. 2, realizada sobre uma procissão de Corpus-Christi; uma possível teoria e uma experiência* (São Paulo: Irmãos Ferraz, 1931).

6 / Stigger, "Flavio de Carvalho."

7 / See José Lira, "Modernismo, erotismo e domesticidade masculine: a casa Capuava de Flavio de Carvalho," in *Domesticidade, gênero e cultura material*, ed. José Lira, Joana Mello, Flavia Brito, and Silvana Rubino (São Paulo: Edusp/CPC, 2017), 283–312.

8 / Flavio de Carvalho, *Mecanismo da emoção amorosa* (São Paulo, 1934).

9 / Daher, *Flavio de Carvalho*, 153; Osorio, *Flavio de Carvalho*, 29; Ishida, *Desenho, desejo e designio*, 6.

10 / Dulce Carneiro, "A casa de Flávio de Carvalho," *Casa and Jardim*, no. 40 (January–February 1958): 37.

11 / Michel Delon, *Le savoir-vivre libertin* (Paris: Hachette, 2000).

12 / The main room measured 54.125 feet (16.5 meters) long, 24.5 feet (7.5 meters) wide and 26.25 feet (8 meters) high.

13 / Carneiro, "A casa de Flávio de Carvalho," 40.

14 / Ghislaine Wood. "The Illusory Interior," in *Surreal Things: Surrealism and Design*, ed. Guislaine Wood (London: Victoria and Albert Museum, 2007), 2–15.

15 / Flávio de Carvalho, *Os ossos do mundo* (São Paulo: Ariel, 1936), 42–49.

16 / In the original: "Un hommage chaleureux à son talent de la lumière. Un souvenir d'un journée dans sa maison où le gout de la vie, le gout délicieux d'être au monde . . . anime le frisson d'un long et déréglé baiser."

17 / In the original: "des heures dans la compagnie d'hommes et femmes qui ont le culte de l'art, de la beauté. Merci."

18 / Flávio de Carvalho *Livro dos comensais*, n.d., file 2, Flávio de Carvalho Papers, Centro de Documentação Alexandre Eulálio/ Universidade Estadual de Campinas, Campinas-SP.

19 / Beatriz Preciado, *Pornotopia: An Essay on Playboy's Architecture and Biopolitics* (New York: Zone Books, 2014), 110–111.

20 / Flávio de Carvalho, "Experiência número zero," *Diário de S. Paulo*, July 6, 1943.

21 / Rui Moreira Leite,"Flavio de Carvalho: Media artist avant la lettre," *Leonardo* 37, no. 2 (2004): 150–157.

22 / Flavio de Carvalho, "Uma these curiosa," *Diário da Noite*, São Paulo, July 1, 1930.

23 / José Lira, "The Anthropofagic Body and the City: Flávio de Carvalho," in *Are We Human? 3rd Istanbul Design Biennial*, ed. Beatriz Colomina and Mark Wigley (Istanbul: Istanbul

Foundation for Culture and Arts, 2016), 418–421.

24 / A reasonable part of his private library, as well as much of his writings, correspondence, photographs, drawings, films, newspaper scrapbooks and more is kept in the Alexandre Eulálio Documentation Center at Campinas State University in Cedae, in the state of São Paulo.

25 / Flávio de Carvalho, "A Nova Forma Poética: Conversa com Tristan Tzara," *Diário de São Paulo*, August 27, 1935; Carvalho, "O Voluptuoso e o Inesquecível: entrevista com Man Ray," *Diário de São Paulo*, 31 August 1935; Carvalho, "Sciencia e lyrismo: Entrevista com Roger Caillois," *Diário de São Paulo*, September 10, 1935; Carvalho, "Surrealismo: entrevista com Andre Breton," *Cultura* (February–March 1939).

26 / Flávio de Carvalho, "A Nova Orientação: Um laboratório de experiências para a arte moderna," *Diário da Noite*, May 1, 1933; Carvalho, "O caso do Teatro da Experiência (carta aberta ao Dr. Costa Netto, delegado de Costumes)," *Diário da Noite*, December 8, 1933.

27 / Paulo Mendes de Almeida, *De Anita ao Museu* (São Paulo: Perspectiva, 1976), 76–78.

28 / Carvalho, *Experiência no. 2*, 15.

29 / A wordplay, something like "Magic objects/Made objects." See Bruno Latour, *Reflexão sobre o culto moderno dos deuses fe(i)tiches* (Bauru, SP: Edusc, 2002).

30 / Carvalho, *Experiência no. 2*, 16.

31 / "O ideal anthropophágico no IV Congresso de Architectos," *O Estado de Minas*, 9 July 9 1930.

32 / Carvalho, *Experiência no. 2*, 35.

33 / "O 'test'psychológico do engenheiro não se repetirá . . . Querendo conhecer a força da multidão, fugiu e acabou sendo preso." *Diário da Noite*, June 8, 1931. See also, "Uma experiência perigosa: cada qual com a sua mania." *Diário Popular*, June 8, 1931; "Lyncha! Lyncha! Gritou a multidão; e o psychologo que durante a procissão de 'Corpus Christi' queria fazer uma experiência sobre a psychologia das multidões, refugiou-se na Leiteria Campo Bello." *Correio do Povo*, June 8, 1931; "Experiência mal succedida: queria estudar a psychologia das multidões e o povo, indignado, quasi lynchou o curioso engenheiro." *A Gazeta*, June 8, 1931.

34 / Carvalho, *Experiência no. 2*, 56.

35 / In 1950, Brazilian art sociologist and critic Gilda de Mello e Souza—in her PhD dissertation, "Fashion in the nineteenth century," in which she analyzed Brazilian literature and photography, foreign travelers' accounts, and other historical sources—would look at fashion and particularly women's costumes as an anthropological system of signs, based on class, gender, and psychological functions and thus to be read as a form of art on the crossroads between the visual arts and minor arts, like the arts of the body and of rhythm. See Gilda de Mello e Souza, *O espírito das roupas: A moda no século dezenove* (São Paulo: Companhia das Letras, 1987).

36 / Daniel Linguanotto, "Flávio de Carvalho estreou seu New Look—é de nylon e de brim, acalma os nervos, evita as guerras, previne resfriados," *Manchete*, October 27, 1956, 72–75.

37 / "Um novo figurino: Os homens usarão saiote," *Visão*, March 30, 1956, 72.

38 / "Saiote e blusão," *Tribuna da Imprensa*, March 21, 1956, 7.

39 / Flavio de Carvalho, "A moda e o novo homem," *Diário de São Paulo*, March 31, 1956.

40 / "Playboy at work," *Time*, Latin American Edition, June 25, 1956, 30

41 / "Saiote e blusão," *Tribuna da Imprensa*, March 21, 1956, 7.

42 / Toledo, *Flávio de Carvalho*, 516.

43 / Toledo, 528.

44 / Mello e Souza, "A moda como arte," in *O Espirito das Roupas*, 26–51.

45 / Stigger, "Flavio de Carvalho."

46 / "Vida Musical da Juventude Musical Brasileira, Ano I-outubro–novembro de 1955 no. 4," cited in Fernando Menon, *Jeunesses Musicales e sua representação civil no Paraná: Juventude Musical Brasileira, 8a. Região PR/SC, setor do Paraná* (master's thesis, UFPR, Curitiba, 2008), 57.

47 / Mário Cabral, "Universidade Internacional de Música," *Tribuna da Imprensa*, August 16, 1955, 3; "Paisagens, paz e poesia cercarão a Universidade Estadual de Música," *Ultima Hora*, April 3, 1956; "Isolada dentro do mundo a Universidade de Eleazar," *Tribuna da Imprensa*, September 6, 1956, 2; "Já foi entregue o projeto da Universidade Internacional das Artes," *O Estado de S. Paulo*, September 20, 1956; "Transformação do Vale do Paraíba em Centro Internacional de Artes," *O Globo*, November 23, 1959. See also Rossetti, *Flávio de Carvalho*, 242–250.

48 / Alan Hess, *Googie Redux: ultramodern roadside architecture* (San Francisco, CA, Chronicle Books, 2004).

49 / Luis Martins, "Ar condicionado," *O Estado de S. Paulo*, April 13, 1961, cited in Rui Moreira Leite, "Flavio de Carvalho: Modernism and the Avant-garde in São Paulo, 1927–1939," *Journal of Decorative and Propaganda Arts* 21 (1995): 208.

50 / Daher, *Flavio de Carvalho*, 61.

51 / Marcel Mauss, "Les techniques du corps," in

Techniques, Technologies et Civilisation (Paris: PUF, 2012), 365–394.

52 / Flavio de Carvalho, "A casa do homem do século XX," *Diário de São Paulo*, February 27, 1938.

53 / Flavio de Carvalho, "A máquina e a casa do homem do século XX." *Dom Casmurro*, March 2, 1940.

54 / "Novos modelos de casa de aluguel: Flávio de Carvalho e as suas experiências; o homem que fugiu de Deus para fazer o diabo! Casas ou macumba; arquitetura ou feitiço," *O Governador*, June 16, 1938.

FORM AND SENSIBILITY Discursive Discrepancies in Concrete and Neoconcrete Art

2

Michael Asbury

The advent of the neoconstructivist avant-gardes in Brazil during the mid-twentieth century has become consolidated as a local art historical canon. As always, canonization takes place at the expense of the complexities and even contradictions of those movements and artists it celebrates. The denomination "local canon" may itself be misleading, for in this particular case it has been to a large extent legitimized internationally through the projection, reception, and collection of Brazilian art abroad. More problematic still is the association between locale and a particular form of discourse, one that is seen to belong to the character and "temper" of a particular place. Nowhere is this more explicitly affirmed than in the so-called rift between *paulistas* (São Paulo natives) and *cariocas* (Rio de Janeiro natives), through art critical discourse pertaining to the concrete and neoconcrete movements. The association between place and "artistic temper," particularly when viewed from the "outside," becomes therefore all the more problematic. Writing from such a position and, precisely because of this, aware of the dangers of essentializing such production, I explore in this essay some of the inconsistencies within the respective discourses in order to open new avenues for debate and (art) historical understanding. This is therefore not a grand historical survey but a brief investigation into certain discrepancies that were already present within contemporaneous critical discourse, intent to escape the somewhat reductive light to which such movements have become exposed.

Reviewing the early São Paulo Biennials for a special edition of the *Folha de São Paulo* newspaper in 2001, the concrete poet Décio Pignatari recalled the controversy behind the national painting award at the occasion of its second edition in 1953. Known as the Guernica Biennial, it surveyed the pioneering efforts of European modernism, yet Pignatari's focus was on the Brazilian participation. His emphasis related to the consolidation of concrete art in Brazil, a movement that he himself, together with poets Augusto and Haroldo de Campos, had become closely allied to over the course of the 1950s. Pignatari's choice to remember how Alfredo Volpi came to share the national painting prize with Emiliano Di Cavalcanti may not seem at first the most obvious subject for review by a concrete poet, yet precisely because of this it is all the more revealing of the complex interconnections across critical discourses in mid–twentieth-century Brazilian modern art.

It was in fact only natural that Pignatari would wish to undermine a painter such as Di Cavalcanti, whose paintings had sought to represent the "Brazilian people," their customs and habits, in short, their character. A central figure in the figuration versus abstraction debate, Di Cavalcanti had protested the wave of abstraction that, in his opinion, had been uncritically imported and presented at the first São Paulo Biennial in 1951. It may seem reasonable to assume that it was not so much the manner in which Di Cavalcanti's subjects were represented but representation itself that bothered Pignatari. Yet at that moment, Volpi could hardly be called an abstractionist himself. On the contrary, a self-taught painter of modest background, his compositions of vernacular façades, festive flags, and buntings also celebrated popular Brazilian scenes and were often wrongly interpreted as naïf. In his review, Pignatari sought to repel the latter as a misguided conception:

> At the 2nd Biennial, . . . the Jury was composed of a mixture of Brazilians and foreigners. These, at the first edition, concerned themselves with the international prizes, taking little notice of the national representation: the Brazilians were left to share their cake as their taste demanded. Being as such the great prize had already been promised to Di Cavalcanti.
>
> Yet the Brazilian group had not counted with the ethical integrity of Herbert Read, that great name of art criticism and literature from England (also a poet), who is said to have argued: "If there is someone here who should receive a prize it is Alfredo Volpi." Utter national shock. Read was ready to go to the press to denounce the plot. In the end, the prize was conceded to both, with Read insisting that Volpi's name appeared first. It was from that point that the São Paulo concrete art group (to which I belonged), under the leadership of Waldemar Cordeiro, became enamored with admiration for Volpi, who I audaciously and polemically considered and still consider, as the "first and last great Brazilian painter" who the ignorant, in the American fashion, call the "painter of buntings."[1]

His reference to "the American fashion" might in fact have been a rhetorical means of disassociating himself from the binary logic, articulated by the *Modernistas* in their critique of the first Biennial, one that associated abstraction with North

American cultural imperialism and representation with national identity and thus cultural liberation. One could add that Volpi would himself disrupt other quite distinct dichotomies, as will be discussed below.

Over the course of the 1950s, the concrete art group's adulation of Volpi's work would contradict some of their own fiercely held premises. Such a contradiction is somewhat camouflaged by the fact that Volpi, perhaps in response to the attention he received, began to elaborate complex geometric compositions and motifs that at first sight appeared increasingly concrete in nature. It is worth remembering that the term concrete art had been created by Theo van Doesburg in 1930 as a way of distinguishing a particular form of abstraction that drew directly from geometry to create "concrete" forms, rather than abstracting from the observable world. In this respect, Volpi's geometric compositions never fully escaped the condition of being abstractions from nature, given their undeniable relation to his former paintings of buntings, facades, and rooftops, in short, to those themes he never entirely abandoned and indeed would always return to.

Pignatari's statement is thus somewhat discordant from the orthodox art historical view that stresses the dichotomy between the mathematical basis ruling concrete creation that the consensus sees as characteristic of the São Paulo–based concrete art Ruptura Group (active from 1952) and that is juxtaposed with the intuitive approach pursued by the Rio de Janeiro–based neoconcrete artists. The latter had emerged toward the end of the 1950s out of the loose gathering of artists formally associated with the Grupo Frente (established in 1954). Discrepancies such as this, whether stemming from the discourse relating to São Paulo concrete art or the Rio de Janeiro neoconcrete movement (officially established in 1959), are the subject of this essay. It focuses on the figures of painter Alfredo Volpi in São Paulo and sculptor Franz Weissmann in Rio de Janeiro, drawing on the respective critical discourses that evolved around each of them.

THEORETICAL CONVERGENCE

There is a marked interest in Volpi's work expressed by Mário Pedrosa following the 1953 São Paulo Biennial painting awards, most notably in his organization of a retrospective exhibition on the artist in 1957 when the art critic described Volpi as the Brazilian master of his time.[2] Later, Pedrosa would organize a special gallery dedicated to Volpi at the 6th São Paulo Biennial in 1961 for which, as director of the Museum of Modern Art in São Paulo, he acted as curator as was then customary practice. Yet, it would be a little too simplistic to attribute Pedrosa's interest in Volpi as stemming purely from recognition and respect for the British critic

Herbert Read. Indeed, it is possible to identify certain common traits and interests from the writing of both art critics.

It seems quite clear that Volpi represented for Pedrosa a critical link between contemporaneous art in Brazil, the theoretical paradigm he had been developing since his studies on Gestalt psychology—exposed in his 1949 thesis, "The Affective Nature of Form in the Work of Art"—and his political views on the nature and the possibilities of art within modern societies. Within such a broad spectrum of interests, Pedrosa attempted to articulate the notion of the autonomy of art, or a scientific approach as he saw it, in the context of constructivist-orientated abstraction. He understood this position in opposition to the excessive subjectivity defended at the time by figures such as André Breton.

Projecting itself as universal, Pedrosa's intellectual and aesthetic outlook had the added requirement of combating the legacy reminiscent of socialist realism that is present within the figurative modernist tradition in Brazil, a legacy that had informed Di Cavalcanti's attacks on abstraction during the Biennial in 1951.[3] Being himself a Trotskyist militant, it was important for Pedrosa to separate left-wing politics from figurative art through a critical perspective that evaded the simplistic binary formulation that had been conjured within the context of Cold War politics. For Pedrosa, evidence for such a perspective would arise from quite unexpected quarters.

Invited by Almir Mavignier, Pedrosa had come into contact with extraordinary examples of so-called outsider art. The art critic would articulate such work in relation to notions of symbolic form and the universalist potential of abstraction.

Employed in the late 1940s at the National Psychiatric Hospital in the Engenho de Dentro neighborhood in Rio de Janeiro, Mavignier, together with Dr. Nise da Silveira, established art therapy workshops for the patients as an alternative to medication and electroconvulsive therapy (ECT). Having witnessed the extraordinary work produced by inmates, Mavignier invited artists Ivan Serpa and Abraham Palatnik as well as art critic Mário Pedrosa to contribute to those workshops. Later, other artists such as Lygia Pape and exhibition organizers such as Leon Degand, the then director of São Paulo's Museum of Modern Art, would also attend. Yet for the four initial contributors (Mavignier, Serpa, Palatnik, and Pedrosa) the experience with the patients would be particularly significant.

Mavignier, Palatnik, and Serpa also participated in that first edition of the São Paulo Biennial in 1951, with the latter being awarded the young painter's prize. Palatnik, who became so impressed by the work of the patients, had by then abandoned painting all together and submitted, with Pedrosa's encouragement, his first Kinechromatic apparatus. The artwork left the Biennial's awarding jury so perplexed that they could not categorize it under any of the running prizes (painting, sculpture, or prints) and so it remained *hors concours*.[4]

Perhaps the most visually striking proximity between concurrent avant-garde practice and the work of the psychiatric patients was the cover of the first Grupo Frente exhibition catalog in 1955. It is undoubtedly significant that in the years preceding that first Frente Group show a number of high-profile exhibitions by Engenho de Dentro interns took place. Perhaps not so coincidently, given Ivan Serpa's leading role within Grupo Frente, the cover for its first exhibition catalog is somewhat reminiscent of Artur Amora's paintings, one of the Engenho de Dentro patients who approached painting through a process of simplification of patterns found in domino pieces.[5]

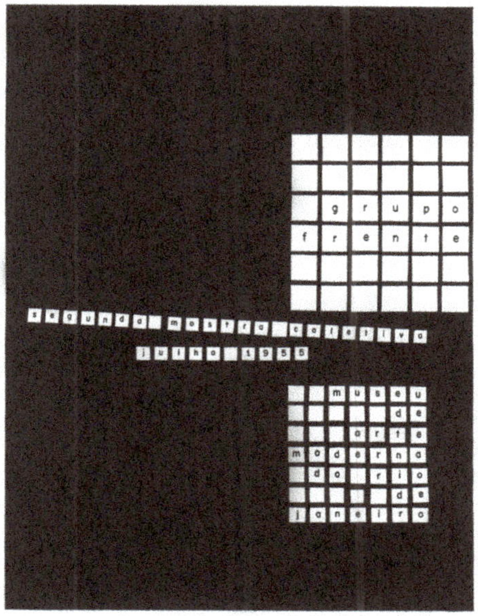

Catalog of Grupo Frente second exhibition,1955. Collection of the Museu de Arte Moderna do Rio de Janeiro.

In 1949, through Mavignier's intervention, the Museum of Modern Art in São Paulo hosted what turned out to be a somewhat controversial exhibition of work by Engenho de Dentro patients, selected by Leon Degand. For that occasion, Pedrosa wrote an article entitled "Arte: Necessidade Vital" (Art: Vital necessity) that refers to Dubuffet's notion of Art Brut (of 1945). It is not clear whether, other than by Pedrosa himself, such a term was known among the artists working at Engenho de Dentro. However, according to Glaucia Villas Boas, Pedrosa from the outset of his involvement with the psychiatric hospital possessed knowledge of Hans Prinzhorn, who he later cites in his 1951 essay "Forma e personalidade" (Form and personality).[6] Prinzhorn published *Artistry of the Mentally Ill* in 1922 based on his work on diagnosed schizophrenics.[7] Dubuffet's own collection and articulation of Art Brut is said to owe a great debt to Prinzhorn's study. In relation to the latter, the artist affirmed, for instance: "[The] innate necessity for expression could only be satisfied with the construction of forms [, giving his theory] a universal character . . . by the admission that the art of the insane could only be understood by the identification of pulsations towards the game, the ornamental, order, imitation and symbolization. [As such] there was no reason to discriminate the art of schizophrenics from the Fine Arts, except if considered by a dogmatic and outdated attitude."[8] In 1947, reviewing an earlier exhibition of 245 works by Engenho de Dentro inmates at the Ministry of Education and Culture in Rio de Janeiro, Pedrosa had already argued that "no one would deny that such works are harmonious, seductive, dramatic, alive or beautiful, in short, true works of art."[9] In

1949 however, Pedrosa was forced to paraphrase Prinzhorn's argument in response to accusations by the academic artist and art journalist Quirino Campofiorito, who argued that such work could not be considered art but instead consisted of "simply a means to provide the unfortunate creature an escape from the mental torments that affect his normal equilibrium."[10] Pedrosa's response to Campofiorito was blunt: "Worst of all is that there really is an analogy and similarity between one art and the other, as there is with that of children. This proves only that the reporter does not know what art is and takes nudes and the conventional statues of the academics as artistic expressions. . . . The artist is not that who has a diploma from the National School of Fine Arts, otherwise we would not have artists amongst the primitive peoples, including our native Indians."[11] Works from that 1949 exhibition were shown in 1950 at the Psychopathic Art exhibition in Paris during the 1st International Congress of Psychiatry. Moreover, in 1957 Carl Jung inaugurated an exhibition of paintings from Engenho de Dentro interns, archived within the then newly formed Museum of the Unconscious, during the 2nd International Congress of Psychiatry in Zurich.[12]

A sense of wonder and timelessness was expressed by Dr. Nise da Silveira upon her discovery of certain motifs found in the work of her patients which she promptly associated with Jungian archetypes. Beyond their common, if unconnected, correspondence with Carl Jung, Silveira shared with Herbert Read an intellectual allegiance with the political ideology of anarchism, which in the case of the art critic, informed his interpretation of the significance of such archetypal imagery.

We find in Read's writing similarities with Pedrosa's project for the affirmation of the universal qualities of such works, despite the fact that Pedrosa never ascribed to the Jungian archetypal repertoire.

In a similar experience to that of Silveira, Read, in what he described as "something of an apocalyptic experience," became "deeply moved . . . upon immediately recognizing [in the drawing of a five-year-old girl, the figure of a] 'mandala,' an ancient symbol of psychic unity, universally found in prehistoric and primitive art and in all principle cultures of history."[13]

According to art historian David Thistlewood, the discovery would make of Read "in all major respects, a follower of Jung" from the early 1940s onward.[14] Moreover, for Thistlewood, the conversion would affect the way in which Read would identify the practice of modern art with psycho-political patterns of creative power:

> A fixing upon abstract unities; a collation of personality traits specifically outside of the self; the celebration of maternity; an acknowledgment of belonging to the land—all these projections-beyond-self, Read thought, were fundamentally anarchistic. Moreover, objectified in creative works which he knew very well indeed—the mandala in Gabo's constructions; the Dark Shadow in his own novel *The Green Child*; maternal and terrestrial forms respectively in Moore's and Hepworth's sculpture—they helped substantiate Jung's demand for a reconciliation of individuals and the group.[15]

Perhaps it was precisely this combination of themes—the sense of belonging; the rhythmic patterns, and the maternity theme—which may have attracted Read to Volpi's paintings at the Biennial in 1953. Another supposition would be that he identified in Volpi's themes and style an approximation with the work of Alfred Wallis, a self-taught painter from St. Yves, whose work was discovered by Ben Nicholson in the late 1920s.[16]

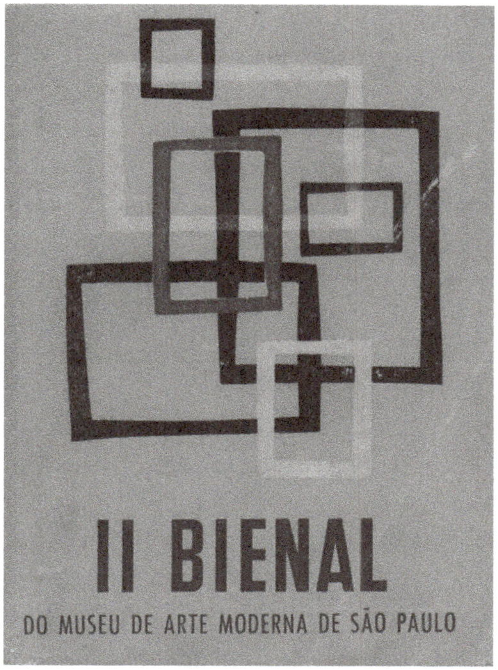

2nd São Paulo Biennial, 1953. Catalog cover design by Danilo Di Prete. Fundação Bienal de São Paulo / Arquivo Histórico Wanda Svevo.

For Pedrosa, on the one hand, it seems clear that Volpi would represent a synthesis of both frontlines in his aesthetic-ideological ethos. As Arantes has argued: "returning his attention to primitive art, [Pedrosa] mobilizes knowledge that allows him to relate those artistic forms with the ways of life of archaic civilizations. Similarly, comparing the child, the schizophrenic and the artist, he is obliged to pay attention to the issues related to the unconscious."[17] Arantes describes Pedrosa's gradual incorporation of the psychoanalytical approach, arguing that although totally discarded in 1949 due to its purely subjective emphasis (and here Arantes adds: "which is incompatible with a concrete psychology"), by 1951, in his essay "Forma e personalidade" (Form and personality), the debate revolves around the emotional subtracts that could perhaps be behind aesthetic pleasure, even if the intent is to prove that such a phenomenon escapes both Freudian and Jungian psychoanalytical interpretations.[18]

According to Arantes, there is already a shift toward an interior model of reasoning which is made all the more evident by the text's emphasis on "the primitive manifestation in art" which ultimately led Pedrosa to question the relation between symbolic values and formal structures. Moreover, Arantes argues that it is through his reading of Susanne Langer that Pedrosa (expressed in a paper given at the Fourth International Art Critics Association in Dublin 1953, the very year of Volpi's prize) would finally loosen his position by recognizing that visual perception "is not merely a sensorial and mental process of the surface" but comes from the unconscious and crystallizes itself in consciousness after "a battle between several perceptive layers."[19] Read's response to Langer, on the other hand, seems strikingly similar to descriptions of concrete art: "The whole of Langer's work . . . considered the work of art as to be received as a vivid presentation of itself. It is not to be regarded as a stimulus to spurious feeling, but rather as the symbolic form of a specific, extended or heightened experience. Such finely articulated symbols might not be translated into other modes of expression; and the pretense to interpret them discursively is vain."[20] Through Langer's work—on Gestalt in "Presentational Forms" or "Life Symbols" and its references to primitive abstraction, or indeed through other studies such as the "Roots of Myth"—Read's and Pedrosa's views on the universalism of abstract form, as well as the symbolic transformation and sensibility in art in the broadest sense of the word, approach each other's, at precisely the moment Volpi is awarded the National Painting Prize.[21]

To consider Volpi as somewhat of an "outsider" was therefore a necessary consequence of such a theoretical framework developed in parallel by the respective art critics. It was however one that did not fully respect the actual creative conditions of the artist himself. Tracing Volpi's early trajectory, art critic Lorenzo Mammi stated how the artist was not as isolated as Pedrosa implied but that he had direct contact with events considered as historically significant within Brazilian modernism. Volpi attended for instance the 1917 controversial exhibition of expressionist paintings by Anita Malfatti as well as Fillipo Tommaso Marinetti's 1926 public address in São Paulo. During the 1920s, as Mammi argues, Volpi had already suppressed in his painting the desire to merely reproduce nature but was already engaged with romanticist, impressionist, and later expressionist genres. Such work earned him the gold medal at the 1928 Salão de Belas Artes Muse Italiche, at the Palácio das Indústrias, São Paulo, for artists of Italian descent. Italian art from Giotto to that of the nineteenth and early twentieth centuries, together with a working class and lower middle-class network of Italian artists living in São Paulo constitute Volpi's broad art apprenticeship.[22]

The participation within the local salons continued with varying success and in the 1930s Volpi integrated the circle of the Santa Helena group: a studio formed by artists, many of whom were of Italian descent. Key protagonists of *modernismo* would occasionally participate in meetings organized by the group, figures such as Sérgio Millet, Bruno Giorgi, Lasar Segall, and Tarsila do Amaral. In 1938 Volpi had the opportunity to see the work of Josef Albers, an artist he claimed to have always admired. Several accounts also state how Volpi had absorbed the work of Cezanne at the occasion of the exhibition of French Art "From David to Picasso" held in 1940 in São Paulo. Volpi is also said to have been influenced by artists such as Oswaldo Goeldi, considered as a unique figure of expressionist sensibility within Brazilian art. Lasar Segall, the Lithuanian expressionist who became a central figure within the 1920s São Paulo modern art movement, also held a significant role in Volpi's artistic formation.

2nd São Paulo Biennial, 1953. President Juscelino Kubitschek, Francisco Matarazzo Sobrinho, and guests viewing Pablo Picasso's *Guernica*. Fundação Bienal de São Paulo / Arquivo Histórico Wanda Svevo.

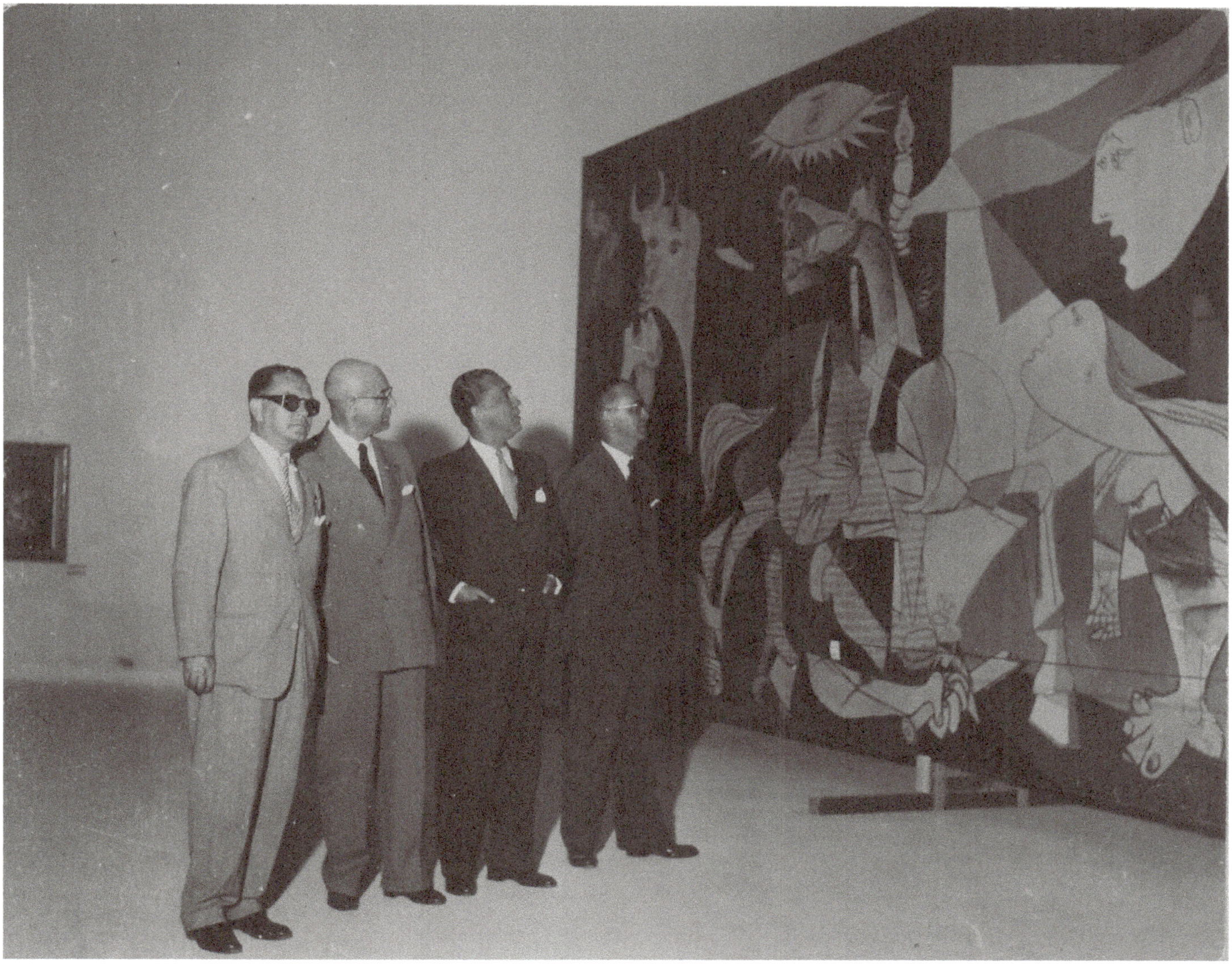

Such a brief summary of Volpi's artistic trajectory prior to his "discovery" by Herbert Read in 1953 suggests an artist with a solid foundation and awareness of early twentieth-century movements with significant connections within the local artistic milieu.

It is however one of Mammi's remarks that would place Volpi more in relation to the sophistication of a Ben Nicholson than the "outsider" character of a painter such as Alfred Wallis. In the late 1930s Volpi began frequenting the coastal town of Itanhaém where he came across the work of "naïf" painter Emygdio Emiliano de Souza. This encounter became one of the sources for his stylistic shift which can be noted in the paintings of house façades and later with the introduction of bunting motifs.[23]

Although it is difficult to trace a precise line of development, given that the artist rarely dated his paintings, Volpi's work did not progress in a linear fashion. It also seems that several distinct themes and "styles" were worked on concurrently. What is certain is that such shifts in Volpi's technique and compositions—the switch in technique from oil on canvas to tempera or the adoption of naïf-like motifs, after his encounter with the works by Emiliano de Souza—were taken consciously, as opposed to being merely stylistic whims of an untrained, intuitive artist.

Equally, within the transition from the painter of popular festivities and façades to the celebrated concrete artist, the bunting in Volpi's work assumed an iconic role: a pivot through which the artist detached himself from figuration to become a producer of geometric, if not entirely, concrete forms.

Pedrosa's emphasis on Volpi's progression from the craftsmanship of his profession as a painter-decorator to that of the professional artist hints at a possible reason for the concrete group's interest in the artist from Cambuci—the working-class and lower middle-class São Paulo neighborhood where Volpi lived for most of his life.[24] Waldemar Cordeiro, spokesman for the Ruptura Group, himself an artist of Italian origin, drew on Gramscian Marxist theory to argue that the simplicity of the concrete geometric visual language held a direct appeal that transcended erudition and Volpi seems paradigmatic in this respect: "We believe with Gramsci that culture only exists historically when it creates a unity of thought between the 'simple [people]' and the artists and intellectuals. In effect, only within this symbiosis with the simple does art rid itself from the intellectual elements and from its subjective nature, and so becomes life."[25] However, if Volpi over the course of the 1950s transcended erudition, he did so, arguably, by contradicting the very premises of the concrete art movement. The figure of the bunting, the graphic mechanism through which Volpi's work integrates the concrete visual vocabulary, is at one and the same time the iconic abstracted symbol that denies that association.

It is true that Volpi did produce work that to all intents and purposes could be described as concrete art. Such is the case of *Composição Concreta Branca e*

2nd São Paulo Biennial, 1953. Awarded artists on front row: Maria Martins, Tereza d'Amico, Antonio Bandeira, Arnaldo Pedroso D'Horta, Alfredo Volpi, Di Cavalcanti, José Fábio Barbosa da Silva, Bruno Giorgi, and Robert Tatin. Fundação Bienal de São Paulo / Arquivo Histórico Wanda Svevo.

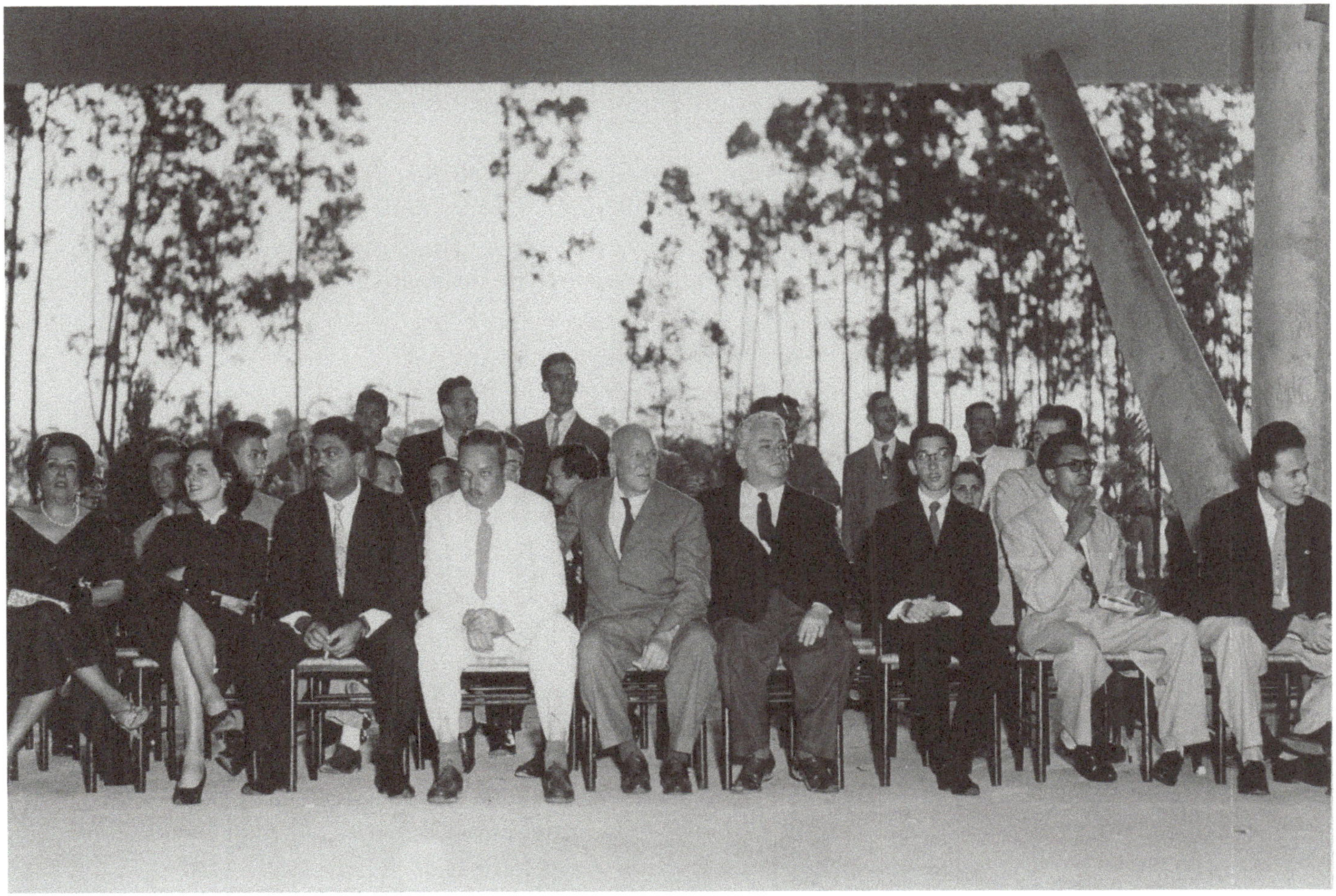

Vermelha (Concrete Composition in White and Red) of 1955, one of the rare works that is titled and dated, a work Pignatari described as follows: "The dynamic structure in his extraordinary checkered painting in white and red, where a refraction phenomenon takes place through the interference of the elements (that reconcile themselves at the center of the rectangular picture: the incidence of the eye), confers the same white two diverse qualities. This work is precisely a concretist work, even if for Volpi, probably it does not matter which 'ism' it belongs to."[26] Other works by Volpi from the second half of the 1950s present clear constructivist-oriented compositions. Volpi's participation in the First Exhibition of Concrete Art, held at the Museum of Modern Art in São Paulo in 1956, which traveled to Rio de Janeiro the following year, attests the level of his integration within that group. His inclusion in that exhibition raises nevertheless some interesting issues with regard to the consensual narratives on the concrete and later neoconcrete movements in Brazil.

Pignatari's description of Volpi's *Composição Concreta Branca e Vermelha* is in this sense somewhat discordant with orthodox definitions of concrete art. By dismissing the process through which the artist achieved the composition, Pignatari inadvertently associates Volpi with what would become a central tenet within the neoconcrete discourse: one that called for the sole critical focus on the finished work rather than the process which led to it.[27]

As discussed earlier, the mathematical basis ruling concrete art production is often placed in opposition to the intuitive approach pursued by the neoconcrete artists. The divergence between the two groups is said to have emerged precisely at the moment in which they were brought together at the occasion of the national concrete art exhibition.

Volpi's role within such an exhibition was ambivalent and therefore all the more art historically significant. This fact did not escape the attention of Rodrigo Naves who argued that:

> Perhaps most of Volpi's oeuvre within the constructive art's sphere of influence is closer to the aestheticism of concrete art. Several other works, however, feature solutions . . . which imply a deeper involvement with neoconcrete art.
>
> . . .
>
> According to his output during the second half of the 1950s, Volpi seemed to straddle the influence of both groups, and always because of his unique solutions.[28]

For Naves the complexity of Volpi's work, one that is evidenced through its ambivalence with respect to the constructivist movements in Brazil, reveals the very contradictions present within that optimistic moment of rapid industrialization of the nation. His stubborn artisan processes that combined sophisticated colorist skills in

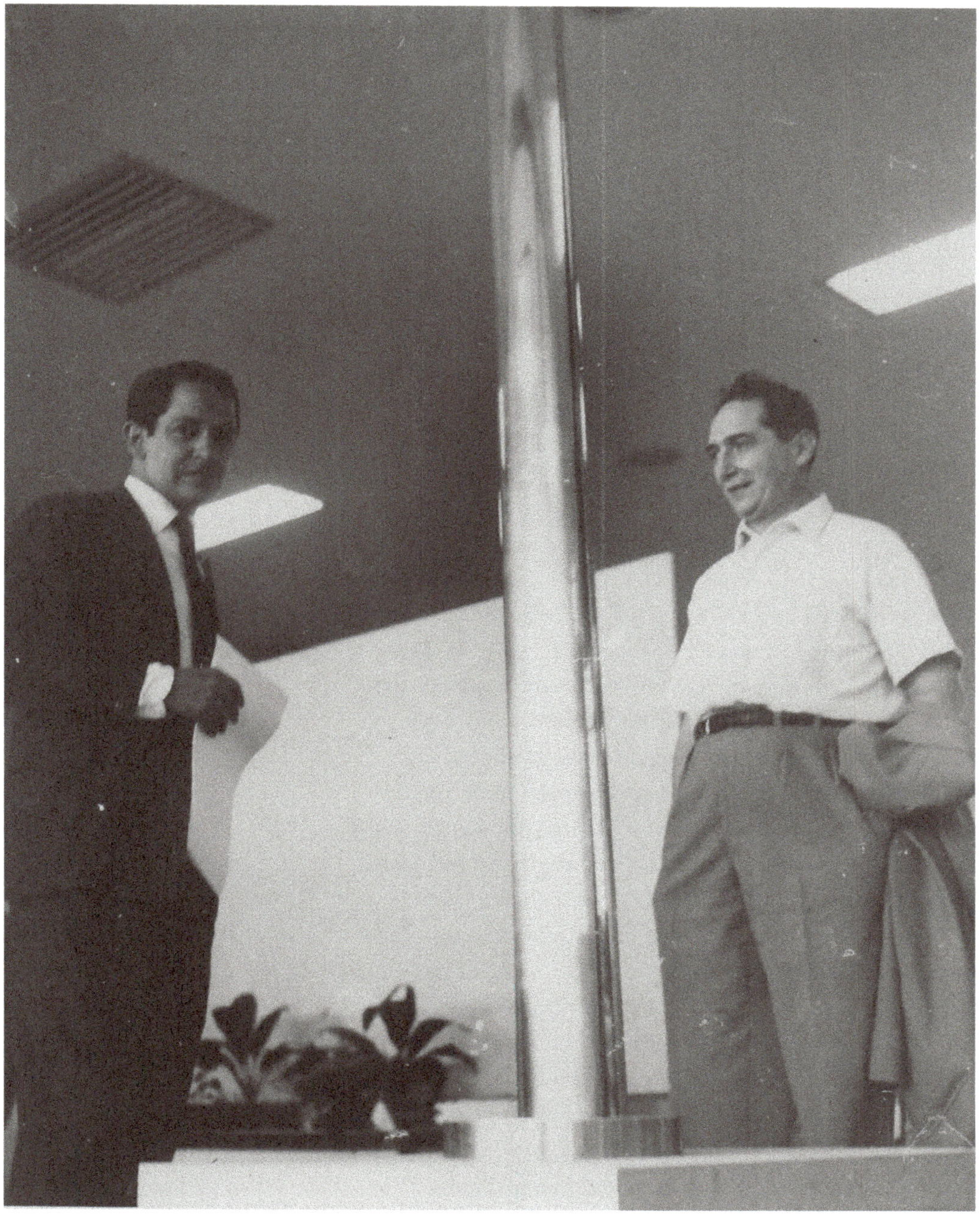

2nd São Paulo Biennial, 1953.
Guided tour with Jayme Maurício and Mario Pedrosa.
Fundação Bienal de São Paulo / Arquivo Histórico Wanda Svevo.

contrast with the most unpretentious themes and motifs, a personal incorporation of the modernist tradition, would have a profound impact on the generation of artists that followed—most notably, as Naves argued, among the neoconcrete artists.

Naves's supposition is confirmed by a letter Ferreira Gullar sent to Mário Pedrosa prior to the publication of the Neoconcrete Manifesto. The letter is dated February 1959 and in it, after discussing some business about the forthcoming AICA conference that would be held in Brazil later that year, Gullar states: "In short, we [the neoconcretes] seek to put things back in their places: let us do away with this scientific demagogy that only frightens the bourgeois and confuses the artist himself. Art is not taught in school, and one need not be a doctor (rather, someone like Volpi) to make it."[29]

DIVERGENCES BETWEEN SUSANNE LANGER AND FERREIRA GULLAR

According to consensual art historical accounts, neoconcretism's rejection of mathematics as a premise for creation was at the heart of its reaction to the concrete art group in São Paulo. Although this referred initially to poetry, specifically to Ferreira Gullar's abhorrence of the proposed "Plano piloto para poesia concreta" (Pilot plan for concrete poetry), it was later applied, but arguably never fully elaborated, within the overall neoconcrete critique.[30] It is true that one of the most significant contributions of neoconcretism was precisely the questioning of disciplinary distinctions within cultural production. We witness for instance the close relation between neoconcrete poems and works that required manipulation by the spectator, while Gullar's "Teoria do não-objeto" (Theory of the nonobject) brought the fields of painting and sculpture together through a phenomenological understanding of their presence in space, in the world.[31] The neoconcrete manifesto, in this way, privileged the perception of the finished work as an object (a nonobject as would be argued later), a unique apparition within the world, over and above the process that led to its constitution: "It does not matter what mathematical equations are to be found at the root of a sculpture or painting by Vantongerloo. It is only when someone perceives and experiences the work of art, that its rhythms and colors have meaning. Whether or not Pevsner used figures of descriptive geometry as his starting point is without interest, if placed alongside the new space that his sculptures give birth to and the cosmic-organic expression which his works reveal."[32] Mathematics thus stood as "diametrically" opposed to the organic, intuitive, and expressive act itself: qualities held dear by the neoconcretists and that the São Paulo concretists are said to have avoided at all costs. For Gullar, art that was constituted or perceived through mathematical premises submitted the object to "the machine-eye" rather than the "body-eye." Proposing

Members of the international jury gathered on December 12, 1953, to select the winners of the 2nd São Paulo Biennial. Participants included Herbert Read, James Johnson, Sweeney, Bernard Dorival, Emile Langui, Max Bill, Mario Pedrosa, Sandberg, Hofenstaegel, Palluchini, Brest, Pefeiffer, Sérgio Milliet, and Santa Rosa. Photograph Folhapress.

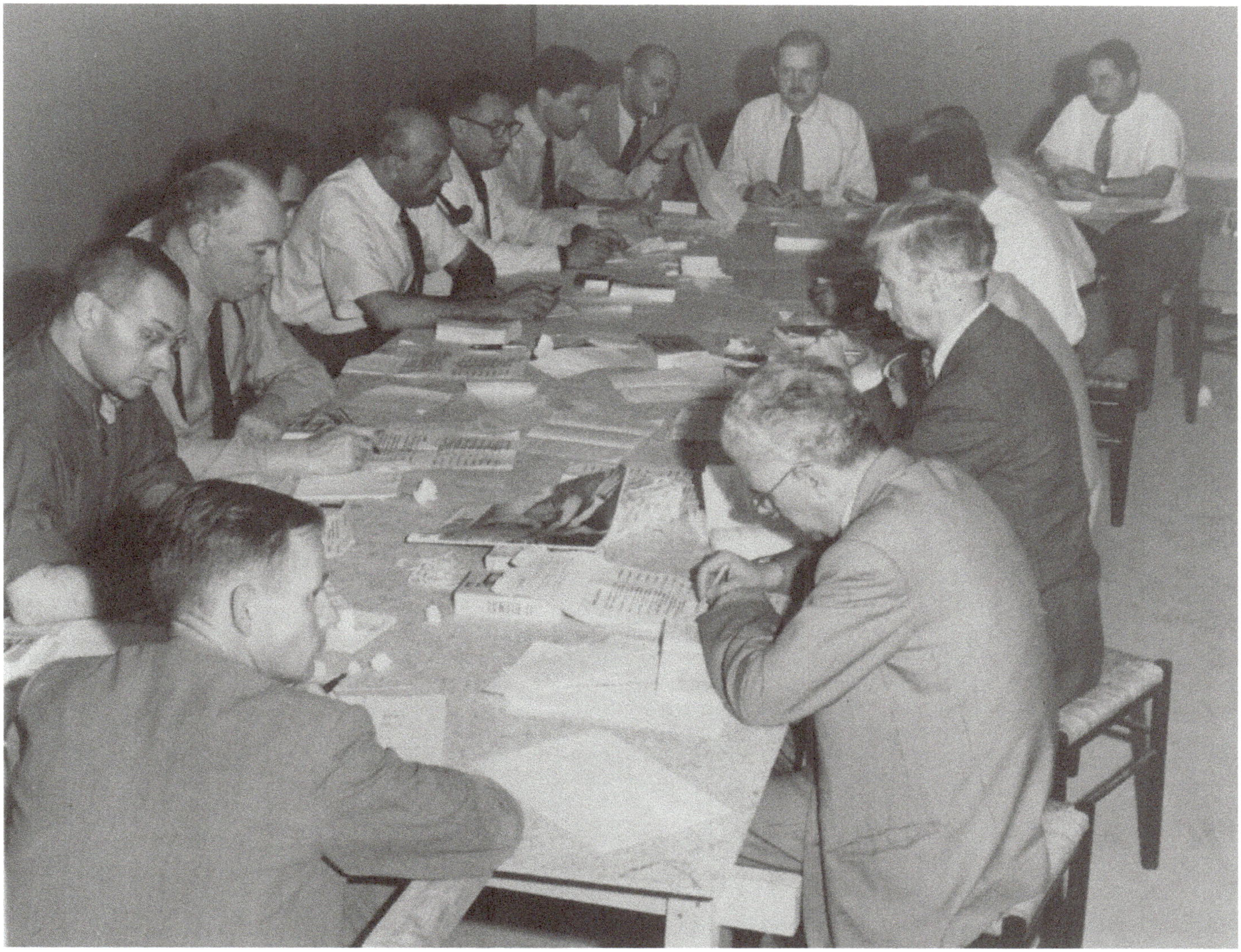

nothing less than a reevaluation of the legacy of modernism itself, the manifesto therefore laid out a revisionist critique of works by European pioneers of modern art:

> Neoconcrete art asserts the absolute integration of these elements and believes that the 'geometric' vocabulary it utilizes can render the expression of complex human realities as proved by a number of artworks created by Mondrian, Malevich, Pevsner, Gabo, Sophie Taeuber-Arp, etc. Even if these artists themselves mistook the concept of expressive form for the notion of mechanical form, it must be clear that, in art language, the so-called geometric forms totally loose the objective character of geometry to turn into vehicles for the imagination.[33]

This revisionist approach to historic works becomes the method for analysis for the production of the neoconcrete group itself, and Franz Weissmann is perhaps the most obvious example of such a posteriori theoretical procedure.

The very idea of the "organic," heralded by Gullar through the image of the object as "quasi-corpus" as a principle relation to geometry within neoconcrete works, could be seen to have been explored, keeping in mind the specificity of each case, by Herbert Read in his writing on Henry Moore. Such a coincident use of terminology seems pertinent if only because Moore had been one of Weissmann's early references within his sculptural work over the course of the 1940s. Read in 1952 drew on D'Arcy Thompson's *On Growth and Form* as an example of how mathematics can describe form in nature stating that in "the organic type of art . . . [it is] really a choice between applying the values of a particular formula or varying the values of a general formula. It is only necessary to add that the artist, even if he is a constructivist, proceeds by intuitive rather than calculative methods."[34] It is clear that the notion of the organic invoked for Read, in this particular instance, the idea of a process of abstracting from nature. Read's analysis of Pevsner and Gabo is quite distinct, however, which leads to the conclusion that he, like Pedrosa had done concurrently, was in fact attempting to establish some sort of scientific analogy for the understanding of art in general.

> The particular vision of reality common to the constructivism of Pevsner and Gabo is derived, not from superficial aspects of a mechanized civilization, nor from a reduction of visual data to their "cubic planes" or "plastic volumes" . . . but from an insight into the structural processes of the physical universe as revealed by modern science. The best preparation for a true appreciation of constructive art is a study of Whitehead or Schrödinger. But it must again be emphasized that though the intellectual vision of the artist is derived from modern physics, the creative construction which the artist then presents to the world is not scientific, but poetic. It is the poetry of space, the poetry of time, of universal harmony, of physical unity. Art—it is its main function—accepts this universal manifold which science investigates and revels, but reduces it to the concreteness of a plastic symbol.[35]

Read's articulation of the relation between art and science within constructivist art approaches the premises of neoconcretism not so much through what is said but by reference to Alfred North Whitehead and the notion of "the concreteness of the plastic symbol," which I would suggest, although not exactly analogous, approaches Gullar's idea of the art object as a "quasi-corpus."

Gullar cited the philosopher Susanne Langer in his elaboration of the theoretical premises of neoconcretism, yet in order to do so while simultaneously maintaining a critical distinction from concrete art, he was obliged to ignore key aspects of Langer's thinking. While concentrating primarily on Merleau-Ponty's phenomenology, Gullar, in other words, ignored the principle conclusions Langer drew from her PhD mentor, Alfred North Whitehead, namely what she defined as "symbolic transformation" within nondiscursive forms of creation. Langer saw mathematics as an island of abstract thought in the sea of positivistic empiricism, which she described as dominating mid–twentieth-century thinking: "And so, a scientific culture succeeded to the exhausted philosophical vision. An undisputed and uncritical empiricism—not skeptical, but positivistic—became its official metaphysical creed, experiment its avowed method, a vast hoard of 'data' its capital, and correct prediction of future occurrences its proof."[36] Langer argued in 1942 that a philosophy of reason that connects Descartes to German idealism had come to an end brought by a particular form of positivistic empiricism that held a "naïve faith in sense-evidence."

This submission of subjectivity within empiricism, through the scientific equation of truth with fact, was exemplified by Langer in the efforts produced to align psychology with scientific methods, and although not explicit within the text itself, we could extrapolate this to include the Marxist rejection of idealism through historical materialism. Published in the United States during World War II, Langer's critique of the faith in the objectivity of the scientific method, as the notion of *Weltanschauung* (worldview) itself, transcended national and political divisions.

As such, can we not think of Langer's critique in relation to the ideology of developmentalism which swept through Brazil during the post–World War II era? Is it not the case that such a scientific, technocratic culture, empirical yet arguably positivistic (as in the understanding of Langer) in its approach, serves rather well as a broad definition for the ideology of rapid industrialization during the Juscelino Kubitschek government?

Is it a coincidence that neoconcretism claimed its "independence of artistic creation in the face of objective knowledge (science) and practical knowledge (ethic, politics, industry, etc.)"?[37] Perhaps, since (if considered under Langer's perspective) this statement would suggest that at the crux of neoconcretism's autonomy—its a-political laboratory-like approach to cultural production, as Ronaldo Brito has suggested—was the negation of a productive (positivistic) relation with society at large. Was this negation not the very source of its innate political and aesthetic tensions that would ultimately lead to its dissolution during the 1960s?[38] If seen through Langer's notion of symbolic transformation, we do not find rupture (other than Gullar's own defection from avant-garde practice in 1961 to become a Marxist playwright) but continuity and autonomy or even detachment in an existential sense.[39]

The tension within neoconcretism outlined by Ronaldo Brito can perhaps be traced to Gullar's own reluctance to accept a reciprocal relationship between author and reader. Underlying the development of the poem-object lies Gullar's frustration that a poem had not been read as the author had intended.[40] It required thus a mechanism to secure its "poetic" objectivity, that is, the disposition of the poem over several pages so that its content could not be immediately disclosed but revealed gradually according to the author's intention. Symbolic transformation here is discursive (in which the word *Verde* becomes, through repetition, *Erva*) rather than open and subjective, particularly when compared to experiments carried out by contemporaneous poets such as Wladimir Dias-Pino whose poem "Solida" (1956) invited the readers themselves to determine the order of the word-signs.

Objectivity, claimed in the name of mathematics, was also not so straight forward in the case of the presence of formulations within concrete art. If Langer saw science as having been submitted to "practical knowledge" through a positivistic agenda dictated by the ideology of technology and industrialization, mathematics remained for her an exception within her philosophical enquiry into "symbolic transformation": "A mathematician does not profess to say anything about the existence, reality, or efficiency of *things* at all. His concern is the possibility of *symbolizing things*, and of symbolizing the relations into which they might enter with each other. His 'entities' are not data but *concepts*."[41] Langer is referring to a level of complexity within the mathematical field that transcended simple descriptive geometry. However, given the metaphysical investment that Langer places on mathematics as a nonpositivistic domain of symbolic formation, Mário Pedrosa's essay entitled "The Problematics of Sensibility" (which draws on Langer's "Feeling and Form") is perhaps a better means of understanding the position held by Weissmann's organization of intuition through geometrical and later nongeometrical abstract forms.[42] As we shall see, mathematics in itself is still not sufficient as a means of unravelling the nondiscursive, in short, semantically complex character of the work, if perceived as process rather than finished object.

Weissmann's relation to neoconcretism can only be understood as retrospective since during the short lifespan of the movement itself (1959–1961) the sculptor was in the midst of experimenting with nongeometric production. The fact that he traveled to Europe almost immediately after the official launch of the Neoconcrete Manifesto is conveniently ignored, possibly because during that period he would turn to the *Informel*—that dreaded, hot bloodied, adversary of the neoconcrete geometric yet intuitive expression. Weissmann is therefore a paradoxical figure, which makes him all the more interesting, being neoconcrete before neoconcretism and *Informel* during much of the existence of neoconcretism itself.

If we admit that Weissmann's neoconcrete work was produced before the advent of the movement itself, then his relation to concrete art is also problematized. We find clues to this through an analysis of what is usually considered his "first" abstract geometric work, the *Cubo vazado* (Hollowed cube).

Weissmann's own accounts of whether or not he had been aware of Max Bill or Bill's *Tripartite Unity* at the moment of conception of *Cubo vazado* (1951) are contradictory as can be noted in the following statements:

> The *Cubo vazado* was the definite severance with the figure. During this period, I liked Max Bill's work a lot. He stimulated me and from this stimulus *Cubo vazado* was born. I start off with the cube as a three-dimensional element and the square as a flat element. The cube was the original element which gave me the impulse to move on.[43]

And:

> At that time, I didn't know who Max Bill was. I didn't know his work. . . . How did the perforated cube [*cubo vazado*] come about? Perhaps due to a need to break with everything. That madness. So, I wanted to invent the simplest geometric form. I thought the simplest geometric form was the cube. Then I saw Max Bill's work.[44]

Whatever the case, today one can affirm that *Cubo vazado* was a pivotal work in Weissmann's career as it relates to key concepts and works within the concrete art movement in Brazil during the course of the 1950s while possessing (quite literally) at its core what would become the artist's own procedural logic within the construction of geometric-based sculpture: namely, the configuration of space via the articulation of lines and planes.

Among the busts, torsos, and feminine figures present in photographs of Weissmann's studio in Belo Horizonte in the 1940s are a plethora of constructions in wire, metal plate, and string which clearly indicate the pressing necessity Weissmann felt for a renewal in his formal research.

Among the early works in wire we find a work in the form of what he would later call a "linear cube." It is barely visible because of the fact that its void is denied by a series of threads in the style of Pevsner or Gabo, that crisscross the three planes established by the parallel lines within the six-sided structure. The *Cubo vazado* formed by a line, rather than a more volumetric square cross-sectioned strip, was therefore already present as a prototype circa 1948, and if linear virtual volumetric construction was already present within the work, albeit in the form of studies following Gabo and Pevsner, perhaps it also answers the ambivalent relation that *Cubo vazado* has with the legacy of Max Bill. That is to say that an affinity was

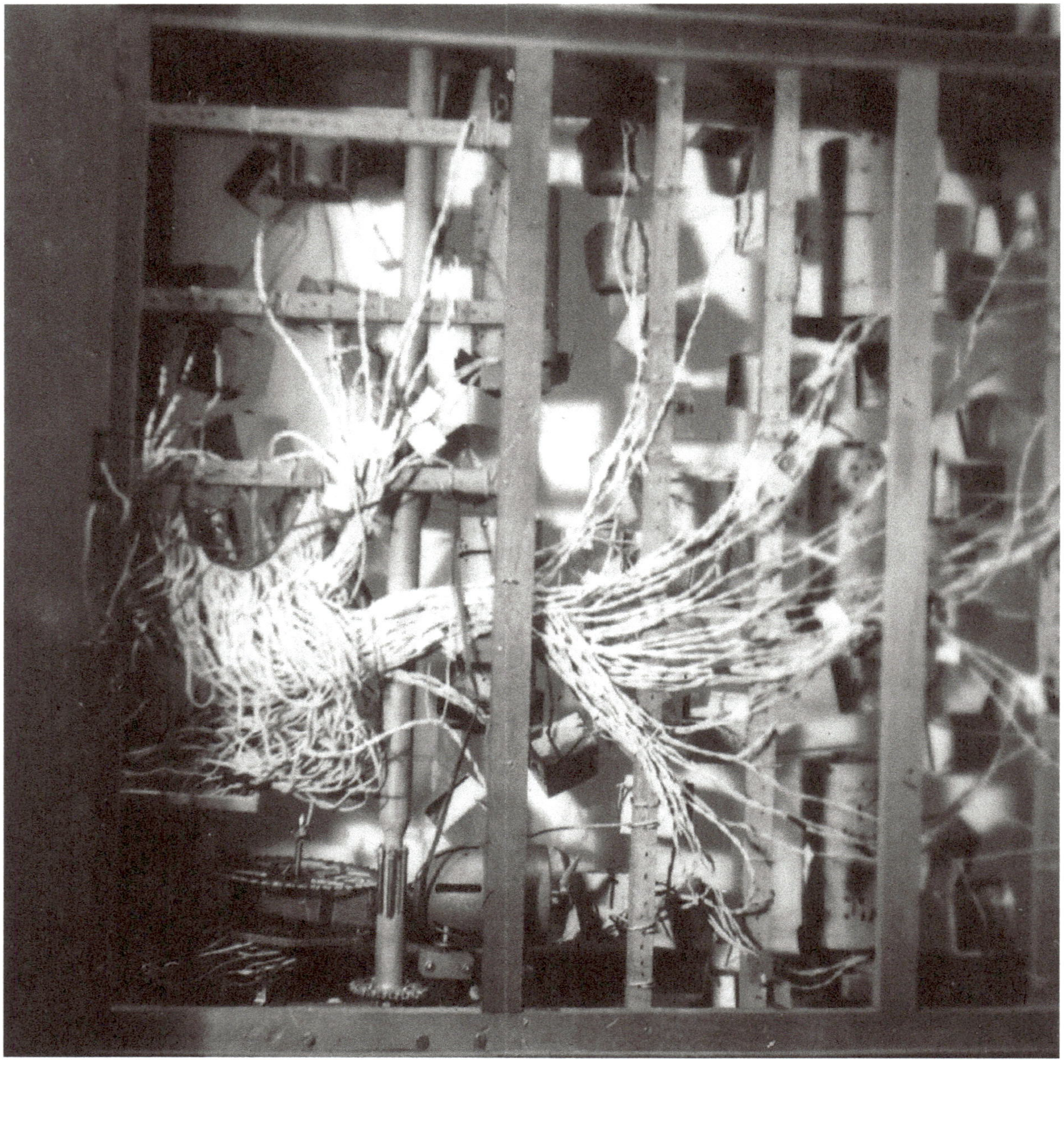

Abraham Palatnik, *Kinechromatic Device: First Movement in Blue and Purple*, 1951. Rear view of the work depicting electric mechanism. Courtesy of The Estate of Abraham Palatnik.

Abraham Palatnik, *Kinechromatic Device: First Movement in Blue and Purple*, 1951. Artist working on electric mechanism. Courtesy of The Estate of Abraham Palatnik.

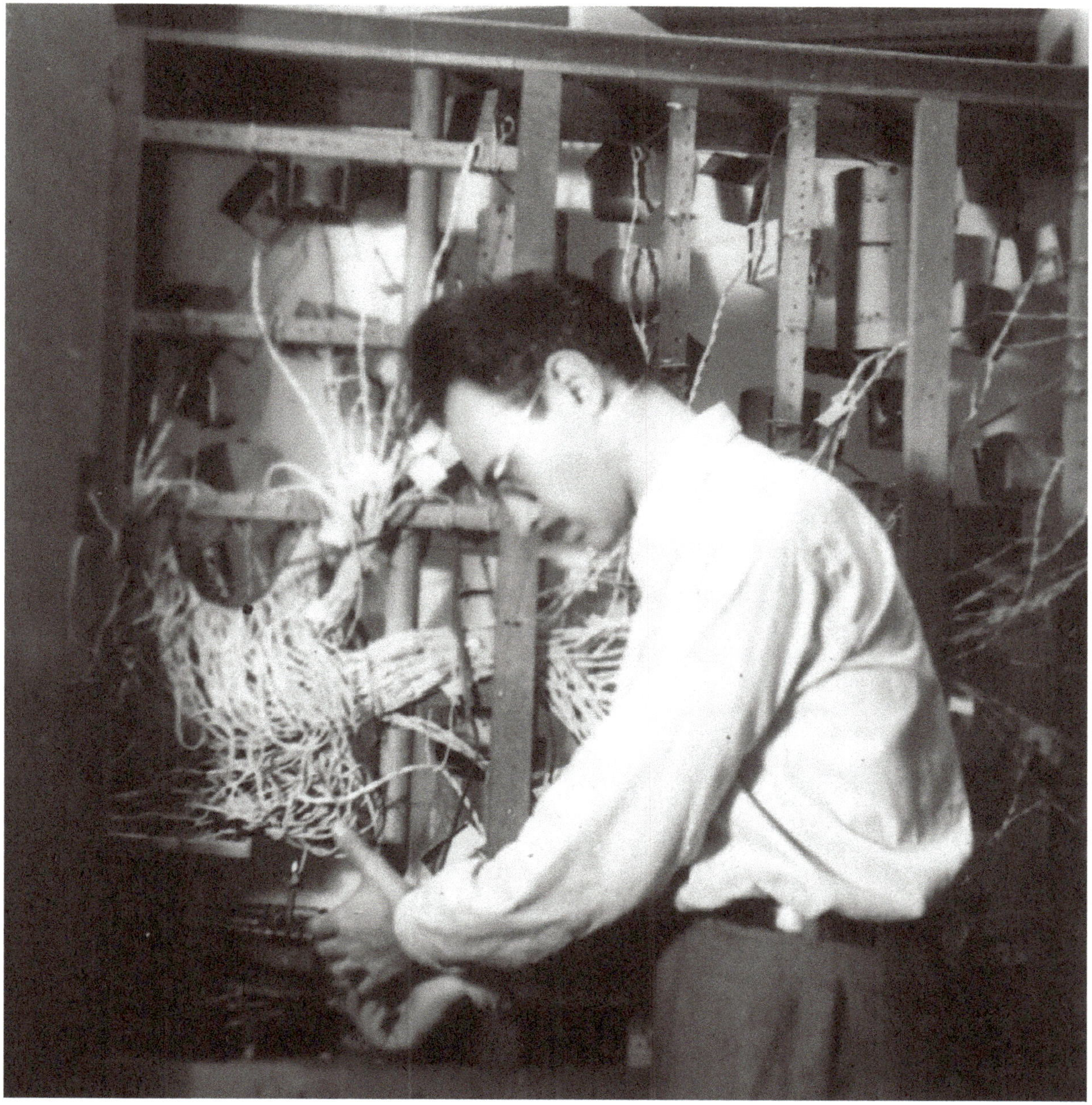

obviously recognized but not through directly referring to Bill but instead to the very sources of European constructivism itself.

If Weissmann's work with the line was achieved through a process of abstracting, a moment of rupture must have occurred in which the point of departure was no longer the figure but geometry itself. In this sense the line in Weissmann's work still holds a significant relation to concrete art.

The wire sculptures, in their invocation of geometric figures, suggest that it is still possible to conceive the form a priori even if maquettes were used as an initial means of intuitive experimentation, while the complexity of the geometric progressions created from planes suggest that the form could only be achieved by experimentation, as the artist himself admitted on several occasions. The former would suggest the proceedings of a concrete artist, the latter the intuitive approach of a neoconcrete artist. Yet, both these procedures occur concurrently with Weissmann. The works in wire, in suggesting volumetric form by providing certain but not all of the form's outlines, can be considered to function within the domain of Gestalt psychology, which shows how cognitive processes operate in order to "complete" a suggested pattern. With the works from planes no such clarity is provided. In these the form remains mysterious, even when its composition, after some consideration, is deduced. When this ambivalence is combined with Weissmann's transition to creative procedures closer to the *informel* tendency around 1960, it becomes evident that his work and intuitive approach to art making had more in common with Pedrosa's broad advocacy of abstraction than any position that the concrete/neoconcrete dichotomy would allow. As Pedrosa, drawing on Langer's *Feeling and Form*, argued:

> However much the habit of extrinsic rationalism wants to make us believe that a gesture, an action, a thought resulting from pure neutral cerebral effort attached to the rules of deductive thinking to biological fatality, the primary sensory reaction, the spontaneous organizing force of the perceptive apparatus, the awakening of sensitive memory, the interaction, after all, of the entire psychic complex placed in movement do not permit this absolute separation between logical discursive process in search of an abstract and transferable conclusion and the subjective-emotive complex which is the ego. Not only the artist but also the philosopher, the scientist, the politician are beings motivated by sensibility. As with all products of mental activity, the work of art participates in the symbolic nature of human thinking. Only its symbolic essence is very different from that of the discursive verbal symbol.[45]

Notes

This essay brings together certain themes that I have been working on during and since the Arts and Humanities Research Council (AHRC) funded my "Meeting Margins: Transnational Art in Latin America and Europe 1950–78" research project that was run jointly by the Art History Department at the University of Essex and the TrAIN research center at the University of Arts, London. A presentation at our final conference in 2011, at Tate Modern in London, drew on many issues that I explore here and which themselves were based on several papers published over the course of the project. Of particular relevance here: Michael Asbury, "Franz Weissmann: Mitos Vazios," in *Franz Weissmann: A síntese e a lírica construtiva* (Rio de Janeiro: Centro de Arte Hélio Oiticica, 2012), 22–27. I have since published an essay on Volpi that draws on sections of this essay; see Michael Asbury, "Alfredo Volpi: At the Crossroads of Brazilian Modern Art," in *Volpi: At the Crossroads of Brazilian Modern Art*, ed. M. Asbury and C. Brunson (London: Cecilia Brunson Projects, 2016), 7–15 (English) and 61–69 (Portuguese).

1 / Décio Pignatari, "Desvio para o concreto," *Folha de São Paulo, Caderno Especial 2*, May 20, 2001. Unless otherwise noted, all translations are mine.

2 / See Mário Pedrosa, "Volpi, 1924–1957" (Rio de Janeiro: Museu de Arte Moderna, 1957), exhibition catalog, translated into English by Steve Berg in Glória Ferreira and Paulo Herkenhoff, eds., *Mário Pedrosa: Primary Documents* (New York: Museum of Modern Art, 2015), 281–285.

3 / See Michael Asbury, "The Bienal de São Paulo: Between Nationalism and Internationalism," in *Espaço Aberto/Espaço Fechado: Sites for Sculpture in Modern Brazil*, ed. P. Curtis and G. Feeke (Leeds: Henry Moore Institute, 2006), 72–83, exhibition catalog.

4 / See Michael Asbury, "Some Notes on Abraham Palatnik's Kinechromatic Apparatus," in *Abraham Palatnik: A reinvenção da pintura* (Brasilia: Centro Cultural Banco do Brasil, 2013), 61–77.

5 / Mavignier upon seeing the contemporary work of artist José Patricio at the 2008 ARCO art fair, again recalled Artur Amora. See Michael Asbury, "José Patricio: Painting by Numbers/Pinturas Numerosas" (São Paulo: Galeria Nara Roesler, 2008), 1–10, exhibition catalog.

6 / Later published in M. Pedrosa, *Arte, forma e personalidade* (São Paulo: Kairós, 1979), 83–118.

7 / G. Villas Boas, "A estetica da conversão: O atelier do Engenho de Dentro e a arte concreta carioca," *Tempo Social, Revista de Sociologia da USP* 20, no. 2 (2008): 210. Hans, Prinzhorn, *Bildnerei der Geisteskranken* (Berlin: Springer, 1922), translated by Eric von Brockdorff as *Artistry of the Mentally Ill* (New York: Springer Verlag, 1972).

8 / Villas Boas, 210.

9 / Mário Pedrosa, "Ainda a Exposição do Centro Psiquiátrico" [Still the exhibition at the psychiatric center], *Correio da Manhã*, February 2, 1947.

10 / Villas Boas, "A estetica da conversão," 206.

11 / Villas Boas, 207.

12 / For an insightful study of the relations between the psychiatric hospitals in Brazil and the art historical reception of Brazilian art of the mid-twentieth century, see Kaira M. Cabañas, *Leaning from Madness: Brazilian Modernism and Global Contemporary Art* (Chicago: University of Chicago Press, 2018). For a detailed biographical trajectory of Nise da Silveira, see Luiz Carlos Mello, *Nise da Silveira: Caminhos de uma psiquiatra rebelde*, 2nd ed. (Rio de Janeiro: Automatica, 2015).

13 / D. Herbert Read Thistlewood, *Formlessness and Form: An Introduction to His Aesthetics* (London: Routledge and Kegan Paul, 1984), 112.

14 / Herbert Read's *Education Through Art* had been published in 1943.

15 / Thistlewood, 115.

16 / For a discussion on the themes and issues surrounding Volpi and the 1953 Biennial prize, see Michael Asbury, "Alfredo Volpi: At the Crossroads of Brazilian Modern Art," in *Volpi: At the Crossroads of Brazilian Modern Art*, ed. M. Asbury and C. Brunson (London: Cecilia Brunson Projects, 2016), 7–15 (English) and 61–69 (Portuguese).

17 / Otilia B. F. Arantes, *Mário Pedrosa: Itinerário critico* (São Paulo: Cosac Naify, 2004), 98.

18 / Arantes, 98.

19 / Arantes, 99.

20 / Quoted in Thistlewood, *Formlessness and Form*, 152.

21 / See Susanne K. Langer, *Philosophy in a New Key: A Study in the Symbolism of Reason, Rite and Art* (London: Oxford University Press, 1951 [1942]). At the Meeting Margins conference held at the university of Essex in December 2010, Suzana Vaz elaborated on the significance of Jung within the work at the Engenho de Dentro Hospital, and Sérgio Martins investigated the articulation of Gestalt psychology and Merleau-Ponty's phenomenology within the historiography of neoconcretism. A report of that conference was published as a special dossier in Michael Asbury, "The Popularization of Scientific Thought," in Dossier Meeting Margins, *Concinnitas Journal*, Instituto de Artes, Universidade Estadual do Rio de Janeiro (2011), 14–23.

22 / See L. Mammi, *Volpi* (São Paulo: Cosac & Naify, 1999). See also M. Asbury, "Alfredo Volpi," in Asbury and Brunson, *Volpi*, 7–15 (English) and 61–69 (Portuguese).

23 / Mammi, *Volpi*, 105.

24 / Pedrosa, "Volpi, 1924–1957."

25 / W. Cordeiro, "O Objeto," in *Revista Arquitetura e Decoração*, no. 20 (December 1956); reprinted in Aracy A. Amaral, *Projeto Construtivo Brasileiro na Arte (1950–1962)* (Rio de Janeiro: Museu de Arte Moderna do Rio de Janeiro, 1977), 75, exhibition catalog.

26 / D. Pignatari, "A Exposição de Arte Concreta e Volpi," Suplemento Dominical, *Jornal do Brasil*, January 19, 1957. Reprinted in Augusto de Campos, Decio Pignatari, and Haroldo de Campos, eds., *Teoria da poesia concreta: Textos criticos e manifestos 1950–1960* (São Paulo: Livraria Duas Cidades, 1975), 60.

27 / Pignatari, 60.

28 / R. Naves, "A complexidade de Volpi," *Novos Estudos* 4 (July 2008): 150.

29 / Ferreira Gullar, letter to Mário Pedrosa, February 16, 1959. Reprinted in Ferreira and Herkenhoff, *Mário Pedrosa*, 417.

30 / According to Gullar, the spokesman for the neoconcrete group, the initial disagreement emerged from a proposal from the brothers Augusto and Haroldo de Campos and Décio Pignatari, wishing to publish a plan outlining the next ten years of concrete poetry along mathematical principles of composition. See statement by Gullar in *Neoconcretos*, documentary film, directed by Katia Maciel, produced by N-IMAGEM (UFRJ, 2001).

31 / Ferreira Gullar "Teoria do Não Objeto," Suplemento Dominical, *Jornal do Brasil*, December 19, 1959. For the translated facsimile, see *Neoconcrete Experience*, Gallery 32 (blog), 2009, http://gallery-32.blogspot.com/2010/02/neoconcrete-experience-11-dec-2009-30.html.

32 / "Manifesto neoconcreto," Suplemento Dominical, *Jornal do Brasil*, March 22, 1959. Facsimile translated at http://gallery-32.blogspot.com/2010/02/neoconcrete-experience-11-dec-2009-30.html. Note that although the manifesto is signed by members of the Neoconcrete Group, including Weissmann himself, it is common knowledge that its author was Ferreira Gullar.

33 / "Manifesto neoconcreto."

34 / Herbert Read, *The Philosophy of Modern Art* (London: Faber and Faber, 1969 [1952]), 201.

35 / Read, 233.

36 / Susanne Langer, *Philosophy in a New Key: A Study in the Symbolism of Reason, Rite and Art* (Oxford: Oxford University Press, 1951). For a greater insight into what Langer possibly imagined to be the transcendental potential of mathematics, refer to Bertrand Russell, *An Essay on the Foundations of Geometry* (Cambridge: Cambridge University Press, 1892).

37 / "Manifesto neoconcreto."

38 / Or, as Ronaldo Brito has argued, its condition of representing the apex and rupture of the constructivist tendency in Brazil. See Ronaldo Brito, *Neoconcretismo: Vértice e ruptura do projeto construtivo brasileiro* (São Paulo: Edições Cosac & Naify 1999.)

39 / Lygia Clark is perhaps the most obvious example within this proposition of neoconcrete symbolic transformation, but Oiticica's transition from the 1950s to the 1960s could also be understood within the context of continuous "metaphysical" enquiry through the artist's reading of Bergson. See Michael Asbury, "O Hélio não Tinha Ginga," in *Hélio Oiticica: Fios soltos do experimental*, ed. Paula Braga (São Paulo: Perspectiva, 2007): 27–51.

40 / Gullar statement in *Neoconcretos*.

41 / Langer, *Philosophy in a New Key*, 19.

42 / Mário Pedrosa, "Problemática da sensibilidade," Suplemento Dominical, *Jornal do Brasil*, July 11, 1959. Facsimile translated at http://gallery-32.blogspot.com/2010/02/neoconcrete-experience-11-dec-2009-30.html.

43 / Artist statement made in 2002, *Franz Weissmann: 1911–2005* (Rio de Janeiro: Edições Pinakotheke, 2011), 217, exhibition catalog.

44 / Weissman, interview by Paulo Sergio Duarte, Paulo Venancio Filho, and Vanda Klabin, *Gávea, Revista de História da Arte e Arquitetura*, 14, no. 14 (September 1996). Reprinted in *Franz Weissmann* (São Paulo: Instituto Tomie Ohtake, 2008), 199, exhibition catalog.

45 / Pedrosa, "Problemática da sensibilidade."

THE BAUHAUS IN BRAZIL Pedagogy and Practice

3

Adele Nelson

On seeing the recent Brazilian works on view as a juror at the 4th São Paulo Biennial in 1957, Alfred H. Barr Jr. notoriously characterized them as "Bauhaus exercises" and mere "diagrams."[1] Geometric abstract works by Lygia Clark, Waldemar Cordeiro, Hermelindo Fiaminghi, Hélio Oiticica, Lygia Pape, Luiz Sacilotto, Franz Weissmann, and others prominently displayed at the exhibition were undoubtedly the target of Barr's dismissive remark.[2] Instantly controversial in Brazil, the remark was understood, then as now, as dismissive of Brazilian abstract art as a latter-day, derivative replaying of the innovations of early twentieth-century European modernism—by no one less than the founding director of the Museum of Modern Art in New York.[3] In his rebuke of Barr's assessment, prominent Brazilian art critic Mário Pedrosa noted the neocolonial attitude at work in the demand by foreign critics that Brazilian art either parrot the currently favored style in New York and Paris, in this case gestural abstraction, or literally include "flocks of parrots."[4]

Barr was not wrong in identifying the German school and its philosophy of design as an important reference for Brazilian artists, a relationship made all the more vivid by the Biennial's special exhibition dedicated to the Bauhaus. What he failed to recognize or value were the ways artists in Brazil were engaged not in imitation but in transformation. Barr judged the Brazilians with a suspicion similar to that evinced by Peter Bürger in his 1970s analysis of the avant-garde, which viewed the neo-avant-garde as depoliticized imitators of the historical avant-garde.[5] However, as Barr's comments also make clear, artists working in a developing nation placed claims on the history of European modernism in a context of particular contestation. Benjamin Buchloh, in his critique of Bürger, has called for an investigation of "the actual conditions of reception and transformation of the avant-garde paradigms" on the part of the European and US postwar avant-gardes, a project equally crucial for study of the postwar avant-gardes of Latin America and beyond.[6] Engagement with Bauhaus ideas, at the institutional and individual levels, proved a key forum for Brazilian actors in the 1950s to articulate tactics of citation and adaptation and to assert nonderivative, radical conceptions of modernism.[7]

In their respective landmark studies from the 1970s, Brazilian art historians Aracy Amaral and Ronaldo Brito established that European constructivist tendencies—including De Stijl, the Russian avant-garde, and the Bauhaus—found a powerful resonance and redefinition in Brazil following World War II among concrete and neo-concrete artists.[8] The claims on the Bauhaus, in particular, are ripe for reappraisal, as the manifold reinterpretations of the Bauhaus in the 1950s, in Brazil and abroad, allow us to critically reflect on the postwar Brazilian avant-garde and its relationship to European modernism. Scholars have analyzed individual Brazilian artists' transformations of the formal and conceptual ideas of Bauhaus students and teachers, including Josef Albers, Max Bill, and Paul Klee.[9] Others have drawn attention to the effort in the late 1950s and early 1960s to create an art school in Rio de Janeiro based on the Hochschule für Gestaltung (School of Design, HfG) in Ulm, Germany (1953–1968)—an initiative that would result in the creation of the Escola Superior de Desenho Industrial (School of Industrial Design) in 1963.[10] Emphasis on the figure of Bill and narratives of influence centered on Bill's transmission of concretism to Latin America, however, have overshadowed a nuanced interpretation of the context and stakes of artists' considerations of Bauhaus pedagogy and practice. Yet important developments related to art education in the early 1950s, which had little direct connection to Bill's activities or were positioned in opposition to them, are essential to understanding the conditions in which ideas about the Bauhaus became relevant and useful for artists in Brazil.

To speak of the Bauhaus in the singular and to use the term both as a historical reference and as an ostensibly stable and unified set of design and pedagogical principles is, of course, inaccurate. Walter Gropius, the institution's first director, aimed not simply to provide an alternative to traditional art academies but to eschew the notions of art for art's sake and of design in the strict service of industry. Indeed, the Bauhaus was to be an interdisciplinary and international school where creative expression engaged the "practical work of the world."[11] Hal Foster and Barry Bergdoll employ narrative metaphors—fiction and myth—to explain the capacities of Gropius's "Bauhaus idea" not only to assimilate the artists and principles of De Stijl and Russian

4th São Paulo Biennial, 1957. Installation view with works by Franz Weissmann and Hermelindo Fiaminghi. Fundação Bienal de São Paulo / Arquivo Histórico Wanda Svevo.

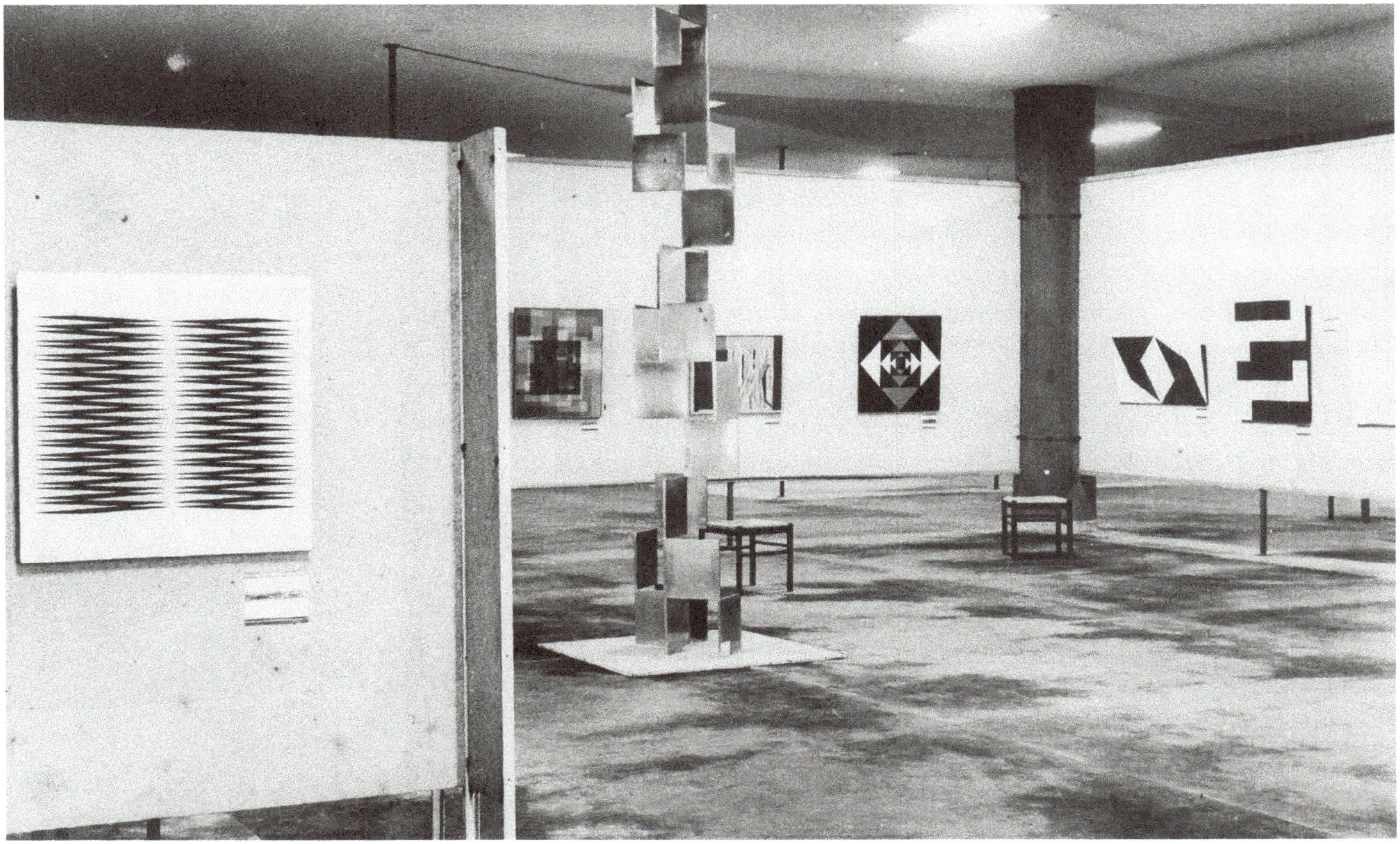

constructivism, the school's historical contemporaries, but to endure and attract new adherents.[12] From its inception in Weimar, Germany, in 1919 and subsequent moves to Dessau and Berlin (until its closure in 1933), to the permutations that its masters and students developed—first while in exile in the United States and later in Europe and Latin America after World War II—the Bauhaus was always multifaceted. Historian Paul Betts has argued that in the 1950s, West German and US institutions in the context of the Cold War stripped the Bauhaus of its historical socialist and communist associations, rendering it a "bold yet innocent school of fine arts," and understood its design approach as a tool of capitalist development and an embodiment of liberal humanism.[13] In the Brazilian context, politicians and the leaders of a spate of new modern art institutions, including the São Paulo Biennial, adopted discourses linking artistic freedom, democracy, and capitalist "progress" in light not only of the Cold War but also of rapid state-supported economic development and the country's return to democracy following the Estado Novo dictatorship of Getúlio Vargas (1937–1945).

Two art schools that opened their doors in the early 1950s at the recently established museums in São Paulo and Rio de Janeiro were key interlocutors in the negotiation of claims on the German school and its pedagogy for the emerging Brazilian postwar avant-garde. The first was the Instituto de Arte Contemporânea (Institute of Contemporary Art, IAC) at the Museu de Arte de São Paulo (São Paulo Museum of Art, MASP), inaugurated by MASP's director Pietro Maria Bardi in 1951, with architect Jacob Ruchti as a key teacher. The second was the art school of the Museu de Arte Moderna do Rio de Janeiro (Museum of Modern Art in Rio de Janeiro, MAM-RJ), which opened in 1952 with artist Ivan Serpa as lead teacher. The IAC was short-lived, lasting less than three years in its original configuration, and Serpa's courses at MAM-RJ were suspended when he departed for extended travel in Europe in 1958.[14]

The schools offered instruction grounded in nonobjective abstraction and immersed students in modern art history, alternatives to the training oriented by naturalism, expressionism, and cubism at Rio's Escola Nacional de Belas Artes (National School of Fine Arts, ENBA), São Paulo's Liceu de Artes e Ofícios (School of Arts and Crafts), and the private schools in both cities. In this essay, I examine the curricula of the new schools, highlighting the important roles of certain thinkers and teachers, including Bardi and Ruchti at the IAC and Pedrosa and Serpa at MAM-RJ, and works by artists trained at the respective schools, including an analysis of the series of paintings by Clark that in part elicited Barr's comments. The pedagogy and practice that these artists and thinkers created, far exceeding exercises, reveal that the Bauhaus served as a crucial point of both avowal and disavowal for the emerging Brazilian avant-garde and its supporters, which they used to establish connections to European modernism, assert a basis of art-making in nonobjective abstraction, and proffer an ethos of research-based and materially grounded experimentation.

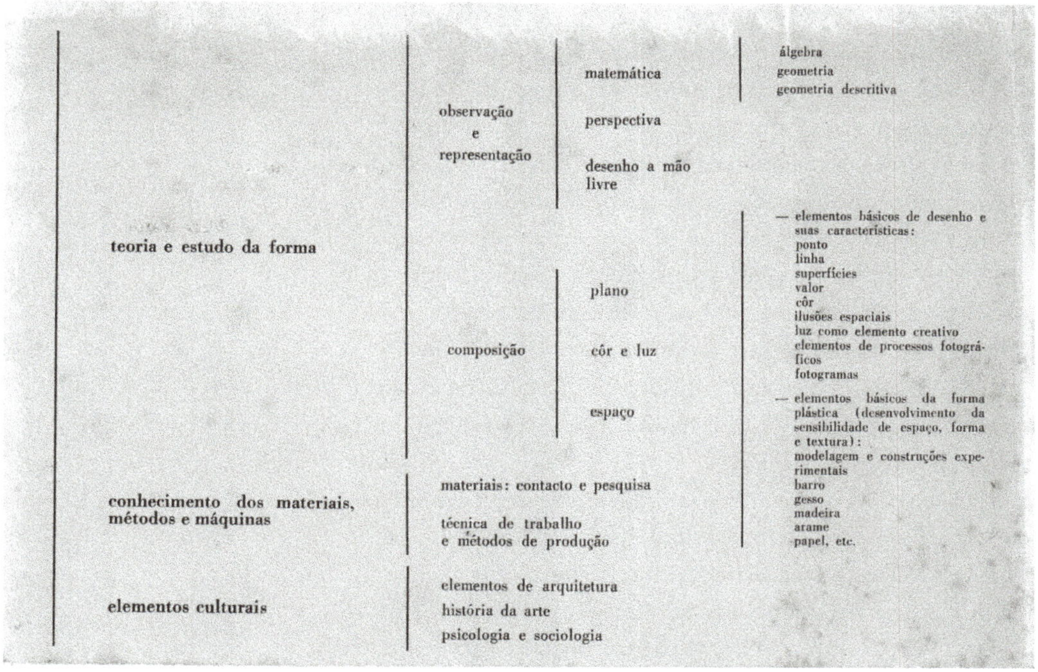

Curriculum diagram for the introductory course at Instituto de Arte Contemporânea, 1957. Arquivo do Centro de Pesquisa do Museu de Arte de São Paulo.

INSTITUTO DE ARTE CONTEMPORÂNEA

The IAC opened its doors at MASP on March 1, 1951, the same day the museum inaugurated a retrospective dedicated to Bill.[15] In public and private communications, the MASP and IAC leadership declared a relationship between the new school and the Bauhaus.[16] The Bauhaus was, at mid-century, an effective shorthand for the ambition of Bardi and his collaborators to brandish the IAC as a new form of education—international in orientation and distinct from the traditional fine art academies and vocational training available to Brazilians. Design historian Ethel Leon has argued that the repeated evocations of the Bauhaus (the Dessau Bauhaus, in particular) and of the Institute of Design in Chicago, where László Moholy-Nagy had sought in the late 1930s to establish a new Bauhaus, served strategic purposes of legitimization and derived from a desire to forge a relationship with industry over and above any fidelity to Bauhaus models.[17] Although there is truth to Leon's analysis, the organization and execution of the IAC curriculum nevertheless evinces a rigorous examination and adaptation of Bauhaus pedagogy and, in particular, of the approaches of the self-declared inheritors of Bauhaus instruction in the United States.

In essays for local and international periodicals, Bardi and Ruchti stated matter-of-factly that the school was modeled on the Bauhaus and, above all,

Chicago's Institute of Design, which Ruchti had visited during an extended stay in the United States in 1947.[18] Like Moholy-Nagy in Chicago, the founders of IAC framed their ultimate goal as creating designers and justified the school's creation with the material needs of the rapid industrial expansion of the city of São Paulo.[19] In the year before the school's inauguration, Bardi contacted art and design schools in the United States that had positioned their approaches, to varying degrees, as Bauhaus-based and announced his museum's intention to found an art school. He requested curricula and reading lists, writing, "we should like to accomplish something similar of [*sic*] what you are doing always in the same spirit of the Bauhaus."[20] While Bardi was aware of the then-nascent plans for a new Bauhaus in Ulm and hoped that Bill would teach as a visiting professor at the IAC, the HfG was not a model for the IAC. Bardi did not request information from Bill about his plans, nor did the IAC leaders mention the German institution in their representation of the IAC.[21]

The IAC founders adopted the Bauhaus preliminary course, albeit one revised to the specific intellectual and economic conditions in Brazil and with particular attention to Moholy-Nagy's curriculum in Chicago. The course asserted the cornerstone of Bauhaus pedagogy: that an experiential and abstract study of color, form, texture, and materials was the foundation of visual expression. [22] A brochure for the IAC explained the curriculum in two diagrams, the first of which detailed the preliminary course.[23] The brochure quoted the well-known diagrams of the curricula of the Bauhaus from 1922 and the Institute of Design from 1937, without appropriating their distinctive circular form. The IAC diagram instead maps, from left to right, the breakdown of large subjects into specialized topics and, ultimately, long lists of materials. The privileged term in the IAC diagram is not the field of study but the concept of *form*, and drawing is understood as the principal means to study and theorize form. If the Bauhaus and the Institute of Design diagrams suggested equality among the two- and three-dimensional media in a training that culminated in the elevated fields of architecture and urban planning, the IAC in its curricular diagram privileged two-dimensional design and drawing. Industrial design—the burgeoning field for which Ruchti saw the school preparing its students—is absent in the first-year curricular map.

Bardi and his collaborators followed Moholy-Nagy's division of the preliminary course into three units, describing them as "Teoria e estudo da forma" (Theory and Study of Forms), "Conhecimento dos materiais, métodos e máquinas" (Knowledge of Materials, Methods, and Machines), and "Elementos culturais" (Cultural Elements). The first unit, however, dominated the curriculum, subsuming elements that at the Institute of Design were divided between analytical and constructive drawing and a basic design workshop. In contrast to the Institute of Design's emphasis on the physical and life sciences, the IAC instead underscored "cultural elements" and offered courses in psychology and sociology—a focus in

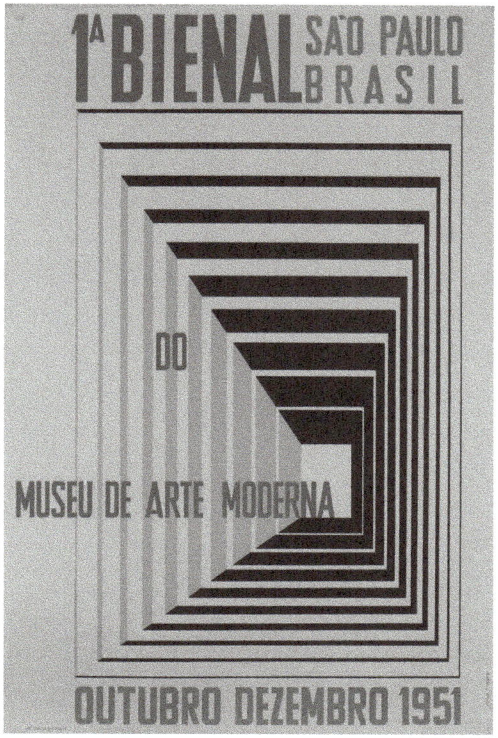

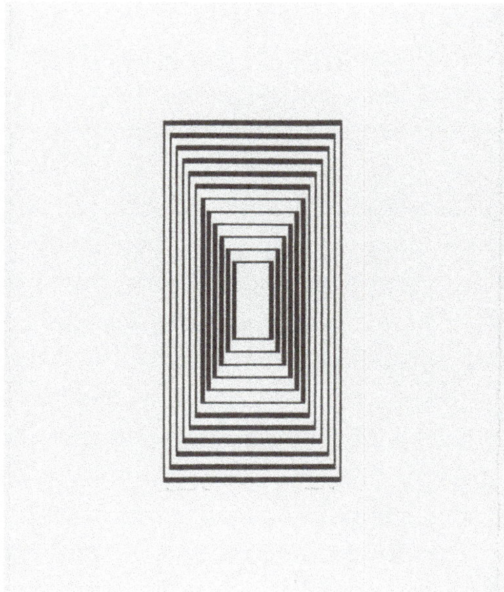

Antonio Maluf, poster for 1st São Paulo Biennial, 1951. Fundação Bienal de São Paulo / Arquivo Histórico Wanda Svevo.

Josef Albers, *Introitus (Dedication)* from the series *Graphic Tectonics*, 1942. Lithograph. The Museum of Modern Art, gift of the artist.

concert with the widespread interest among intellectuals in postwar Brazil in visual perception, Gestalt psychology, and psychiatry.

In the school's first months of existence, three of the four studio courses were devoted to drawing—a focus foretold in the "Teoria e estudo da forma" unit of the preliminary course.[24] Ruchti, instructor of IAC's composition course, viewed Bauhaus-based instruction in drawing as inseparable from the formation of designers, whom he envisioned acting as technical experts and problem-solvers in the new Brazilian economy.[25] In a 1951 text on the school, he argued that drawing and design must be understood as fundamentally intertwined as a "critical and analytical activity."[26] Ruchti saw the incorporation of intellectual and systemic analysis into the process of creation as one of the key contributions of Bauhaus pedagogy.

The emphasis on drawing, and on drawing as a means of critical visual analysis, can be seen in the design that Antonio Maluf, then an IAC student, completed for the poster of the first São Paulo Biennial in 1951.[27] In Maluf's work, concentric rectangles converge in a white rectangular void in the center right of the composition. The Bauhaus "sources" are at least twofold. Maluf based the poster design on a gouache drawing he had completed during his first month of study at the IAC, likely in Ruchti's composition class, where he learned about Vasily Kandinsky's precepts for creating dynamic equilibrium in a composition utilizing formal organization and color theory.[28] He also adapted the composition of a print from Josef Albers's *Graphic Tectonic* series from 1942, which he may have encountered reproduced in a 1948 poster designed by Bill that was included in the artist's 1951 retrospective at MASP.[29]

In the series, Albers gave the works titles that evoke sacred and ancient spaces and arranged patterns of concentric rectangles—delineated in bands of varying thicknesses that retain the crisp lettering pen profile of his preliminary drawings—to suggest architectural and virtual spaces that simultaneously recede and project. Maluf's design retains the overall organization of Albers's composition in *Introitus (Dedication)*, including rendering the sharp turns of Albers's line in the less amenable medium of gouache. Maluf, however, shifts the white void off-center—carrying out a formal strategy encouraged by Kandinsky, emphasized by Ruchti, and implemented by Albers himself in other prints in the series—to create perceptional tension and a sense of a simultaneously recessional and ascendant space. The two-dimensional text Maluf superimposes contradicts the three-dimensional quality of the concentric rectangles. Maluf also introduces color into Albers's black-and-white scene, deploying red and yellow in a manner that accentuates the qualities Kandinsky attributed to each color: the red type lays "firmly on the plane," while the yellow parallel lines seem to expand.[30] The final poster design is thus both Bauhaus-inflected and unorthodox, as the works and ideas of revered artists became templates for the younger Brazilian artist's compositional play. If space compresses and shifts within Albers's centered composition, Maluf's spatial registers—here architectonic, there graphic, here cast shadows, there typography—seem to overlay and slide past one another. Departing from Albers's references to the monumental and the spiritual, Maluf's crisp geometric abstract design instead calls to mind speed and the cinema, effects in keeping with the efforts, at the Biennial and elsewhere, to portray Brazil as a modernizing state.

IVAN SERPA AT THE MUSEU DE ARTE MODERNA DO RIO DE JANEIRO

Like the IAC, which sought to train designers through drawing, MAM-RJ distanced itself from the notion of educating "fine artists." In the case of MAM-RJ, the archetypal student was not the designer of posters and products but a child dressed in a smock with a paintbrush in hand. According to Pedrosa, Serpa's approach to the instruction of children, in particular, was a testament to the larger role that art education should play in a democratic society.[31] In contrast to Bardi and Ruchti's efforts to position the IAC as a successor to the Bauhaus in Brazil, the teachers at MAM-RJ did not purport to share a unified approach. Local artists taught a range of courses at the museum, but it was the museum's first teacher, Serpa, whose painting classes for children and adults captured the popular and critical imagination of his contemporaries and provided an identity for the new school.[32] Having won the prize for best painting by a young Brazilian artist at the first São Paulo Biennial in 1951, Serpa had a reputation as both an emerging abstract artist and a children's art instructor.[33] At MAM-RJ, he taught a number of burgeoning abstract artists—many of whom, including Aluísio Carvão and Oiticica, would soon fill the ranks of the mid-1950s avant-garde Grupo Frente (Front Group), and later the neo-concrete movement.[34]

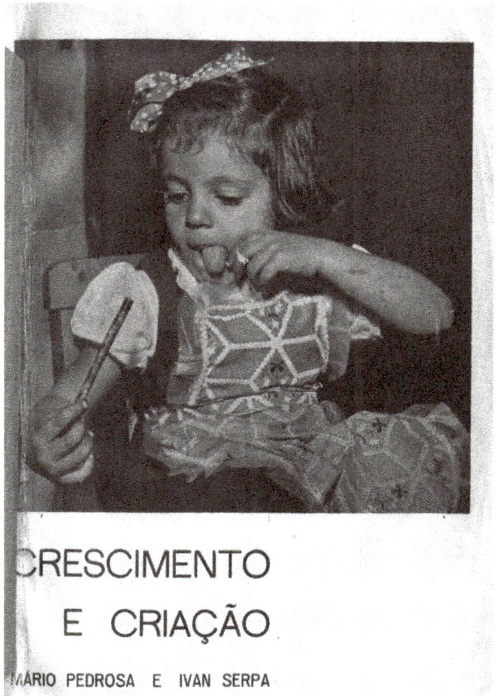

Ivan Serpa and Mário Pedrosa, *Crescimento e Criação*, 1955. University of Texas Library, Austin.

Contemporary commentators, historians, and Serpa alike often discussed his pedagogy in terms of his openness to experimentation and freedom of expression.[35] Although this is an accurate assessment—a hallmark of Serpa's teaching was his mentoring of both figurative and abstract artists—the rhetoric has overshadowed a more nuanced account of his approach. Moreover, the vision of Serpa's classrooms as self-directed, unstructured spaces accounts neither for the rigorous study of geometry, color, and materials evident in the visual production of students in his painting class for adults nor for the degree to which Serpa's instruction was informed by Bauhaus pedagogy. If the IAC's relationship to the Bauhaus was overdetermined, Serpa's incorporation of Bauhaus techniques in his teaching at MAM-RJ is a conspicuous blind spot in both contemporaneous and historical accounts.

Pedrosa, Serpa's most vocal advocate and interpreter, largely set the parameters for our understanding of the artist's teaching in texts from the late 1940s through the mid-1950s. In *Crescimento e criação* (Growth and creation), the book-length publication Pedrosa and Serpa produced in 1954, Pedrosa emphasized that the artist synthesized experimentation with technical and compositional know-how. He argued that Serpa countered "academic preconceptions," but did so while improving his students' ability to manipulate materials and to organize forms and marks in a composition.[36] Focusing on Serpa's instruction of children, Pedrosa cast Serpa as an educator-cum-social-reformer participating in an international reimagining of the education of youth.[37] At the international level, the intellectual context for this valorization of the creativity of children included the development-oriented discourse of organizations such as the United Nations and UNESCO and the conception of "visual thinking" by early- and mid-twentieth-century pedagogues and psychologists, including Rudolf Arnheim, about whom Pedrosa wrote in detail in *Crescimento e criação*. In Brazil, and specifically within Serpa and Pedrosa's milieu, Serpa's classroom was understood to stand alongside the studio that artist Almir Mavignier established in 1946 for psychiatrist Nise da Silveira's mentally ill patients at the Centro Psiquiátrico Nacional Pedro II (commonly referred to as Engenho de Dentro, the neighborhood in which it was located) as a model for a reorientation of the understanding of creativity. Never the exclusive domain of artists, art and creativity were, according to Pedrosa, "universal acquisitions."[38]

Pedrosa elected to understand Serpa's approach in relationship to Arnheim and theories of visual perception rather than suggesting parallels with the interests in the creativity of children and outsiders by surrealists, members of the Bauhaus, or the likes of Jean Dubuffet. It was not for lack of knowledge or contact—in fact, he was related to surrealist poet Benjamin Péret by marriage and participated in art-critical circles in France as well as Germany and the United States where he had resided in the late 1920s and late 1930s through the mid-1940s, respectively.[39] Pedrosa's larger intellectual project—orienting an inclusive conception of modernism on the art of nonartists and providing a place for "autochthonous resistance to international taste"—as well as his skepticism toward what he saw as a misconstruing of Bauhaus principles, and Klee's ideas in particular, as a basis for "solipsistic self-absorption" among gestural abstract artists and their champions, made the likelihood of him asserting a one-to-one lineage between Serpa's teaching and the Bauhaus remote.[40]

Moreover, Bill's presence in Brazilian artistic discussions in the early 1950s, dating back to his aforementioned exhibition in São Paulo, and in particular the substance of and controversy surrounding his visit to Brazil in May and June 1953, meant that relating Serpa's pedagogy to the Bauhaus was a decidedly unattractive option for Pedrosa. Bill's lectures at MAM-RJ, the occasion for his visit, are best known for the scandal his critique of Brazilian architecture caused in the local artistic and architectural communities.[41] Yet he also spoke at length about his plans for the new Bauhaus in Ulm, which would teach its first classes in August of that year.[42] Bill acknowledged the significance of early Bauhaus instruction, particularly the teachings of Kandinsky and Klee, but in his remarks he was more critical of that early pedagogy than he had been in contemporaneous publications (where he emphasized that the HfG in Ulm directly descended from the Bauhaus).[43] In Rio, Bill explained that he understood the approach at HfG to represent an advancement over what he viewed as Kandinsky's and Klee's more rudimentary, less scientific theories. The interpretation of the Bauhaus that Bill put forward thus differed significantly from the interests of Serpa, Pedrosa, and their cohort of artists and thinkers for whom consideration of the practices steeped in mathematics of mid-century artists such as Bill's did not supplant thinking about the work of Kandinsky, Klee, Kazimir Malevich, Piet Mondrian, and other early twentieth-century figures, nor about the art of children, untrained artists, and the mentally ill.

Although it does not appear that Serpa followed a structured curriculum comparable to that of the IAC or some of his fellow teachers at MAM-RJ, Paulo Herkenhoff, Mari Carmen Ramírez, and Irene V. Small have demonstrated that he led his adult students in explorations of nonobjective abstraction focused on color theory, application of materials, and modern art history, requiring his pupils to complete an extensive number of works, often serial investigations of form and color.[44] The experimental and abstract studies of color, material, and form taught in various iterations in the Bauhaus preliminary course were, undoubtedly, the source of many, if not all, of the exercises Serpa employed. Ramírez has noted, for example, that albums containing material and texture experiments displayed at the 1955 Grupo Frente exhibition were likely an outgrowth of Serpa's classroom.[45] Pedrosa described the albums as "containing the most varied experiments with textures, with every sort of material from bobbin lace and typewriter letter keys to cheap wrapping paper"—an account that distinctly recalls the texture and material studies in the Bauhaus preliminary course.[46]

Grupo Frente's material experimentation was not confined to the collectively executed notebooks, a fact on display at the group's second exhibition in 1955. Hélio Oiticica and his brother César, who studied with Serpa in 1954 and possibly in early 1955, exhibited mixed-media works, including experimental prints by Hélio composed of carbon paper impressions and gouache on cardboard, in which the artist ran an iron over elements of the composition.[47] Carvão, a student of Serpa's since 1953, included a medium-format suspended sculpture constructed of thin, painted slats of wood that resembled a mass of stacked matchboxes in various states of disassembly.[48] Members of the group who had not studied with Serpa also contributed to the panoply of materials on display. Abraham Palatnik showed furniture, and Pape and Clark, in addition to woodcuts and paintings, exhibited jewelry and architectural maquettes, respectively.[49]

Pedrosa interpreted the Grupo Frente notebooks, as well as the new material study evident in the artists' practices, as being foundational for the creation of enlightened design and art for an industrialized society that would be on a par with medieval craftwork.[50] The analogy between the modern and the medieval is reminiscent of Walter Gropius's conception of the Bauhaus as a "new guild of craftsmen" in the mode of medieval masons' lodges in all but name.[51] Pedrosa's larger proposal that the group share not a style but an ethos of disciplined and ethical experimentation, which he described as "the freedom of creation," was grounded in his observation of Serpa's classroom.[52] Without evoking the Bauhaus, the vision Pedrosa proposed of an ethical, experimental postwar avant-garde nevertheless corresponded with elements of the Cold War reinterpretation of the German school: both share an understanding of creativity as a wellspring of humanism and an optimism about the utility of a nonobjective, abstract artistic training for industry. However, Pedrosa, a Trotskyist and active political activist, believed that art must engage society and viewed the materially grounded conception of art forged by Grupo Frente as revolutionary.

LYGIA CLARK AND THE 4TH SÃO PAULO BIENNIAL

Among the works on display at the 4th São Paulo Biennial (1957) were Clark's *Planos em superfície modulada* (Planes in Modulated Surface), a new series of low-relief paintings begun that same year. Clark employed materials and methods that were, at first glance, easily understood: industrial paint, plywood, and airbrush. Upon closer examination, the work's unusual construction comes into focus, namely actual gaps between the elements of the painting. What first appear to be hand-drawn, ruler-aided compositions—equivalents to Josef Albers's crisply rendered and incised *Structural Constellations* (1949–1958), engravings on laminated plastic—are, in fact, assemblages that retain the jigsaw puzzle character of their preliminary collages and foretell the articulation of three-dimensional space found in Clark's hinged sculptures a few years later.

The relationship between Clark's own work and Albers's was widely commented on at the time by both the artist and critics. Pedrosa, in particular, contested critics who viewed Clark's works as indistinguishable from those of Albers. While noting the importance of "the old Bauhaus master" to the Brazilian artist's recent series, Pedrosa underscored the innovation of the *Planos em superfície modulada*, writing, "Lygia's current painting reveals space to us as composed of vectors that allow us to have a phenomenologically affective rather than a purely sensorial awareness of it."[53] Whereas space in Albers's works and the consequent viewing experience remain solely optical, Clark integrated real space via the grooves within her paintings and thereby created a tangible experience of space.[54] Clark similarly emphasized her interest in the multidimensional, ambiguous space Albers created in his *Structural Constellations*, as well as her integration of "external space" in the *Planos em superfície modulada*.[55] Clark and critic Ferreira Gullar would later understand the phenomenological orientation expressed in this series as foundational to the conception of neoconcretism.[56]

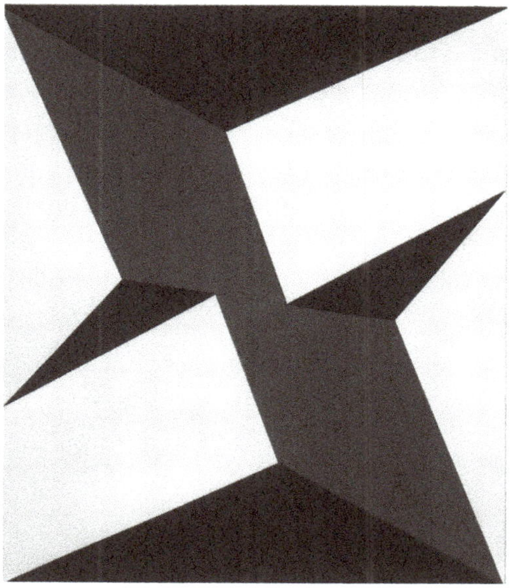

Lygia Clark, *Planes on Modulated Surface #5*, 1957. Museum of Fine Arts Houston. Courtesy of "The World de Lygia Clark" Cultural Association.

An equally radical component of Clark's series, however, is how the artist points to the sequential variation of geometric forms—a key operation of Bauhaus pedagogy as practiced by Albers and others—only to then undermine the expectation of a mappable sequence or formal evolution.[57] In early texts, Clark criticized works, including her own earlier production, that depended on "serial form," arguing that her work beginning in 1957 operated differently.[58] Clark assembled differently scaled geometric shapes of sundry types (triangles, trapezoids, rectangles, squares, parallelograms) into medium- to large-format compositions of largely black, white, and gray. The result is a group of works that range from sparse near monochromes to dense, multifaceted geometric patterns. Moreover, she produced pairs of works that share identical compositions but differ in dimensions or palette. For example, she created slightly smaller but otherwise indistinguishable versions of several works, including *Planos em superfície modulada no. 5*. As signaled by a myriad of seemingly simple, readily legible formal alterations in the series, Clark builds the operation of repetition into her practice, and she marks repetition as an act not of imitation, but of transformation.

Leah Dickerman has argued that "experience, not knowledge, was the Bauhaus watchword," and Eva Díaz has traced how "the rhetoric of experiment" was central to the reception of the Bauhaus by artists in the US context.[59] Pedrosa articulated a nexus of terms—*freedom* and *creation*, *ethics* and *discipline*—for pedagogical and artistic activities of the 1950s that point to the high societal stakes of art making in mid-century Brazil. Pedrosa's best-known slogan for the Brazilian avant-garde—"the experimental exercise of freedom"—belies an unspoken relationship to Brazilian interpretations of Bauhaus ideas.[60] The expression dates to 1967, but it finds its origins in what Pedrosa saw as the productive tension between instruction and experimentation in Serpa's pedagogy. On the continuum of experience, experiment, and experimentation, Brazilian artists and thinkers positioned themselves as inheritors and usurpers of European modernism. By 1959 the neo-concrete movement would declare that artists operating in a developing nation more completely fulfilled the ideas and praxis of the historical avant-garde than did the earlier artists themselves. In the early and mid-1950s, by contrast, Clark, Maluf, and others maintained an active tension between inheritance and usurpation in their works. The potential for misrecognition as a form of derivation that was implicit in *Planos em superfície modulada* and other series was, and is, a vital entry point into the artists' tactics of citation and adaptation—and to their critical relationship with modernism.

Notes

Curator Regina Teixeira de Barros commissioned this article in conjunction with the Pinacoteca do Estado de São Paulo's publication, in 2015, of a facsimile edition of the landmark volume *Projeto construtivo brasileiro na arte (1950–1962)* of 1977. Because of funding constraints, the essay was not published. I am grateful to the editors of *ARTMargins* for reviewing the present work and providing a home for it. Portions of this text were delivered at the Museum of Modern Art, New York; the American Comparative Literature Association Annual Meeting; and Temple University. I thank Gwen Farrelly, Claire F. Fox, Esther Gabara, Jay Levenson, Peter Logan, and Heather Ann Thompson for the invitations to speak. This essay is indebted to the thoughtful and critical insights of Libby Hruska, Jennifer Josten, and the two anonymous readers for *ARTMargins*. I also thank Rhys Conlon, Emily Hall, and Paulina Pobocha for their suggestions. For their research assistance, I am grateful to Ivani Di Grazia Costa, Romeu Loreto, and Bárbara Bernardes (Biblioteca e Centro de Documentação, Museu de Arte de São Paulo Assis Chateaubriand); Elizabeth Varela, Cláudio Barbosa, and Aline Siqueira (Pesquisa e Documentação, Museu de Arte Moderna do Rio de Janeiro); Ana Paula Marques (Arquivo Histórico Wanda Svevo, Fundação Bienal de São Paulo); and Daniela Baumann (HfG Archiv-Ulm). A Summer Research Award, a Vice Provost for the Arts Grant, and a Grant-in-Aid for Research from Temple University supported this work.

1 / C. A., "Conversa com Alfred Barr Jr.," *O Estado de São Paulo*, September 28, 1957, Suplemento literário, 7. Unless otherwise noted, translations are mine.

2 / *IV Bienal do Museu de Arte Moderna de S. Paulo* (São Paulo: Museu de Arte Moderna de São Paulo, 1957), 58–70, 73–81, exhibition catalog.

3 / For an analysis of the reaction to Barr's remark in Brazil, see Ana Cândida de Avelar, "Controversies of a Juror: Alfred Barr Jr at the 4th São Paulo Bienal," *Third Text* 26, no. 1 (January 2012): 29–39.

4 / Mário Pedrosa, "Brazilian Painting and International Taste" (1957), in *Mário Pedrosa: Primary Documents*, ed. Glória Ferreira and Paulo Herkenhoff (New York: Museum of Modern Art, 2015), 192.

5 / Peter Bürger, *Theory of the Avant-Garde* (1974), trans. Michael Shaw (Minneapolis: University of Minnesota Press, 1984).

6 / Benjamin Buchloh, "The Primary Colors for the Second Time: A Paradigm of Repetition of the Neo-Avant-Garde," *October*, no. 37 (Summer 1986): 43. For extended considerations of Buchloh's proposals regarding the neo-avant-garde, as well as those of Bürger and Hal Foster in relation to postwar Latin American avant-gardes, see Andrea Giunta, "Farewell to the Periphery: Avant-Gardes and Neo-Avant-Gardes in the Art of Latin America," in *Concrete Invention: Colección Patricia Phelps de Cisneros, Reflections on Geometric Abstraction from Latin America and Its Legacy*, ed. Gabriel Pérez-Barreiro (Madrid: Museo Nacional Centro de Arte Reina Sofía, 2013), 105–117; and Sérgio Martins, *Constructing an Avant-Garde: Art in Brazil 1949–1979* (Cambridge, MA: MIT Press, 2013), 2–9.

7 / Pedrosa identified a "radical attitude" toward modernism among Brazilian postwar artists as well as Alexander Calder and Paul Klee, whom he saw as models for young Brazilian artists. See Adele Nelson, "Radical and Inclusive: Mário Pedrosa's Modernism," in Ferreira and Herkenhoff, *Mário Pedrosa*, 35–43. Sérgio Martins and Irene V. Small use the notions of hijacking and destabilization in their analysis of the Brazilian avant-garde's relationship to modernism. See Martins, *Constructing an Avant-Garde*, 2; and Irene V. Small, "*Pigment Pur* and the *Corpo da Côr*: Post-Painterly Practice and Transmodernity," *October*, no. 152 (Spring 2015): 82–102.

8 / See Aracy A. Amaral, *Projeto construtivo brasileiro na arte (1950–1962)* (Rio de Janeiro: Museu de Arte Moderna do Rio de Janeiro, 1977); and Ronaldo Brito, *Neoconcretismo: Vértice e ruptura do projeto construtivo brasileiro* (Rio de Janeiro: Funarte, 1985). Portions of Brito's text first appeared in the mid-1970s.

9 / See, for example, Paulo Herkenhoff, "A aventura planar de Lygia Clark—De caracóis, escadas e caminhando," in *Lygia Clark*, ed. Paulo Herkenhoff (São Paulo: Museu de Arte Moderna de São Paulo, 1999), 21–22; Mari Carmen Ramírez, "The Embodiment of Color—'From the Inside Out,'" in *Hélio Oiticica: The Body of Color*, ed. Mari Carmen Ramírez (London: Tate, 2007), 37–38; and María Amalia García, "Max Bill on the Map of Argentine-Brazilian Concrete Art," in *Building on a Construct: The Adolpho Leirner Collection of Brazilian Constructive Art at the Museum of Fine Arts, Houston*, ed. Mari Carmen Ramírez and Héctor Olea (Houston, TX: Museum of Fine Arts, 2009), 53–68. I discuss Oiticica's evocations of Klee in my contribution to *Hélio Oiticica: To Organize Delirium*, ed. Lynn Zelevansky, Elisabeth Sussman, James Rondeau, and Donna De Salvo (Pittsburgh, PA: Carnegie Museum of Art, 2016).

10 / See, for example, Silvia Fernández, "The Origins of Design Education in Latin America: From the HfG in Ulm to Globalization," *Design Issues* 22, no. 1 (Winter 2006): 3–19; and Aleca Le Blanc, "Palmeiras and Pilotis: Promoting Brazil with Modern Architecture," *Third Text* 26, no. 1 (January 2012): 103–116.

11 / Walter Gropius, "The Viability of the Bauhaus

Idea" (1922), in *The Bauhaus: Weimar, Dessau, Berlin, Chicago*, ed. Hans M. Wingler (Cambridge, MA: MIT Press, 1969), 52.

12 / Hal Foster, "The Bauhaus Idea in America," in *Albers and Moholy-Nagy: From the Bauhaus to the New World*, ed. Achim Borchadt-Hume (New Haven, CT: Yale University Press, 2006), 92–102, 173–175; and Barry Bergdoll, "Bauhaus Multiplied: Paradoxes of Architecture and Design in and after the Bauhaus," in *Bauhaus, 1919–1933: Workshops for Modernity*, ed. Barry Bergdoll and Leah Dickerman (New York: Museum of Modern Art, 2009), 40–61.

13 / Paul Betts, "The Bauhaus as a Cold War Weapon: An American-German Joint Venture," in *Bauhaus Conflicts, 1919–2009: Controversies and Counterparts*, ed. Philipp Oswalt (Ostfildern: Hatje Cantz, 2009), 190–208.

14 / On the closure of the IAC in late 1953, see *Alexandre Wollner, Alexandre Wollner: Design visual: 50 anos* (São Paulo: Cosac and Naify, 2003), 72; and Ethel Leon, "IAC, Instituto de Arte Contemporânea: Escola de Desenho Industrial do MASP (1951–1953)" (master's thesis, Universidade de São Paulo, 2006), 67–70, 158–78. On Serpa's European travels, see Vera Beatriz Siqueira, "Insistently Current," in *Ivan Serpa*, ed. Fabiana Werneck Barcinski et al. (Rio de Janeiro: Silvia Roesler; Instituto Cultural The Axis, 2003), 169–175. The IAC was reestablished temporarily in 1957.

15 / Invitation, folder 14, box 3, Exposição de Pintura de Max Bill (hereafter, Exp. Bill), Biblioteca e Centro de Documentação, Museu de Arte de São Paulo Assis Chateaubriand (hereafter, Biblioteca MASP); "Uma escola e um centro de atividades artísticas: Inicia-se amanhã o funcionamento do Instituto de Arte Contemporânea," *Diário de São Paulo*, February 28, 1951, folder 1, box 1, Instituto de Arte Contemporânea (hereafter, IAC), Biblioteca MASP; and Jacob Ruchti, "Instituto de Arte Contemporânea," *Habitat: Revista das artes no Brasil*, no. 3 (April–June 1951): 62.

16 / Bardi's collaborators at the IAC (some of whom taught at the school) included the artists and architects J. Villanova Artigas, Lina Bo Bardi, Eduardo Kneese de Mello, Rino Levi, Jacob Ruchti, and Lasar Segall, who convened on March 20, 1950, to discuss the school's curriculum. The archival holdings at Biblioteca MASP only record Bardi's organizational role in establishing the school, though scholars, former participants, and contemporary accounts often view Bo Bardi as Bardi's primary collaborator. See, for example, Zeuler R. M. de A. Lima, *Lina Bo Bardi* (New Haven, CT: Yale University Press, 2013), 47.

17 / Ethel Leon, "The Instituto de Arte Contemporânea: The First Brazilian Design School, 1951–53," *Design Issues* 27, no. 2 (Spring 2011): 116–119.

18 / Ruchti, "Instituto de Arte Contemporânea," 62; and Pietro Maria Bardi, "Diseño industrial en São Paulo," *Nueva Visión: Revista de cultura visual*, no. 1 (December 1951): 9. On Ruchti's trip, see Marlene Milan Acayaba, *Branco e preto: Uma história de design brasileiro nos anos 50* (São Paulo: Instituto Lina Bo e P. M. Bardi, 1994), 34.

19 / See, for example, "No Museu de Arte: Instalação do 'Instituto de Arte Contemporânea': O belo a serviço da indústria—Fundamentos no desenho," *Diário da Noite*, February 8, 1950, folder 1, box 1, IAC, Biblioteca MASP; and Ruchti, "Instituto de Arte Contemporânea," 62. On Moholy-Nagy's pedagogical goals in Chicago, see Foster, "Bauhaus Idea in America," 96–97, 101.

20 / Bardi wrote, in English, to directors and registrars at Black Mountain College, Cranbrook Academy of Art, and Rhode Island School of Design, as well as at the Akron Art Institute (now Akron Art Museum) and the Toledo Museum of Art. Although Bardi's correspondence to Serge Chermayeff, Director of the Illinois Institute of Technology—where, since 1949, the Institute of Design had been based—is not preserved in the archive, Chermayeff's reply, in which he shared information on the institute's curriculum and recommended books, is. See Pietro Maria Bardi to Director, Cranbrook Academy of Art, March 10, 1950; and Serge Chermayeff to P. M. Bardi, March 13, 1950, both to be found in folder 1, box 1, IAC, Biblioteca MASP.

21 / The archival holdings at MASP include no mention of HfG in Bill and Bardi's copious correspondence regarding Bill's 1951 exhibition, although Bardi did write to others of his desire for Bill and other international figures to teach at the IAC. Bill was involved in the planning of HfG by 1950, and he revised his text "Beauty from Function and as Function" (originally delivered as a lecture at the Swiss Werkbund in 1948) to include a mention of Ulm when it appeared in the São Paulo magazine *Habitat* in 1951. Max Bill, "Schönheit aus Funktion und als Funktion," *Werk* 36, no. 8 (August 1949): 272–274; Max Bill, "Beleza provinda da função e beleza como função," *Habitat: Revista das Artes no Brasil*, no. 2 (January–March 1951): 61–64; Bardi to Cranbrook Academy of Art, March 10, 1950; Paul Betts, *The Authority of Everyday Objects: A Cultural History of West German Industrial Design* (Berkeley: University of California Press, 2004), 142–143; Karin Gimmi, "On Bill," in Max Bill, *Form, Function, Beauty = Gestalt*, ed. Brett Steele (London: Architectural Association London, 2011), 11.

22 / On the Bauhaus preliminary course, see Rainer K. Wick, *Teaching at the Bauhaus* (Ostfildern-Ruit: Hatje Cantz, 2000);

Leah Dickerman, "Bauhaus Fundaments," in Bergdoll and Dickerman, *Bauhaus, 1919–1933*, 15–18; and Hal Foster, "Exercises for Color Theory Courses," in Bergdoll and Dickerman, *Bauhaus, 1919–1933*, 196–199.

23 / The curriculum detailed in the circa 1957 version is identical to a printed curriculum from 1951, except for the elimination of the "Cursos complementares" (Complementary courses), which were to be taught by visiting international professors. See "Cursos," folder 1, box 1, IAC, Biblioteca MASP; "Finalidades do I.A.C. no Museu de Arte: Pretende colocar os modernos métodos de produção a serviço da arte contemporânea," *Diário de São Paulo*, June 15, 1950, folder 1, box 1, IAC, Biblioteca MASP; "Programa," folder 1, box 1, IAC, Biblioteca MASP; Ruchti, "Instituto de Arte Contemporânea," 63; and a brochure in the box Relatórios 1957, IAC, Biblioteca MASP.

24 / "Cursos regulares do Instituto de Arte Contemporânea, Museu de Arte," attendance book, folder 2, box 1, IAC, Biblioteca MASP; and Ruchti, "Instituto de Arte Contemporânea," 62.

25 / Ruchti, "Instituto de Arte Contemporânea," 62.

26 / Ruchti, 62.

27 / Maluf attended the IAC from its opening in March 1951 until at least June 1951. "Cursos regulares do Instituto de Arte Contemporânea, Museu de Arte."

28 / The gouache, entitled *Equação dos desenvolvimentos em progressões crescentes e decrescentes* (Equation of Developments in Ascendant and Descendant Progressions), dates to March 1951, when Maluf was enrolled in Ruchti's class. Leon has published notes from Ruchti's class (created by Lauro Prêssa Hardt in August 1951) which replicate a diagram and cite ideas in Kandinsky's 1926 Bauhaus book *Punkt und Linie zu Fläche* (Point and Line to Plane), a book held in the Biblioteca MASP. See Vasily Kandinsky, *Punkt und Linie zu Fläche: Beitrag zur Analyse der Malerischen Elemente* (1926), 2nd ed. (Munich: A. Langen, 1928); Jacob Ruchti, *Composição: Notas de aula* (São Paulo: Instituto de Arte Contemporânea, 1951), in Leon, "IAC, Instituto de Arte Contemporânea," appendix 5, 205–225; and Regina Teixeira de Barros, ed., *Antonio Maluf* (São Paulo: Cosac and Naify; Centro Universitário Maria Antonia da Universidade de São Paulo, 2002), 12.

29 / Scholars have not previously suggested that Albers or his series *Graphic Tectonic* was a reference for Maluf's poster design, although the series was widely reproduced at the time and the formal parallels are evident. It is possible that Bill's poster for the exhibition *Josef Albers, Hans Arp, Max Bill* at Galerie Herbert Hermann in Stuttgart in 1948—which illustrates Albers's *Introitus (Dedication)*—was among the posters and books displayed in the 1951 MASP exhibition. Max Bill, "Constatations concernant la participation de Max Bill à la 'Bienal de São Paulo,'" Zurich, August 2, 1951, folder 13, box 3, Exp. Bill, Biblioteca MASP. Late in his life, Maluf related his poster design to Albers by casting the poster as a predecessor to Albers's *Homage to the Square* series (1949–1976). Antonio Maluf to Adolpho Leirner, November 23, 1998, folder 2005.1016, Antonio Maluf Files, Adolpho Leirner Archives at the ICAA, Museum of Fine Arts, Houston. I am grateful to Mari Carmen Ramírez for the opportunity to access the Leirner archives.

30 / Vasily Kandinsky, *Point and Line to Plane* (1926), trans. Howard Dearstyne and Hilla Rebay (New York: Solomon R. Guggenheim Foundation, 1947), 62, 65.

31 / Mário Pedrosa, "A força educatora da arte" (1947), in Mário Pedrosa, *Textos escolhidos*, Vol. 2: *Forma e percepção estética*, ed. Otília Arantes (São Paulo: Edusp, 1996), 61–62. For an interpretation of MAM-RJ's education program in light of discourses of democracy, see Aleca Le Blanc, "Tropical Modernisms: Art and Architecture in Rio de Janeiro in the 1950s" (PhD dissertation, University of Southern California, 2011), 180–232.

32 / Serpa began teaching courses at MAM-RJ on May 10, 1952, and his classes in the early 1950s included painting classes for children and adults as well as a theory of painting course. See "Artes plásticas: Aulas de desenho e pintura," *Correio da Manhã*, May 9, 1952, 7; and *Museu de Arte Moderna do Rio de Janeiro* (Rio de Janeiro: Museu de Arte Moderna do Rio de Janeiro, 1967), n.p.

33 / Serpa had taught children's art classes at his home since 1947. Siqueira, "Insistently Current," 159.

34 / When Grupo Frente first exhibited in 1954, five of its eight members had studied with Serpa. By 1955, ten of its fifteen members were Serpa's former or current students.

35 / See, for example, "Pincel e calças curtas: O que é e como funciona a escolinha de Ivan Serpa—Horário sem rigidez e nenhuma obrigação—Criança, artista inato," *Tribuna da Imprensa*, May 29, 1954, folder MAM-Cursos, 1954 (hereafter Cursos 1954), Acervo Museu de Arte Moderna do Rio de Janeiro (hereafter Acervo MAM-RJ); Siqueira, "Insistently Current"; and Hélio Márcio Dias Ferreira, "Ivan Serpa, Artist-Educator," in Barcinski, *Ivan Serpa*, 201–207.

36 / Mário Pedrosa and Ivan Serpa, *Crescimento e criação* (Rio de Janeiro, 1954), reprinted as Mário Pedrosa, "Crescimento e criação," in Pedrosa, *Textos escolhidos*, 2:72.

37 / Mário Pedrosa, "Arte infantil" (1952), in Pedrosa, *Textos escolhidos*, 2:63–70; and Pedrosa, "Crescimento e criação," 71–80.

38 / Mário Pedrosa, "The Vital Need for Art" (1947), in Ferreira and Herkenhoff, *Mário Pedrosa*, 105.

39 / He also lived in Paris later in his life, and in Belgium and Switzerland as an adolescent.

40 / Mário Pedrosa, "A Bienal de cá para lá" (1970), in Mário Pedrosa, *Arte: Ensaios*, ed. Lorenzo Mammi (São Paulo: Cosac Naify, 2015), 489, 491. See also Nelson, "Radical and Inclusive," 35–43.

41 / Bill visited Brazil twice in 1953, in May and June (when he lectured at MAM-RJ) and in December (when he served on the jury of the second Biennial). For analysis of Bill's widely covered criticisms of Brazilian architecture, see Valerie Fraser, *Building the New World: Studies in the Modern Architecture of Latin America, 1930–1960* (London: Verso, 2000), 252–255; and Le Blanc, "Palmeiras and Pilotis," 103–105.

42 / See "Artes plásticas: A conferência de Max Bill," *Correio da Manhã*, May 31, 1953, 11; "Artes plásticas: Max Bill esclarece pontos de vista e desfaz mal entenidos (I)," *Correio da Manhã*, June 7, 1953, 11; and "Max Bill: Visita ao Brasil do famoso escultor modernista," *Boletim do Museu de Arte Moderna do Rio de Janeiro*, no. 9 (July 1953): 5–6, 8.

43 / See, for example, Max Bill, "The Bauhaus Idea from Weimar to Ulm," *Architects' Year Book* 5 (1953): 29–32. Bill also sharply distinguished HfG and the Bauhaus in private correspondence in 1953. See Nicola Pezolet, "Bauhaus Ideas: Jorn, Max Bill, and Reconstruction Culture," *October*, no. 141 (Summer 2012): 100–101.

44 / Paulo Herkenhoff, "Rio de Janeiro: A Necessary City," in *The Geometry of Hope: Latin American Abstract Art from the Patricia Phelps de Cisneros Collection*, ed. Gabriel Pérez-Barreiro (Austin: Blanton Museum of Art, University of Texas at Austin, 2007), 56–57; Ramírez, "The Embodiment of Color," 35–36; and Irene V. Small, "Hélio Oiticica and the Morphology of Things" (PhD dissertation, Yale University, 2008), 46n22.

45 / Ramírez, "The Embodiment of Color," 35, 71n43. To the best of my knowledge, researchers have not located the Grupo Frente notebooks. I believe, however, the albums are partially visible in an installation view held by Acervo MAM-RJ: Pasta de fotografias: MAM-EXP: 29 "Grupo Frente," Arquivo Fotográfico, Acervo MAM-RJ.

46 / Mário Pedrosa, "Grupo Frente" (1955), in Ramírez, "Embodiment of Color," 71n43.

47 / See my essay in Zelevansky et al., *Hélio Oiticica*.

48 / Eric Baruch, Alusío Carvão, João José da Silva Costa, Elisa Martins da Silveira, et al. to MAM RJ, January 5, 1954, folder Cursos 1954, Acervo MAM-RJ; "Museu de Arte Moderna do Rio de Janeiro, matrículas dos cursos" (1954), folder Cursos 1954, Acervo MAM-RJ; "Museu de Arte Moderna do Rio de Janeiro, matrículas dos cursos (segundo semestre)" (1954), folder Cursos 1954, Acervo MAM-RJ.

49 / See *Grupo Frente: Segunda mostra coletiva* (Rio de Janeiro: Museu de Arte Moderna do Rio de Janeiro, 1955).

50 / Pedrosa, "Grupo Frente," in Ferreira and Herkenhoff, *Mário Pedrosa*, 270.

51 / Walter Gropius, "Program of the Staatliche Bauhaus in Weimar," 1919, in Wingler, *Bauhaus*, 31. On Gropius's use of medieval allusions, see Charles W. Haxthausen, "Walter Gropius and Lyonel Feininger, Bauhaus Manifesto, 1919," in Bergdoll and Dickerman, *Bauhaus, 1919–1933*, 64–67.

52 / Pedrosa, "Grupo Frente," trans. in *Arte contemporáneo brasileño: Documentos y críticas/ Contemporary Brazilian Art: Documents and Critical Texts*, ed. Glória Ferreira (Santiago de Compostela: Artedardo, 2009), 476.

53 / Mário Pedrosa, "Lygia Clark, or the Fascination of Space" (1957), in Ferreira and Herkenhoff, *Mário Pedrosa*, 287.

54 / Pedrosa, 287.

55 / Lygia Clark, "The Influence of Albers" (1957), in *Lygia Clark: The Abandonment of Art, 1948–1988*, ed. Cornelia H. Butler and Luis Pérez-Oramas (New York: Museum of Modern Art, 2014), 56.

56 / See, for example, Ferreira Gullar, "Clark: Uma experiência radical," *Jornal do Brasil*, March 22, 1959, suplemento dominical, 3; and Lygia Clark, "Lygia Clark and the Concrete Expressional Space" (1959), in *Lygia Clark*, ed. Manuel J. Borja-Villel (Barcelona: Fundació Antoni Tàpies; Marseille: MAC, Galleries contemporaines des Musées de Marseille; Porto: Fundação de Serralves; Brussels: Sociéte des Expositions du Palais des Beaux-Arts, 1997), 84.

57 / On Albers's approach to variation, see Eva Díaz, "The Ethics of Perception: Josef Albers in the United States," *Art Bulletin* 90, no. 2 (June 2008): 260–285.

58 / Lygia Clark, "1957" (1957), trans. in Butler and Pérez-Oramas, *Lygia Clark*, 56. See also Lygia Clark, "Ideas about Diverse Points" (1957), in Butler and Pérez-Oramas, *Lygia Clark*, 57; and Lygia Clark, "1957" (1957), in Butler and Pérez-Oramas, *Lygia Clark*, 57–58.

59 / Dickerman, "Bauhaus Fundaments," 17; and Eva Díaz, "We Are All Bauhauslers Today," *Art Journal* 70, no. 2 (Summer 2011): 118.

60 / Mário Pedrosa, "The 'Silkworm' in Mass Production" (1967), trans. in Ferreira and Herkenhoff, *Mário Pedrosa*, 148.

GRUNDLEHRE AT THE ULM SCHOOL OF DESIGN A Survey of Basic Design Teaching

4

Martin Mäntele

The Hochschule für Gestaltung (HfG), also known as the Ulm School of Design (1953–1968), was one of the most progressive educational institutions in the field of industrial design and visual communication that emerged from the ruins of postwar Germany. Located in the southern German city of Ulm, the school was cofounded by Inge Scholl—sister of Hans and Sophie Scholl, who were executed by the Nazis in 1943 as core members of the White Rose resistance group—and her future husband, Otl Aicher, in collaboration with the internationally renowned Swiss artist and architect Max Bill.

For both Scholl and Aicher, reconstructing Germany was not just a matter of rebuilding the country's infrastructure but also its educational institutions. In the immediate postwar period, many of Germany's intellectuals, among them the writer Hans Werner Richter and the philosopher of religion Romano Guardini, formed a group around Scholl and Aicher. In 1947 they founded an adult education center, the Volkshochschule Ulm, with the aim of promoting Germany's democratic reconstruction. Out of their work with this center came the idea of establishing a private university that focuses mainly on political education.

On a trip to Switzerland in 1948, Scholl and Aicher met with Bill—a former student at the Bauhaus in Dessau—who proposed to them the idea of continuing the progressive Bauhaus experiment in Ulm and whose contact with the former Bauhaus director, Walter Gropius, could be helpful in realizing this ambitious goal.

In 1949 Scholl, through an American friend, met Shepard Stone, then assistant director of Public Affairs for Occupied Germany and consultant to High Commissioner of Germany John J. McCloy. Stone was so impressed by Scholl's plans that he procured a dinner invitation at the high commissioner's residence in Bad Homburg. The people she met on this occasion were daunted by her ambition and promised financial support. A few days later McCloy spoke so highly of her at a lecture in Boston, Massachusetts, that she made the news. The headline in the German newspaper *Die Neue Zeitung* (January 30, 1950), edited under the auspices of the Americans, read: "Ein Mädchen—Symbol für Deutschland" (A girl—Symbol for Germany).

In the beginning of 1950 McCloy and Scholl forged a tacit agreement that the reeducation fund of the Office of the High Commissioner in Germany would cover half of the costs if Scholl would succeed in procuring the other half—in form of either money or building materials—on the German side. But time was of the essence—on July 1, 1950, the Americans expected an outline on which to base their request.

Scholl approached potential sponsors and partners, while discussing the school's scope, curriculum, and likely lecturers and drawing floor plans with Aicher. Their plans and ideas also had to be discussed with Bill, who was busy with his own projects in Zurich. Also, with the Cold War gaining momentum, the Americans wanted to check the political leanings of the applicants as well. In a memorandum in which he declared that he was not a communist, Bill also softened the leftist image of the Bauhaus, stating that people at that time were looking full of hope to the East, but most of them had since changed their minds.

However, the project suffered a serious setback in 1951, when a defamation campaign claimed that Hans and Sophie Scholl had been communists and that Scholl and Aicher were communist sympathizers. Bill had to change the building plans and go with a concrete structure because the prospected donation of steel was withdrawn. Almost an entire year would pass before they could convince all interested parties that the rumors were unsubstantiated. Finally, in June 1952, the Americans handed over a check in a ceremony at the Lord Mayor's Hall in Ulm.

It took two years, from 1953 to 1955, to build the HfG. The finished campus comprised the main school building, a students' hall, and a couple of semidetached houses for the lecturers. It was one of the first university campuses built in Germany. In the process of writing this essay I read all of Bill's letters which are held at the HfG Archive. My goal was to find out how he developed the concept for his *Grundlehre*, a basic design course. Because his concept was gradually evolving, the core ideas for the *Grundlehre* can more easily be grasped in several brochures which were issued by the Geschwister Scholl Foundation in 1950 and later years. More importantly,

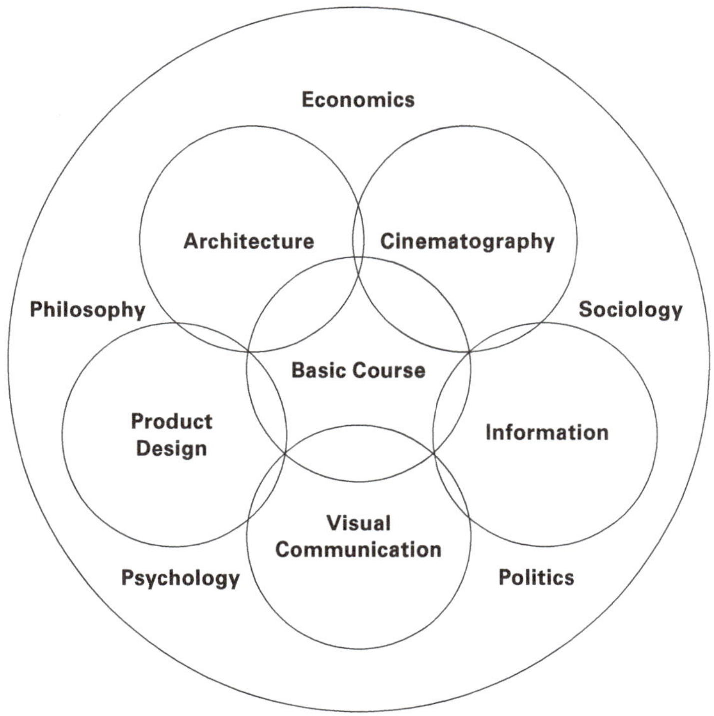

Schematic teaching at HfG Ulm.

the letters provide important insight in how intensely the cofounders of the HfG discussed every detail of the course.

In the first printed program from 1950, Bill insists that the basic design course was supposed to shake up established ideas and assumptions. His intent was to hire some former "Bauhäusler," whom he considered to be up for the challenge. He was particularly interested in Walter Peterhans, who had headed the photography department at the Bauhaus from 1929 to 1933 but now lived and taught in the United States, and Josef Albers, who had taught at the Bauhaus from 1923 to 1933. In fact, Bill repeatedly asked Albers to leave the United States and join the HfG faculty, but Albers refused as he did not want to give up his US citizenship.

Bill's design for the HfG program, visualized in a schema using interlocked circles, was included in the first printed brochure. It reminds one of a similar schema of the Bauhaus with the major difference that the *Grundlehre* sits at the center, and in the first year, students were supposed to take this basic course. Bill insisted that the course should be compulsory. Although students could opt to join one of five departments—Product Design, Visual Communication, Architecture, Information, and City Planning (which was never established; in its stead a Film Department was added in 1961)—the basic course assignments had no specific function: students were not yet given the task of designing a product or building or creating an applied graphic design.

Josef Albers and Almir Mavignier. Courtesy of HfG Archive / Museum Ulm.

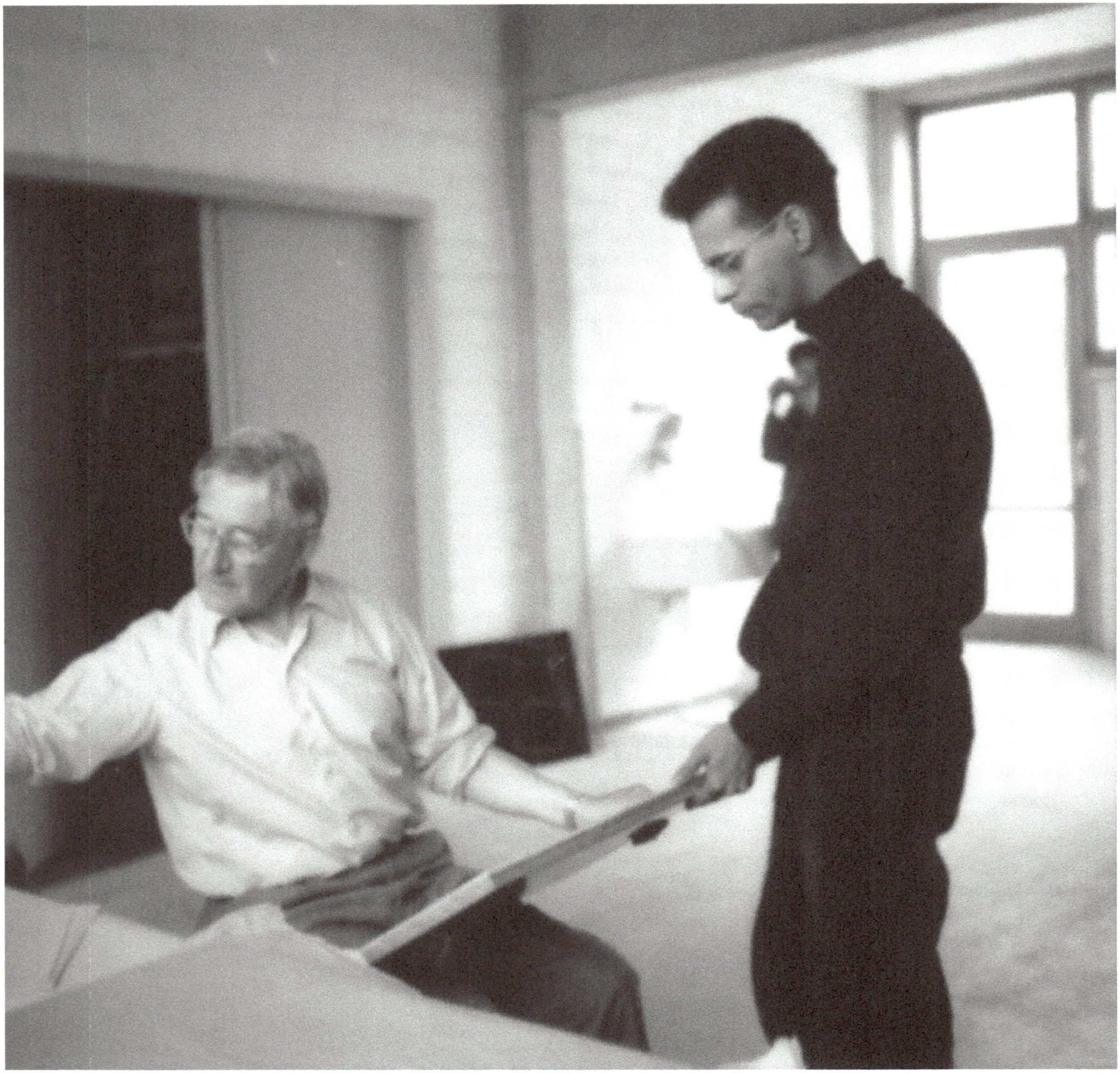

After many letter exchanges and planning sessions, classes finally began on August 3, 1953, with a three-month course in visual training with Peterhans as instructor. Based on the Visual Training course he had conceived for the Architectural Department at the Armor Institute (today's Illinois Institute of Technology, where the course is still taught), the course included numerous exercises that were regarded as the foundation for the specialized work of designers. By using abstract tasks, students were taught to develop sensitivity to proportional relations and achieve ultimate precision, concentration, and discipline during process and execution. In his course, Peterhans requested that students use equal size sheets of a certain kind of cardboard paper, which, given its high quality are kept in excellent condition until today.

Until its closure in 1968, 640 students attended the Ulm School of Design, including 278 international students. Among the foreign students, 30 were from Latin America, including 10 from Brazil. Many historical links exist between the HfG and museums and design schools in Brazil. In 1951 Bill won the grand prize for sculpture at the São Paulo Biennial. In 1959 and 1960 Tomás Maldonado and Otl Aicher taught at the Federal University in Rio de Janeiro. The Escola Superior de Desenho Industrial (ESDI) in Rio is often regarded as a Brazilian affiliate of the HfG. Maldonado devised ESDI's first curriculum on the basis of his experience in Ulm. In 1958, HfG graduate Karlheinz Bergmiller moved to Brazil, and in 1963 he became a member of ESDI's founding committee. Alexandre Wollner, a pioneer of visual communication in Brazil, also studied at the HfG and went on to teach at ESDI starting in 1963.

In November 1953 and from May to August 1955, Josef Albers was guest lecturer at the HfG. Albers's reputation had only grown since his days at the Bauhaus. After his training as a teacher, he enrolled at the Bauhaus in 1920 and was asked to join the staff in 1925. In 1939 he immigrated to the United States where he taught at Black Mountain College until 1949. His influence on basic design and fundamental training cannot be overstated. When Bill approached him, Albers was already teaching at Yale. In 1958 Aicher taught a course there himself. Albers placed practical experience at the center of his teaching. Students should learn to observe and develop a visual vocabulary of expression. His basic course was divided into three areas: design—drawing—color.

Brazilian sculptor Mary Vieira was one of the students attending Albers's *Grundlehre* course. Previously, she had been working with Bill in Zurich. Another student from Brazil to become a renowned graphic designer and painter in Germany was Almir da Silva Mavignier. Central to Albers's teaching was color. Albers conveyed the effect of colors and their mutual influence and dependence on each other: the interplay between color and color, color and form, color and quantity, or color and position.

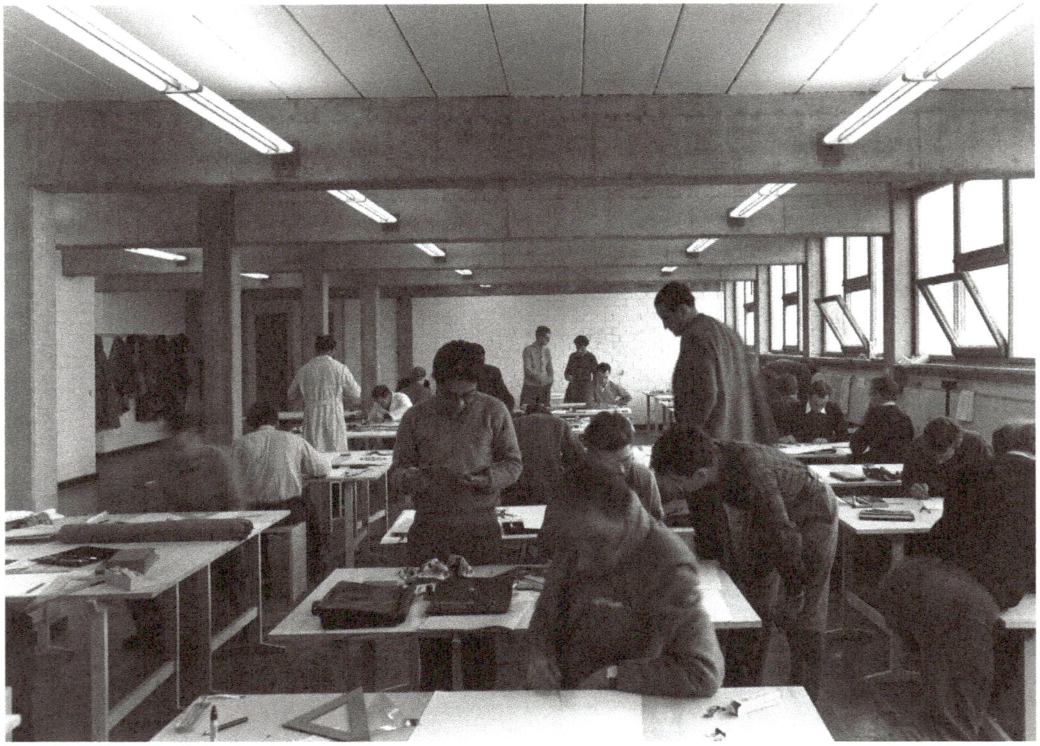

Workshop in progress, 1955.
Photograph by Ernst Hahn.
Courtesy of HfG Archive /
Museum Ulm.

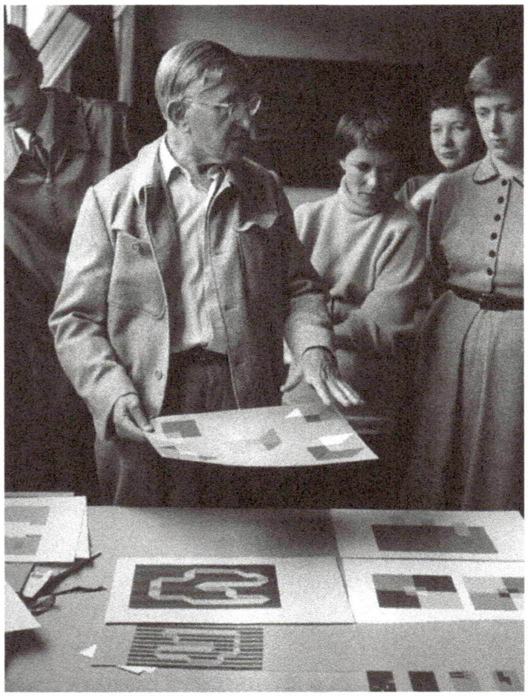

Josef Albers with students.
Photograph by Eva-Maria
Koch. Courtesy of HfG
Archive / Museum Ulm.

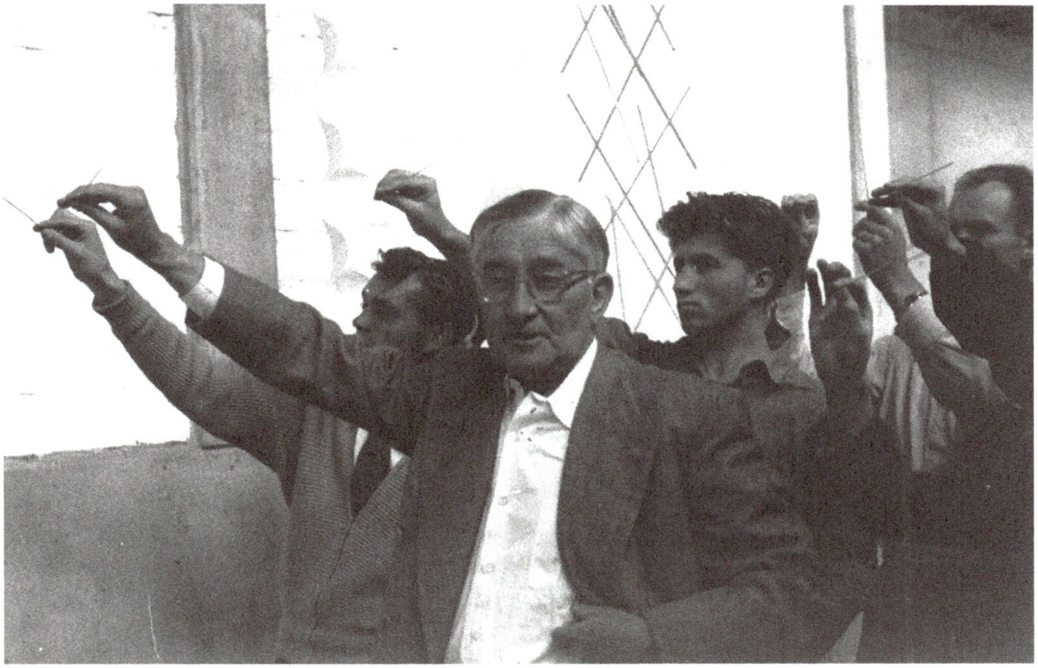

Josef Albers and students. Courtesy of HfG Archive / Museum Ulm.

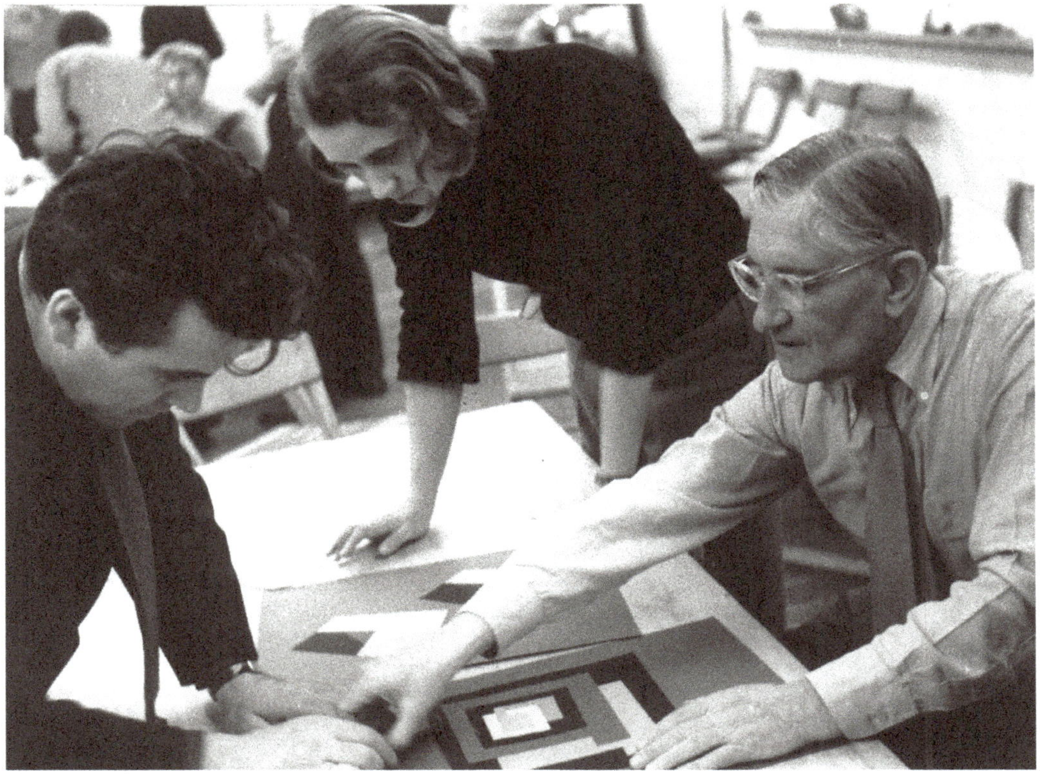

Josef Albers with Otl Aicher and student. Photograph by Eva-Maria Koch. Courtesy of HfG Archive / Museum Ulm.

However, the instructor from whom the students received the most direct reference to the Bauhaus was Helene Nonné-Schmidt. Formally trained as a technical drawing and crafts teacher, Nonné-Schmidt was involved in the Bauhaus weaving mill and from 1928 concentrated on theoretical works as a student of Paul Klee. Nonné-Schmidt taught the basic course based on her own notes on the courses on form and color morphology by Paul Klee and elementary design teaching by Joost Schmidt.

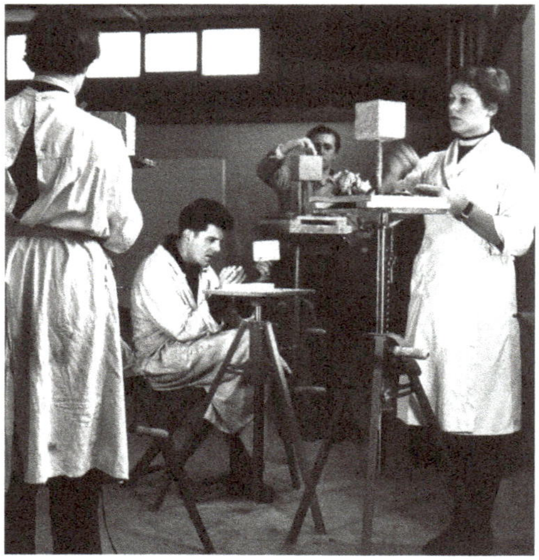

Tomás Maldonado workshop. Photograph by Ernst Hahn. Courtesy of HfG Archive / Museum Ulm.

Bill thought that valid design rules could be studied from works of art. These rules could then be applied to design in general and therefore transmitted to the way things are designed—be it the design of an electrical appliance or the layout of a magazine. In his *Grundlehre*, Bill included elements of the Bauhaus-*Vorkurs* (preliminary course), especially Johannes Itten, Laszlo Moholy-Nagy, and Josef Albers. Unlike at the Bauhaus, individual artistic development was not central to the HfG program, whose *Grundlehre* encouraged a more objective and intellectual approach.

In April 1955 Johannes Itten was hired for one week to give an introductory course on color theory. Similar to Albers, Itten engaged students in some relaxing exercises at the beginning. It is rumored that Albers had warned that he would not come back if Itten were given a second teaching engagement. And indeed, Itten was never invited again. Along with Bill and Aicher, renowned figures such as Max Bense, Hans Gugelot, Friedrich Vordemberge-Gildewart, Alexander Kluge, and numerous visiting lecturers from all over the world taught at the HfG.

Tomás Maldonado from Argentina gave the school a new direction, and his work at the school had far-reaching consequences. He expanded the curriculum to include theory to provide a theoretical basis for design work. When Maldonado joined the staff in 1954, he was immediately given work within the *Grundlehre* course. His focus was on the theory of perception and form, laws of symmetry, and topology. He called his course Visual Introduction. The tasks were based on mathematics and therefore differed from those of the Bauhaus pedagogy, which relied on systematic and intuitive knowledge through self-experience. Maldonado conducted a series of exercises into the design rules. The term *design* describes something whole, with different attributes than its component elements. The rules of design describe regulations, which are followed by perception.

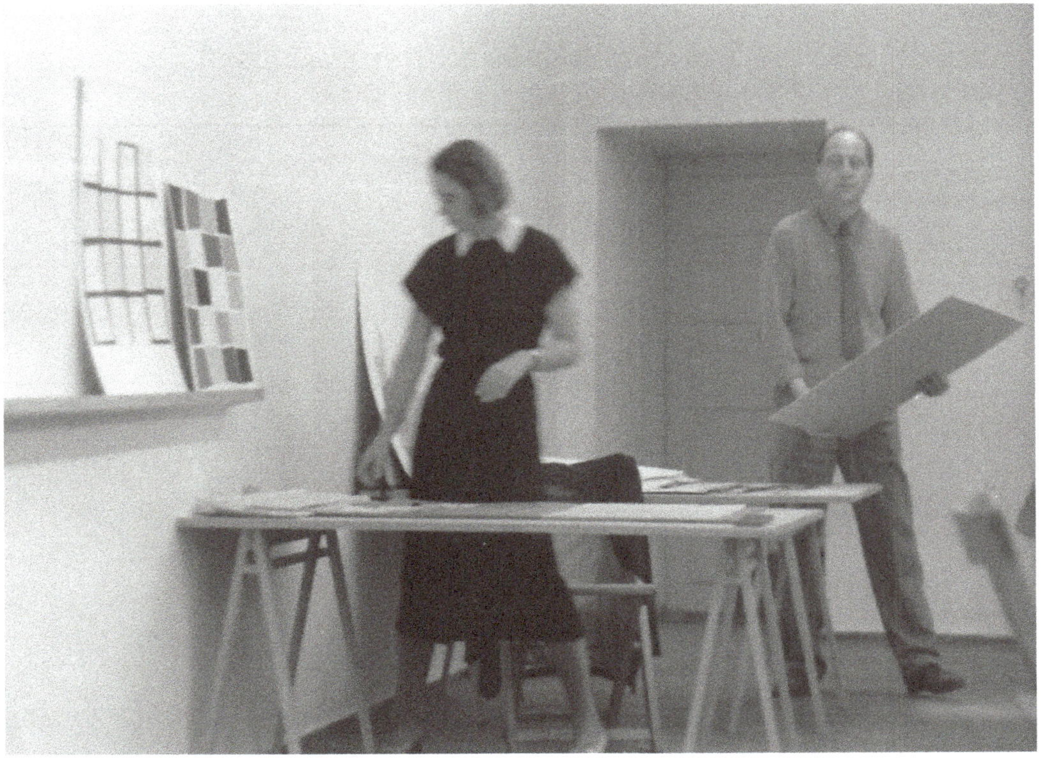

Walter Peterhans and student. Photograph by Eva-Marie Koch. Courtesy of HfG Archive / Museum Ulm.

One of the best works to illustrate the changes Maldonado implemented in the curriculum of the *Grundlehre* course is a compilation of assignments by Klaus Franck from the *Grundlehre* of 1955/56. Assignment 1 explained how a Peano surface is constructed. Assignment 3 was very popular: Use black as a color, meaning that within the whole composition black should not appear like a void but like a color equal to the other colors. Assignment 4 was about symmetry. And assignment 5 was again popular with Maldonado: Precision—Imprecision; using precise means in order to achieve an effect of imprecision. With his interest in higher mathematics and geometry, Maldonado implemented the scientific requirements of the HfG.

Students also were asked to produce three-dimensional works in the *Grundlehre*. Ulrich Burandt constructed a non-orientated surface as a prime example of why topology was such an important subject. Topology studies those properties of geometric forms that remain constant under certain transformations such as bending or stretching. In the course of this highly dynamic development Maldonado and Aicher proposed the "Ulm model." To quote Aicher, "[The Ulm model is] a design model that rests on technology and science. The designer is no longer a lofty artist but an equal partner in the decision-making process of industrial production."[1] Maldonado summarized this viewpoint in the phrase: "Product design is not an art." He dissociated himself from the customary view of the designer as a brilliant artist guided by intuition, thereby making it clear that despite the great achievements of the Bauhaus it was time to say goodbye to Bauhaus ideals. Throughout its existence the Bauhaus represented the view that creative tasks were best left to architects, sculptors, and painters. In the 1920s, this was feasible. However, after World War II technical and economic conditions had changed. Under the aegis of Aicher and Maldonado the Ulm School of Design therefore set itself the task of feeding future designers with the most progressive technical and scientific information available. It devised the occupational profile for a designer and did so in accordance with the principle "product design is not an art."

Bill did not agree with this new direction; he believed that design and art could not be separated and left the HfG in 1957. In 1958, in a lecture given at a design congress in Brussels, Maldonado said: "The designer will be the coordinator. His responsibility will be to coordinate, in close collaboration with a large number of specialists, the most varied requirements of product fabrication and usage; his will be the final responsibility for maximum productivity in fabrication, and for maximum material and cultural consumer satisfaction."[2]

After Bill's departure, a younger generation of lecturers took command. In the academic year 1960/61, the last general basic course was taught under a new name: First Academic Year (Erstes Studienjahr). In the first quarter of the first year, students now were taught a visual grammar that should be applied to find solutions to specific design problems. Afterward, they were asked to engage with specific tasks in their respective departments.

The assumption that there may be one general theory as a basis for creative activity appeared too restrictive in the early 1960s. In the academic year 1961/62 the general *Grundlehre* for all students was abandoned and then resumed separately within the individual departments. All full-time faculty—including Aicher, Friedrich Vordemberge-Gildewart, and Anthony Fröshaug—formulated exercises for the "visual introduction."

A special feature of the Ulm model was the inclusion of theoretical subjects in the curriculum, such as cybernetics, mathematical operations analysis, the then new field of semiotics, scientific theory, philosophy, among others. They were not only viewed as providing fundamental knowledge for design work but to analyze the latest technologies and intellectual issues of the day. In addition, these subjects were added to the curriculum amid an enthusiasm for technology in the second half of the 1950s. In 1957 Sputnik 1 was the first satellite to be launched into space. East and West began a race against time to come up with cutting-edge technological developments.

All this technological and scientific know-how, along with the philosophical schools of thought at the time, is evident in the books in the school library, now housed in the HfG Archive library.

In addition to teaching, the school took on commissions from the industry. Teaching staff and students were involved in this work. Designs drawn up by "development groups" provided a first-hand opportunity to collaborate with various industries and gain practical experience. The best-known examples are commissions done for Braun such as the SK4 radiogram, nicknamed "Snow White's coffin."

For his diploma project Hans (Nick) Roericht developed a system of stackable tableware, which was produced by the German company Thomas and, in 1964, acquired for the design collection at the Museum of Modern Art in New York. The production ran continually between 1961 and 2006, obviously it was a great success and proved the validity of ideals of the school: to design sustainable products, helping people improve their environment.

At the beginning of all these iconic designs stood the methodological approach established by the Ulm School of Design, taught to the students from their very first days at this institution, with the *Grundlehre* as the base for everything.

Sixteen years after the school's founding the experiment came to an end. Chronically short of funds, as a private college it had come to depend on repeated grants from the state of Baden-Württemberg. Amid the inflamed atmosphere of the 1968 student revolts, the political masters were not prepared to continue funding this college with its progressive approach to work. At the end of 1968, the Ulm School of Design was forced to close.

Notes

1 / Otl Aicher, "Die Hochschule für Gestaltung: Neun Stufen ihrer Entwicklung." *Architese* 5, no. 15 (1975): 14; my translation.

2 / Maldonado quoted in D. Rinker, "'Industrial Design is not an art': Tomás Maldonado's Contribution to the Creation of a New Professional Identity," in *Ulmer Modelle – Modelle Nach Ulm*, ed. G Bonsiepe et al. (Ostfildern: Hatje Cantz, 2003), exhibition catalog.

TWISTING THE MODERNIST CURVE Mary Vieira's *Polyvolume: Meeting Point*

5

Luisa Valle

Born in São Paulo in 1927 and raised and educated in Belo Horizonte, Mary Vieira studied at the Escola de Belas Artes do Parque Municipal (School of Beaux Arts of the Municipal Park) under the supervision of Alberto da Veiga Guignard. As a young artist, Vieira exhibited at the Edith Behring atelier in Rio de Janeiro in 1950 and, for a brief period, got involved in the ebullient atmosphere of the emerging Brazilian concrete movement.[1] After attending a Max Bill exhibition at the Museu de Arte de São Paulo (MASP), Vieira started corresponding with the Swiss artist and, in 1951, decided to relocate to Europe. In 1953 and 1954, she attended the Ulm School of Design, under Bill's rectorship, and spent the rest of her career in Italy, Switzerland, and Brazil. Although Vieira missed much of the development of concretism and neoconcretism in Brazil, her public works from the 1960s and 1970s highlight the proximity of her practice to a genealogy of postwar Brazilian art that merged formalistic concerns with perception theories. If some of the distinctions between concretism and neoconcretism rest on the contrast between individual and collective experiences, passive contemplation versus active participation, Vieira's public works, produced in Switzerland and installed in Brazil, complicate these classifications, and challenge nationalist narratives of Brazilian modernism.[2]

Among the most influential of the seminal public works that she produced in that period is *Polivolume: Ponto de encontro* (*Polyvolume: Meeting Point*). Commissioned in 1960 for the lobby of the Itamaraty Palace, the headquarters of the Ministry of Foreign Affairs in Brasilia, the work is an exploration of the totemic form that paradoxically challenges stability and authorship by engaging the viewer's direct interaction while also allowing for temporal transformation. In this essay I offer a transhistorical account of this site-specific work, exploring the ways in which Vieira's work continues to negotiate our perception of concrete art, public art, public space, and public history. Adopting Henri Lefebvre's triad model for the production of space as an organizational tool—designed, lived, and symbolic space—I approach Vieira's work as an ongoing interaction of social and spatial relationships, a process of production rather than an autonomous object.[3] Looking at the individual and collective experiences proposed by the work, I also examine the political potency of Vieira's *Polyvolume* in negotiating public art and public space as both a constitutive part of Brasilia's utopian modernism and as evidence of its failure.

DESIGNED SPACE

Polyvolume: Meeting Point is composed of a central column of industrially cut rectangular aluminum blades stacked horizontally onto a metal axis. The sheets of metal are spaced apart by thin metallic washers. The separation allows for light to pass through the blades and the viewer to see through the work and into the 98-foot-long free span of the 17,000-square-foot area of the Itamaraty Palace's ground floor. The gaps between the blades not only render the work visually lighter but also indicate that its metal sheets can be moved by tactile manipulation. Arched marble benches, designed as broken sections of two circles of different size, surround the central column. The curved marble benches mark the perimeter of the work. The broken circumferences allow for multiple points of access to the central column. The seating arrangements invite viewers to gather around, meet, and socialize around the work. At first titled just *Polyvolume*, the work was spontaneously renamed "meeting point" by the workers overseeing the installation.[4] The marble benches are the same height as the circular pedestal upon which the artwork stands. Both the concentric seats and the pedestal are slightly elevated from the floor, creating the illusion of suspension, in contradiction to the weight of the material.[5]

A diagram detailing the development of the *Polyvolume* project indicates that its design evolved from the rupture of a spiral progression composed of several tangent circles, where the diameter of the smaller circles are equal to the radius of the larger ones.[6] Vieira followed a similar pattern of conception in many of her two-dimensional, sculptural, and public works, such as *Polivolume: conexão-livre-homenagem a Pedro de Toledo* (*Polyvolume: A Free Connection Homage to Pedro de Toledo*), installed in 1979 at the Eisenhower Square, an extension of the

Ibirapuera Park in São Paulo.[7] From 1952 to 1953, Vieira executed a series of prints in homage to Max Bill that gives insight into her design process, including into the sculptural works that were to come.[8] *Zeiten einer Zeichnung* (Times of a drawing), is composed of two series of eight plates consisting of lines and curves that move progressively from plate to plate and meet at the end of each progression. Upon moving to Switzerland in 1951, Vieira joined Allianz, a group of local concrete artists, and participated in their last exhibition in Zurich in 1954.[9] Despite establishing a close relationship with Bill and other members of the group, such as Leo Leuppi and Camille Graeser, Vieira never considered herself strictly a concrete artist.[10] Insisting that her research started in Belo Horizonte in 1943, Vieira chastised her Swiss, German, Belgian, Dutch, and English peers for "being interested only in the static and univocal shapes, or in elementary colors in structural fields, not optically vibrating."[11] Diagrams of Itamaraty's *Polyvolume* suggest that the work was designed in a similar fashion to Vieira's homage to Bill, in which geometric forms are deconstructed and reconstructed anew.[12] However, instead of following a single progressive pattern established by the artist, the reconstruction process of Vieira's *Polyvolume* is contingent on viewer participation and social and spatial relationships.

LIVED SPACE

Polyvolume: Meeting Point offers the public multiple forms of circulation, allowing viewers to linger or pass quickly, to sit down and meet friends, or to play with the sculpture itself, changing the position of the blades and the shape of the totem and in the process altering views of the environment and other people using the space. Housing four major components—the spiral staircase designed by Milton Ramos and Joaquim Cardoso, the bas-relief on the wall and the gridded floor patterning created by Athos Bulcão, and Vieira's *Polyvolume*—the ground floor of the Itamaraty articulates a spatial, dynamic, and immersive experience. When people access the space from the mezzanine using the stairs, the viewer's perception of space is altered at every step. The geometric relationships created by the overlay of abstract shapes—the grid of the façade, the orthogonal lines on the floor and ceiling, the trapezoid shapes of Bulcão's wall relief, the curvature of the mezzanine's edge, of Vieira's benches, the diagonal lines of the stairs, and the *Polyvolume*—together generate the perception that the space is in constant flux. The viewer's downward descent together with the concatenated geometric elements of the space bestow the Itamaraty lobby with what Vieira coined as the "optical vibrancy" typical of her work.[13]

From the ground floor, at eye level, the spiral staircase and Vieira's *Polyvolume* stand as vertical elements cutting across the free span of the lobby, mirroring and

Mary Vieira, *Polivolume: Ponto de encontro*, 1969–1970. Permanent installation at Itamaraty Palace, Brasilia. Photograph by Matheus Costa. Courtesy of Consulado Geral do Brasil, New York.

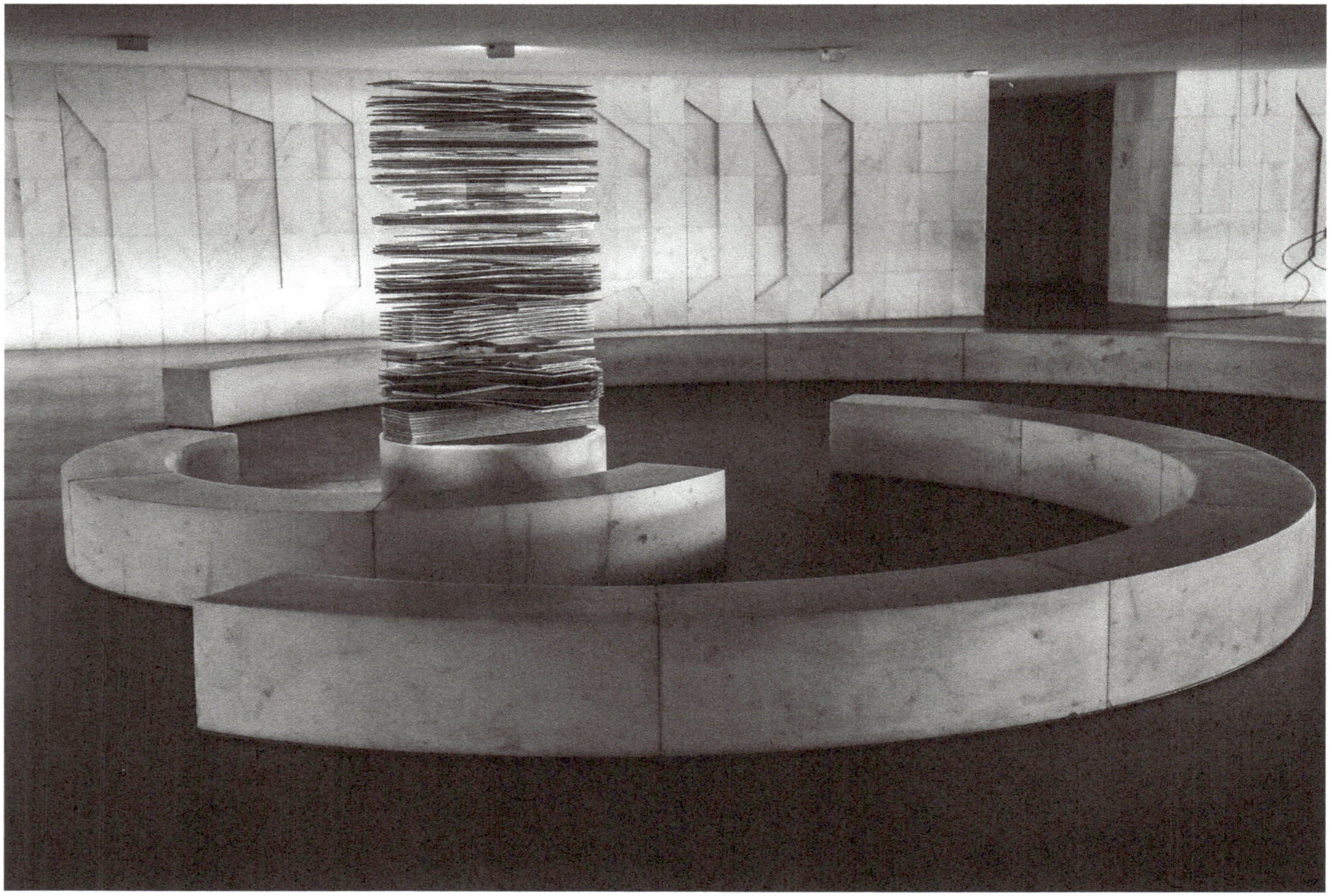

feeding off each other. The viewer finds multiple paths around the marble benches to approach Vieira's column, and tactile engagement with the work creates the possibility of infinite modulations of its blades. The viewer's manipulation of the metal sheets again activates the environment through the optical apparatus and bodily movement around and through the gaps of the blades stacked onto the *Polyvolume*'s centrifugal core. By turning the metal sheets, the viewer intensifies the dialogue between Vieira's column and the impression of movement suggested by the spiral staircase. As multiple viewers walk around the *Polyvolume*, new perspectives and vistas are created as eyes, touch, and bodily movement come together in creating subjective and collective orthogonal, curved, and diagonal lines that cut through the space and their outlook on each other.

SYMBOLIC SPACE

Vieira started her first kinetic investigations—such as in *Formas eletrorotatorias, espirálicas, a perfuração virtual* (Electro-rotary Spiral Shapes to Virtual Perforation), commissioned for and put on display at the 1948 exhibition of the "producers class," an organization of wealthy farmers from Minas Gerais—in Belo Horizonte.[14] The work consisted of a laminated metal structure that spun at alternate times driven by an electric motor and producing a spiral effect.[15] Vieira also designed the exhibition space, creating a sculptural environment to surround her work. Many years later, Vieira would again take on the role of exhibition designer on the occasion of Brazil's participation in the 1957 *Interbau*, Berlin's international architecture exhibition, where plans and projects for Brasilia, Brazil's new modernist capital were presented for the first time to the European public.[16] Vieira designed the exhibition space, entitled *Brasilien baut Brasília*, as well as the poster and catalog for the exhibition. Understanding Vieira's background is important to fully appreciate how she came onto a constructive practice independently from the Rio-São Paulo axis and preceding her relocation to Switzerland. Most important, Vieira's early production situated her in the middle of Belo Horizonte's intellectual elite, whose close ties to the region's industrial economy gave her easy access to metal factories and specialized labor essential to her sculpture.

In many ways, Vieira's practice embodied the ambiguities that were typical of Brazil's official modernist architecture program. These ambiguities were most apparent in the design and construction of Brasilia, a state-of-the-art urban experiment developed in an uncharted area of the country. By the late 1950s, concrete artists in Brazil had departed from the movement's early adherence to the rationalist principles disseminated through European manifestos and educational programs—

mainly the Bauhaus and the Ulm School of Design in Germany.[17] Brazilian concrete art reappraised European models in terms of the modulation of time, space, and movement. Modernist architecture in Brazil had also departed from the rationalist postulates of Corbusian and Bauhaus architecture and had assumed an organic and gestural quality early on, from Niemeyer's dynamic design for the Pampulha Park (1940) to the curves of Brasilia's temporal monumentality (1960). In 1959, Ferreira Gullar's "Manifesto neoconcreto" (Neoconcrete manifesto) pushed the Brazilian constructivist project into the realm of social relationships and phenomenology.[18] Neoconcretism's emphasis on subjective and collective experiences gestured toward a worldwide questioning of top-down state mandates, such as the architecture/everyday life dichotomy and the developmentalism associated with both concrete art and modernist architecture in Brazil. Neoconcrete artists turned to the multifaceted character of everyday life for rethinking the division of urban spaces. The construction of Brasilia from 1955 to 1963 occurred at the same time as the rise of neoconcretism in Brazil. Yet, works produced by neoconcrete artists were never considered for the capital's innovative program that aimed at the integration of art and architecture.

In 1959, the International Extraordinary Conference of Art Critics took place in Brazil. Art critic Mário Pedrosa presented the theme of the first session, "The New City—Synthesis of the Arts," which revolved around Brasilia. Pedrosa identified the new capital as both an architectural object and a work of art, calling attention to its social, cultural, and artistic totality.[19] Lúcio Costa's dynamic pilot plan and Niemeyer's gestural architecture bestowed the capital with the character of a monumental work of Brazilian concrete art. Pedrosa had imagined a synthesis of the arts for Brasilia that included works derived from the Brazilian constructivist project, not the "stars of easel painting in Brazil," which he deemed "stripped from any spatial imagination."[20] He affirmed that Brazil's new generation of spatial and constructivist investigators was closer to the true synthesis of the arts. However, Brasilia's urban modernism included more figurative works by artists active since the 1930s who had worked with Niemeyer and Costa on previous official projects—such as Bruno Giorgi, Candido Portinari, and Emiliano Di Cavalcanti—than abstract works by artists such as Alfredo Volpi and Athos Bulcão.[21]

A presentation by Costa at the International Congress of Artists in Venice, organized by UNESCO in 1952, sheds some light on the disjuncture between the constructive genealogy of Brasilia's modernist architecture and the new capital's predominantly figurative visual arts program.[22] Costa suggested that architecture should itself have a plastic dimension and emphasized his preference for the term *integration* with rather than *synthesis* of the arts in order to preserve the particular aesthetic dimension of each discipline—thinking perhaps of Mies van der Rohe's Barcelona Pavilion of 1929 rather than in terms of the *Gesamtkunstwerk* of Victor

Horta, Charles Mackintosh, and Walter Gropius's Bauhaus, for example.[23] In a 1953 text called "Desencontro" (Yielding), Costa responded to Max Bill's critique of the decorative façade of the former Ministry of Education building in Rio de Janeiro. Bill took issue with Portinari's mural in particular.[24] Costa's response to Bill reinforced his preference for an integration of figurative and abstract elements rather than a synthesis of modernist architecture and abstract art.[25]

However, perhaps because the Itamaraty Palace was one of the last structures to be built in Brasilia, its interaction with art is also one of the less figurative in the capital. The building was raised late in the transition between what constituted a national vocabulary in the visual arts in the 1940s (figurative art) and in the 1960s (geometric abstraction). The capital's visual arts program holds a mix of abstract and figurative works, a blend that indicates the resistance to abandoning the figurative style while also foreseeing the impossibility of embracing only one system of representation to translate the national identity. The Itamaraty's art and architecture belong mostly to a then established genealogy of Brazilian constructivist investigation.[26] Yet, on the ground floor of the Itamaraty, the nationalist claim lay in both the synthesis and dynamism of its geometric postulates and the desire for a participatory and socially produced space.

Polyvolume: Meeting Point was commissioned by Oscar Niemeyer and Ambassador Wladimir Murtinho as a permanent artwork for the Itamaraty Palace while the building was still under construction.[27] In a lecture given in 1958 in St. Petersburg, titled "The Contemporary City," Niemeyer argued: "Cities will be modern when they are not limited only to a grand display of technique and taste, but rather when they will be cities of free and happy men, who would look to each other without superiority or envy, as brothers and comrades of this harsh and short journey that life offers them."[28] *Polyvolume: Meeting Point* embodied this urban vision. In a 1969 interview in Rio de Janeiro's newspaper *Jornal do Brasil*, Vieira explained: "[My] sculpture [was] made to give air to the viewer's artistic, creative capacity. A menial worker will perhaps be able to create something better than the president if both are given the opportunity to touch the same art piece. . . . I am convinced that in front of one of my art pieces, the worker, used to dealing with brick and cement, will have fewer inhibitions to deal with its materials than a bureaucrat who has always been limited to dealing with office work."[29] Niemeyer and Vieira both convey the ambiguous nature of Brasilia, an authoritarian top-down project in search for democratic participation, freedom, and social equality.

I would like to suggest that the ambiguous character of Brasilia's project—however symbolic a place it came to occupy in the national imaginary—can also be found inside its buildings, such as in the role played by Vieira's *Polyvolume: Meeting Point* in the lobby of the Itamaraty Palace. Vieira was already living abroad when

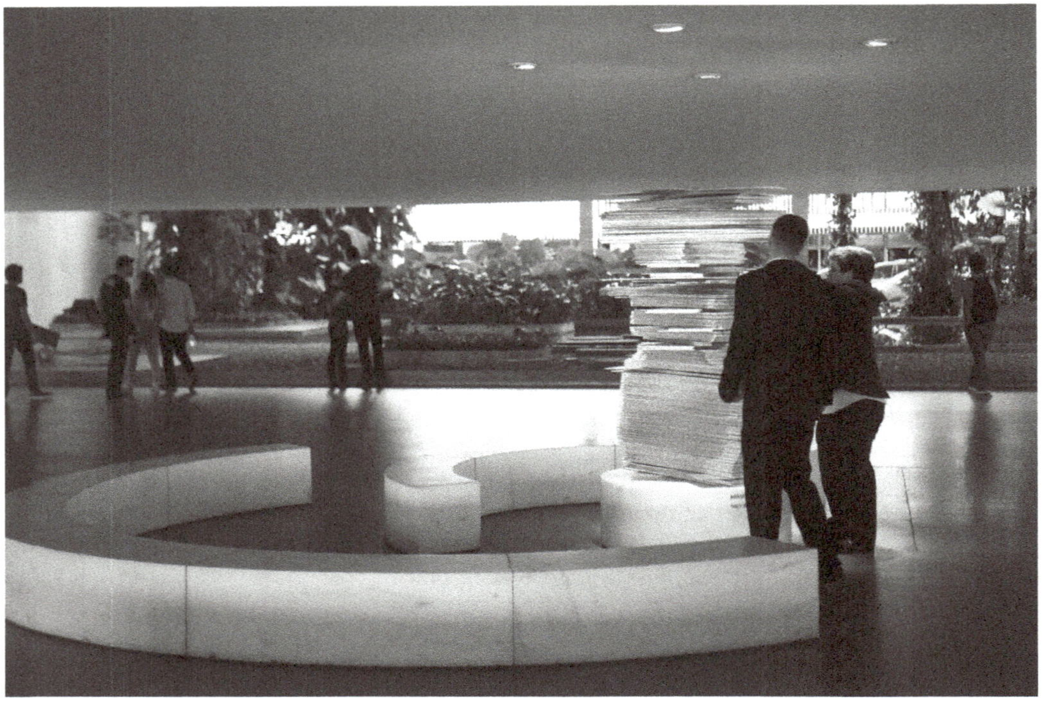

Mary Vieira, *Polivolume: Ponto de encontro*, 1969–1970. Permanent installation at Itamaraty Palace, Brasilia. Photograph by Dammer Martins, 2019. Courtesy of Consulado Geral do Brasil, New York.

Gullar's "Manifesto neoconcreto" pushed the country's constructivist investigation toward the realm of social and spatial relationships. Yet Vieira had already been exploring the neoconcrete themes of collective gathering, tactile manipulation, and the participatory nature of art in her artistic investigation and pedagogical practice leading up to the commissioning of *Polyvolume*, such as in the paper exercise of constructing and deconstructing a cube in three sections, which she assigned in her Structuring Space class at the Kunstgewerbeschule in Basel, Switzerland, today's Basel School of Design.[30] The exercise gave insight into how the production of space was as much about structuring form as it was about the participation of the students or, as Vieira suggested, the "times of motion in various directions."[31] Besides fostering creative ways to build and split a solid, however, Vieira's pedagogical exercise, which derived from her polyhedric design studies, also demanded students to achieve the "truth" or "beauty" of a predetermined form.[32] Thus, unlike the neoconcrete artists, Vieira never abandoned the rationalist postulates of a universal techno-utopia central to the modernist project in Brazil and abroad. In addition, the industrial character and orchestration of space of Vieira's work gestured toward principles of usefulness and efficiency being furthered by corporate modernist projects that were challenged worldwide by the artistic and architectural avant-garde, including neoconcretism.

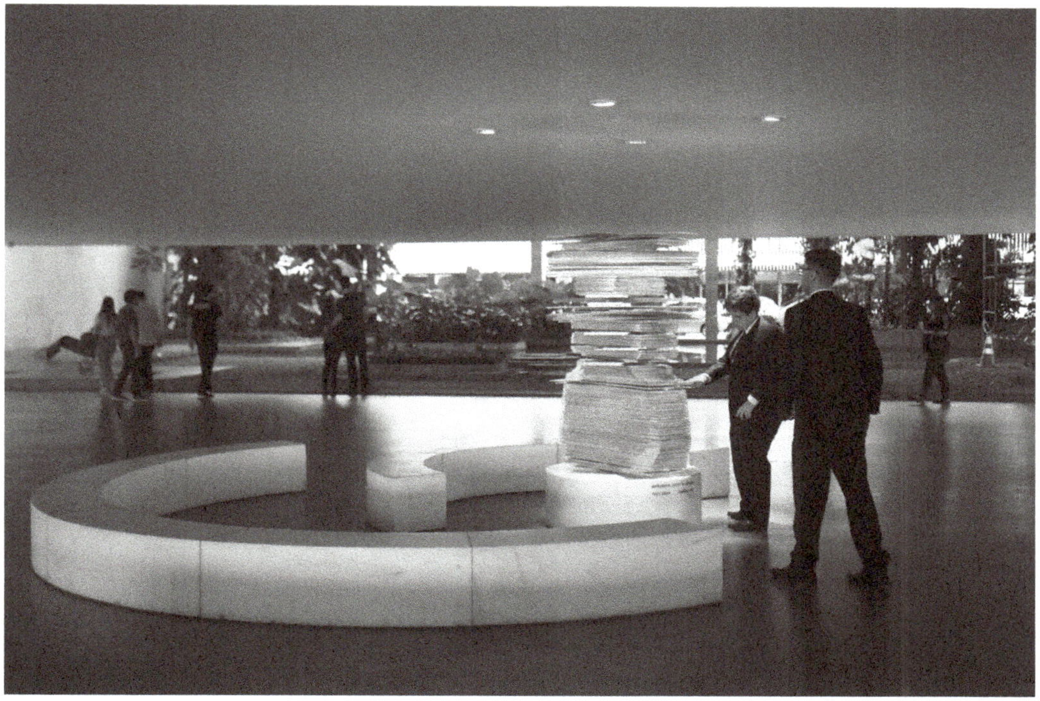

Mary Vieira, *Polivolume: Ponto de encontro*, 1969–1970. Permanent installation at Itamaraty Palace, Brasilia. Photograph by Dammer Martins, 2019. Courtesy of Consulado Geral do Brasil, New York.

Though living abroad, Vieira kept in dialogue with postwar Brazilian art and architecture through shared exhibitions, and her work converged with those of many artists with whom she shared space at exhibitions in Brazil and abroad: the kineticism of Abraham Palatnik; the spatial practice of Hélio Oiticica, Franz Weissmann, and Amílcar de Castro; the design inquiries of Almir Mavignier; and the phenomenology of Lygia Clark and Oiticica's participatory art. Questions central to Vieira's work include the use of industrial processes paired with freehand manipulation, the leap into three-dimensional space, and the sensual and rational engagement of the viewer with the artwork via object-body, sight-form associations. While Vieira did not participate in the 1960s development of a new vocabulary for the Brazilian avant-garde, her investigations of form and space are in keeping with central ideas of both the concrete and neoconcrete programs and an integral part of the genealogy of Brazilian constructive practice. Although Vieira's work reflects the constructive lineage of Brazilian abstract art, it departs as much as it converges with the principles of both movements.

Because of delays in production and Brazil's social and political instability after the 1964 military coup, Vieira's work was not installed at Itamaraty until 1970, almost ten years after its commission and during the worst years of the dictatorship. In 1964 the military had appropriated the capital for its autocratic project, thwarting any of the capital's surviving socialist aspirations.[33] By the 1970s, Vieira's *Polyvolume: Meeting Point* was associated with the official developmentalism and authoritarianism of the new regime. The "precision of [the *Polyvolume*'s] Swiss-produced industrial blades," as Pedrosa described it, was perceived as a corrupt form of forging an official Brazilian avant-garde.[34]

The period of installation of *Polyvolume: Meeting Point* inevitably raises questions about its designation as "public art." What does the term *public* mean in such a repressive context? Does *Polyvolume: Meeting Point* retain its democratic intentions of accessibility, participation, inclusion, and accountability to the people? How does it relate to its context in the Itamaraty Palace, an institution that arguably never fully possessed the characteristics of an open, public place? Although government employees circulate in the building, public access to the lobby, and thus to Vieira's sculpture, is limited—viewers need to take part in a guided visit. Hence, *Polyvolume: Meeting Point* must be interpreted in the context of Niemeyer's architecture, Costa's plan, and the government's marshalling of vast resources to build Brasilia—all top-down projects that never proposed accountability to the general public.

Vieira's industrially produced *Polyvolume: Meeting Point* concomitantly embraced and rejected the ideal of permanence, timelessness, and aesthetic essence that gives it independence from historical contingencies. The site-specificity, usefulness, and durability of the work allowed it to be swept into the realm of a transhistorical continuity and neutrality. The dictatorship led to a polarized society divided between those who supported and those who resisted the coup. Marginalized sectors of the society remained excluded from the political debate. A now multifaceted Brazilian avant-garde questioned positions both of the left and of the right by embracing the marginal, the amateur, and the absurd.[35] Living abroad, Vieira missed the Brazilian avant-garde's deliberate process of "de-skilling" as a form of resistance, the articulation of a new vocabulary that embraced utilitarian, rudimentary, and precarious materials, popular culture, kitsch, parrots, palm trees, bromeliads, the art of children, the insane, their accumulation and exaggeration.[36] These "postmodern" systems of art making (as Pedrosa defined Oiticica's project of environmental anti-art in 1965, for example) challenged the elitism of the rationalist principles of concrete art and official modernist architecture in Brazil.[37] The new vocabulary denounced Brasilia's project by pointing to undemocratic theories both of the left and of the right.

The new vocabulary of the 1960s Brazilian avant-garde opened art making to history, politics, and everyday life. The 1960s avant-garde still built on the geometric shapes and rationalist postulates of modernist architecture and concrete art as tools in the struggle for social emancipation, active participation, and ongoing codification of Brazilian cultural identity but now also challenged it.[38] On the ground floor of the Itamaraty, the rationalist principles of the country's constructivist project intersected with those of the country's official modernist architecture. Yet, this merger of modern architecture and concrete practices created an immersive and participatory ensemble that challenged traditional breaks established in the history of Brazilian constructive research, such as between concrete and neoconcrete art. Thus, even though *Polyvolume: Meeting Point* contains within it all the possibilities of Brasilia's utopian project and the dream of cultural emancipation of Brazilian concrete art, it also exposes all the contradictions, paradoxes, and frustrations of these two projects.

Associated with official developmentalism and authoritarianism, the "precision of Swiss-produced industrial blades" enabled *Polyvolume: Meeting Point* to assume a transhistorical and political neutrality—a claim that can sadly be made for the entire project of Brasilia.[39] As Vieira proposed, her work searched for the space where "the viewer conjugated the polyvolumetric verb."[40] Yet, the rationalism of the geometric principles, industrial precision, and controlled participation that are inherent to *Polyvolume: Meeting Point* came to represent the obsolescence of the utopian dream it belonged to. In the 1970s, the verb that the avant-garde conjugated to represent the national used a radically different vocabulary of precarious walls, plugged-in television sets, and electric guitars, accumulation, and exaggeration.[41] Authenticity and purity became myths. But have the form and feeling of Vieira's silver metal blades become mute? More than fifty years after Brasilia's construction and thirty years into the country's process of redemocratization can we find new ways to "conjugate the polyvolumetric verb"?[42] Have we had enough time to look back at the modernist curves of Vieira's *Polyvolume* with the distance necessary to reengage with the object outside nationalist frameworks of nostalgia or defeat? Investigating past and present experiences of Vieira's *Polyvolume* and the ambiguity of its site may be an attempt at restoring the work's process of production and its potency in engaging with public art, public space, and public history.

Notes

1 / Edith Behring taught drawing at the Escola de Belas Artes do Parque Municipal in Belo Horizonte and left for Rio in 1950, where she studied printmaking with Axl Leskoschek whose students included Ivan Serpa and Almir Mavignier, two of the founders of Brazilian concrete movement.

2 / The shift from individual to collective experiences of artworks is a traditional mark in the transformation of the Brazilian constructive project in the 1960s. See Regina Teixeira de Barros, *Arte construtiva na Pinacoteca de São Paulo* (São Paulo: Pinacoteca do Estado de São Paulo, 2014), 31.

3 / Henri Lefebvre, *The Production of Space*, trans. D. Nicholson-Smith (Oxford: Basil Blackwell, 1991).

4 / Denise Mattar, *Mary Vieira: O tempo do movimento* (São Paulo: Centro Cultural Banco do Brasil, 2005), 35.

5 / Pedro Augusto Vieira Santos, *Preservação e restauro das obras de Mary Vieira em espaços públicos no Brasil* (master's thesis, School of Architecture and Urbanism, University of São Paulo, 2017), 45.

6 / Vieira Santos, 70.

7 / Vieira Santos, 70.

8 / Vieira Santos, 48.

9 / Mattar, *Mary Vieira*, 25.

10 / Mattar, 25.

11 / Mattar, 25.

12 / Ferreira Gullar, "Mary Vieira: Ideia e forma," in *Revista Continente*, July 2005, http://www.revistacontinente.com.br/index.php/component/content/article/165-traduzir-se/1930.html (site discontinued).

13 / Mattar, *Mary Vieira*, 25.

14 / Mattar, 22.

15 / Mattar, 22.

16 / Mattar, 27.

17 / Aracy Amaral, *Projeto construtivo brasileiro na arte* (Rio de Janeiro: Museum of Modern Art and São Paulo: Pinacoteca do Estado, 1977).

18 / Ferreira Gullar, "Neo-Concrete Manifesto," in *Art in Latin America*, ed. Dawn Ades (New Haven, CT: Yale University Press, 1989), 335–337

19 / Mário Pedrosa, *Mário Pedrosa: Primary Documents*, ed. Gloria Ferreira and Paulo Herkenhoff, trans. Stephen Berg (New York: Museum of Modern Art and Duke University Press, 2016), 365.

20 / Pedrosa, 366.

21 / Costa and Niemeyer had worked with these artists before in official projects, such as the former building of the Ministry of Education and Public Health in Rio de Janeiro (1936–1945), today Palacio Gustavo Capanema.

22 / Lucio Costa, "O arquiteto e a sociedade contemporanea," in *Lucio Costa: Registro de uma vivencia* (São Paulo: Empresa das Artes, 1995), 270.

23 / Discussions on the synthesis of the arts have permeated the history of art for centuries. In the nineteenth and twentieth centuries, the idea of a *Gesamtkunstwerk* flourished in the work of artist-architects such as Victor Horta, Charles Mackintosh, Antonio Gaudi, Eliel Saarinen and, of course, Walter Gropius's Bauhaus. Giedion and Sert also brought attention to the collaboration of architects and urbanists with landscape designers, painters, and designers in their "Nine Points of Monumentality" in 1943.

24 / Costa, "Desencontro," in *Lucio Costa*, 202.

25 / Costa, 202.

26 / Figurative sculpture by Bruno Giorgi punctuates one of the gardens designed Roberto Burle Marx for the Itamaraty building, for example.

27 / Vieira Santos, *Preservação e restauro das obras de Mary Vieira*, 67.

28 / Oscar Niemeyer, "Depoimento," *Módulo*, no. 9 (February 1958): 6.

29 / Mattar, *Mary Vieira*, 30.

30 / Mary Vieira, "'La structuration de l'espace' cours 1969 a la kunstgewerbeschule du canton de bâle," reprint from *Graphis revue internationale d'arts graphiques e appliqués anné* 25, no. 146 (December 1969–January 1970): 560.

31 / Vieira, 560.

32 / Vieira, 561.

33 / Mattar, *Mary Vieira*, 43.

34 / Mário Pedrosa, "Da dissolução do objeto ao vanguardismo brasileiro," in *Acadêmicos e modernos*, ed. Otília Arantes (São Paulo: Edusp, 1998), 363.

35 / The social-political role of the art workshop led by Pedrosa and Dr. Nise da Silveira in a facility for the mentally ill in Rio de Janeiro and Pedrosa's workshop for children at the Museum of Modern Art in Rio de Janeiro in the 1960s, for example, intertwined pedagogical, psychiatric, and aesthetic investigations.

36 / Hal Foster, *Art since 1900: Modernism, Antimodernism, Postmodernism* (London: Thames and Hudson, 2004), 531.

37 / Mário Pedrosa refers to Oiticica's work as "postmodern" in "Arte Ambiental, Arte Pós-Moderna, Hélio Oiticica," *Correio da Manhã*, June 26, 1966. Paulo Herkenhoff cites the article "Crise do conhecimento artístico," *Correio da Manhã*, July 31, 1966, as yet another instance when Pedrosa referred to Oiticica's art as "postmodern." Herkenhoff also reveals that Pedrosa repeatedly did so many times over the years. See Paulo Herkenhoff, "Rio de Janeiro: A Necessary City," in *The Geometry of Hope:*

Latin American Abstract Art from the Patricia Phelps de Cisneros Collection, ed. Gabriel Pérez-Barreiro (Austin: Blanton Museum of Art, University of Texas, 2007), 61n49.

38 / Hélio Oiticica's environmental anti-art, for example, deconstructs traditional ways of art-making and art-viewing essential to previous movements by dissolving the polarity between artist and viewer, low and high culture, between art and life. According to Pedrosa, these represented crucial shifts in the parameters that informed Brazilian art until the 1950s.

39 / Pedrosa, "Da dissolução do objeto," 363.

40 / Mattar, *Mary Vieira*, 35.

41 / Oiticica's architectural environment *Tropicália* (1967)—composed of two *Penetrables*, narrow corridor-like structures where participants enter and walk in, out, and around as they please—was composed of walls of plywood and textile. Tropical plants and birds were juxtaposed with written signs inside the structure. One of the signs reads "Pureza é mito," or purity is a myth, which addressed the inadequacy of the industrial universalism of concrete art and modern architecture.

42 / Vieira, quoted in Mattar, *Mary Vieira*, 25.

LINA BO BARDI AND THE CREATION OF THE SCHOOL OF VISUAL ARTS IN PARQUE LAGE

6

Claudia Saldanha

During his brief tenure as director of the School of Visual Arts (1975–1979), Rubens Gerchman was widely recognized for setting up a program of art classes and events that met the demands of an emerging new art scene in Rio de Janeiro a decade after the military coup of 1964. Extrapolating its role as an educational institution, the school positioned itself as the city's cultural beacon promoting the work of young artists and connecting them with professionals from various cultural backgrounds. Structured as a multidisciplinary space, the school offered regular educational activities in tandem with a vibrant program of exhibitions, lectures, and performance. These events—which included dance, theater, and art installations—transformed the school into a cultural magnet that attracted a young audience that yearned for connectivity and a sense of purpose. The genesis of the School of Visual Arts, however, was a complex affair set in motion a decade prior to Gerchman's arrival, and this essay addresses the important confluence of events that made possible the implementation of this important institution.

Brainstorming for the creation of the School of Visual Arts started in December 1964, when then Governor of Rio de Janeiro Carlos Lacerda extended an invitation to Italian architect Lina Bo Bardi (1914–1992) to plan, organize, and manage an art studies center for the city. He thus set the foundation for an ambitious program that privileged innovation and experimentation, aiming to engage young artists and art professionals. As for the site, Lacerda was successful in securing a palatial home built in the 1930s that by 1957 had become city property. Commonly referred to as Parque Lage, the eclectic-style building is perched in a 125 acres urban park in Rio's upper-middle-class Zona Sul (South Zone) area amid greenery and century-old trees on the edge of the Atlantic Forest.[1]

In looking back at Bo Bardi's architectural works realized in Brazil—more specifically the works produced from 1960 to 1980, such as the Unhão Museum in Salvador, the Museu de Arte de São Paulo (MASP), the Pompeia Factory, and the Oficina Theater—one is impressed by the architect's extraordinary versatility in adapting historic spaces or creating entirely new structures. The construction or adaptation of existing spaces is punctuated by a great sensibility for preservation and conservation of the original buildings' characteristics and in proposing new constructions to answer the need of new activities. Thus, a church and a warehouse from the seventeenth century were transformed into an ocean-front museum for modern art in Salvador; an old oil tank factory was transformed into a community center to host and promote art forms and diversity in a São Paulo working-class neighborhood; in a large lot in Avenida Paulista a new three-story building was built to house Brazil's largest art collection. In all these projects, Bo Bardi introduced educational programs, seminars, exhibitions libraries, documentation centers, and performance and other interactive spaces. Informed by her architectural training in Europe and early collaborations with Gio Ponti and Bruno Zevi, Bo Bardi's projects aimed at not only to restructure the spaces but to redefine the cultural occupation of those constructions as well.

Besides architecture and furniture design, Bo Bardi's professional activity also comprehended editorial projects, museology, curatorial work, and art criticism. She was responsible for the editorial management of the Italian magazine *A-Cultura della Vita* and the Brazilian *Habitat*, first published in 1950 as the catalog for MASP. Together with her husband, Pietro Maria Bardi (1900–1999), she was responsible for the magazine's first ten issues focusing on articles related to art, architecture, and matters related to art education. In 1947, the Bardis in collaboration with fellow architect Jacob Ruchti created the Instituto de Arte Contemporânea as an educational branch of MASP, one of the first schools in Brazil to train young designers under a strong functionalist direction influenced by the Bauhaus. In her introduction to *Habitat* 4 (1951), an issue dedicated to architectural projects for schools, Bo Bardi wrote:

> If anything must be done to "transform" mankind, the first step is to "form" them. And it is natural that the process must start in the schools. To build schools is fine, a task that fits well within the realm of abstract initiatives and resounding ministerial decisions; but the burning intent, and the sense of urgency is lacking. It is necessary to dramatize the problem of the schools and bring it to life, make it present, quotidian.

> What is a school? It is a place where one learns to read and to write, where one learns to check one's watch and to count time, where above all, one learns to be proud of one's country. At school, one also studies the progressive order of time, many disciplines, infinite other things until the day when one graduates and this complex of learned things forms a baggage, the means to start one's voyage through humanity.
>
> The premise for building according to school needs seems at first beyond the problem of architecture, yet it is closely related. The forms that expand and that connect with the exterior, the garden, the large windows, the foreboding atmosphere are the first step for abolishing barriers. The school bunker—Gothic, Norman, or without style but with the common denominator of a prison reminding the student that to study is an agonizing endeavor—this kind of school has become antiquated and obsolete. Let's start with the schools, and above all, let's start with architecture.[2]

The idea to invite Bo Bardi to spearhead research for the art center in Rio came from the engineer and landscape designer Lota de Macedo Soares, a close friend of the governor who at the time was in charge of the important structural urban redesign for the city. Motivated not only by Bo Bardi's capabilities as an architect but above all by her vast cultural knowledge, Soares promoted a meeting between Bo Bardi and Lacerda and suggested her appointment to run the newly created art center.

The concept of an art center in Parque Lage was part of a broader plan conceived by Lacerda to restructure Rio de Janeiro's complex urban layout and optimize the use of public spaces. Soares's successful experience of designing and developing the Flamengo Park in a landfill area by the Guanabara Bay, with its high-speed routes running through tropical gardens designed by Roberto Burle Marx, had strengthened the bond between the engineer and the governor. Together they discussed how Flamengo Park might be developed to include sports courts and the new home for Rio's Museum of Modern Art. Soares helped select architects, urban planners, landscape designers, and technicians to collaborate in the creation of a major urban work connecting Rio's commercial center to its posh neighborhoods of Zona Sul. In the early 1960s, such advanced understanding of urban design would transform the region indelibly and propose a new benchmark in terms of how public spaces in Rio could be used.

Hence the implementation of an art center in Parque Lage, whose property had been incorporated to the state by Lacerda as a way to give public access and new productive use to that portion of the Atlantic Forest. In August 1966, Lacerda created a foundation with the charge for capturing funds to maintain the new arts center. Bo Bardi's responsibilities included the creation of a preliminary work project for Parque Lage, setting budget plans, hiring staff, and overseeing renovation construction. According to its initial plan, the purpose of the foundation was to create pathways for youth to develop "a clear and constructive understanding of the issues affecting the contemporary world," to cultivate "their interests and individual talents in the

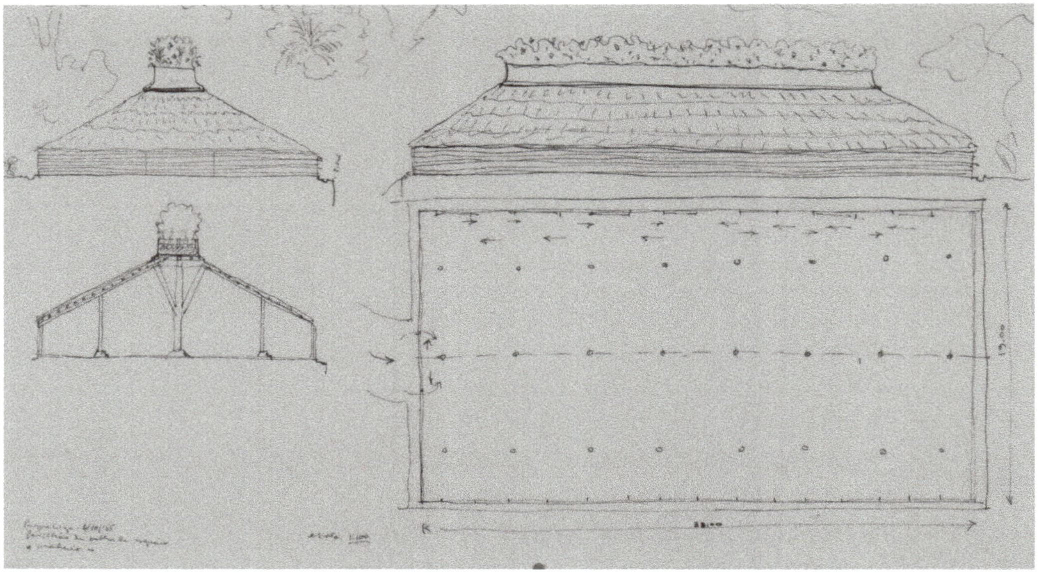

Lina Bo Bardi, Project for a pavilion at Parque Lage, 1965. Pen, graphite and China ink on vegetal paper. Copyright Instituto Bardi / Casa de Vidro.

field of the arts and of technique," and to foster "a sense of community through the exchange and dialogue with other universities and schools in Brazil and abroad."[3]

Bo Bardi's contribution to Brazilian culture remains the subject of continuous study and is far from being understood in its broadest spectrum. With each new project and venture, she implemented innovative ideas that revealed her keen intelligence, versatility, and profound interest in Brazilian popular culture. Her vast technical and theoretical knowledge about art, architecture, urban planning, and design, together with her interest and respect for the vernacular, popular culture, and craft, made her an key asset for Lacerda's ambitious plans.

When she began working on the MASP project, she jotted down this note:

> A remembrance place? A mummy tomb for the noteworthy? A warehouse or a collection of artworks made by people for people, already obsolete and must be managed with a sense of pity. None of that. The new museums must open their doors; let fresh air and new light pour in. Between past and present there is no continuity solution. It is necessary to intertwine modern life, unfortunately melancholic and distracted by all kinds of nightmares, in its new grand art trend.

And also:

> The museum's mission is to create an atmosphere, a visitors experience that helps them comprehend art and make no distinction between ancient or modern art.[4]

Since its inception, the MASP educational programs followed directives set forth

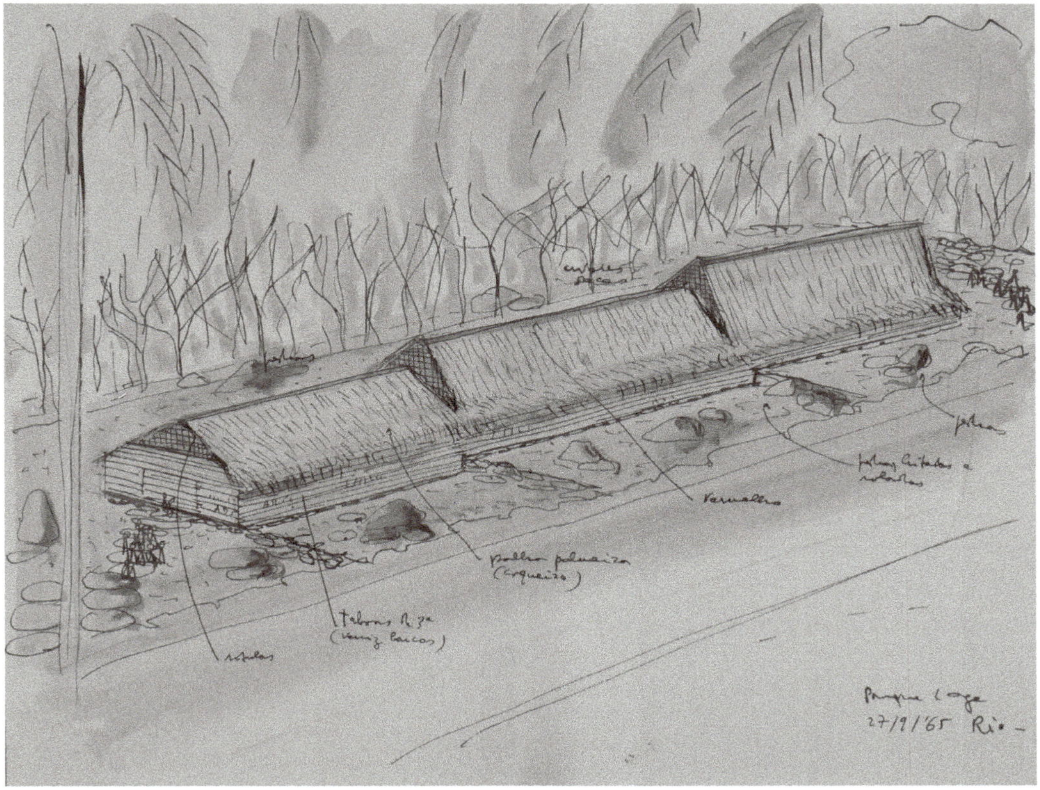

Lina Bo Bardi, Project for a pavilion at Parque Lage, 1966. Watercolor, graphite and China ink on paper. Copyright Instituto Bardi / Casa de Vidro.

by UNESCO, which understood museums as cultural formation centers of pivotal relevance to their visitor's education. The International Museum Council (ICOM), a UNESCO branch, was created following the need to establish norms for modern museums. In an article published in the first issue of *Habitat*, Bo Bardi addressed the didactic activities at MASP citing the special classes of drawings from nature, music history, printmaking, photography, and a dedicated space for children—the Children's Art Club, which offered painting, music, and dance classes. Articulated on the premise of a modern concept of museum, MASP became a dynamic center, engaging large audiences through culture and art education.

In a 1975 thesis presented in Mexico, art critic Mário Pedrosa reflected on the roles of art institutions of that period, arguing that only a modern art museum could understand and value art in its proper nature and the museum's role in promoting it.

> Different from the ancient and traditional museum, the one that keeps masterpieces in static positions, today's museums are above all a home for experiences. A "*paralaboratorio*." Inside it one understands what experimental art is. And these days, a place where the contemporary critics can assimilate the blending of all art genres. Sculpture turns into painting, painting

> into sculpture, and so on. Another characteristic of contemporary activities is the unlimited attention to research, experimentation, and invention. . . . The modern museum's role fits right here: it is the privileged ambience where this experience should take place.[5]

Bo Bardi's ideas for the structuring of MASP education outreach were essential for the creation of the Center of Studies Foundation at Parque Lage. Although her project was never fully implemented because of the lack of incentive and resources, she was able to outline basic ideas that Rubens Gerchman would later use to create the School of Visual Arts.

Given this background, it is not surprising that Gerchman would invite Bo Bardi to join the planning group in charge of restructuring the School of Visual Arts. Besides contributing to the creation of a new curriculum, Bo Bardi proposed, in collaboration with set designer Hélio Eichbauer, the first course under Gerchman's tenure, titled Multidimensional Workshop. The course was offered in the summer of 1976, with Eichbauer as instructor. Because of her hectic schedule during the completion of MASP, Bo Bardi was unable to teach. However, her collaboration with Gerchman extended for a significant period, and her proposal for the foundation, titled *Academia*, included notes on activities such as the following:

> Seminars; production of documentary movies with a scientific angle (human sciences and facts) produced by specialists; documentation center (documents, exhibitions, recorded material and publications exclusively about Brazil); library (from the beginning subscribed magazines and bibliography services); publication of a monthly newsletter; national forum covering Brazilian issues; occasional participation of foreign guest contributors; public issues exhibitions; coffee shop and restaurant; an art gallery in the plant nursery and concerts; theater for 300 guests.[6]

In the project sent to the foundation in charge of creating the Arts Studies Center, Bo Bardi emphasized the need for a vast curriculum for the formation of artists and art professionals. Beyond the program's interdisciplinary character, she also insisted on the creation of a project that included the restoration of the entire estate (the mansion, its stables and gardens) as well as changes to the buildings' interiors to better suit the new school. And she stressed her priorities in a terse list of directions: "The relationship between intellectual and industrial work; avoid dilettantism and improvisation, against verbiage and self-aggrandizing; all work must be clearly stated in WRITING, criticism also must be conveyed in writing; against prolixity; against 'folkloristic' concepts of a moral, social, and political order."[7] Furthermore, Bo Bardi's proposals such as forums, seminars, festivals, exhibitions, documentation center, library, auditorium, newsletter, invitations to foreign art professionals, and hosting of nonresident professors demonstrated the cosmopolitan philosophy on which the Parque Lage art center was built. The program departs from the intellectual and artistic production honed in workshops, studios, classes, and seminars and culminates in the dissemination of this production through exhibitions and publications, a production that was further solidified through artist-to-artist exchanges and international residence programs.

In "Cinco anos entre os brancos" (Five years among the whites), an article in which she talks about the time she lived in Salvador and created the city's Museum of Modern Art, Bo Bardi wrote:

> The Modern Art Museum is a phenomenon typical of a new country where the word *museum* has a meaning other than preservation. The old-world countries create museums based on their relevant collections; there are no museums with reduced or no collections. Salvador's Museum of Modern Art wasn't a traditional museum: given the state's low budget, it could hardly "preserve." Its activities were geared toward the creation of a cultural movement that embraced the values of a historically poor culture that could overcome Western historical standards. Supported by a popular experience (distinct from folklore), the museum penetrates a modern culture world, with the craft, methods and strength of a new humanist.[8]

Bo Bardi's 1966 program for the Parque Lage Studies Center reflected the same ideas that punctuated almost all her previous projects. To the recovery of existing spaces she added the need for new ones, to fulfill the new activities. In that sense, an art school would assume the relevance and function of a museum—"The museum's mission is to create an atmosphere, an environment to enable the visitor to comprehend artworks, where there is no distinction between ancient or modern art." Both in renovation projects such as the Unhão Museum and the Pompeia Factory and in new constructions such as MASP, Bo Bardi allowed for new-use plans. For the Unhão she created an adjoining building for workshops and arts and crafts courses; for the Pompeia Factory she changed a creek's course and built a fireplace for the community space as well as a library and restaurant; for MASP she built an enormous open space under the museum for shows and large public gatherings. For Parque Lage, she designed external wood pavilions covered in palm tree fronds to house workshops and open-air exhibitions. In designing the pavilions, Bo Bardi connected the typology and technique proper to storage warehouses to a new concept of workspace. As the sketches for the pavilions demonstrate, Bo Bardi was keen in establishing connections with the environment: the stone floors and the fence of tree logs would create a transition between the mansion and the park's vegetation.

One cannot ignore the similarities to her various projects: "I chose a simple architecture that could immediately communicate what in the past was called 'monumental,' meaning in the sense of 'collective,' of civil dignity. I used my previous experience of five years living in Brazil's Northeast region, the exposure to folk popular culture, not with a romantic folklore angle, but with a simplifying experience. Through that experience I landed what one could call 'poor architecture.' I insist, not from an ethnical point of view."[10] Bo Bardi's contribution was fundamental for

Gerchman's restructuring of the School of Visual Arts in 1975. Although Gerchman surrounded himself with highly qualified collaborators who promoted debate and reflection on a daily basis, it was inevitable that a great portion of the teaching structure still followed outdated practices in the studios and workshops. In the school's inaugural brochure several courses revealed a sense of sameness as in any art school. This impression that nothing had changed could be erroneous and overshadow the relevance of one of the most innovative experiences in Brazil.

Art critic Wilson Coutinho said: "Rubens Gerchman got to this month of August 1970 with a few special characteristics. He had seen the ousting of president João Goulart, witnessed the ascension of the military junta to power . . . participated in progressive movements in the 1960s and lived in the United States—center of progressive ideas, replacing Paris—and therefore, due to his credentials, he is the one best suited to champion the changes at Parque Lage."[11] Throughout the years of its existence, the School of Visual Arts was shaped in various configurations. It hosted transformations in the art field and important debates promoted by society in general. Lately, various issues faced by the School of Visual Arts have limited its resources for the advancement of education and cultural center. The opening of other schools, free courses, and postgraduation programs in art transformed the art and cultural scene, necessitating the implementation of a new management model and an education program complemented by exhibitions and other activities that restructure the relationship between the three pillars since 1975: education, exhibition, and circulation of its artistic and intellectual production. While the education deficiencies have been evident, the School of Visual Arts plays a prominent role in Brazil and has been on the radar of artists, curators, art critics, and other art professionals worldwide.

Notes

1 / The area had been a private orchard since 1811 and after several iterations a mansion was built on the site by Henrique Lage, an industrialist married to Gabriella Besanzone, a Italian opera singer. Around 1936, the house was the center for Brazil's Lyric Theater Society, and in 1957, the family used the property to settle debts.

2 / Lina Bo Bardi, introduction to *Habitat: Arquitetura e artes no Brasil*, no. 4 (São Paulo: Habitat Editora Ltda., MASP, 1951).

3 / Lina Bo Bardi, unpublished manuscript, collection of Instituto Lina Bo Bardi.

4 / Lina Bo Bardi, "Cinco anos entre os brancos," in *Mirante des Artes* (São Paulo: Serviço Social do Comércio [SESC], Instituto do Patrimônio Histórico e Nacional [IPHAN], 2015), 4.

5 / Mário Pedrosa, "Arte culta e arte popular" [Erudite Art and Popular Art], *Arte em Revista*, no. 3 (1980): 22–26. The thesis was first presented at the Popular Art Seminar, México City, 1975.

6 / Bo Bardi, unpublished manuscript.

7 / Bo Bardi, unpublished manuscript.

8 / Bo Bardi. "Cinco anos entre os brancos," 4.

9 / Bo Bardi, unpublished manuscript.

10 / Bo Bardi. "Cinco anos entre os brancos." 4.

11 / Wilson Coutinho, "O jardim da oposição" [The opposition garden], in *O jardim da oposição*, ed. Helio Eichbauer, Heloísa Buarque de Hollanda (Rio de Janeiro: Escola de Artes Visuais 1975–1979, 2009), 26–29.

II

TROPICAL REASON The Making of a Counterculture in Brazil

7

Frederico Coelho

In his memoir, *Verdade tropical*,[1] Brazilian singer-songwriter Caetano Veloso suggested that certain groups of artists connected to the late 1960s Tropicália movement—which he cofounded with Gilberto Gil, Torquato Neto, and others—owed their successes to a productive tension between two extremes in Brazil's complex artistic traditions that pitched rationalism against intuition. The first group was made up of artists and intellectuals involved in 1950s constructivism, teetering on the edge of the modernist avant-gardes, such as the concrete artists and poets, the composers and conductors associated with the Música Nova movement,[2] as well as some of the neoconcrete artists. The second group featured artists and intellectuals engaged with the Brazilian counterculture of the 1960s.[3] And the third group—which included artists such as Torquato Neto, Jorge Mautner, Rogério Duarte, José Agripino de Paula, Waly Salomão, and Julio Bressane, among others—explored transgressive forms of aesthetic experimentation. In his remarks, Veloso was hinting at the pivotal chasm that happened in the late 1950s, when a group of artists based in Rio de Janeiro formulated a response to what they perceived as the rigid rationalism of the concretist program set forth by Max Bill and his followers.

Veloso traces a historical arch that roughly spans from 1951, the year of the first São Paulo Biennial (the most thorough genealogy of the constructivist movements of the era), to 1968, the official end of the Tropicalismo and Arte Marginal (outsider culture) movements[4]—or from the high modernism of the 1950s avant-garde and its

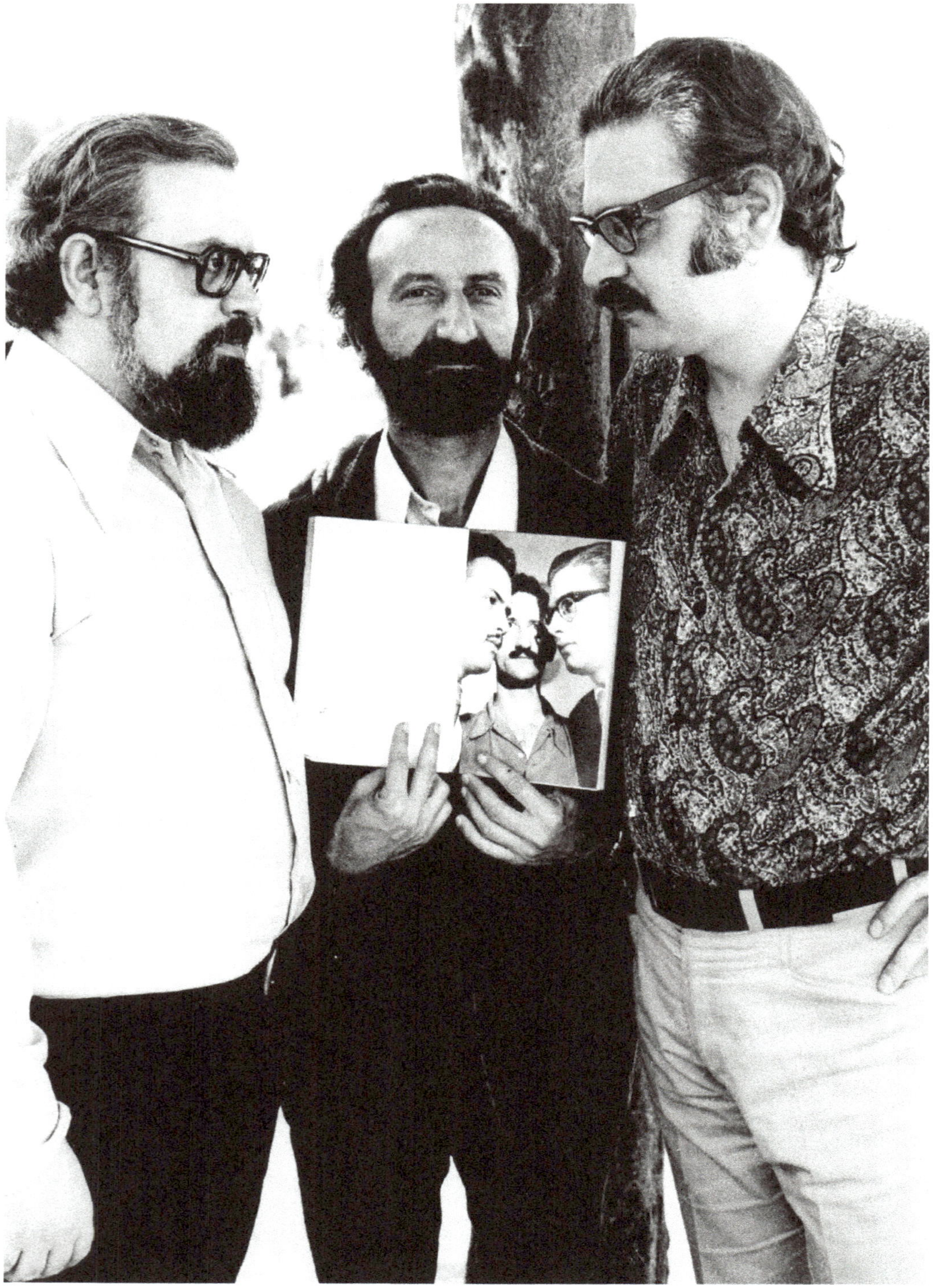

Haroldo de Campos, Décio Pignatari, and Augusto de Campos. Photograph by Ivan Cardoso.

interest in rationalism, geometry, architecture, design, and poetry to the "postmodern" counterculture movement of the late 1960s which comprised pop, psychedelia, hedonism, mass culture, popular music, television, cinema, and the desecration of the literary code. The same artists (the brothers Augusto and Haroldo de Campos and Hélio Oiticica, for instance) that had helped shape the constructivist avant-gardes of the 1950s reunited some ten years later, this time around popular music and related events. As Veloso points out, however, the groups converged in different ways.

What distinguished the artists and intellectuals of the late 1960s from those of the 1950s, according to Veloso, could be summed up in one word: reason (or lack thereof). Why would these two seemingly disparate groups—the "high modernists," or "rationalist," of the 1950s and the "postmodernists," or irrationalists, of the 1960s[5]—forge an alliance amid the last modern avant-gardes in Brazil? What caused the concrete poets to move away from their strong rational-mathematical premises in the 1950s and embrace the chaos of language at the limits of prose as Haroldo de Campos did in his *Galáxias*?[6] What brought the crisis of form in the work of neoconcrete artists closer to the crisis of the word in the work of, for example, counterculture poets such as Waly Salomão, Rogério Duarte, and Torquato Neto? What led Hélio Oiticica to bring together *culture* and *madness* in the same flash of ideas, as he did in a seminar presented at the Museum of Modern Art in Rio in 1968? Is it the tropical climate that debunks occidental reason in favor of folly? Or can we embrace the "Tropical Cartesianism" suggested by Max Bense as a paradigm for this meeting of forces?[7] What leads a reader of constructivist theories, such as Oiticica, to embrace the delirium of language and of the body?

The convergence stressed by Veloso unfolds beyond the short Tropicalist moment (1967–1968) and consolidates in the early 1970s, mainly through independent magazines. Two of them stand out as historic objects: the legendary *Navilouca*, a single-issue magazine that the poets Torquato Neto and Waly Salomão began to put together in 1972 and published in 1974, and *Pólen*, published in 1974 by Duda Machado and Susana de Moraes (in collaboration with the poet Mauricio Cirne and the visual artists Antonio Dias and Iole de Freitas). The pages of *Navilouca* featured works by Haroldo and Augusto de Campos, Décio Pignatari, Lygia Clark, Hélio Oiticica, Duda Machado, Luis Otavio Pimentel, Caetano Veloso, and Rogério Duarte as well as an innovative layout design by Oscar Ramos and Luciano Figueiredo. The connection between the 1950s avant-garde and the generation that embraced the 1960s counterculture zeitgeist in their personal lives and work found in *Navilouca* an ideal platform for expressing the experimental format and performative character that characterized the encounter between the "rationalists" and "irrationalists." In contrast, *Pólen* created a bridge between the visual artists that went beyond the generation of neoconcrete artists. Many of the artists that were published in *Navilouca* also appeared in *Pólen*, but the editors also featured Carlos Vergara, Waltércio Caldas, Antonio Risério, and Rubens Gerchman, among others. The permanence of the Campos brothers, Oiticica, Veloso, Waly Salomão, and Torquato Neto denotes how the alliances and partnerships of the Tropicalist era unfolded and brought to an end the destructive polemics that pitched neoconcrete artists against their concrete counterparts.

Beyond the media exposure afforded by the Tropicalista pop stars, what caused these two productive forces of Brazilian art of the 1950s and 1960s to converge? Granted, between 1968 and 1972, those who were excluded from the debate about what direction the country might take—whether to adopt school-taught Marxism, socialist realism, or militarized conservatism—formed a political and an aesthetic alliance. But which threads exactly caused this web of relationships and discourses to form? Was it Oswald de Andrade's risks and writings to rethink Brazilian culture?[8] Were intellectual affinities and aesthetic compromises converging toward a cosmopolitan and transgressive strategy of cultural debate? And why does Veloso invoke *reason* as the basis for his analysis?

My hypothesis is that the "rationalists" and "irrationalist" shared a common perspective. The creative tension among the constructivist artists of the 1950s and the experimental artists of the 1960s and 1970s lies between reason and madness (or rationalism and irrationalism, to use Veloso's terms). For the country's cultural tensions at that moment reenacted the clash between societal boundaries based on mathematically rational aesthetic principles and lives whose embrace of delirium opened new perspectives on art. How can we reconcile the fact that at the same time that young poets in São Paulo dedicated themselves to the rigorous foundation of a new creative paradigm for Brazilian and world poetry, a group of artists in Rio de Janeiro had become involved with inmates of a psychiatric hospital and accepted madness not as a defect of the brain but as an aesthetic possibility? What were the implications of "the positivity of madness" in the context of Cartesian control of the mind over the creator-body?

The presence of visual artists dedicated to constructivist research at the Engenho de Dentro hospital under Dr. Nise da Silveira's leadership produced a node in the narrative line of Brazilian constructivism. Recent research on the subject suggests that one cannot understand the specificity of the neoconcrete experience in Rio without mentioning the impact that Silveira's work exerted on the artistic milieu in Rio in contrast to the primacy of mathematical rigor among São Paulo concrete artists and poets. This, perhaps, opens the door for a possible understanding of how madness—and its impact on art—was able to foster unexpected connections among artists of different generations in Brazil.

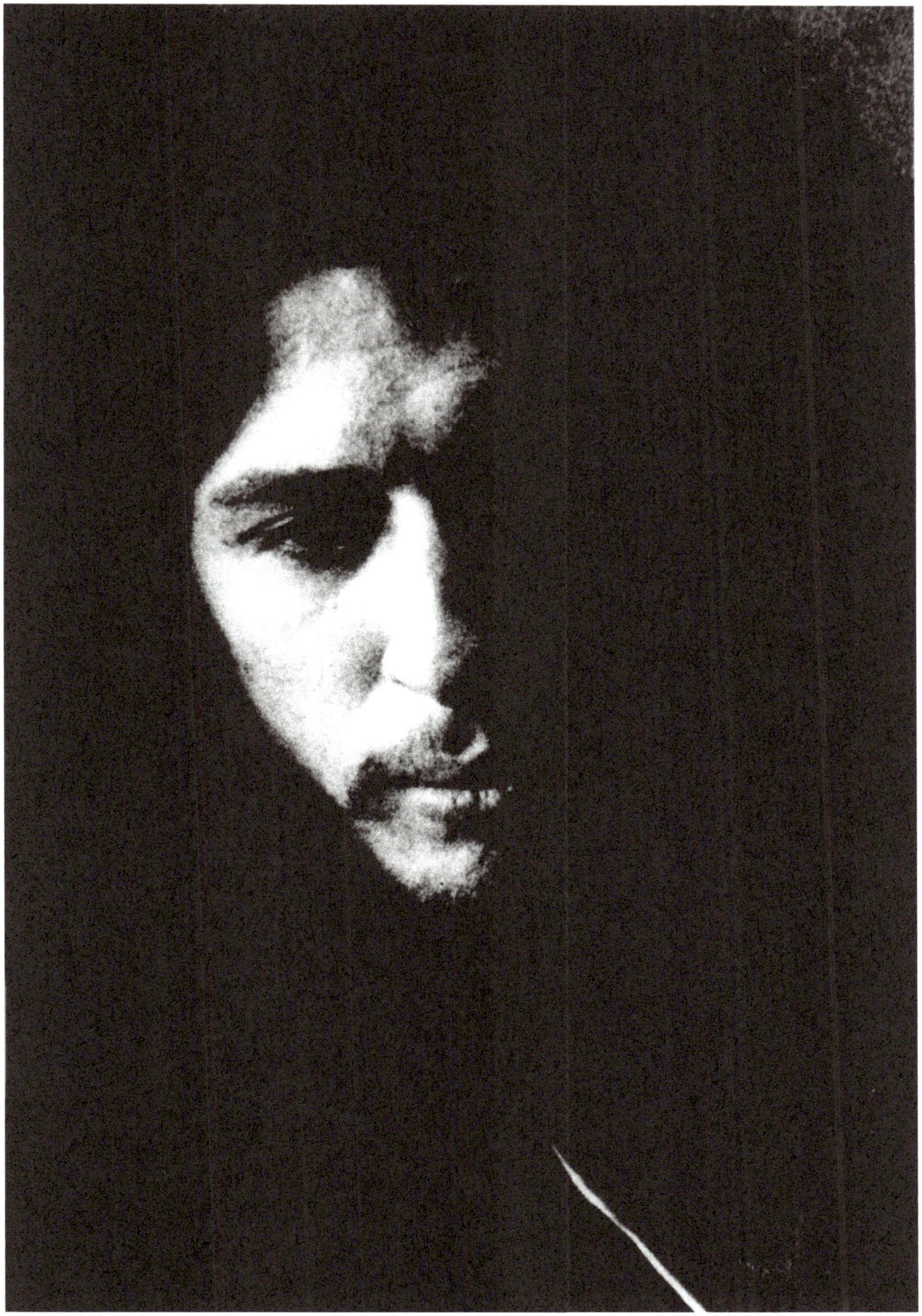

Torquato Neto. Photograph by Ivan Cardoso.

The feud between concrete and neoconcrete poets and artists was prompted by the critique raised by the latter onto the former's dogmatic application of rationalistic-mechanistic principles. The articles and debates that circulated in the press at that time focused on how the poet and art critic Ferreira Gullar was keen on emphasizing their distinct perspectives. The first sentence in his "Manifesto neoconcreto" (1959) already refers to the "rationalist exacerbation" of the concrete art practiced then. He also uses expressions such as "experiment" and "expressive possibilities" and underscores the critical aloofness of the rationalist approach, accusing it of stealing "all autonomy" from art by subjecting it to a "mechanical objectivism."

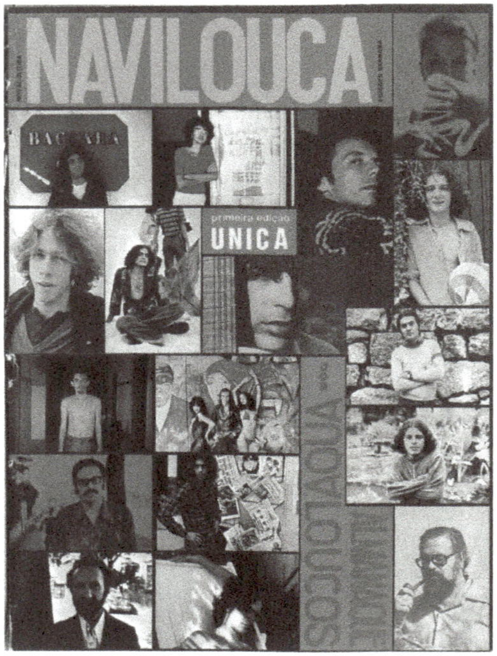

Navilouca, 1974. Front cover design by Óscar Ramos and Luciano Figueiredo.

Two years earlier, in 1957, when the term *neoconcrete* had not yet been coined to distinguish between the São Paulo and Rio factions, Gullar, Oliveira Bastos, and Reynaldo Jardim (three poets and critics connected with the group of artists in Rio) published "Poesia concreta: Experiência intuitive" (Concrete poetry: Intuitive experiment) in the Sunday supplement of *Jornal do Brasil*. The article was written in response to an essay published in the same newspaper by Haroldo de Campos titled, "Da fenomenologia da composição à matemática da composição" (From the phenomenology of composition to the mathematics of composition).[9] The intention on the part of Gullar et al. was to demarcate to what extent reason could dominate over poetic intuition—in their minds, one of the radical principles informing the production of the São Paulo group at that time.

What Campos proposed as "mathematical operation," a key innovation in concrete poetry, entailed a process no longer based on "word-draws-word" (a term used by Campos to exemplify the traditional method of writing) but rather one taking into consideration the poem's structure as a formal possibility for calculating space-time—a proposition that would plunge poetry deeper into "the realm of constructivist rationality." In Gullar, Bastos, and Jardim's text, however, the use of the term "intuitive experiment" is a direct retort to Campos's deprecating phrase "intuition availability." They defended as "concrete" principles the contingency of actions and the capacity to apprehend the world beyond rational and verifiable procedures. They assumed the reader has a crucial role in completing the poetic work rather than just treating it as an object, an isolated form, admired for its internal mathematical perfection.

In addition to stirring the public debate about the term *concrete*, their text would signal a definitive break with the rationalist paradigm by deriding it as a "scientific misunderstanding," stating: "The alleged submission of poetry to mathematic structures has all the hallmarks of this misunderstanding." Concrete poetry, for the Rio group, should count as a daily experience—affective, intuitive—so as not to become mere illustration, in the field of language or of catalogued science laws.

The rupture between art and science, between rational technique and intuitive technique, between man-machine and man-experiment might relate to situations that, somehow, take us back to the contact between those art critics and artists and Dr. da Silveira's research. Many of her patients throughout the late 1940s and 1950s took classes with Almir Mavigner, who, as has been amply documented, brought Ivan Serpa, Mário Pedrosa, and Abraham Palatnik among others to the Hospital Psiquiátrico in Engenho de Dentro. Already in 1949, the São Paulo Museum of Modern Art held the exhibit *Nove artistas de Engenho de Dentro* (Nine Artists from Engenho de Dentro), although it was never mentioned in any documents or official timelines as an event important to the São Paulo concrete group.

In Rio, Dr. da Silveira's work reached the principal players of critical and artistic production. Mário Pedrosa, the most important art critic at the time, had witnessed firsthand the art workshops in progress at Engenho de Dentro and even discussed the quality of their work with other critics. Based on that debate, Pedrosa, in 1951, wrote an essay titled "Forma e personalidade" (Form and personality) that focused exclusively on the relation between art and its critical limits vis-à-vis the so-called nonartistic creations (in primitive cultures or by children and schizophrenics).[10] The essay is clearly influenced by his visits to the hospital atelier and the exhibitions he had helped organize.

Pedrosa and Léon Degand had organized the 1949 exhibition *Nove artistas de Engenho de Dentro* at the São Paulo Museum of Modern Art which sparked a long study by Pedrosa that already presented ideas that would later overlap with Gullar's texts. (Incidentally, Pedrosa and Gullar shared an apartment from 1954 to 1960, the period in which the Grupo Frente and neoconcretism emerged.) Indeed, Pedrosa uses the expression "creative intuition" in his 1951 essay, already countering the rigid rationalist/scientific parameters in art criticism. Pedrosa posits the question of *intuition*, thus countering the rigid rationalist/scientific parameters in art criticism. Pedrosa would revisit the theme of intuition again in his 1960 essay, "Das formas significantes à Lógica da expressão" (From signifying forms to the logic of expression), in which he elaborates on the term based on his readings in continental philosophy by Henri Bergson, Ernest Cassirer, and others.

In 1958 Gullar approached the theme Pedrosa had examined in the two aforementioned articles. In his article "Louco faz arte? A propósito de um debate" (Do the insane make art? Apropos of a debate),[11] Gullar also opposed the negative reaction by critics to the art produced by Engenho de Dentro's patients Emygdio de Barros, and Adelina and Fernando Diniz. Denoting close familiarity with Pedrosa's thoughts, Gullar brought up Gestalt theory and Cassirer to substantiate the "reevaluation of the individual and the latent forces of individual expression." Gullar's article was published around the same time as his reflections on nonobject theory and on Lygia Clark's art. This alignment with the experimental and intuition as escape routes to the rationalist/mathematical dogma of São Paulo constructivism profoundly influenced the work of Hélio Oticica, Lygia Clark, and Lygia Pape—three artists who had professional and personal connections with the two art critics. The individual works of Pedrosa and Gullar, and their brief experience living together during the neoconcrete era stresses the role of the individual, the inclusion of the viewer/reader as an active part of an artwork.

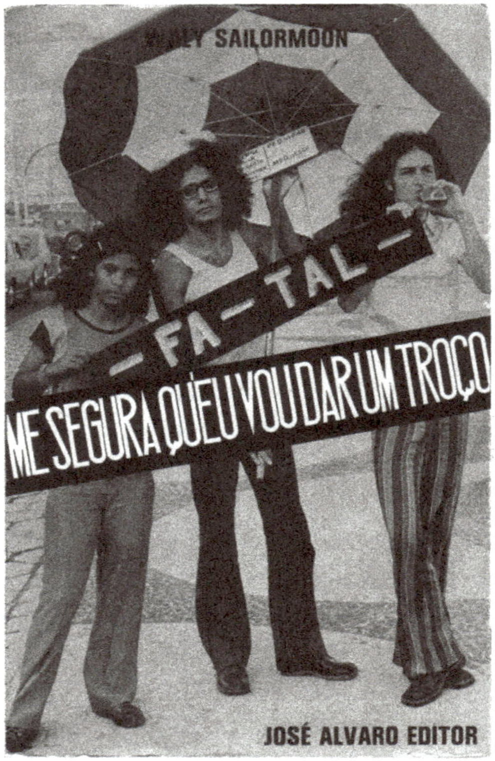

Waly Salomão (Sailormoon), *Me segura qu'eu vou dar um troço*, 1972. Front cover design by Oscar Ramos and Luciano Figueiredo. Courtesy of Marta Braga.

Of course, it is not prudent to leap from the crises of rationalism among constructivist artists to the crisis of language in the art of schizophrenics as proof of a connection between the "rationalists" and "irrationalists." Still, we can point to certain aspects that indicate that *word* and *image* are unstable concepts in Brazil in the 1960s. The national dream of a defined path toward national development with the help of the most modern techniques of industrialized society (advertising, cybernetics, design, visual poetry, and more) shipwrecked before the excesses of Tropicalismo and the primacy of the body as a space of experimentation and rupture—political, existential, and aesthetic. The body that insinuated itself into Gullar and Pedrosa's texts as a counterpoint to the Cartesian reason of concretism becomes symptomatic of this crisis of language, in which the word is subsumed by sensations and the mechanical control of the body empties into experiment-limits and new significance in its use in arts.

In the 1970s, the asylum at Engenho de Dentro was once again the focus of attention in Rio de Janeiro, albeit not as a center for patient-artist interaction but rather as a shelter for psychiatric help. Graphic designer Rogério Duarte and poet Torquato Neto—two of Oiticica's closest friends and, like Veloso, key figures in the Tropicalismo movement—checked themselves into the hospital in 1970 and 1971, respectively.[12] Both men were multitalented intellectuals equally at ease in music, journalism, cinema, poetry, criticism, and art; and both faced personal situations that bordered on "critique and clinic" to paraphrase the title of Gilles Deleuze's final work.[13] These extreme episodes unfortunately were not isolated cases for the generation that, in the aftermath of the Tropicália movement, assumed a degree of radicalism that Veloso deemed "irrational."

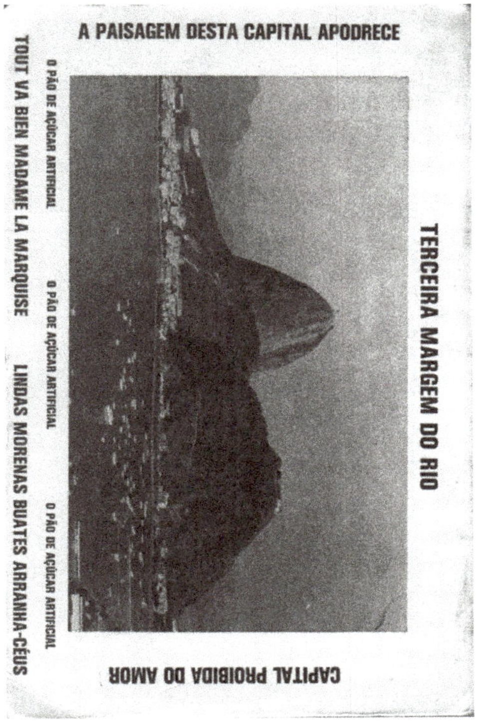

Waly Salomão (Sailormoon), *Me segura qu'eu vou dar um troço*, 1972. Back cover design by Oscar Ramos and Luciano Figueiredo. Courtesy of Marta Braga.

The "irrationalists," that is, the outsiders of Brazil's cultural mainstream, found in madness and its philosophical and aesthetic unfoldings a constant theme. It is not by chance that Antonin Artaud's work arrived in Brazil with such force through the efforts of this younger generation, through the alternative press, and through intellectuals such as the journalist and philosopher Luiz Carlos Maciel. The author of a column titled "Underground" in the weekly *O Pasquim*, Maciel published insightful essays on the widespread debate about antipsychiatry, drawing a parallel between artists such as Artaud and the chronic problems of mental health assistance in Brazil and abroad. Around the same time, Gilles Deleuze and Felix Guattari's *Anti-Oedipus* (1972) was published in Brazil. It became clear in this context that Dr. da Silveira's successful experiment in the early 1950s pioneered the productive nexus of art, madness, and alternative treatments of mental problems that intellectuals such as Deleuze, Guattari, and Foucault were to explore two decades later.

The relationship proposed by Deleuze between the *critical* (mediated by productive reasoning, which enables us to achieve a minimum of creative discipline in the middle of chaos) and the *clinical* (whose creator succumbs to language and does not produce "sense") allows us to think about how to situate works that oscillate between these two poles. The title of Neto and Salomão's magazine, *Navilouca*, is a reference to the medieval ships that collected the mad from coastal cities and took them to an unknown destination.[14] Launched in 1972, the same year that Michel Foucault visited Brazil for a series of lectures at Pontifical Catholic University of Rio de Janeiro, *Navilouca* was published around the same time as the work of one of the principal scholars on the theme of madness in the West. To quote Salomão, it was an era that radically proposed "the obliteration of the former separation between the individual and the object."[15]

Torquato Neto clearly demonstrated this in his journals written during his voluntary confinement at Engenho de Dentro. Little by little, his texts suggested his abandonment of what he called his "faith in words." He found the word, prime material for poets—and for reason—to be at an insoluble impasse. The coda of his artistic discourse was conditioned by this bankruptcy of the word. Torquato Neto was a young intellectual devotee of the idea of concrete paideuma (the tangle of precursors that inform our present). A reader of the São Paulo poets, he also followed the work of the masters they promoted (Pound, Joyce, Mallarmé) and mastered the production of his own poems as if in dialogue with the concrete school. His personal life, however, dragged him little by little to a space where reason could no longer resist delirium. The critical became clinical.

My thoughts are but embryonic ideas about the relations between Cartesian aesthetic principles in a country such as Brazil and their limits through the presence of a conjunction of discourses and practices that dislocate from mathematics to the disordering of forms. In some of Oiticica's, Clark's, and Pape's works, the body takes on the preponderant role of invention of other principles (intuitive, experimental) that escaped the dogmas of the country's first constructive moment. In reclaiming a subject and a body open to the chance of experience, the dialogue with artworks, authors, and events linked to the boundaries of language and the discourses guaranteed by reason—schizophrenics, marginal people, immigrants, women, Brazilian natives, blacks—is permanent. The critical and the clinical walk hand in hand, even when sometimes the clinical swallows the critical in a country that alleviates a crisis of language with a political crisis.

If in the 1950s the concrete and neoconcrete groups had to stake out antagonistic positions in search of a relation with European constructivist models, in the 1970s a reencounter was possible because of the degree of compatibility that came to exist in their work. The new approach of Oiticica and the Campos brothers during their time together in Manhattan is proof that even if principal constructivist artists were still deeply rooted in the work of the São Paulo poets, rather than the work of the poets from Rio, fidelity to the Poundian paideuma of invention connected them all. Rationalists or irrationalists, mathematicians or hedonists, tenuous creative lines were traced so that the avant-garde contributed a specific profile to the Brazilian counterculture—and new life to the concrete poets and their theoretic texts.

Notes

1 / Caetano Veloso, *Verdade tropical* (São Paulo: Companhia das Letras, 1997).

2 / Grupo Música Nova was a Brazilian musical movement dedicated to promoting modernist classical music founded in 1963. The original members were composers who had studied in Germany: Gilberto Mendes, Willy Corrêa de Oliveira, Damiano Cozzela, Rogério Duprat, and Júlio Medaglia.

3 / The Brazilian version of the international phenomenon known as the counterculture gained steam after 1968, emulating the concepts and fashions of American hippie culture. The outlandish look and antiestablishment behavior displayed by its followers immediately garnered the attention of the mainstream press, for it exposed a rift between a new generation and the military rule. Standing against mass culture and in its process of globalization, the image of the hippie rebel, was also a sign of transgressions vis-à-vis conservative ideology—both on the right and the left. See Christopher Dunn, *Contracultura—Alternative Arts and Social Transformation in Authoritarian Brazil* (Chapel Hill: University of North Carolina Press, 2016).

4 / "Outsider culture" or "outsider art" were some of the terms used to denote some experimental or alternative art works created between 1968 and 1972 in Brazil. The terms were later used to include alternative movies, poetry, and music. See Frederico Coelho, *Eu, brasileiro, confesso minha culpa e meu pecado—Cultura marginal no Brasil em 1960 e 1970* (Rio de Janeiro: Civilização Brasileira, 2010).

5 / "High modernists" and "postmodernists" are terms used by literary scholar Gonzalo Aguilar. See his *Poesia concreta brasileira—As vanguardas da encruzilhada modernista* (São Paulo: Edusp, 2005).

6 / Haroldo de Campos's *Galáxias* is an experimental book of poetry which consists of fifty fragments written between1963 and 1976. The first fragments (each a one-page prose poem) were released in avant-garde magazines around the world. The collected version was finally published in Brazil in 1984.

7 / German philosopher Max Bense visited Brazil several times during the1960s. His memoir of his travels—*Brasilianische Intelligenz* (1965)—was published in Brazil as *Inteligência brasileira* (São Paulo: Cosac Naify, 2009).

8 / A poet, journalist, playwright, and polemicist, Oswald de Andrade was one of the founders of Brazilian modernism. As the author of the *Manifesto antropofágico* (Cannibalist manifesto), his philosophical ideas and aesthetics have played a major role in the rethinking of Brazilian culture, influencing the generations that succeeded him, including concrete poetry, Tropicalia, and the Brazilian counterculture.

9 / Both essays were published side by side in *Suplemento Dominical do Jornal do Brasil*, June 23, 1957.

10 / Mário Pedrosa, "Forma e personalidade," in *Arte, ensaios: Mário Pedrosa*, ed. Lorenzo Mammi (São Paulo: Cosac Naify, 2015), 160.

11 / *Suplemento Dominical Jornal do Brasil*, April 20, 1958.

12 / Although happening around the same time, these dramatic episodes in the lives of Rogério Duarte and Torquato Neto are unrelated. On April 5, 1968, Rogério and his brother, Ronaldo, were arrested by the State Police (DOPS) and tortured over the period of a week on a military base in Rio de Janeiro. After his release, Rogério suffered a series of emotional and professional setbacks which required successive psychiatric assistance. Neto, on the other hand, expressed suicidal tendencies early on, in addition to struggling with alcoholism. According to his diaries, the psychiatric internments were his efforts to overcome the symptoms related to these chronic ailments.

13 / Gilles Deleuze, *Critique et clinique* (Paris: Les Édition du Minuit, 1993).

14 / Waly Salomão came up with the idea for the title after reading Michel Foucault's *Histoire de la folie à l'âge claissique*, also released in 1972.

15 / Waly Salomão, *Armarinho de miudezas* (Rio de Janeiro: Rocco, 2005), 63. In the original: "Época de obliteração da anterior distância sujeito-objeto, o próprio poeta sendo o corpo da poesia, o poeta sendo o poema."

EPIDERMAL AND VISCERAL WORKS Lygia Pape and Anna Maria Maiolino

8

Claudia Calirman

As feminism gained ground in the United States in the 1970s, its terminology was called into question by many leading artists in Brazil.[1] Lygia Pape (1927–2004), one of the most prominent female Brazilian artists of the twentieth century, was among those who rejected the nomenclature, stating she was not interested in "any ideological feminist discourse."[2] The work of Anna Maria Maiolino (b. 1942) from the 1960s seemed to be motivated by experiences such as women's daily lives. She recalls that many critics considered these themes prosaic, banal, and obvious.[3] Both critics and the public had long disallowed such domestic subjects in women's art and to a large extent continue to do so today. Although adamant about rejecting the feminist label, both Maiolino and Pape were engaged in questioning and redefining constructions of women's identity, a central feminist pursuit.

Despite their professed lack of allegiance to feminism as a cause, both artists contributed seminal works to the feminist canon. Although both Pape's and Maiolino's artistic practices were rooted in the Brazilian neo-concrete movement from the 1950s and 1960s,[4] my focus here is on these artists' later "contaminated" production, their so-called "epidermic" or visceral works which address the abject and the sensorial.

Through these themes, they were able to question traditional gender roles and introduce topics related to women's constructed identity in Brazilian art without any overt engagement with the discussion of gender. This separation, albeit subtle, likely represented an important tactical gambit: in Brazil and elsewhere, women artists who addressed feminist issues frequently found themselves pigeonholed or critically lambasted. "It seems quite clear to me," writes Aracy Amaral in 1993, "that, at the moment, any artist who represents social problems in his or her works will always be discriminated against in Brazil by the country's formalist critics."[5] These critics have also dismissed the multiculturalism that has permeated visual art criticism since the 1990s, accusing it of being an imported fashion from the United States, and disdaining it as part of the minority quotas program and the politically correct mindset.

Despite their lack of embrace of feminism, women artists have enjoyed a predominant role in Brazilian society since the advent of what is known in Brazil as *modernismo.* In 1917, Anita Malfatti (1889–1964) was instrumental in introducing expressionism to Brazil. In the 1920s, Maria Martins (1894–1973) explored surrealism, and Tarsila do Amaral's (1886–1973) paintings powerfully evoked the notion of anthropophagia, or cultural cannibalism, as described by her partner, the poet and writer Oswald de Andrade, in his "Anthropophagite Manifesto" (1928).[6] The 1960s saw a veritable explosion of prominent women artists, including Lygia Clark (1920–1988), Lygia Pape, Anna Bella Geiger (b. 1933), Anna Maria Maiolino, and Regina Silveira (b. 1939), among others.[7] In more recent generations, Jac Leirner, Beatriz Milhazes, Rosangela Rennó, and Adriana Varejão—all born in the 1960s—have gained marquee status in the international art market and in global exhibitions. The discussion in Brazil has never been based on the same issues raised by Linda Nochlin's influential 1971 essay, "Why Have There Been No Great Women Artists?," because women artists have had a seat at the table for over a century. A more compelling question, then, is why so many leading women artists so vehemently rejected feminist discourse, even as their works addressed the same issues tackled by their feminist counterparts in the United States and elsewhere.

For the art critic Paulo Herkenhoff, Brazilian artists, regardless of gender, have always striven not to be considered derivative of hegemonic centers of artistic production; therefore, the discussion of center versus periphery has always been more salient than the debate on gender issues. Herkenhoff points out that artists from Latin American countries are "constantly being pressured with the burden of proving that they are not mirrors but full individualities, perfectly capable of participating in the contemporary system of symbolic exchanges."[8] From this perspective, the desire to bridge the confining territory of "Latin American art" and to participate as "equals" on the international scene was always a more important issue for these artists than inwardly focused discussions of identity politics. As Lygia Pape said, "I think it is outrageous that an exhibition can still be titled Latin American Art. . . . This is self-discriminating, it is very reductive."[9] The art critic Guy Brett concurs: "No European artists are asked that their work give proof of their European identity, but this is always the first thing expected of a Latin American."[10] Brazilian artists constantly sought to singularly define themselves by the quality and innovation of their work, independent of any specific context or culture.

However, as the cultural theorist Nelly Richard astutely claims, "The judgment of 'quality' seeks to make itself trustworthy (equitable) by pretending to rest on the neutral institutional recognition of women and men with works of equivalent merit. But how can we not doubt this judgment when we know that the formalist category of quality is not neutral (universal) but rather forged by a prejudicial culture that defends among other interests, masculine supremacy as the absolute representative of the universal?"[11]

As Latin Americans, then, women artists in Brazil already faced certain unwanted and unwarranted expectations about what their art would stand for; to adopt a feminist identity in their practice would only add another, potentially narrowing, stamp. In attempting to avoid any specific label, many women artists understandably opted out of feminist discourse. In time, discussion of feminist art in Brazil and elsewhere in Latin America became all but taboo.

Amaral suggests an additional explanation for the lack of feminist interests in Brazilian art, writing: In reality it is necessary to recognize the practical reason why women in Brazil had so much availability to dedicate themselves to the arts. The presence, even today, of one or more domestic helpers in the household providing services for the middle class and the upper middle class always gave Brazilian women the possibility to dedicate themselves to the arts, a condition that their North American counterparts could not afford in contemporary times.[12] Although this argument does not explain the phenomenon, it does raise an interesting point about the discrepancy of class in Brazilian society. It was not until 2014, in light of the then recent massive street demonstrations in Brazil in response to the government's lavish expenditures to host the 2014 World Cup, that this gross social and economic inequality had been being publicly challenged.

A complete account of the lack of interest in gender issues in Brazil throughout the 1970s must also take note of the country's history of brutal social and political realities. In the late 1960s and 1970s, Brazil was in the midst of the most repressive years of a military dictatorship that came to rule the country for twenty years (from 1964 to 1985). In December 1968, the military regime decreed the Institutional Act #5 (AI-5), which abolished civil rights in the country, instituted censorship of the media and the arts, and implemented torture as a practice of the state.[13] All attentions were turned toward the struggle against the repression and censorship imposed by the military regime, overshadowing other important debates such as gender differences, social inequalities, and racial discrimination. In the wake of globalization, Latin American artists became better known, yet for the most part, the work of Latin

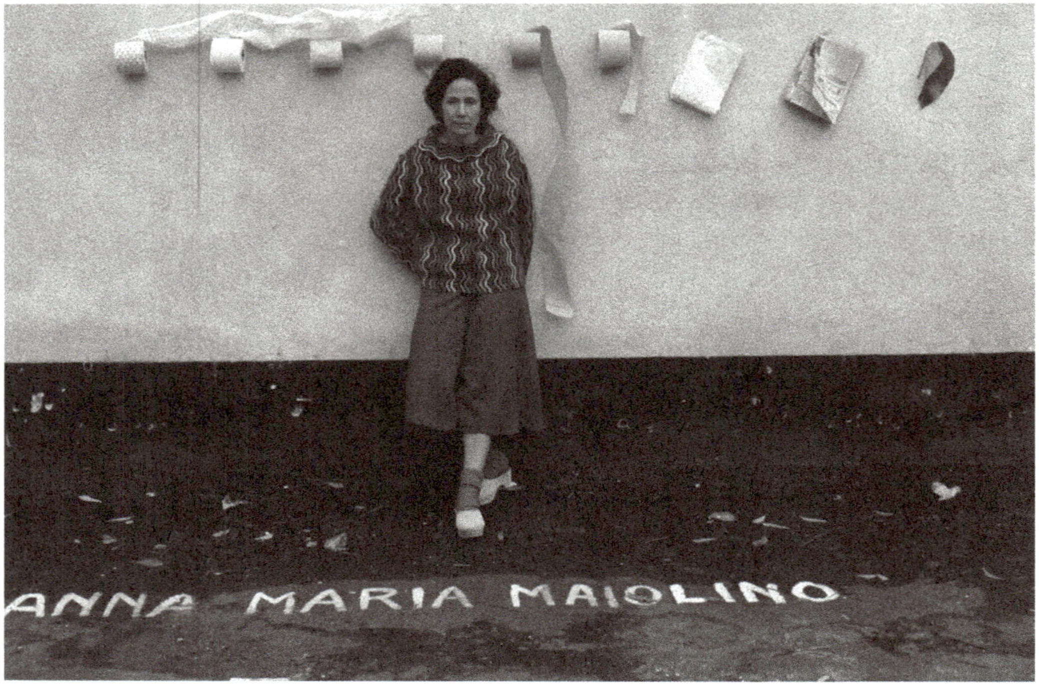

Anna Maria Maiolino, *Estado escatológico (Scatological State)*, 1978. Installation for the exhibition Mitos vadios, São Paulo, Brazil. Courtesy of Studio Anna Maria Maiolino.

American women artists from the late 1960s and 1970s—a period characterized by both artistic innovations and political repression—remains largely unexamined.[14]

Born in Rio de Janeiro, Lygia Pape participated in the seminal 1967 exhibition *Nova objetividade brasileira* (New Brazilian Objectivity) organized by Hélio Oiticica at the Museu de Arte Moderna do Rio de Janeiro (Museum of Modern Art of Rio de Janeiro, MAM-RJ). Pape contributed two sculptures to the exhibition: *Caixa de formigas* (Box of ants) and *Caixa de baratas* (Box of cockroaches), both from 1967. In *Caixa de formigas*, an acrylic box encloses a piece of raw meat, placed on top of a mirror at the bottom of the box, that is being devoured by live ants. Inside the box, three painted circles bear the inscription "a gula ou a luxúria" (gluttony or lust). *Caixa de baratas* is also an acrylic box with a mirror affixed to the bottom—this one containing a grid of dead cockroaches, with the larger ones glued to the bottom of the box.

At the time, these sculptures were interpreted as a critique of museums and the stagnant, "dead" art contained therein. In retrospect, however, *Caixa de formigas* and *Caixa de baratas* were also significant in their attempt to break with the reigning constructivist order promoted by the concrete movement. By provoking disgust and repulsion in the viewer—whose face is reflected among the dead cockroaches in the mirror at the bottom of the box—these works offer a stark repudiation of the rationality promoted by geometric abstraction. For Herkenhoff, "These works contaminated the aseptic constructivist project, through the parochial female fear of cockroaches and its scatology."[15]

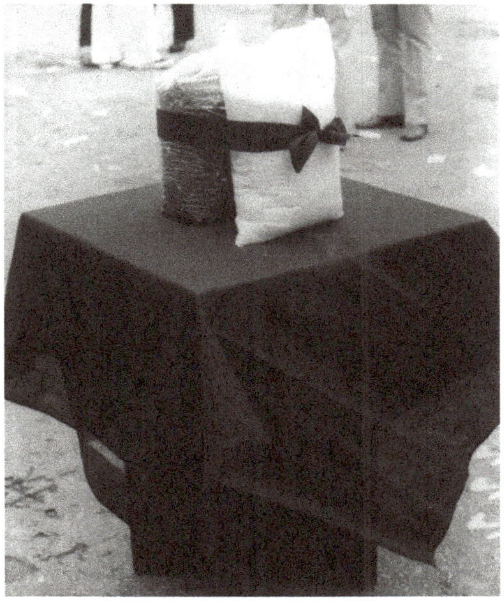

Anna Maria Maiolino, *Monumento à fome (Monument to Hunger)*, 1978. Installation for the exhibition Mitos vadios, São Paulo, Brazil. Courtesy of Studio Anna Maria Maiolino.

A year later, Pape participated in the happening "Apocalipopótese" (a play on the words "apocalypse" and "hypothesis" in Portuguese)—a weekly series of outdoor artistic interventions at Aterro do Flamengo, in the gardens of Museum of Modern Art of Rio de Janeiro.[16] At this event, Pape performed *O ovo* (The egg) (1967), which centered on metaphors of birth and destruction. *O ovo* incorporated a series of giant wooden cubic structures (not ovoid-shaped, as the title might suggest) covered with colored plastic. From inside these breakable boxes, members of a samba school burst out dancing and playing music in a clear analogy to a birth.[17] The surface of the cube, which was made of a thin plastic material, acted like a second skin or epidermis, and was easily torn apart by the dancers in a visceral act. The violence and spirit of transformation implicit in the act also referenced the political repression of the times, and the need to break free. Like *Caixa de formigas* and *Caixa de baratas*, *O ovo* also functions as a critique of geometric abstraction, since the participant has to break the box, violating the cube to be "reborn."

The sensorial experience of breaking through a surface to create a transformative state was similarly promoted by Pape's *Divisor*, which premiered in 1968 and has since been performed several times in multiple venues. *Divisor* consists of dozens of people poking their heads through gridded holes made in a large sheet of white cloth. The piece is a collective and amorphous moving body, a kind of expanded ghost figure moving in space, with multiple heads and openings not unlike the serpent-like Learnaean Hydra in Greek mythology. Speaking simultaneously to the one and the many, Pape's *Divisor* resonates with Antonio Negri and Michael Hardt's notion of the "multitude," which they describe as an organization based on the free singularities that converge in the production of the common.[18] The multitude is neither fully a collective agent nor a collection of individual agents—it takes shape mainly as agency, a "productive potential" of human life for those who perform

Anna Maria Maiolino, *Entrevidas (In Between Lives)*, 1981. Courtesy Studio Anna Maria Maiolino.

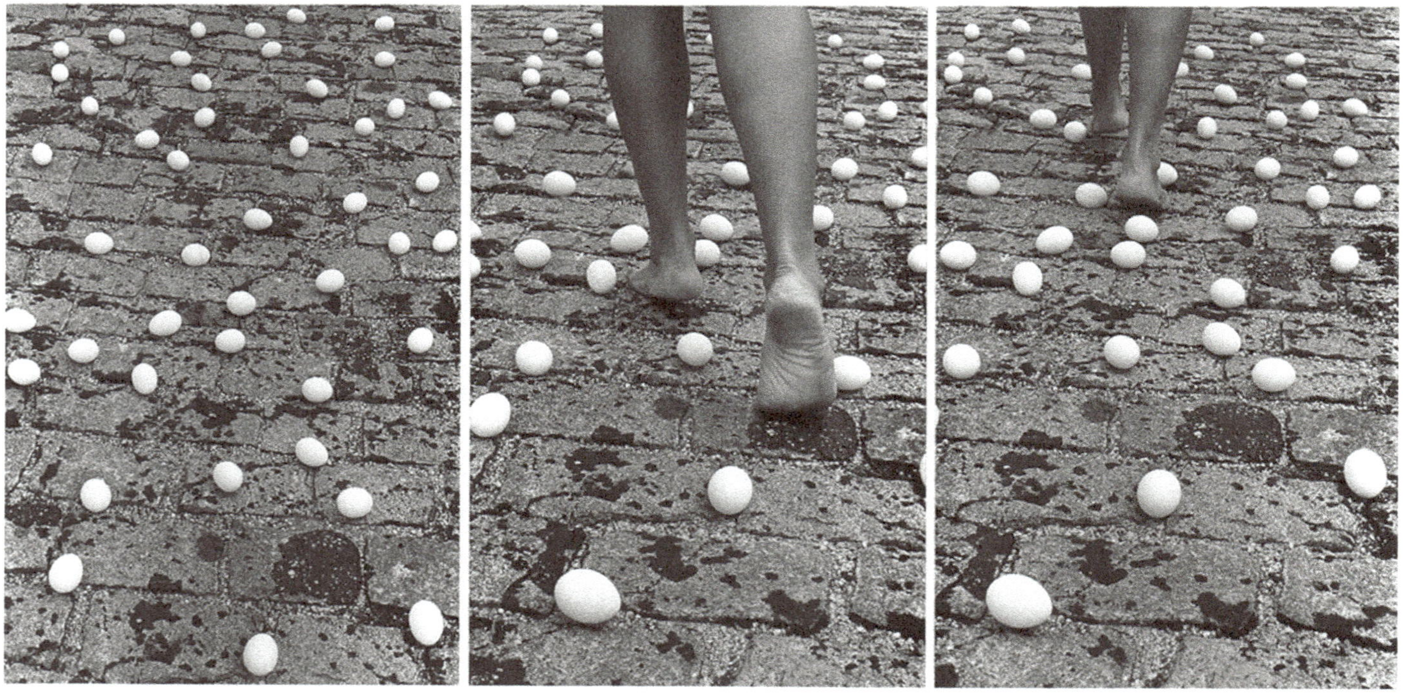

through or within it. The symbolic meaning of Pape's *Divisor* changes every time it is performed and shifts based on the viewer's individual experience; this is intentional, as the artist was more interested in proposing ideas than authoring a finished work of art. *Divisor* has a transformative power, suggesting a change of perception once the participant is immersed in its collective experience.

The work comes to life, sharing a sensibility with Mikhail Bakhtin's description of "grotesque realism"—a grandiose, exaggerated body that is not individualized but rather hybrid and social.[19] Peter Stallybrass and Allon White suggest: "[In order] to complete the image of the 'grotesque realism,' one must add that it is always a figure in process, it is always becoming. It is a mobile and hybrid creature, disproportionate, exorbitant, and outgrowing all limits, decentered and off balance, a figural and symbolic resource for parodic exaggeration and inversion."[20] For Bakhtin, the grotesque realist body violates classical aesthetics, which favors a unique, individualized, autonomous, closed, polished, proportionate, and symmetrical body.[21] If anything, *Divisor*, like her earlier works *Caixa de formigas* and *Caixa de baratas*, also represents a contamination of the classical order, a bold challenge to the prevailing claim of formalism and modernist autonomy in the visual arts in Brazil.

In her influential film *Eat Me* (1975),[22] Pape once again provoked sensations of attraction and repulsion. Here the viewer is confronted by a close-up of a female and a male mouth, suggestive of a vagina, sucking and expelling objects, partially inviting and partially threatening. In one shot, a mustached, lipstick-covered mouth—incidentally belonging to the artist Artur Barrio—fills the entire screen. It sucks a red stone (actually an object made of plastic), which soon changes color, becoming blue. This image cuts to a female mouth sucking on a sausage smothered in ketchup, and then goes back to the cavity of the man's mouth. Male and female mouths are alternated among voices in different languages rhythmically uttering the phrase "*a gula ou a luxúria?*" (gluttony or lust?).[23]

The growing sound of female groans, sexual in nature, culminates with a scream, creating an unsettling experience for the viewer. At the end of the film, an abrupt transition to the sounds of an advertisement suggests an interrupted sexual act.

Playing even further with notions of bad taste, debauchery, and kitsch, the following year Pape created the installation *Eat me: A gula ou a luxúria?* (Eat Me: Gluttony or lust?, 1976), which referenced and strongly criticized the idea of women as both objects and agents of consumption.[24] Tents containing small white paper bags carried the inscription "objects of seduction." Inside the bags were kitschy objects—calendars with naked women, pubic hair, aphrodisiac lotions, peanuts, and mirrors. She stamped the bags, kissed them with red lipstick, and then signed them. Everything could be bought by the audience at the bargain price of one cruzeiro—the Brazilian currency at the time. [25]

When the installation was later recreated at the Museum of Modern Art of Rio de Janeiro, viewers were once again invited to inspect and purchase vulgar objects of desire—dentures, wigs, eyelashes, apples, miniatures of fake female breasts bearing the word "darling," red lipsticks with the inscription *promessa* (promise). Pape defined these items as instruments from daily life and offered them to the public as a critical vision of debauchery and consumerism.[26] By mimicking salacious trinkets sold by street vendors, Pape sarcastically exposed female strategies of seduction, unmasking false promises of ideal female beauty in society.

This installation is even more striking when considered within the context of the "economic miracle" that was underway in Brazil at the time, with sales of consumer goods for the lower middle class soaring even as the military regime was at its most repressive. Pape points to the impoverished aesthetic of kitsch pervasive in the suburbs of Rio de Janeiro, stressing issues of class difference and inequality through the cheapness of the objects and their discarded quality.

Summoning the comic-tragic, Pape's installation offers a sardonic view of the beautification of women both as objects to be desired and as avid consumers of objects of seduction. In 1976, a version of the project *Eat me: A gula ou a luxúria?* was published in the second issue of *Malasartes*, a celebrated (albeit short-lived) journal in Brazil that disseminated theoretical and visual projects by artists.[27] In the pages of *Malasartes*, Pape elaborated on the concept of *epidermização* (epidermization), emphasizing the sensorial aspect of her work as opposed to a rational one. She wrote: "It is not a discourse or a thesis. I unfold the project at the level of an epidermization of an idea, the sensorial as a form of knowledge and consciousness."[28] Pape's "epidermal" works dealing with the body through notions of the abject and contamination, the breaking of the cube/skin, and the consumptive desire to go beyond the discussion of women's construction of identity in society. Her feminist legacy, even if she did not intentionally embrace it, belongs to a larger critical project—one that reminds us that consumerism and mechanisms of seduction can unleash but never fulfill desire.

For Anna Maria Maiolino, as for other artists enduring the climate of fear and censorship under military rule in Brazil, the notion of the "visceral" was a poignant and common theme: works dealt with body parts, viscera, and the fragmented and dilacerated flesh. According to Herkenhoff, "In the Brazilian art milieu the words 'visceral' and 'viscerality' were used [by many artists] to indicate the body's expressive intensity; as well as the organic production of meaning."[29]

In Maiolino's work from the 1960s, this concept of the "visceral" came through references to food and excrement. In one of her earlier works, the soft sculpture titled *Glu, Glu, Glu . . .* (1966) which is made of upholstery stuffing, a male torso above bears the inscription *Glu, Glu, Glu*. In the lower section, padded volumes depict digestive organs, including the stomach and the intestines. These body parts, nakedly protruding in space like overexposed viscera, supposedly alluded to the torture inflicted on political prisoners during the military regime in Brazil.

Born in 1942, in wartime Italy, Maiolino immigrated with her family to South America at age twelve. The family first lived in Venezuela and then moved to Rio de Janeiro in 1960. Like many European artists from her generation, Maiolino lived through the experience of war, exile, and the need to adapt to new environments. From 1968 to 1971, she lived in New York City, where she felt once again like a displaced immigrant, writing, "Without a green card, without anything, I am but one more 'illegal' in the American paradise."[30] Also during this time, overburdened by household tasks and the obligations of motherhood, she produced no new work. Eventually, following a suggestion by Oiticica, she began taking personal notes and commenced a fertile period of writing poetry. In her interviews about those years, there is a sense of silently bearing the unspeakable, deprived of her personhood and her voice. Of this difficult yet formative period, Maiolino wrote: "The words, with their weight and meaning, originated metaphors of sentiments, in angst to find answers to the many questions from my personal life and also to constitute a way to elaborate my reencounter with the military dictatorship upon my return to Brazil."[31]

In 1978, back in Brazil, Maiolino was invited by Oiticica and Ivald Granato to participate in the happening "Mitos vadios" (Vagrant myths) in a vacant lot in Rua Augusta, in São Paulo. The title was a direct response to the I Bienal Latino-Americana de São Paulo, which was one of the first important international cultural events held during Brazil's transition back to democratic rule. The I Bienal Latino-Americana was called "Mitos e magias" (Myths and magic), an allusion to the predominance of magic realism and surrealism in Latin America, a trend frequently pilloried by many artists as regionalist.

Maiolino participated in this happening with two installations: *Monumento à fome* (Monument to Hunger) and *Estado escatológico* (Scatological State). *Monumento à fome* consisted of two sacks, one filled with white rice and the other with black beans. The sacks were tied together with a ribbon and placed on a table covered by a black cloth. In this work, Maiolino addressed the food staple of the lower class in Brazil: rice and beans. In *Estado escatológico*, she displayed various types of toilet paper on the wall, arranged from the cheapest to the most expensive, and humorously included a newspaper and a plant leaf. With these two works, Maiolino connected the ends of the digestive system—ingesting and excreting food. She implied that what enters the body must subsequently be eliminated. In associating food to excrement, she comments on the masses of flotsam and jetsam, the discarded items—or in this case, people—left adrift at the margins of society.

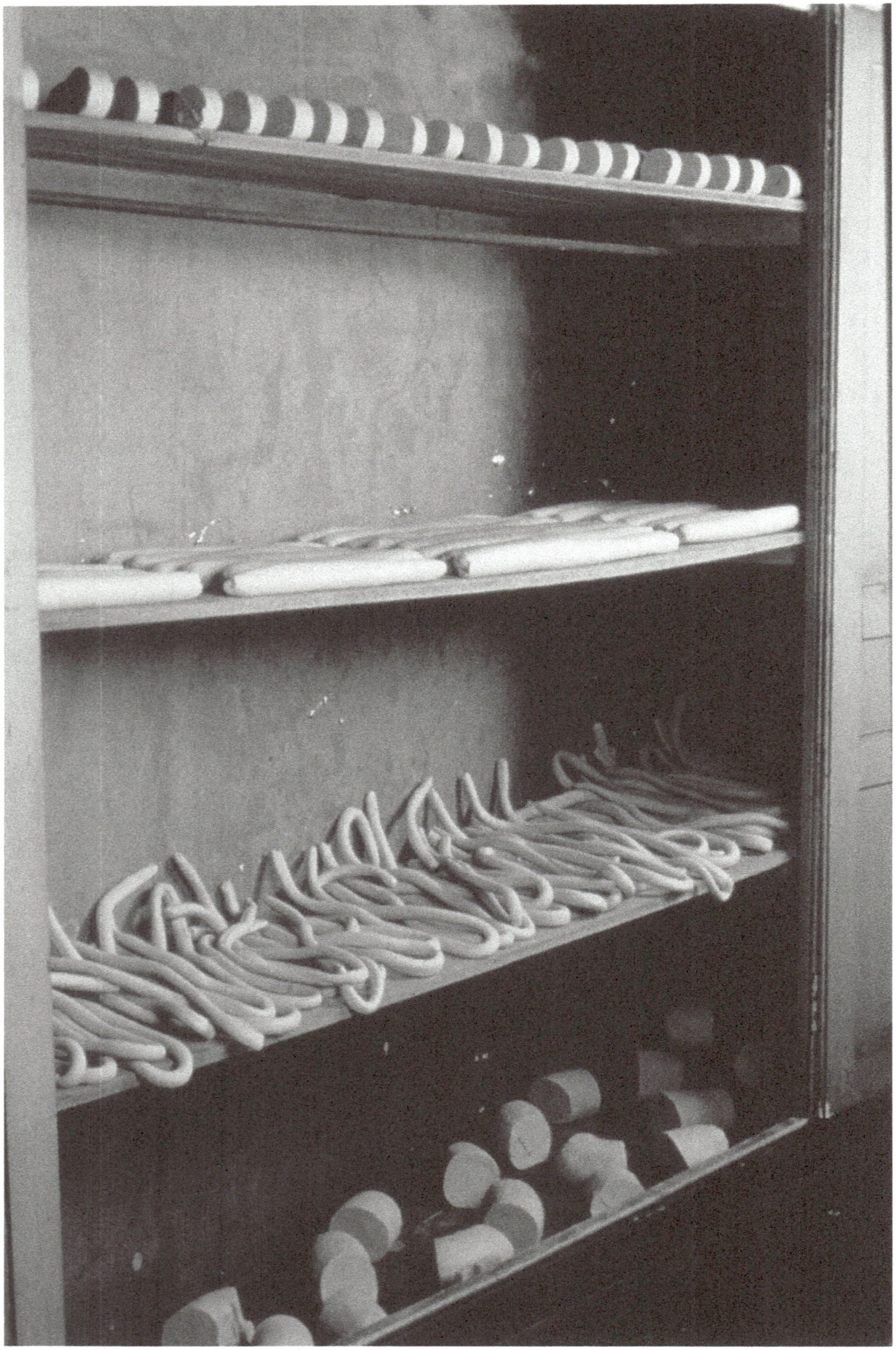

Anna Maria Maiolino, *Muitos (Many)*, 1995. Installation at Kanaal Art Foundation, Kortrijk, Belgium. Courtesy of Studio Anna Maria Maiolino.

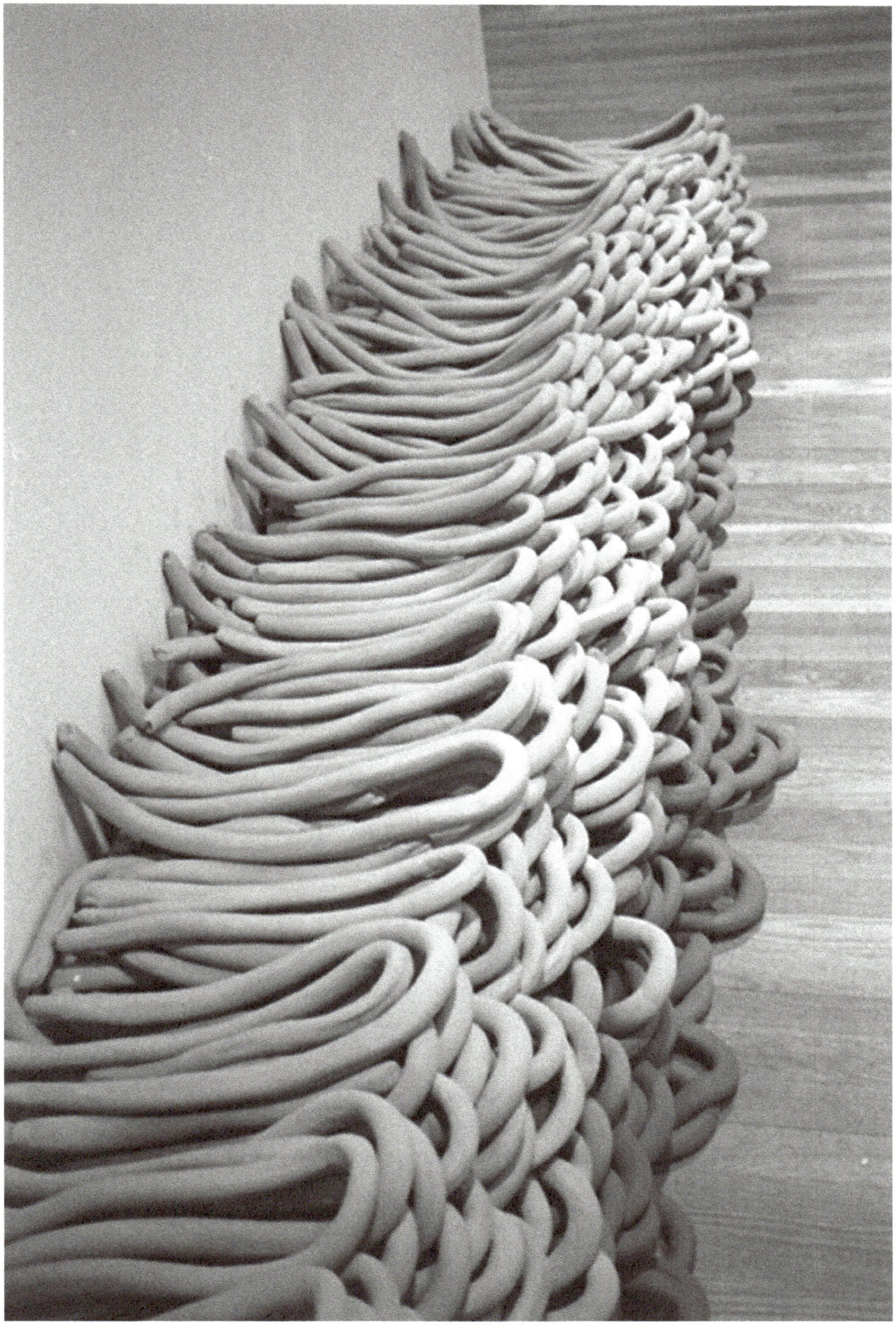

Anna Maria Maiolino, *Mais de mil (Over One Thousand)*, 1999. Installation at the Institute for Contemporary Art, Boston. Courtesy of Studio Anna Maria Maiolino.

Likewise, her 1979 installation *Arroz e feijão* (Rice and beans), remade for the 29th São Paulo Biennial (2010), also addressed disparate social access to consumerism, discriminating high from low, those with means from those who are disenfranchised from consumer society. It consists of a large table covered with a black cloth set up for a meal. Seeds of rice and beans germinate from white plates filled with soil. Hope and hunger are intertwined. The art critic Frederico Morais ironically noted that it is precisely in the excremental function of the body that low and high meet indiscriminately, with no class distinction.[32] Maiolino's work draws on the notion of abject art: the abject occupies the place of unfulfilled desire. She writes, "The intestine is a cavity that we never can fill in, in the same way that we can't fulfill desire."[33]

From the mid- to late 1930s, Georges Bataille wrote about the abject in a group of unpublished texts titled "L'Abjection et les formes misérables" as a way to describe attraction to the rotten and the wasted.[34] For Bataille, "What the system cannot assimilate must be rejected as excremental."[35] In examining Bataille's writings on the abject, Rosalind Krauss pointed out their association not necessarily to bodily abjection but instead to social exclusions. According to Krauss, "These texts identify social abjection with a violent exclusionary force operating within modern State systems, one that strips the laboring masses of their human dignity and reproduces them as dehumanized social waste."[36]

Krauss claims that much of abject art is founded in the multiple forms of the "wound," which is always the place of the feminine. She asserts that "whether or not the feminine subject is actually at stake in a given work, it is the character of being wounded, victimized, traumatized, marginalized that is seen as what is in play within this domain."[37] Indeed, underlying Maiolino's practice is a pervasive sense of the precarious, the fragile, the visceral, and the sensorial: for better or worse, all qualities traditionally related to the female body.

The feminine struggle against the male, patriarchal, and univocal sense of order is also played out in Maiolino's work through language (or better, the lack of proper language). Maiolino attests to the utterance of language as an impossible task, an unfinished business, in her Super-8 film *In-Out (Antropofagia)* (1973–1974). Two mouths, one female and one male, alternately occupy the full screen. At the beginning, a black adhesive tape covers the mouth on screen, like a censor box, making the act of speech impossible. The mouth then tries to convey some sound, to formulate a sort of speech, to no avail. In subsequent shots, nonlinear images unfold: menacing teeth, a mouth ingesting a long black thread, lips spilling colored filaments, a mouth holding an egg.

Despite their articulation of different bodily motions such as eating, talking, and arguing, ultimately, these mouths are stripped of an important function: the ability to articulate cohesive linguistic meaning. There is nothing epic about these mouths' movements; on the contrary, they are banal, noneventful, mere exercises in space. They attest to the failed attempt to communicate through language. The anthropophagic act of cultural cannibalism is also evoked through word (the title) and image (the mouth).

As in Pape's 1975 film *Eat Me*, the mouth devours and swallows, appropriates and regurgitates, thus creating symbolic meanings. The verbal and the preverbal, nature and culture, images and words are intertwined in a disruptive way. Both films generate a state of chaos and confusion undermining qualities predominantly associated with masculinity, such as efficiency and clarity. They also allude to the mouth as a means for consumptive unfulfilled desire which relentlessly cannibalizes us.

Also, like Pape's 1967 *O ovo*, Maiolino's 1981 installation *Entrevidas* (Between lives) tidily knits notions of birth and destruction. Consisting of a floor dotted with hundreds of eggs, which the audience is invited to walk through, this fragile egg carpet acts as a minefield potentially charged with the possibility of birth and annihilation. The eggs also represent the passage from nature into the symbolic order existing in a transitional space. According to Herkenhoff, this work occupies an area "between the preverbal (the egg as a metaphor for life before birth), and the nonverbal (the growing fear of experiencing a space of insecurity and alienation)."[38] It is a visual poem alluding simultaneously to fear and censorship, to fragility, precariousness, and temporality.

In the early 1990s, Maiolino further explored the notion of banality, repetition, and the tedious manual labor of women's daily domestic tasks: waiting, passing time, knitting, cooking, and preparing food. She adopted handmade unfired clay as her main medium. Abandoning the mold and shaping forms with her own hands, she worked with large amounts of clay, manipulating them onsite and letting them dry out without firing them. In the 1995 installations *Muitos* (Many) and *Mais de mil* (More than one thousand), both from the series *Terra moldada* (Modeled earth), Maiolino repeatedly emphasized the gesture of creation. Produced in succession, each of these objects bears the mark of the artist's hands, what the art critic Paulo Venâncio Filho called "The Doing Hand."[39]

In a 2002 interview, Maiolino stated: "The installations of unfired clay were the result of the desire to make sculptural works with more hand-molded parts in less time, thus enabling a greater accumulative potential, greater entropy. Once formed, the clay does its natural duty: it dehydrates, petrifies, goes back to the state of being potential dust."[40]

Maiolino's thousands of handmade pieces made of raw clay, called *Rolinhos e cobrinhas* (Little rolls and little snake-shaped coils, 1993–2007), are unformed, fluid, and amorphous. At the 2012 dOCUMENTA in Kassel, the artist filled a small house with myriad unfired clay pieces in different shapes. The installation *Here &*

There exuded the same sense of precariousness and fragility from her early works. These multiple little coils and rolls were taken as reminiscent of food or excrement—handmade pasta from her childhood memories or simply waste. Food and intestines were again entwined.

Although gender difference was not a priority, it is time to revisit the prevailing idea that there was no feminist art coming from Brazil. The works presented here by both Pape and Maiolino incorporate the notions of "viscerality" and "epidermization" through their insistence on ingestion and its expulsion, contamination, failed attempts to communicate through language, metaphors of birth and destruction, and through the vulnerable and the precarious. These works bring an exquisite (dis)order and debasement to the prevailing masculine logical discourse, becoming, despite their utter negation, a hallmark of Brazilian artists' take on feminism in their own terms during this period.

Anna Maria Maiolino, *In/Out (Antropofagia)*, 1973–1974. Film still, Super 8 transferred to DVD, black and white and color, sound. Courtesy of Studio Anna Maria Maiolino.

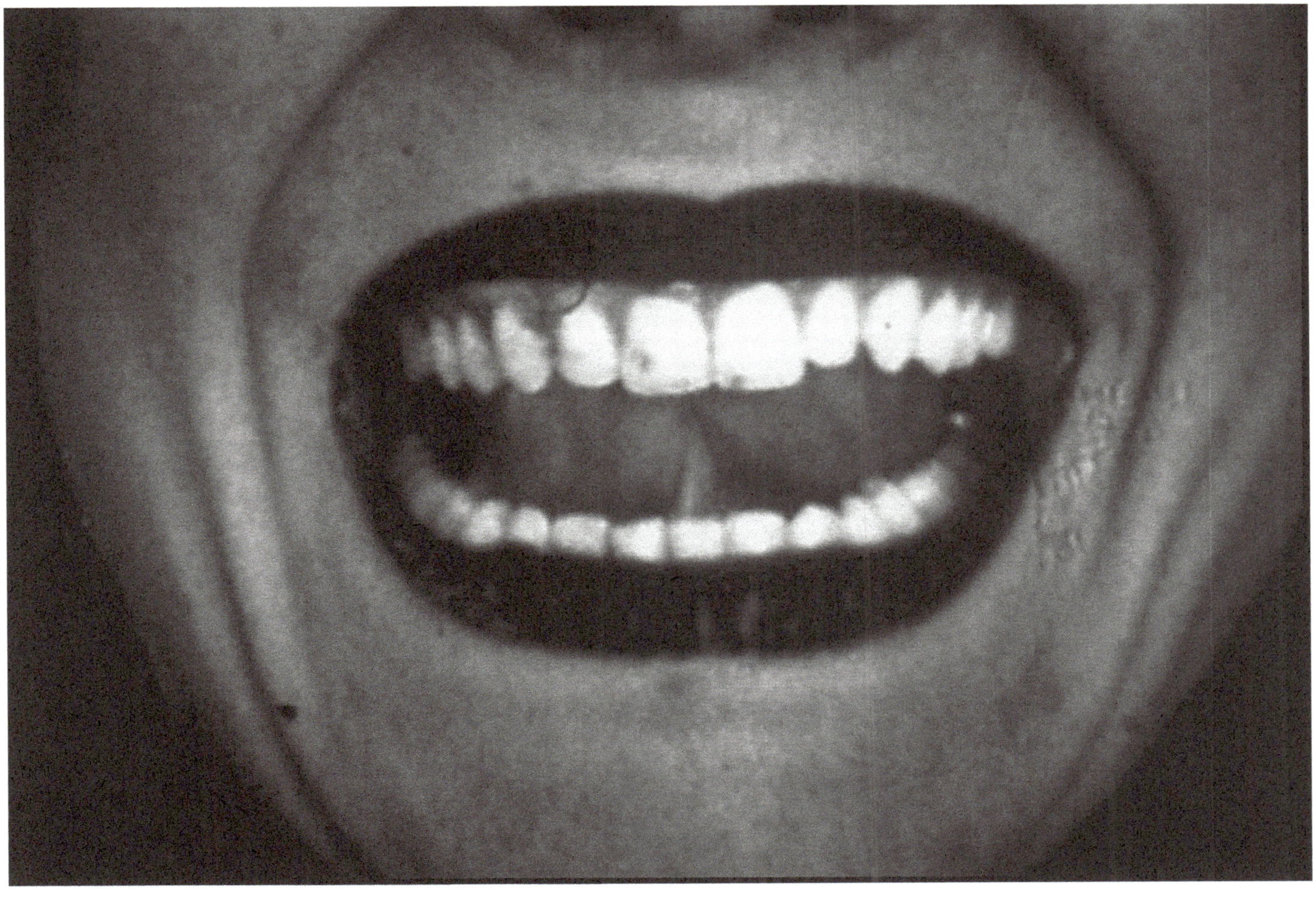

Notes

This article was originally published in *Woman's Art Journal* 35, no. 2 (Fall/Winter 2014): 19–27. We thank the journal's editors for permission to reprint it.

1 / Publications that have included the work of some historical Latin American women artists include: Aracy A. Amaral and Paulo Herkenhoff, eds., *Ultramodern: The Art of Contemporary Brazil* (Washington, DC: National Museum of Women in the Arts, 1993); Catherine de Zegher, ed., *Inside the Visible: An Elliptical Traverse of 20th Century Art In, Of, and From the Feminine*, 2nd ed. (Boston, MA: MIT Press, 1996); Heloisa Buarque de Hollanda and Paulo Herkenhoff, eds. *Manobras radicais: Artistas brasileiras* (São Paulo: Centro Cultural Banco do Brasil, 2006); Cornelia Butler, ed., *Wack! Art and the Feminist Revolution* (Los Angeles: Museum of Contemporary Art, 2007); and Camille Morineau, ed., *Elles @centrepompidou: Artistes femmes dans la collection du musée national d'art moderne, centre de création industrielle* (Paris: Centre Pompidou, 2009). "Re.act.feminism—A Performing Archive" is a comprehensive archival website and traveling exhibition for women performing artists. Its companion book includes an essay by performance theorist Eleonora Fabião: "Performing Feminist Archives: A Research-in-Process on Latin American Performance Art," in *Re.Act. Feminism—A Performing Archive*, ed. Bettina Knaup and Beatrice Ellen Stammer (London: Verlag für moderne Kunst Nürnberg and Live Art Development Agency, 2014), 28–37.

2 / Denise Mattar, *Lygia Pape: Intrinsicamente anarquista* (Rio de Janeiro: Relume Dumará, 2003), 85.

3 / Helena Tatay, "Helena Tatay conversa com Anna Maria Maiolino," in *Anna Maria Maiolino*, ed. Helena Tatay (São Paulo: Cosac Naify, 2012), 37; my translation.

4 / Lygia Pape was a major exponent of the neoconcrete movement, along with Hélio Oiticica (1937–1980) and Lygia Clark (1920–1988). The neo-concrete artists moved away from the finished object of art and embraced the idea of art as process or experimentation. Based on the "Manifesto neoconcreto" written by Ferreira Gullar (1959), they moved away from the rigid geometric abstract forms of the São Paulo concrete group, creating a more tactile, perceptual, and sensorial art. See Ferreira Gullar, "Manifesto neoconcreto," *Jornal do Brasil*, Suplemento Dominical, March 22, 1959; and Ronaldo Brito, *Neoconcretismo: Vértice e ruptura do projeto construtivista brasileiro* [Neoconcretism: Vertex and rupture of the Brazilian constructivist project] (Rio de Janeiro: Funarte, 1985).

5 / Aracy Amaral, "Brazil: Women in the Arts," in *Ultramodern*, 23.

6 / See Gillian Sneed, "Anita Malfatti and Tarsila do Amaral: Gender, Brasilidade and the Modernist Landscape," *Woman's Art Journal* 34, no. 1 (Spring/Summer 2013): 30–39.

7 / A few recent exhibitions have cast light on prominent Brazilian women artists from the 1960s, including: *Mira Schendel* at Tate Modern, London (September 2013–January 2014); *Lygia Clark: The Abandonment of Art, 1948–1988* at the Museum of Modern Art, New York (May–August 2014), with an accompanying retrospective of films and videos "On the Edge: Brazilian Film Experiments of the 1960s and Early 1970s" (May–July 2014) featuring works by Anna Bella Geiger, Sônia Andrade, and Leticia Parente; *Anna Maria Maiolino: Between Senses* at the Hauser and Wirth Gallery, New York (May–June 2014); and a solo project by Regina Vater organized by São Paulo's Galeria Jaqueline Martins at Frieze Art Fair, New York (May 2014).

8 / Paulo Herkenhoff, "The Contemporary Art of Brazil: Theoretical Constructs," in *Ultramodern*, 108.

9 / Lúcia Carneiro and Ileana Pradilla, *Lygia Pape: Entrevista a Lúcia Carneiro e Ileana Pradilla* (Rio de Janeiro: Nova Aguilar, 1998), 60; my translation. From the series Coleção Palavra do Artista.

10 / Guy Brett, "Border Crossings," in *Contemporary Art in Latin America* (London: Black Dog, 2010), 189.

11 / Nelly Richard, *Masculine/Feminine: Practices of Difference(s)*, trans. Silvia R. Tandeciarz and Alice A. Nelson (Durham, NC: Duke University Press, 2004), 30.

12 / Aracy Amaral, "A Mulher nas Artes," in *Textos do Trópico de Capricórnio, Artigos e Ensaios (1980–2005)* (São Paulo: Editora 34, 2006), 3:222; my translation.

13 / For a detailed discussion on the artistic responses to the military regime, see Claudia Calirman, *Brazilian Art under Dictatorship: Antonio Manuel, Artur Barrio, and Cildo Meireles* (Durham, NC: Duke University Press, 2012).

14 / In 2017 Cecilia Fajardo-Hill and Andrea Giunta organized a long overdue exhibition on Latin American women artists at the Hammer Museum in Los Angeles: *The Political Body: Radical Women in Latin American Art, 1960–1985*. The exhibition was part of the Getty Foundation's Pacific Standard Time: Los Angeles/Latin America initiative and broke new ground in the study of feminism in Latin America.

15 / Buarque de Hollanda and Herkenhoff, *Manobras radicais*, 77.

16 / "Apocalipopótese" was coordinated by Oiticica and featured the participation of several artists. It was born of the artist's desire to break the boundaries between the work of art and the public.

17 / Lygia Pape et al., *Lygia Pape* (Rio de Janeiro: Funarte, 1983), 46.

18 / Michael Hardt and Antonio Negri, *Multitude: War and Democracy in the Age of Empire* (New York: Penguin, 2004), 211.

19 / Mikhail Bakhtin, *Rabelais and His World*, trans. Hélène Iswolsky (Bloomington: Indiana University Press, 1984), 19.

20 / Peter Stallybrass and Allon White, *The Politics and Poetics of Transgression* (Ithaca, NY: Cornell University Press, 1986), 9.

21 / Bakhtin, *Rabelais and His World*, 25.

22 / *Eat Me* (1975) was originally shot in 16 mm and later transferred to 35 mm, 10 minutes, and in color.

23 / Eugênio Puppo, ed., *Cinema marginal brasileiro: Filmes produzidos nos anos 60 e 70* (São Paulo: Heco Produções, 2004), 135.

24 / *Eat me: a gula ou a luxúria?* (Eat Me: Gluttony or Lust?; 1976) was first exhibited at Galeria Arte Global in São Paulo.

25 / Denise Mattar, *Lygia Pape: Intrinsicamente anarquista*, 84.

26 / In the outdoor space of Museum of Modern Art of Rio de Janeiro, a film showed the artist seductively inviting the viewers to enter the installation.

27 / Despite the brevity of its existence (only three issues between September 1975 and June 1976) and its relatively small run of five thousand copies, *Malasartes* became one of the most celebrated artists' journals published in Brazil during the mid-1970s.

28 / *Malasartes*, no. 2 (1976): 22–23; my translation.

29 / Paulo Herkenhoff, "A Trajetória de Maiolino: Uma Negociação de Diferenças," in *Anna Maria Maiolino*, ed. Catherine de Zegher (New York: Drawing Center, 2002), 328.

30 / Herkenhoff, 264.

31 / Tatay, "Helena Tatay conversa com Anna Maria Maiolino," in Tatay, *Anna Maria Maiolino*, 42; my translation.

32 / Frederico Morais, *Do corpo à terra: Um marco radical na arte brasileira*, n.p. In an audiovisual work from 1970, Morais relays a quote from the head of the Buckingham Palace garbage collectors, justifying their five-week strike in London: "The garbage of the Queen is like everybody else's: if it is not quickly collected, it will start smelling badly."

33 / Tatay, "Helena Tatay conversa com Anna Maria Maiolino," in Tatay, *Anna Maria Maiolino*, 39; my translation.

34 / Bataille also wrote on the abject in some of his essays first published (posthumously) in English as *Death and Sensuality: A Study of Eroticism and Taboo* (New York: Walker and Co., 1962). Originally published as *L'Erotisme* (Paris: Les Editions de Minuit, 1957) and later published as Georges Bataille, *Erotism, Death and Sensuality: A Study of Eroticism and Taboo*, trans. Mary Dalwood (San Francisco: City Lights Books, 1986). See Georges Bataille, *Ouevres complètes* (Paris: Gallimard, 1970), 2:217–21.

35 / Georges Bataille, "The Use Value of D. A. F. de Sade," in *Visions of Excess: Selected Writings, 1927–1939*, trans. and ed. Allan Stoekl (Minneapolis: University of Minnesota Press, 1985), 91–102.

36 / Rosalind Krauss, "Informe without Conclusion," *October*, no. 78 (Fall 1996): 89–105. Reprinted in Zoya Kocur and Simon Leung, eds., *Theory in Contemporary Art Since 1985*, 2nd ed. (London: John Wiley and Sons, 2013), 119.

37 / Krauss, 121.

38 / Herkenhoff, *Ultramodern*, 63.

39 / Paulo Venâncio Filho, "The Doing Hand," in Tatay, *Anna Maria Maiolino*, 284; my translation. Reprinted in Zegher, *Inside the Visible*, 441–444.

40 / Holly Block, "A Conversation between Holly Block and Anna Maria Maiolino," in Tatay, *Anna Maria Maiolino*, 353–354.

WORD-DROOL The Constructive Secretions of Lygia Clark

Antonio Sergio Bessa

When Lygia Clark returned to Brazil in 1976 after an eight-year stay in Paris, the country she found was a far cry from the ebullient environment she had left behind in 1968. By then a new government-sponsored cultural program that privileged entertainment for the masses had radically supplanted the atmosphere of experimentation, dialogue, and investigation that Clark and her fellow Grupo Frente artists helped articulate in the early 1950s. And as if to corroborate the drastic changing of the guard, the years before and immediately following Clark's return to Rio were marked by upheaval and the death of some of the key figures who, like Clark herself, helped shape Brazil's modernity in the postwar period.

In 1976 the dramatic deaths of former Brazilian presidents Juscelino Kubitschek and João Goulart, two major civil leaders closely identified with the progressive agenda of the 1950s, seemed to effectively seal the end of an era.[1] More specifically to Brazilian culture, the sudden death of Ivan Serpa in 1973, with the consequent closing of his Centro de Pesquisa de Arte, seemed to erase any vestige of continuity with the concretist tradition.[2] As the decade came to a close, the regressive climate only intensified, with tolerance for the avant-garde at an all-time low and once highly regarded artists such as Hélio Oiticica, Glauber Rocha, Júlio Bressane, and Rogério Sganzerla, among others, often characterized as out of touch with reality.

The new reality was dire. In 1975, when poet Ferreira Gullar returned to Rio after living in exile for six years, he could only find work as a scriptwriter for

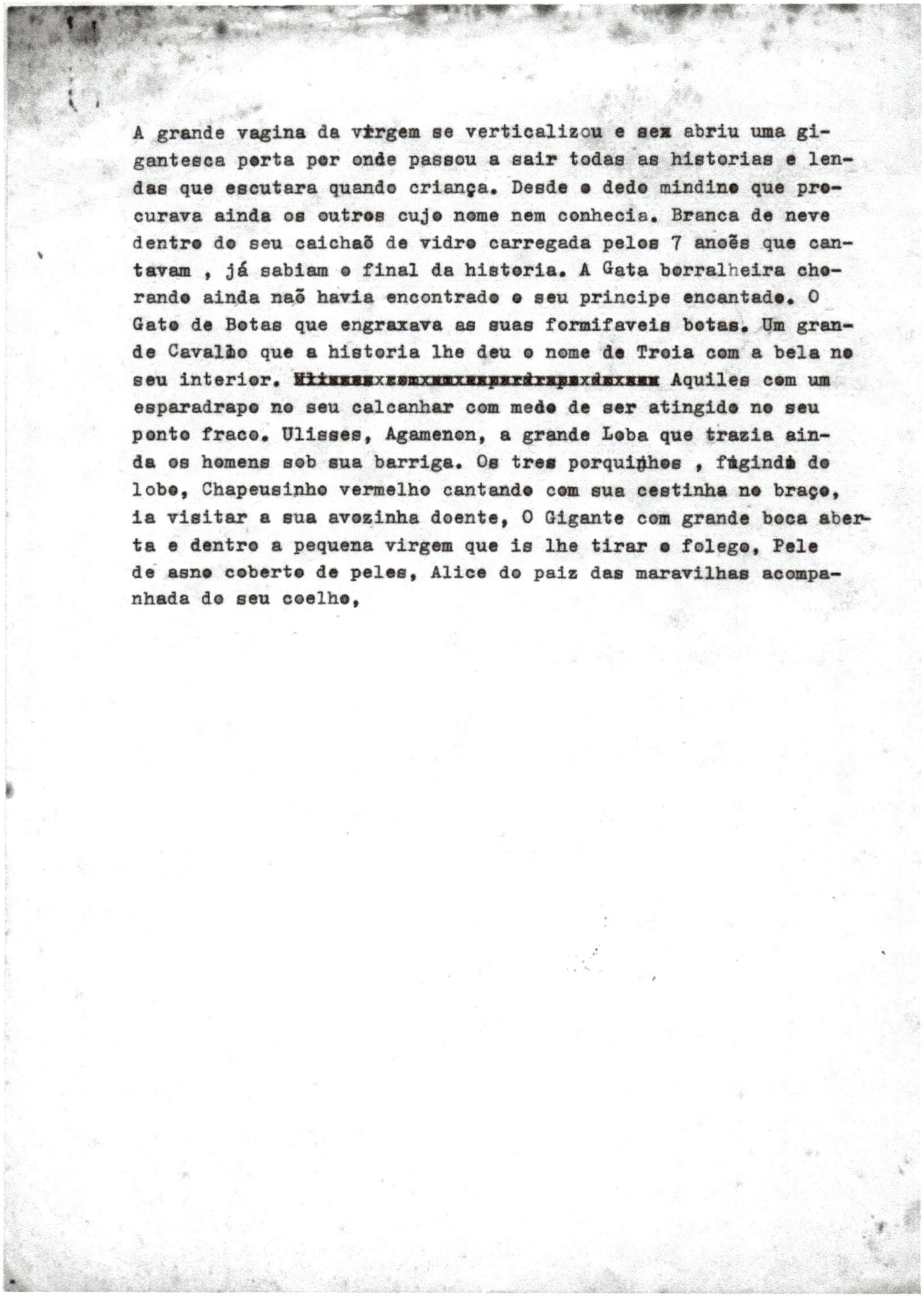

A grande vagina da virgem se verticalizou e sex abriu uma gigantesca porta por onde passou a sair todas as historias e lendas que escutara quando criança. Desde o dedo mindino que procurava ainda os outros cujo nome nem conhecia. Branca de neve dentro do seu caichaõ de vidro carregada pelos 7 anoẽs que cantavam , já sabiam o final da historia. A Gata borralheira chorando ainda naõ havia encontrado o seu principe encantado. O Gato de Botas que engraxava as suas formifaveis botas. Um grande Cavalho que a historia lhe deu o nome de Troia com a bela no seu interior. ~~Ulissesxcomxumxesparadrapoxdaxsem~~ Aquiles com um esparadrapo no seu calcanhar com medo de ser atingido no seu ponto fraco. Ulisses, Agamenon, a grande Loba que trazia ainda os homens sob sua barriga. Os tres porquinhos , fugindo do lobo, Chapeusinho vermelho cantando com sua cestinha no braço, ia visitar a sua avozinha doente, O Gigante com grande boca aberta e dentro a pequena virgem que is lhe tirar o folego, Pele de asno coberto de peles, Alice do paiz das maravilhas acompanhada do seu coelho,

Lygia Clark, *Meu doce rio*, 1984. Published by Galeria Paulo Klabin. Courtesy of "The World de Lygia Clark" Cultural Association.

televised soap operas. Art critic Mário Pedrosa, also returning from exile in 1980, turned his attention to indigenous feather art, disheartened by the cultural scene he encountered.[3] The most alarming indicator of the state of affairs, however, was the tragic 1978 fire at the Museu de Arte Moderna in Rio, once the vibrant site of groundbreaking exhibitions and educational initiatives.[4]

Against this backdrop, the stature (or influence, for that matter) of Lygia Clark among young artists at that particular moment is difficult to gauge. One must consider Clark's self-imposed anonymity, for not only had the work she conducted at the Sorbonne from 1972 to 1975 gone largely unnoticed by Brazilian audiences, but the new work she developed in Rio consisted primarily of one-on-one sessions held in her Copacabana apartment. In the broader international context, with the advent of the Reagan-Thatcher era a few years later, a new conservative agenda would find cultural equivalence in a renewed interest in traditional painting. In Brazil, that new tendency was acknowledged in the 1985 São Paulo Biennial with the installation of *A Grande tela* (The Great Canvas), which featured large-scale neo-expressionist paintings by local and foreign artists hanging side by side in a long hallway. As early as 1969 Clark had written to Oiticica, "The crisis is widespread and terrible," already detecting that the era of experimentation they helped launch was about to come to an end.[5]

It was amid such adverse conditions that in 1984 Clark agreed to develop a new project in collaboration with collector and art dealer Paulo Klabin. Working again in an art gallery context might not have been an easy decision for Clark, as it reversed her gradual distancing from the art system over the previous two decades. The exhibition, it turned out, became a testament of sorts to Clark's entire oeuvre: its centerpiece, *Livro-obra* (Book-work), consisted of a special-edition book surveying her career through miniature replicas of some of her most iconic works, accompanied by her own commentaries. In addition to *Livro-obra*, the gallery also issued an odd artifact for the occasion: *Meu doce rio* (My sweet river), a chapbook edition of texts Clark wrote in Paris while undergoing psychoanalysis. The lack of attention by Clark scholars to this particular moment in her career is in keeping with the very narrow focus through which her work has been examined since her death, often developed along the lines of neoconcretism, or of an ill-defined branch of art therapy. The recurring focus on these two aspects of Clark's career has obscured the broader scope of her enterprise, which the text of *Meu doce rio* complicates further.[6]

Throughout her life Lygia Clark used writing—whether in published texts, journal entries, or letters—with a high degree of precision, to exhaustively examine every new step in her development as an artist and its concomitant existential stakes. Clark's writings offer the rare opportunity to explore her visions based on the most lucid account of the processes that made them unfold. By closely following her writing, and *Meu doce rio* in particular, we can discover the person that Clark endeavored to rescue from cultural constraints.

Clark often alluded to the deepening of an emotional and psychological crisis in her correspondence with Hélio Oiticica. Initially the crisis seemed to be projected outward, often conveying a sense of cultural bankruptcy. It grew increasingly personal, however, as she underwent psychoanalysis with Daniel Lagache and then Pierre Fédida. Hence in 1968 we read, "I am having dramatic experiences: I see an all-encompassing darkness and man at the beginning of things, like a primitive, capturing his own body, recomposing it, rediscovering gesture, the act, the world as another selvage planet."[7] And in the following year she writes, "Many problems as always, but I have grown, so much so that I no longer bite my nails, after having done so for forty-four years, yay."[8] Another important communication from October 1970 details a hallucinatory experience in Carboneras, Spain, in which she detects an "imperious and profound interior process" unleashing from the unconscious. Most tellingly, the same letter closes with a direct reference to patients from the Centro Psiquiátrico Nacional Pedro II, often referred to as Engenho de Dentro: "I am sick of straight people; I'd much rather be in a place like Engenho de Dentro where the fabulous Rogério Duarte checked in; where someone like Emygdio expressed himself or someone like Raphael eats pencils and shit, but what a wonderful character, and how magisterial his production is!"[9]

By 1971 the psychoanalytical process had unleashed painful memories of childhood as Clark rediscovered her own sense of self upon giving up being "the other." A letter dated May 17, 1971, details a painful relationship with her father and memories of abuse. In July 1974 she writes to Oiticica that analysis "has been one of the most creative and mythological things I have lived through to this date. One day I will tell you and will have a fantastic magic mythic world to put in a book with all this experience and my work, which at the bottom are the same."[10] And further on in the same letter she speaks of "a phase of great creativity writing sentences in which the body speaks through its parts. As if the body is being stitched together, which is the phase I am at in my analysis."[11] Oiticica replies with excitement, fully aware of the importance of her statements: "The vibration of the letters that you pull off your typewriter and your euphoria woke me up when I was about to fall asleep (and I have been up for three days since!)."[12] The sense of imminent danger and overwhelming symbolism in Clark's letters throughout this period bring to mind the work of Henry Darger, whose voluminous saga *The Story of the Vivan Girls* shares a thing or two with the slim narrative of *Meu doce rio*, as both texts seem to belong to the category of personal writing not intended for the general public. Access to texts such as these—posthumously released in Darger's case, a melancholic last gesture for Clark—is met with a sense of unease, as if we are breaking into someone else's privacy, our engagement with the writer being less of an aesthetic order.

MEU DOCE RIO

At fifty-six pages, *Meu doce rio* is a condensed compilation of copious drafts produced around 1975. The large quantity of typewritten pages related to this subject in Clark's archives seems to indicate the greater scope of the work as well as its experimental nature. Those manuscripts contain numerous pages crossed out by pen or the same scenario rewritten in different versions. In this section I offer a formal analysis of the published version of *Meu doce rio*, without any attempt to interpret it as a finished work of literature (or art).

The text of *Meu doce rio* is divided into two parts. The first part tries to maintain a sense of narrative, but it seems reasonable to infer that each paragraph was written individually, at different times and on the spur of the moment. In the second part the paragraphs become terser, with a small cast of characters combined in different situations, the narrative progressing as a set of equations.

The first part follows the adventures of a character referred to as "the virgin," in a fantastic landscape in which dragons, lions, bees, serpents, and eagles continuously spar, often devouring or transforming into each other. Throughout, basic ideas that informed Clark's work come through in different guises. Hence, in the fable, the world is a gigantic beast ("o mundo era um grande bicho") whose body movements dictate the everyday activities of those who inhabit it. The beast's piss is the river, and when it changes position it is tantamount to an earthquake. In this text new concerns are hinted at, such as the longing for a primeval body ("man's longing to be surrounded, unified in the greater body").[13] Important works that Clark developed during the sessions at the Sorbonne, such as *Baba antropofágica* (Anthropophagic drool, 1973), *Cabeça coletiva* (Collective head, 1975), and elements of her *Objetos relacionais* (Relational objects, 1976), are alluded to and woven through the narrative. Drooling (baba), or vomiting, represented the formless content that Clark needed to excise in some structured way. Structure in this case seems to have been provided by the writing process itself. In that regard, it is worth noting that Ferreira Gullar, in recalling the gestation of his "Poema sujo" (Dirty poem), explained his process in these terms: "I imagined myself vomiting up my past, creating a meaningless magma out of which I would construct the poem. I would first vomit a universe of words with no order whatsoever, and little by little I would begin extracting the poem from the original magma."[14]

Once the premise is set in the first paragraphs, the narrative switches tone to become a hectic adventure in which the virgin is carried down a river in a makeshift canoe (*piroga*). She has a gigantic head, like a tree, filled with objects, and before the journey starts it must be emptied out. The next phase is an exploration of the body, in which one part talks to the other ("the tear tells the eye: I am a falling star").[15] For the most part passive, the virgin witnesses a series of clashes between animals, until another fablelike character, an ogre, appears, with the task of rousing the virgin from her catatonic state by opening her vagina. This episode prompts an image of the mythical mother from whom everything flows, and the text unfolds into images of fertility. All the while, body parts converse with each other, and the section ends with a flood that exterminates all beings. The virgin then repopulates the world with the eggs inside her body. At this moment she ascends into space and a series of actions culminates in her discovery of the line, here considered as emanating from a spider.

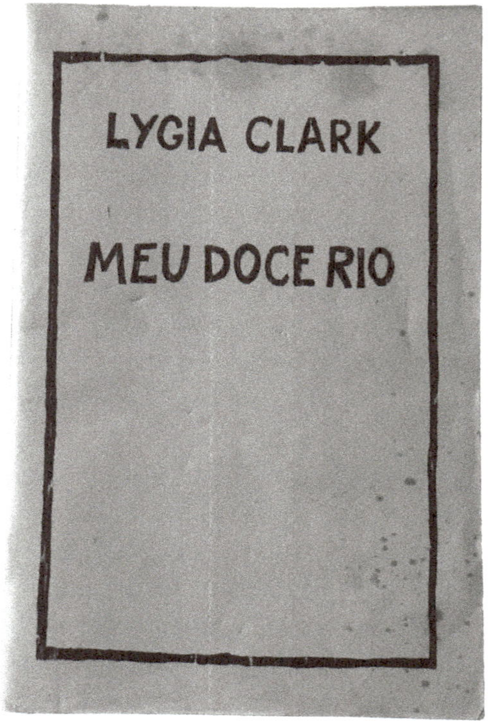

Lygia Clark, *Meu doce rio*, 1984. Published by Paulo Klabin Galeria.

After the discovery of the line (and of writing), the virgin sees her reflection in the waters of "her sweet river" and sees herself as an old woman: "Her image projected on the water, deformed, looks like a thousand-year-old woman, her skin flaccid, the bones twisted underneath. The reflection says to the image: I prove your existence. To which the image replies: You owe me yours."[16] This scene is followed by a fantastic sequence involving a serpent stealing eggs from a bird's nest, and ends with a poetic dialogue between the virgin and the moon: "The virgin pointed her index finger in the direction of the moon, a new dialogue in which the nail says to the finger: 'You point to the moon, but it is in me that the moon ascends.'"[17] Further on, the virgin becomes aware of geometry through the movements of her body: "The virgin raised her legs, folded her knees, thus prompting the dialogue between them and geometry: To kneel down is to discover the right angle. The head pondering: Geometry is born from the reflex of the body projected on my mind."

As the first section comes to a close, Clark reveals her sources in the world of myth, fairy tale, and fable, from Sleeping Beauty, Peter Pan, and Aladdin, to Greek mythology and La Fontaine, ending with author Monteiro Lobato, who endeavored to create a national imaginative literature for children based on Brazilian legends and folklore. Clark's closing words also reflect her discovery of her own breasts and the act of sucking: "The virgin was possessed by intense pleasure, and discovered that to suck was paradise, and that the palate [*céu da boca*] was a perfect name, and into this heaven she allowed herself to enter." In a state of abandon, the virgin seems to be protected by creatures and forces of nature, betraying Clark's deep identification with the natural order.

The second part of *Meu doce rio* features a remarkable change of pace, with the action now centered mostly on the virgin and the ogre. Although other characters appear, the narrative focuses on the tense relationship between these two, its tenor moving from the scatological, to cannibalism, to suggestions of copulation toward the end. It begins with the virgin exploring her anus and discerning between "bad shit" and "good shit," a discovery that leads her to "establish the relationship subject-object." This initial sequence is followed by a series of images of cannibalism mixed with sexual fantasies ("From the virgin's sex a cannibalistic flower blossomed"). After a sequence of exalted violence against the ogre, the virgin screams until her throat is dry. Her mouth still drools, but she is no longer passive, and her body seems to have finally been awakened: "The virgin's body de-petrifies and turns into flesh. The ogre crouches over her, trembling, and the virgin also trembling feels the man."[18]

ARTS AND LETTERS

Understandably, *Meu doce rio* might easily be dismissed as merely a fantasy. However, a memoir written by Clark's older sister, Sonia Lins, indicates that the drive behind Clark's entire oeuvre had deeper roots than the concrete/neoconcrete framework that has informed most of its critical reception—roots that are somehow encoded in the text of *Meu doce rio*. Equally important to a thorough evaluation of *Meu doce rio* are the letters Clark exchanged with family and friends during the period of its composition.

Ambiguously titled *Artes*, Lins's memoir suggests that Clark's trajectory as an artist had its start in the mischievous games (*artes*) they played as children growing up in Belo Horizonte. A gifted storyteller, Lins weaves recollections of family life with sharp considerations of various phases of Clark's work. Although invested with different emotional content, many of Lins's recollections elucidate crucial passages in Clark's texts. For instance, Lins describes their father as an aloof, matter-of-fact character obsessed with cockfighting, traits also confirmed by Clark in her letters, but with devastating implications. Most revealing, Lins's account of Clark's birth and early childhood brings new insight into the analysis she developed under Fédida as well as the works she created with students at the Sorbonne. According to Lins, by the time Clark was born their mother could no longer breast-feed, and the baby screamed for days until a wet nurse was found. Indices of residual memory of this fact abound in both Clark's work and her writings. In a letter dated June 11, 1974, she wrote to Oiticica that a wish to grow "breasts the size of Sugar Loaf" marked the ending of an "androgynous phase" in her analysis.[19] And six months later she communicated the end of yet another important phase, that of the "primitive mother."

> I learned to suck on my arm, for I never knew my mother's breast . . . and discovered wonderful things . . . the palate is what connects the sensation of sucking to a cosmic sensation. My breasts, which had no sensation since the start of this analysis, are now supple as if my body were delineating its geography; my derrière has taken shape and the holes in my body have become more specific: I have discovered that the mouth is for ingesting and that the anus is to expel. I no longer vomit, which happened throughout the whole analysis. My tongue has taken shape and became a plug for the stomach; my teeth are now solid. Isn't it fantastic? I never thought breastfeeding was this whole world, and who was the genius who gave the name palate [*céu da boca*, the roof of the mouth, with *céu* also meaning "sky" and "heaven"] without knowing any of this?[20]

Lins and Clark seem to have shared a strong bond, the older sister keeping a benevolent, if startled, watch on the fragile sibling, "daughter of a wild cat," who would be caught eating dirt, licking the whitewashed walls, or biting her nails. For Clark, however, there seems to be no doubt that childhood was a terrifying experience. With the help of analysis, she hoped to catch up with her actual age and become a functioning adult. But the process was demanding and memories of childhood excruciating. In a heartbreaking letter dated May 5, 1971, she painted a painful picture of growing up feeling like an outcast. In a quick succession of images, Clark recalls the milk bottle that replaced breastfeeding, and sets off on a course to recreate her own birth. The letter also alludes to the image of an archetypal "couple" destroyed in childhood, which she blames for her inability to sustain a relationship. Most strikingly, she refers to her memory of being dragged to a mental hospital for treatment, recalling "dramatic images of childhood such as being pushed in the asylum shower together with other patients, or being thrown in a bathtub with cold water in the middle of the night while still asleep." This episode does not appear in Lins's memoir, and therefore we are unable to determine if it actually occurred or whether it was merely Clark's fantasy. It is noteworthy, nevertheless, that this fleeting remark is found amid a sequence of recollections that mirrors Lins's own narrative. But what Lins offers as bucolic and picturesque Clark invests with menacing connotations: the father's wine cellar is dark and infested with spiders; little Lygia helps the father pluck feathers from the roosters' necks and witnesses with horror a cockfight in which a rooster's eye is punctured; she has nightmares about drooling a vital substance; she bites her nails to the root, despairs at feeling ugly and unwanted, and runs away from home; and finally, there is an allusion to being raped as a child. Clark sums up thus: "An entire life to recover or construct a personality that never becomes full, an enormous gap between interior and exterior."[21]

Relief from such a risky environment was often found in the fantastic stories her grandfather told during occasional visits to his son's family. Mixing local lore and fairy tales with bits of Greek mythology, and related in "crude and real language," Grandfather Lins's stories would cast a long and deep influence, as Clark acknowledged in a letter to her sister dated May 24, 1973: "I never realized how many monsters I absorbed thanks to all the mythology told by Grandfather Lins: I feel incredible symptoms, forms are expelled from the holes in my body and become terrifying octopi or huge black spiders."[22]

BABA-WRITING

However harsh the critical response to this text might be, *Meu doce rio* deserves its place among textual anomalies unbound by aesthetic concerns, the kind that over time play a role in loosening up the strictures of writing. For this text is like the baba that Clark refined into key elements of her later work, exposing the messy, emotionally overwhelming personal stakes of her process. Produced at a time of great fluidity between the visual arts and writing, Clark's text fits comfortably into the category of artist writings that deal with the body, subjectivity, and otherness.[23] But more important, its fantastic imagery and boundless sense of narrative tap into a vigorous vein in Brazilian modernist literature exemplified by classics such as Mario de Andrade's *Macunaíma* and Raul Bopp's *Cobra norato*, narratives that, like Clark's, also address the dissolution of the subject amid the wilderness.[24]

"Madness is a strange reason in twentieth-century Brazilian culture, opposing rationality in panic to its excesses," Paulo Herkenhoff pointed out in his incisive essay for Clark's retrospective in Barcelona.[25] He went on to sketch out a brief network of authors and artists who addressed the clash between reason and madness, starting with Machado de Assis's short story "O alienista" and continuing through the modernist era, up to the work developed in the 1940s by Nise da Silveira with inmates at the Centro Psiquiátrico Nacional Pedro II. For Herkenhoff, the "geometric art of Rio de Janeiro has a distant root" in Silveira's pioneering work, which she developed with the assistance of Almir Mavignier. In the mid-1950s, the increasing polarization between concrete and neoconcrete artists somehow obscured Silveira's contribution to the cultural debate, and Clark's encounter with the unconscious wouldn't take place until well into the 1970s. When it finally occurred, though, she seemed to fully connect not only with her own memories but also with an entire tradition in Brazilian culture that "like certain waters, is deep, free and immense."[26]

Notes

This essay was originally published in *Lygia Clark: The Abandonment of Art* (New York: Museum of Modern Art, 2014). We thank the Museum of Modern Art, 2014, for permission to reprint it.

1 / Widely regarded as the most progressive presidents to rule Brazil in the twentieth century, Kubitschek and Goulart developed their political careers in between two dictatorial periods. It was during Kubitschek's presidency (1956–1961) that the new capital Brasilia was planned and constructed. He died in a car crash on August 22, 1976. Goulart took over the presidency in 1961 after the resignation of Janio Quadros. In 1964 the military junta that would remain in power for the next two decades deposed of Goulart, who lived in exile in Uruguay and Argentina until his death on December 6, 1976.

2 / Ivan Serpa studied art with Axl Leskoschek, an Austrian immigrant who set up a printmaking studio in Rio. In the early 1950s Serpa created Grupo Frente, in which Lygia Clark was a participant. He was an essential collaborator of Nise da Silveira at the Centro Psiquiátrico Nacional Pedro II, and also the founder of the educational program at the Museu de Arte Moderna in Rio. Later he founded the Centro de Pesquisa de Arte, in collaboration with Bruno Tausz. As an educator, Serpa had an important role in the formation of Hélio Oiticica, Waltércio Caldas, Raymundo Colares, and Emil Forman.

3 / For an insightful look at Pedrosa's last years, see the last chapter in Otília Beatriz Fiori's well-researched *Mário Pedrosa: Intinerário crítico* (São Paulo: Editora Cosac Naify, 2004).

4 / The Museu de Arte Moderna (MAM) was created in 1948, first occupying a room at Banco Boavista. It was there that in 1949 Mário Pedrosa organized an exhibition of artworks by patients of the Centro Psiquiátrico Nacional Pedro II. In 1952 MAM occupied the ground floor of Palácio Gustavo Capanema, the famous modernist building that launched the career of Oscar Niemeyer. In 1967 the museum opened its official site at the Aterro do Flamengo, designed by Affonso Eduardo Reidy.

5 / Clark to Oiticica, undated, in Lygia Clark and Hélio Oiticica, *Lygia Clark: Hélio Oiticica—Cartas 1964–1974*, ed. Luciano Figueiredo, with a preface by Silviano Santiago (Rio de Janeiro: Editora UFRJ, 1996), 34.

6 / In the process of researching for this essay, I was fortunate to receive the support of many colleagues and friends to whom I am deeply indebted. Álvaro Clark and his daughter Alessandra Clark generously shared Lygia Clark's manuscripts that are the source of *Meu doce rio*. Moreover, conversations with Alessandra Clark and art historian Paulo Venâncio Filho were crucial in helping me situate *Meu doce rio* in its proper context. Simone Klabin, widow of Paulo Klabin, interviewed at my request a number of key people involved in the production of Clark's last exhibition, also sharing with me her own copies of *Livro-obra* and Sonia Lins's *Artes*.

7 / Clark to Oiticica, October 26, 1968, in *Cartas*, 59. All translations from the Portuguese are mine.

8 / Clark to Oiticica, November 9, 1969, in *Cartas*, 126.

9 / Clark to Oiticica, October 22, 1970, in *Cartas*, 182. In this letter, Clark mentions two patients from the Centro Psiquiátrico Nacional Pedro II, Raphael Domingues and Emygdio de Barros, known for their accomplished artwork. The graphic designer Rogério Duarte, a close friend of Oiticica's, worked for film director and writer Glauber Rocha and for the musicians in the movement known as Tropicália. In 1968 Duarte was arrested for his involvement in the student movement and was subjected to torture. After his release from prison, he was interned at the Centro Psiquiátrico Nacional Pedro II with severe depression. Duarte was later able to resume his design work and became a professor at the Universidade de Brasilia; he currently lives in Salvador. In another letter, Clark mentions being invited to work at a clinic in the Loire: "If it works out it will be my salvation, which is a paradox, for someone like me who makes art to escape the asylum, to end there is incredible! But there is no place for me in the world of normal people"; Clark to Oiticica, March 31, 1971, in *Cartas*, 191.

10 / Clark to Oiticica, July 6, 1974, in *Cartas*, 221.

11 / Clark to Oiticica, 222–223.

12 / Oiticica to Clark, July 11, 1974, in *Cartas*, 226.

13 / Lygia Clark, *Meu doce rio* (Rio de Janeiro: Galeria Paulo Klabin, 1984), 8.

14 / Ariel Jiménez, *Ferreira Gullar in Conversation with Ariel Jiménez* (New York: Fundación Cisneros/ Colección Patricia Phelps de Cisneros, 2011), 111. Also worth noting is Rubens Gerchman's recollection of Clark's first meeting with Fédida: "When she got next to him, she was so moved that she couldn't utter a word . . . she muttered, she wanted to speak, and suddenly she started drooling. There was this dribble coming out of her mouth, and he said: 'Madam, this is a great start.' Because she'd brought out the deepest in her. And the word didn't form itself." In "Archive for a Work-Event," Manifesta Journal 13, no. 9, http://www.manifestajournal.org/issues/fungus-contemporary/archive-work-event-activating-bodys-memory-lygia-clarks-poetics-and-its (site discontinued).

15 / Lygia Clark, *Meu doce rio*, 13.

16 / Clark, 24.

17 / Clark plays with the meaning of *lunula* (little moon), the white base of the nail shaped as a crescent moon.

18 / Clark, 45–54.

19 / Clark to Oiticica, June 11, 1974, in *Cartas*, 247.

20 / Clark to Oiticica, November 11, 1974, in *Cartas*, 256–257.

21 / Clark to Oiticica, May 5, 1971, in *Cartas*, 209–10.

22 / Sonia Lins, *Artes* (Ghent, Belgium: Snoeck Ducaju and Zoon, 1996), 28.

23 / Clark's vivid explorations of her body in *Meu doce rio* share similarities with textual experiments by several of her contemporaries. For instance, Marcel Broodthaers's texts in *Pense-Bête*, despite their acerbic tone and bleak humor, betray the same sense of unease Clark experienced. Of special interest to this discussion is his play on the word *moule*, which can alternately be translated as "mussel" or "mold." An equal sense of estrangement is conveyed by Öyvind Fahlström in his early poem "Müüüüüm and the Megaphones," which leads the reader into a scatological ride down a character's gastric tract. Noteworthy also is the fact that all these texts are based on the fable model common to children's books, in which simple verbal articulations (*baba*, *müüüüüm*, *moule*, *bête*, *bicho*) prompt associations with the fantastic. Most remarkably, Carolee Schneeman's artist book *Parts of a Body House*, published in 1969, echoes Clark's *O casa é o corpo*, a work she exhibited the previous year at MAM in Rio and at the Venice Biennale. For a complete reproduction of *Pense-Bête*, see Gloria Moure, ed., *Marcel Broodthaers: Collected Writings* (Barcelona: Ediciones Poligrafa, 2012). For an English translation of "Müüüüüm and the Megaphones," see *zingmagazine* 2, no. 6 (Summer 1998). For the complete text of *Parts of a Body House*, see Dick Higgens and Wolf Vostel, eds., *Fantastic Architecture* (New York: Something Else Press, 1969).

24 / The important contributions of Mario de Andrade and Raul Bopp to modern Brazilian literature have been obfuscated over the years by the dazzling polemics of Oswald de Andrade's manifestos. That these fantastic narratives take the form of fables, or tales, is highly relevant to our understanding of Clark's story. Indeed, a careful reading of those books will add a new dimension to our understating of what the modernist program entailed. For at the basis of both works is the rescue of an entire folk tradition whose roots extend to a precolonial Brazil, but which also points to the structuralist bent of the postwar generations, a bridging best illustrated by concrete poet Haroldo de Campos's reading of *Macunaíma* based on the theories of Vladimir Propp, in his study *Morfologia de Macunaíma* (1967).

25 / *Lygia Clark* (Barcelona: Fundació Antoni Tàpies, 1998), 47, exhibition catalog.

26 / Clark and Oiticica, February 2, 1971, in *Cartas*, 185.

EMIL FORMAN Removing the Silence of Things

Fernanda Lopes

As a young woman, Antonietta Clélia Rangel Forman's poise and charm was the pride of her family. Born in Rio de Janeiro in 1918, she distinguished herself from most of the women of her generation. As early as 1939, at age twenty-one, she enrolled in flight classes at the Department of Aviation at the city's yacht club, which had a hangar for seaplanes. She was one of the first women in Brazil to earn an aviation license, causing a stir whenever she would fly to Cabo Frio, an exclusive resort town outside Rio. Revisiting her past through photographs, we recognize her interest in gymnastics and sports. She practiced yoga early on before it became fashionable. She also practiced riding at the Sociedade Hípica Brasileira and won several jumping competitions. As the years went by, she put aside her sporting life to dedicate more time to her four children. At old age she was known as Dona Nieta, the mother of Clélia, a chemical engineer; Dora, a psychologist; Hugo, an engineer, and Emil, her youngest son. Another picture reveals she also had two grandchildren: Christiano and Daniel, sons of Dora.

It was Emil who, in August 1975, presented an extensive and unusual "portrait" of this fascinating woman, in a room on the third floor of the Museu de Arte Moderna do Rio de Janeiro (MAM-RJ). The installation *Pictures of Antonietta Clélia Rangel Forman* was a compilation of all the photographic documentation the artist could gather about a single person. "The material to be presented could not be perceived as a closed set (a dead individual) or even a crystallized one (an old person). It was necessary to choose someone who, having lived a long period of time, had not yet reached its definitive image. Antonietta Clelia Rangel Forman, born in Rio de Janeiro during the 1910s, was chosen for being an ordinary person, and for having lived in Brazil (Rio de Janeiro) most of her life," explained the artist in the gallery text that presented the exhibition.

Visitors to the exhibition found themselves surrounded by walls busy with over one thousand images registering the span of over six decades, related not only to the life of an individual but also, possibly, to a period in the history of the city of Rio de Janeiro in the twentieth century, from the early days of modernism to the years of the military regime. The installation also included photographs from the collections of friends and relatives. Unaware of the exhibition plans until the end of December 1974, Antonietta continued to be photographed as usual in familiar situations. Once informed about the project, she actively participated in its production suggesting certain poses or situations, a kind of interference that was welcomed by the artist.

The installation was an investigation of a person, but it was also about the possibilities of photography. The set included studio portraits, photos taken by street photographers, travel photos, photos for identity cards and passports, contact sheets, features in newspapers and magazines, slides, radiographs and 8mm and 16mm films. No technical or aesthetic concerns were taken into account in selecting the materials: some photos were of poor quality, difficult to identify, blurred, overexposed, faded, or double-exposed. In these images, Antonietta appeared alone or with groups of other people, close up or from afar, on her back or even only partially—her forehead, one arm, the tip of her foot. Photos of photos and all kinds of duplicates were also included.

Two photographs showed a friend painting and holding in her hands a photo—now lost—where we could see Antonietta laying in a hammock, in the same pose that generated many duplicate photos. Despite the difficulty in seeing the watercolor, the clash between the two forms of representation produced an interesting effect. There was also a photo taken with a friend after a snow blizzard in New York City in which only their shadows appear: the classic way of denoting presence without showing the subject. With the exception of texts or subtitles in clippings of magazines and newspapers, and the occasional writing in the albums or in photos, the information contained in the documents was withheld.

In the text written for the exhibition brochure, Forman noted that "people nowadays have their lives documented by photography in various and frequent situations . . . the simultaneous presentation of all existing material about a person enables a wider view of the extent that this documentation can reach." The exhibition was not exclusively focused on the past, as the most recent material had equal import in the reading of the ensemble. Overall, Forman's installation was a surprising homage to photography and memory, intriguing in its obsessive and thorough method. More to the point, it faithfully mirrored Forman's personality, temperament, and work process.

Emil Forman was born in Rio de Janeiro in 1954. He studied under concrete art pioneer Ivan Serpa at the Centro de Pesquisas de Arte (Center for Art Research), in Ipanema, from 1971 to 1973. Under Serpa's guidance, he developed an obsession for method and rigor, without allowing it to disrupt the experimental side of his creativity. Alongside the systematic practice of drawing, Forman developed his first works related to accumulation and photography, including *The Cabinet* (1972), an installation in his house coatroom that featured obsolete family objects, and *Concrete Marigold* (1973), an extensive series of photographs about the same object of consumption. At the Centro he also presented his first individual exhibition in 1973. Around that same period he began his series of photographs of social events, registering weddings, birthdays, meetings, and exhibitions that he was invited to, a series that he would continue to work on until 1977.

The artist Jozias Benedicto met Forman in Serpa's classes and wrote about their dynamic in his blog:

> Emil was always late for Ivan's classes. Very young, he was then twenty years old, but already with a strong personality and well defined work; very pale, blond, tall, always in dark clothes; his tone of voice was low, but assured, no coyness about it; a gentleness, a certain aloofness that was always characteristic; but under the quietness there was a strong, determined, and precocious person; he was heir to the wreck of a traditional family, very rich, part of the Rio aristocracy in decline due to the economic changes of the previous decade. The class would be halfway through when he arrived, with a portfolio under his arm. Ivan would ask, "Have you done work, Emil?" He would smile as if embarrassed and say, "I did some drawings on the bus." Then he would open the folder and show dozens and dozens of drawings made with hydrographic pen possibly created on the seat in the back of a bus that would bring him from Praia do Flamengo to Ipanema.[1]

Art critic Ileana Pradilla Cerón, curator of a posthumous exhibition of the artist in 2006, also wrote about Forman's early years:

> As a teenager, Emil Forman used spaces in his home to set up his imaginary universe. Accumulations and nonsense assemblages of objects found or appropriated invaded his room and other surroundings of the family's apartment, altering places usually devoted to domestic privacy. Similarly, with his first solo exhibition in 1973 at the age of 19, Emil began to occupy the public space of art with his private world, exhibiting familiar objects, images of his own room, photographs of his mother, in sum his intimacy eclipsed of privacy.[2]

Forman's first solo exhibition in 1973 provoked shock and irritation not only because of the way it was installed but also because of its content, and it was unanimously referred to in the newspapers of the day as "a curious exhibition." In one of these articles, the artist addressed the project thus:

> I've always been impressed with how people love to keep things throughout their lives. The best way to convey this kind of commitment would be to present all the objects belonging to one person and accumulated throughout her/his life. This was possible to achieve with Ms. Maria Ferreira dos Anjos by recovering all her objects and personal belongings. This woman was born in Vila do Chã, in Portugal and arrived in Brazil in 1919. In May 1920 she was hired by M. A. Rangel, in whose house she remained until her death (April 8, 1973).
>
> Maria dos Anjos preserved, stored, and accumulated all her personal possessions and objects with extreme care. She must have been influenced by the people in the house where she worked and lived at—she was the housekeeper—who had the same habit of keeping everything. In 1967, when she went to visit one of her brothers in Portugal, she took with her six chests full of stuff—here in Rio, she kept only the things that were dearest to her. It is from these things that I made this exhibition.[3]

The 1973 exhibition titled *Objects of Maria dos Anjos Ferreira* resembled very little of what had been produced in Brazil until then. It was in fact "a curious exhibition." Vitrines and drawers installed against a flat backdrop displayed objects left by the family housekeeper, who had died shortly before the show was produced. In an interview to art critic Roberto Pontual,[4] Forman pointed out that his main interest was to indicate when a personal collection comes to a closure; an impetus common to us all, that in his exhibition came to a full cycle. Once someone dies, other objects could not be added to her/his personal collection.

In the catalog produced for Forman's first posthumous survey, art critic Frederico Morais offered an interesting analysis of the exhibition in his testimony about the artist:

> Emil Forman's first solo exhibition, held at the art gallery in Ivan Serpa's Research Center, had an impact. I did not know the artist yet and was impressed by the fact that for his first solo exhibition, he came up with a work so well structured and self-assured while at the same time of great emotional impact.
>
> The exhibition bothered many people. The invitation to the vernissage was conceived as a funeral memorial card, and many people upon receiving it, reacted negatively, disliking the exhibition even before visiting it. They saw Forman's decision to expose personal objects of Dona Iá, his family's Portuguese governess, as a violation of her private life, an intrusion into her privacy.
>
> However, I perceived it in exactly the opposite way, that is, as the manifestation of a profound love for life, and admiration for a person who, throughout her long existence, knew how to protect her solitude by creating a world of her own, absolutely coherent, holistic. And what brought coherence to this world and gave meaning to Dona Iá's life were these objects. All of them perfectly banal, without any economic value, but impregnated with the aura of the subject, biographical objects, Violet Morin would say, true objects-subjects Gaston Bachelard added. Objects that aged alongside the owner, repositories of her memory, connoisseurs of

her idiosyncrasies and virtues, in short, objects closely linked to the individual, (the owner) in a relation of mutual dependence.

> But what Emil Forman took to the gallery, in the form of an *installation*, was not only the objects patiently collected by Dona Iá throughout her solitary existence. He took, to use an expression of Jean Baudrillard, an "arrangement structure." As we know, a simple quantitative survey of the objects proper to a room in 1900 or in a 1960s living-room allowed Abraham A. Moles to draw important conclusions on the socioeconomic and cultural behavior of their owners. Baudrillard went beyond this kind of demographics and analyzed the way objects are distributed in the space of the house, the hierarchy that is created between them; he raised a kind of morality of objects, and wanted to know how objects are experienced, what other desires exist besides functional ones. This is what Emil Forman did, recovering not only the objects left by Dona Iá, but the way she related with them, how she kept them (protected them) in her corner; small objects inside small boxes, small boxes Inside larger boxes, inside chests, inside the furniture. With these objects and in the way she organized them, Dona Iá built her dream house, her protective nest.[5]

After visiting the exhibition, art critic Antônio Bento nominated Forman to the 9th Paris Biennale of 1975, where he presented an audiovisual about Iá's objects, a record of his first show at the Art Research Center. That same year he opened the exhibition *Pictures of Antonietta Clélia Rangel Forman* at the MAM-RJ. The exhibition, which had 3,739 visitors during its first twenty-one days, inaugurated *Área experimental*, a series of exhibitions dedicated to contemporary art at the museum. "A different exhibition"; "An exhibition difficult to understand if the public does not know the artist's thoughts"; "With materials never before thought to be used in an art show"—these were some attempts to define the exhibitions that went on display starting in August 1975 under the *Área experimental* umbrella. The exhibitions were housed in one or more galleries on the museum's third floor, which focused on projects by young Brazilian artists, and lasted from thirty to forty-five days each.[6]

Selected from proposals submitted by artists or commissioned by the Cultural Planning Commission, rather than based on work and portfolio reviews, the exhibitions presented an extremely wide range of responses to the question, "What is experimental?" This variety mirrored the fact that the artists selected for *Área experimental*, as well as those participating in the selection commission, bridged different generations, with artistic productions marked by an array of new references and possibilities, not only in regard to the concepts presented but also in relation to the materials and media chosen by the artists.

The exhibitions were promoted by the MAM-RJ as "presentations of Brazilian artists linked to experimentation," "exhibitions related to research and experimentation," or exhibitions by Brazilian artists "dedicated to research and new creative forms," "involved in research and new artistic proposals," or "linked to new research on language and artistic concepts"; artists whose works "critically address issues related to the art system at production and consumption levels,"

Emil Forman, *Pictures of Antonietta Clélia Rangel Forman*, 1975. Courtesy of Dora Forman.

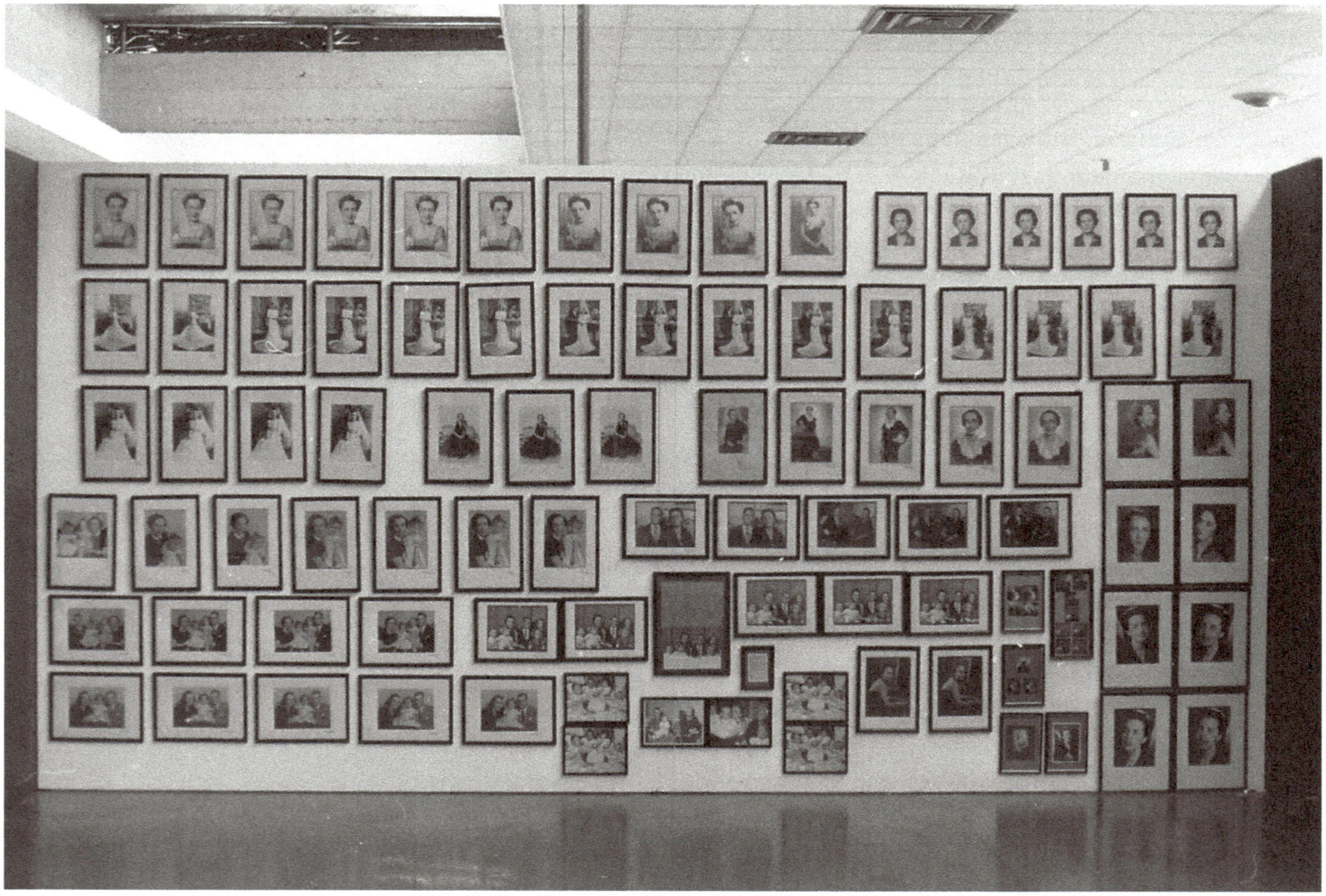

Emil Forman, *Pictures of Antonietta Clélia Rangel Forman*, 1975. Courtesy of Dora Forman.

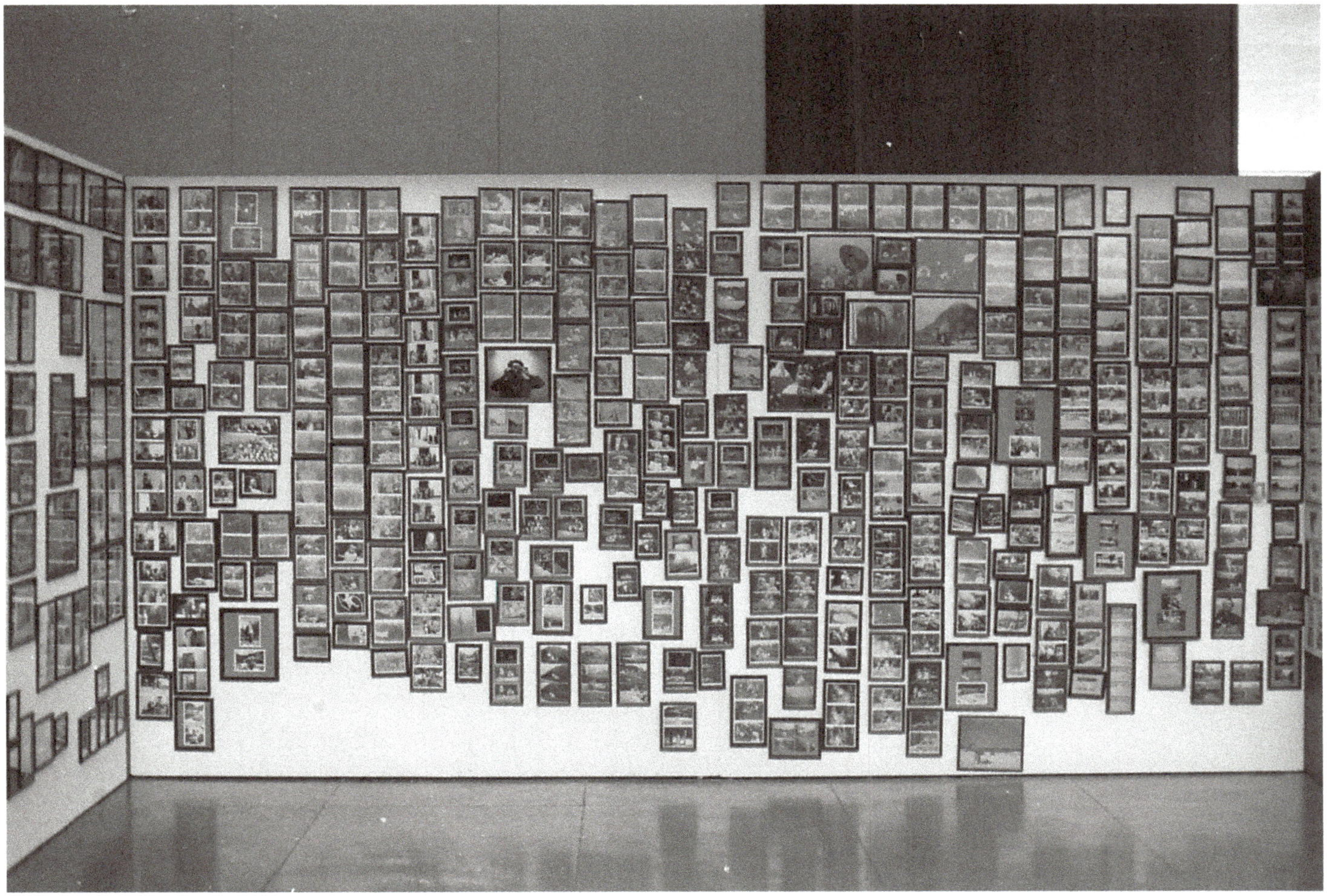

Emil Forman, *Pictures of Antonietta Clélia Rangel Forman*, 1975. Courtesy of Dora Forman.

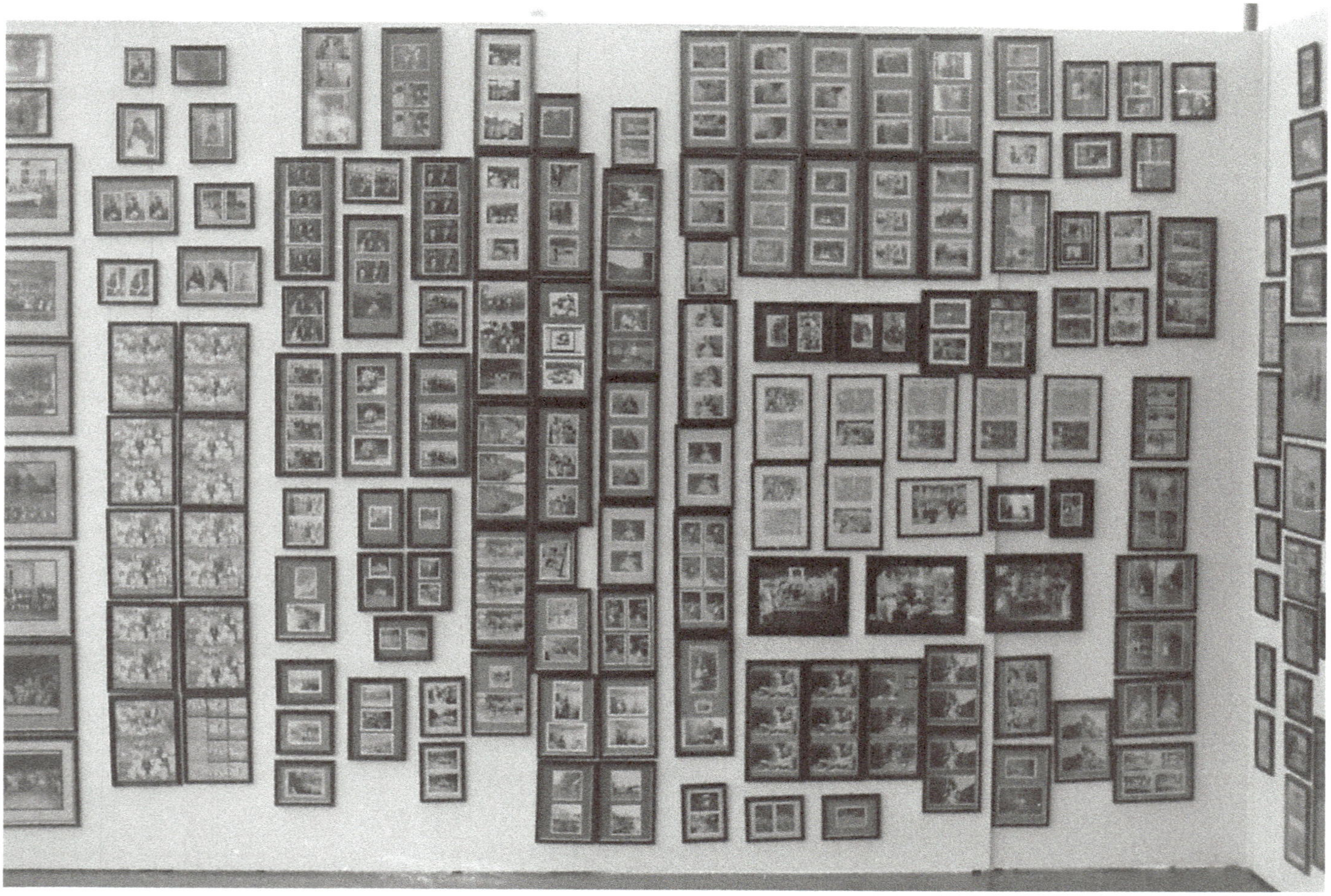

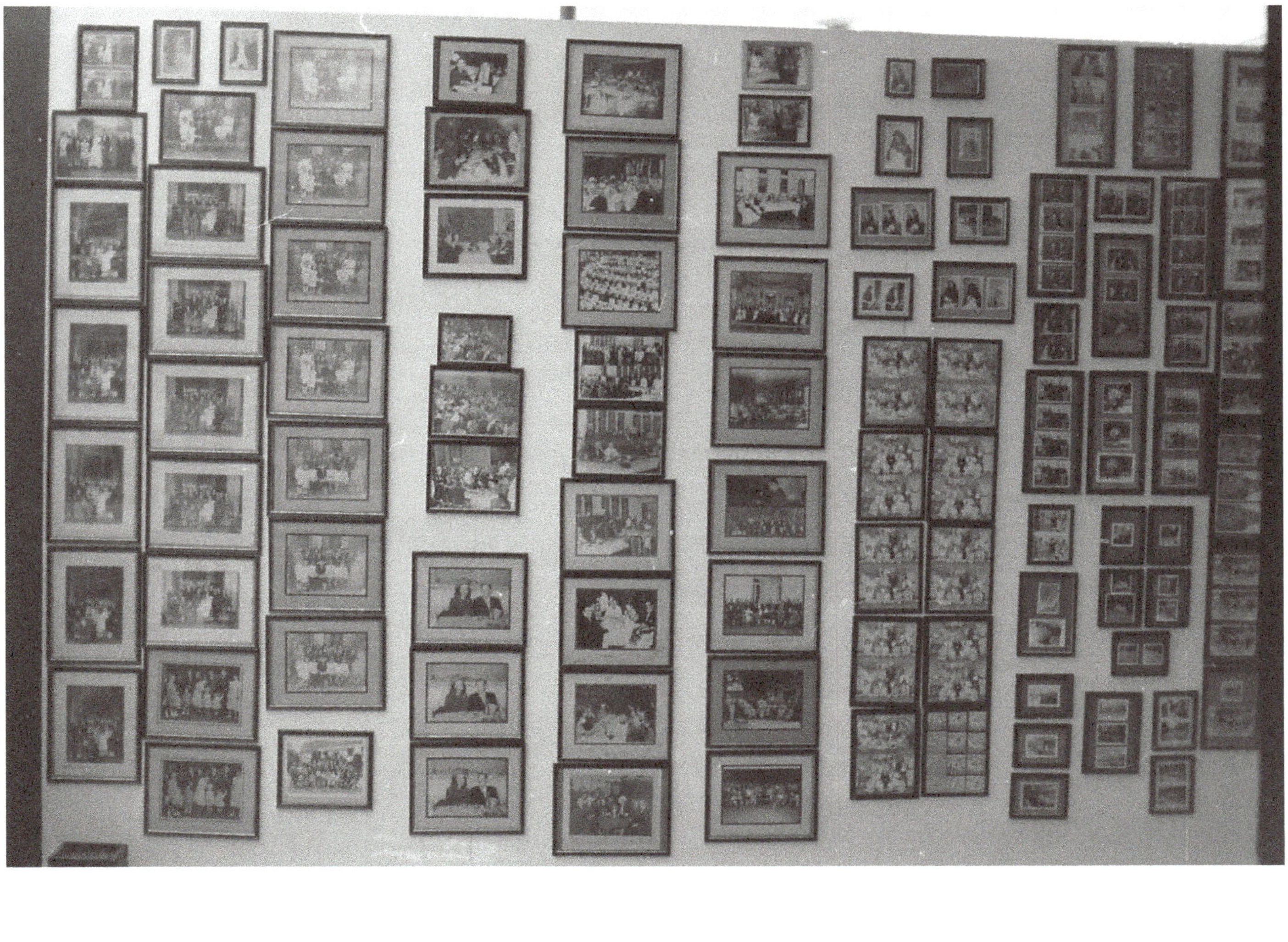

Emil Forman, *Pictures of Antonietta Clélia Rangel Forman*, 1975. Courtesy of Dora Forman.

"critically investigate the system of production and consumption of art," "react and make us think of the current trend in the arts circuit (including artists, galleries, museums, market, etc.)," or artists "whose production is linked to new aesthetic experiences and research, whether in the field of object, photography, audiovisual, or videotape."[7]

At *Área experimental*, other installation projects—by Cildo Meireles, Umberto Costa Barros, and Waltércio Caldas, for example—dealt directly with space in its physical and institutional dimensions, especially taking into account its limitations. Other proposals such as those by Regina Vater, Anna Bella Geiger, Lygia Pape, Carlos Zilio, Ivens Machado, and Paulo Herkenhoff questioned not only the limits of conventional categories and artistic procedures but also the passive attitude of the public in relation to the work of art. And projects such the ones presented by Letícia Parente, Fernando Cocchiarale, and Emil Forman—which were informed by a more conceptual outlook—departed from processes related to cataloging, evaluation, measurement, and classification while questioning their reductionist character, and their value as methods.

An analysis of the list of participants and projects presented in *Área experimental* makes evident the program's three-part structure (with internal variations in each of them) that correspond to attempts to think new paths for Brazilian art at that particular time.[8] One of these possible paths grouped artists interested in possible new readings and developments linked to neoconcrete experimentalism (in some cases, establishing dialogues with more recent productions, such as conceptual art, art povera, and minimalism); another path, more internationalist in tone, featured artists connected to video experimentation and language-based art; yet another path stood in opposition to the other two while remaining tied to a more formalistic position.

Art was no longer considered as merely a historical sequence, in which one reference replaces the other, but rather as a complex of relationships in which the most diverse references are placed on the table, on equal footing, at the same time. It was necessary to make choices. And the lack of consensus on what was *experimental* for the MAM-RJ project meant keeping that possibility open. By not to restricting the *experimental* to a single artistic definition—such as video art, installation art, painting, drawing, or any other medium— *Área experimental* challenged how to rethink art practices. Regardless the specificity of media or technical support, the idea of *experimentation* would have to be rethought in the critical sense, bringing into question the very idea of artistic space, and the terms upon which society and other power systems were structured and managed. At that time in Brazil, it was necessary to expand or reinvent the space of discussion, of debate, and not only in regard to art. Art production at the time was confused with the need to create spaces for the production of art, and in the *Área experimental*, the proposals were presented as projects, which involved the idea of assuming a risk: "Here in this place, we are trying something that one does not know where it will lead to. And that's alright."[9]

In his project for *Área experimental*, Forman embraced all the risks that the program aimed to address. Slender, pale, with an aristocratic demeanor, Forman was the unassuming star of Brazil's new avant-garde. The quiet character of his work, seemingly dissociated from the political upheavals of the 1970s, denoted a personal clash with the ongoing massification of the individual through popular culture and her/his relations, as Ileana Pradilla Cerón points out:

> Apparently oblivious to the transgressive movements of the counterculture that marked the decade of the 1970s; and also far from the noisier attitudes of protest against the country's political situation at that moment, these operations of displacement and grafting of public and private spaces proposed by Emil, were nevertheless disturbing commentaries and procedures on the established order. Although not necessarily innovative (dislocations in art has happened at least since Duchamp and Dadaism) they were sufficiently forceful, however, to create estrangement in a world hardly vulnerable to aesthetic surprise.
>
> In the installations, photographs, and audiovisuals that the artist made between 1973 and 1975, the urge to instill art with life and vice versa was paramount. Paradoxically, at least if contrasted with propositions related to the dissolution of frontiers between art and life promoted by avant-garde artists early in the twentieth century (including the constructivist developments in Brazil in the 1950s), Forman's works was not an affirmation of the present, they rather inventoried fragments of the past, as in a search for lost meaning.
>
> . . .
>
> Forman, however, was a voyeur furtively registering what he saw. But perhaps for seeing the world without filters, with the brutal cruelty with which it presents itself, everything seemed to acquire, in the works of the artist, certain unrealism. His lenses turned the everyday into Fellini-like scenes, where everything and everyone, under the weight of excessive reality, became strange fictional characters.[10]

Paulo Herkenhoff, on the other hand, situates Forman's production, especially the exhibition held at the MAM-RJ, within the very discipline of photography and its multiple aspects.

> The exhibition at MAM inscribes itself in the history of Brazilian art as one of the most profound inquiries about the status and meaning of photography. As important as the turn of the century photomontage of Valério Vieira, the collages of Jorge de Lima (Panic Painting, 1943)[11] and the experimental photography of Geraldo de Barros, José Oiticica Filho, and Athos Bulcão in the 1950s, Emil's work takes us to a discussion about photography, beyond issues related to photojournalism, documentation, or aesthetics (angles, tones, etc.). Emil's work anticipates or coexists with the photography of Artur Omar, Alair Gomes, Hugo Denizart, Pedro Vasques, Vera Chaves Barcellos, Miguel Rio Branco, Iole de Freitas, Essila Paraíso, Ana Vitória Mussi, and Mario Cravo Neto: the radical point of constitution of contemporaneity of this language and the expanding of its hypotheses as images, matter, light, time, space, process, tradition, and practice.

. . .

In this work, Emil's interest is focused in the individual and the language of light. Photography, cinema, x-ray, typographic cliché—images of a world where one no longer has enough time and that he wants to capture. One's life is what photography preserves. Records of moments/facts. What is written is no longer worth anything. What is photographed has worth. This cold and dramatic, curious and insipid, unique, and banal representation is the life of us all, twentieth-century creatures. Industrial societies have turned their citizens into image junkies. What for? Who took these hundreds of photographs? I, you, he, we all, nonphotographers hopelessly doomed to practice the "middle-brow art" of Pierre Bourdieu.

. . .

Emil was not a photographer, yet he was able to confer meaning to it. An innocent photo, banal or beautiful, was a tool to demolish the idealized world. Its transcendent meaning allowed to flow freely from the isolation and pragmatic side of things. The intellectual gesture of organizing things broke their silence.[12]

Few works by Forman gained public notice—not only during his lifetime but unfortunately to this day. The production he left behind is marked by heterogeneity, denoting his curiosity for different media, as was often the case in Brazilian art in the 1970s. Looking back at his production as a whole, it is possible to say that there seemed to be no hierarchy among the images that he appropriated (photographs not taken by him and objects not collected by him, for example) and the ones he crafted himself. There was a powerful and elegant balance between the conceptual universe that was beginning to be explored by young Brazilian artists in the 1970s, and the belief, still prevailing today, in the power of visuality, in the plastic possibilities of each work, which had its dimension as object carefully thought out.

In addition to photography, which occupied a special place in his work, drawing was Forman's language of choice. His relationship with the two media recalls a phrase by Man Ray: "I photograph what I do not want to paint, and I paint what I do not want to photograph." Forman seems to have worked the same way. He made thousands of drawings of situations that he did not want to photograph and used photographs of people and things he did not want to draw. Forman pursued drawing from a very young age, exploring its possibilities exhaustively. Talented and compulsive, he produced graphic work linked to a strong expressive and critical heritage, which straddles an evolution going back to the caricatures of Honoré Daumier to contemporary comics. Ileana Pradilla Cerón commented on the impact of Forman's drawings thus:

Looking at them for the first time, these drawings might surprise with their understated directness. With quick and precise lines, they also remind us of illustrations in children's books. However, as we penetrate this universe, we realize that what first struck us as candor is actually a finger in the wound. Shoes, which appear in myriad ways, the eroticized and

On the following pages:

Emil Forman, *Untitled*, 1974-1977. Courtesy of Dora Forman.

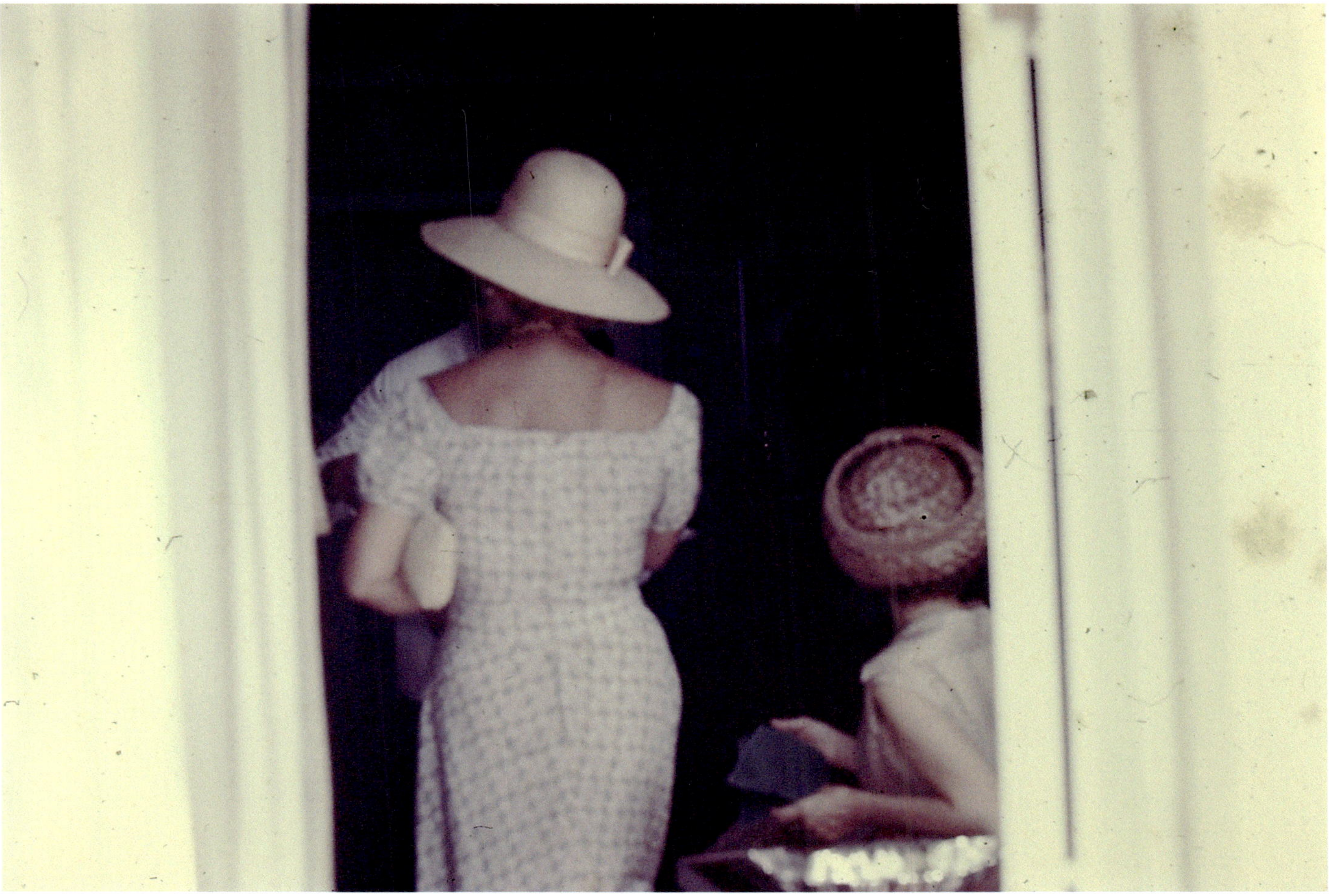

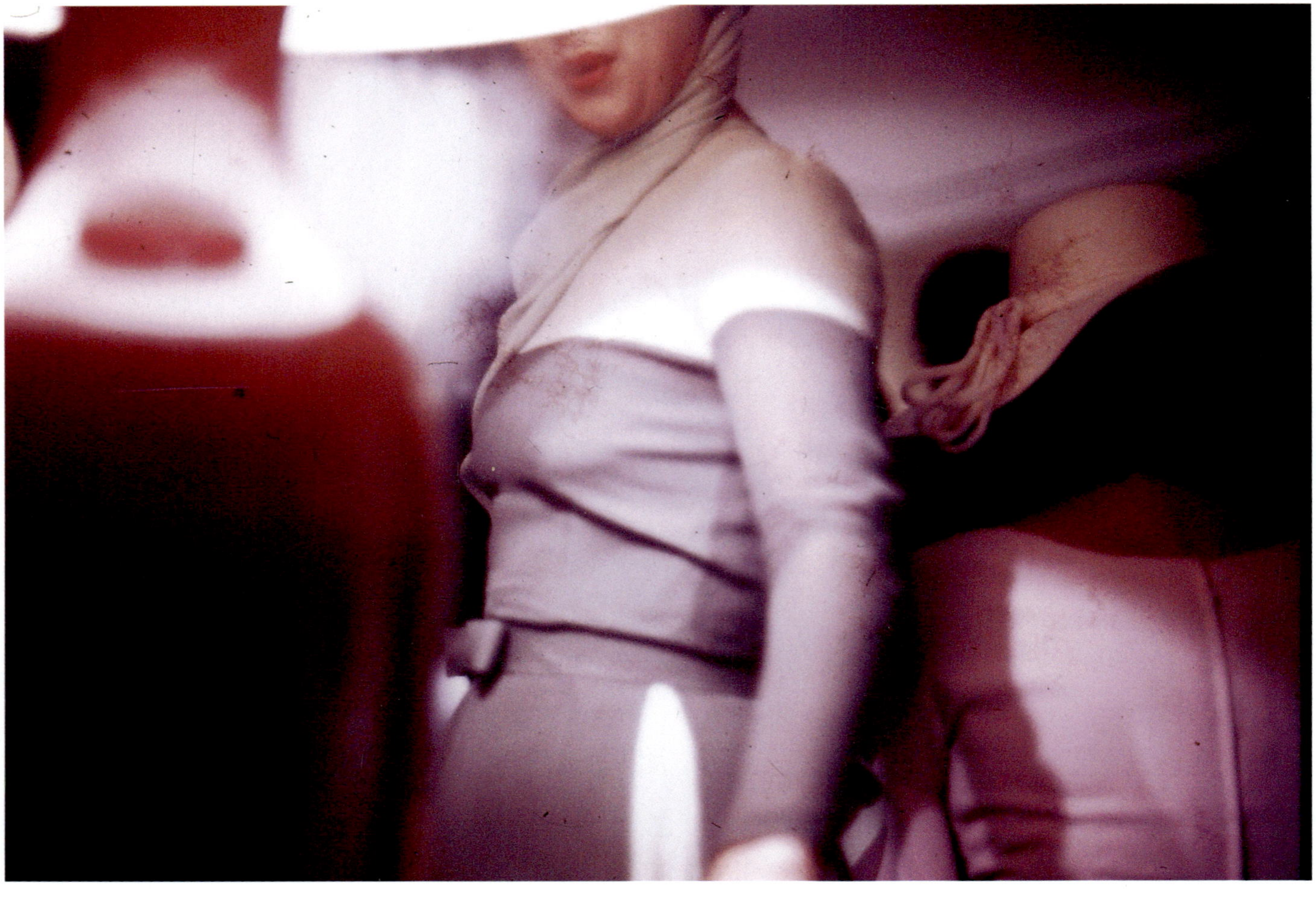

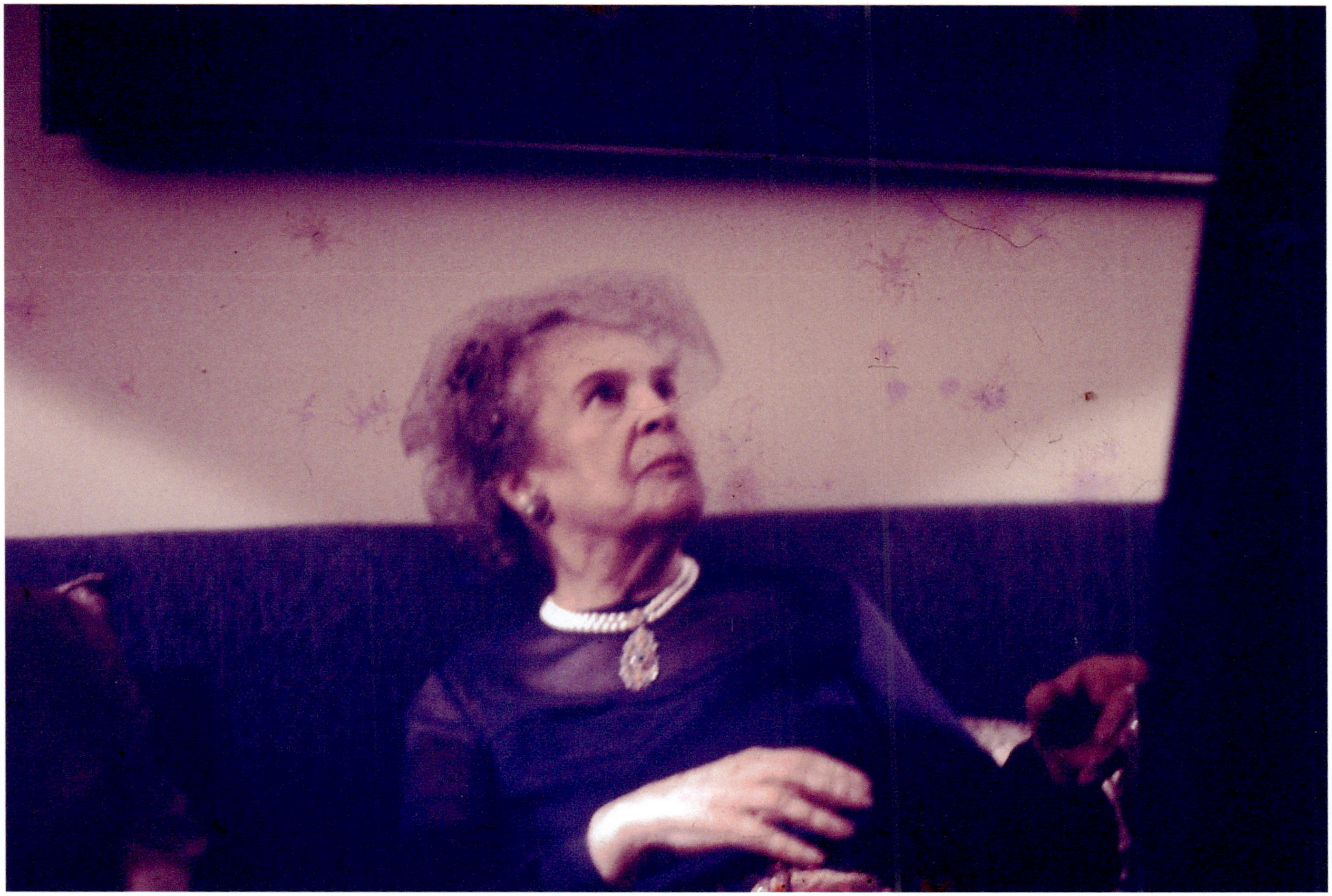

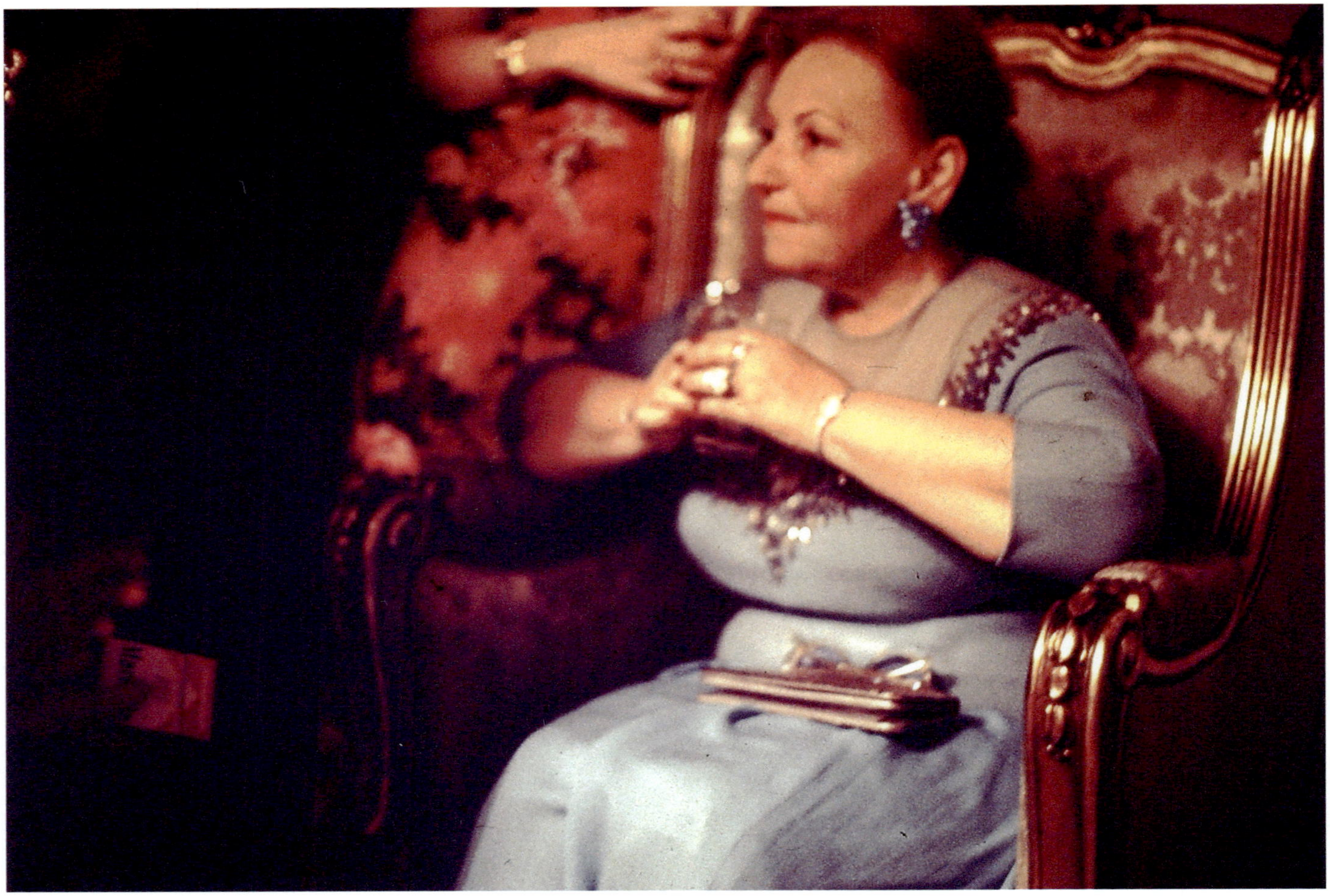

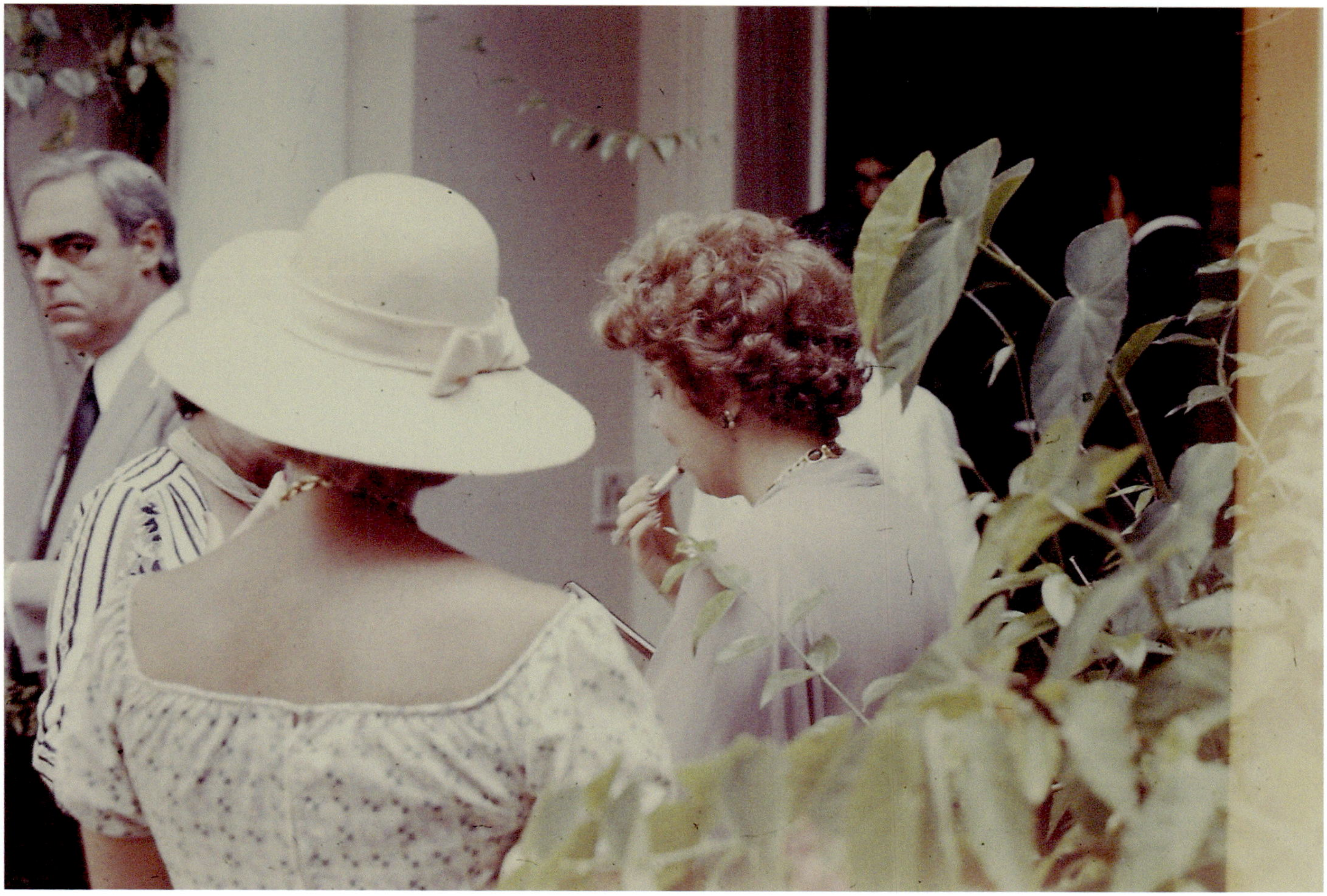

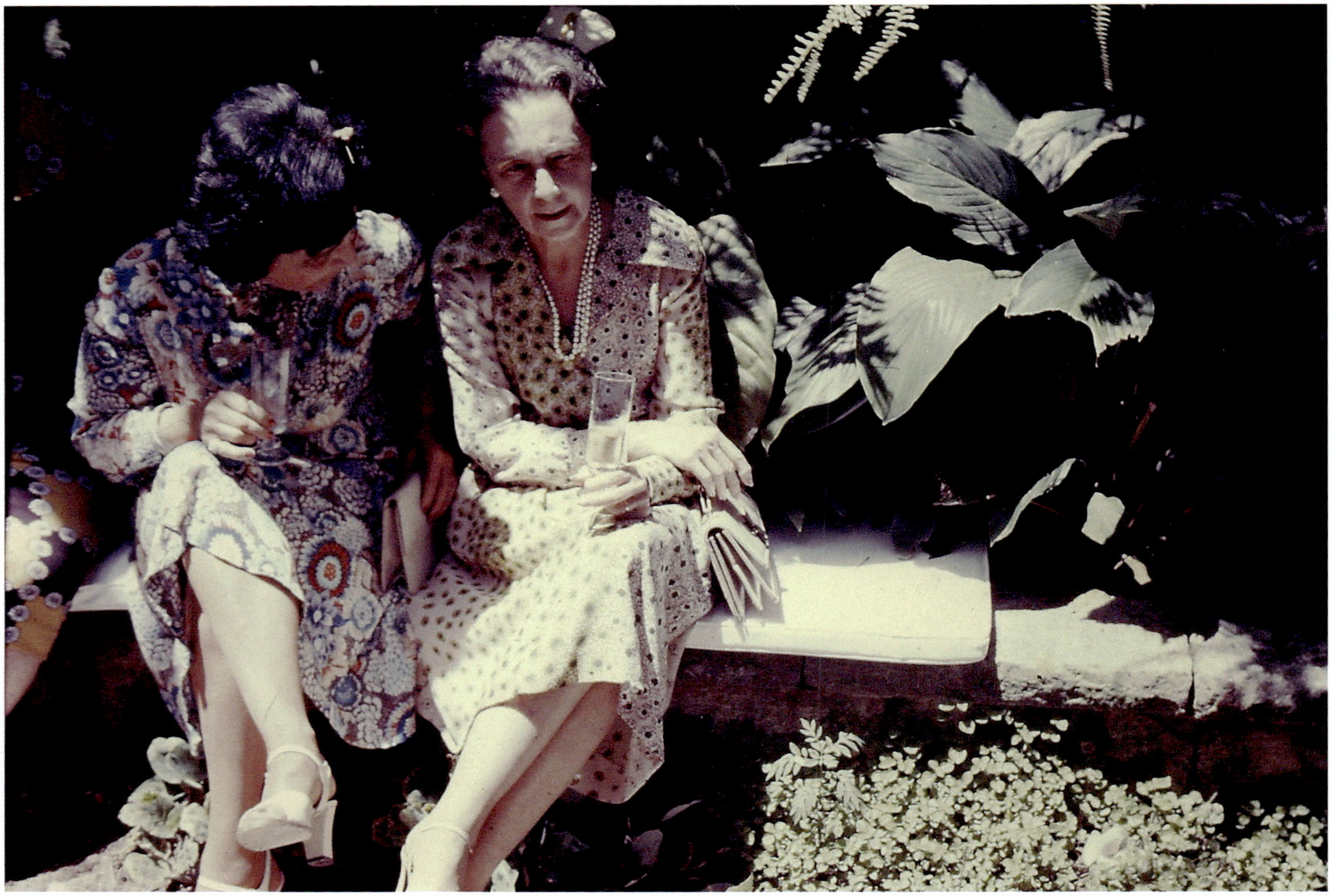

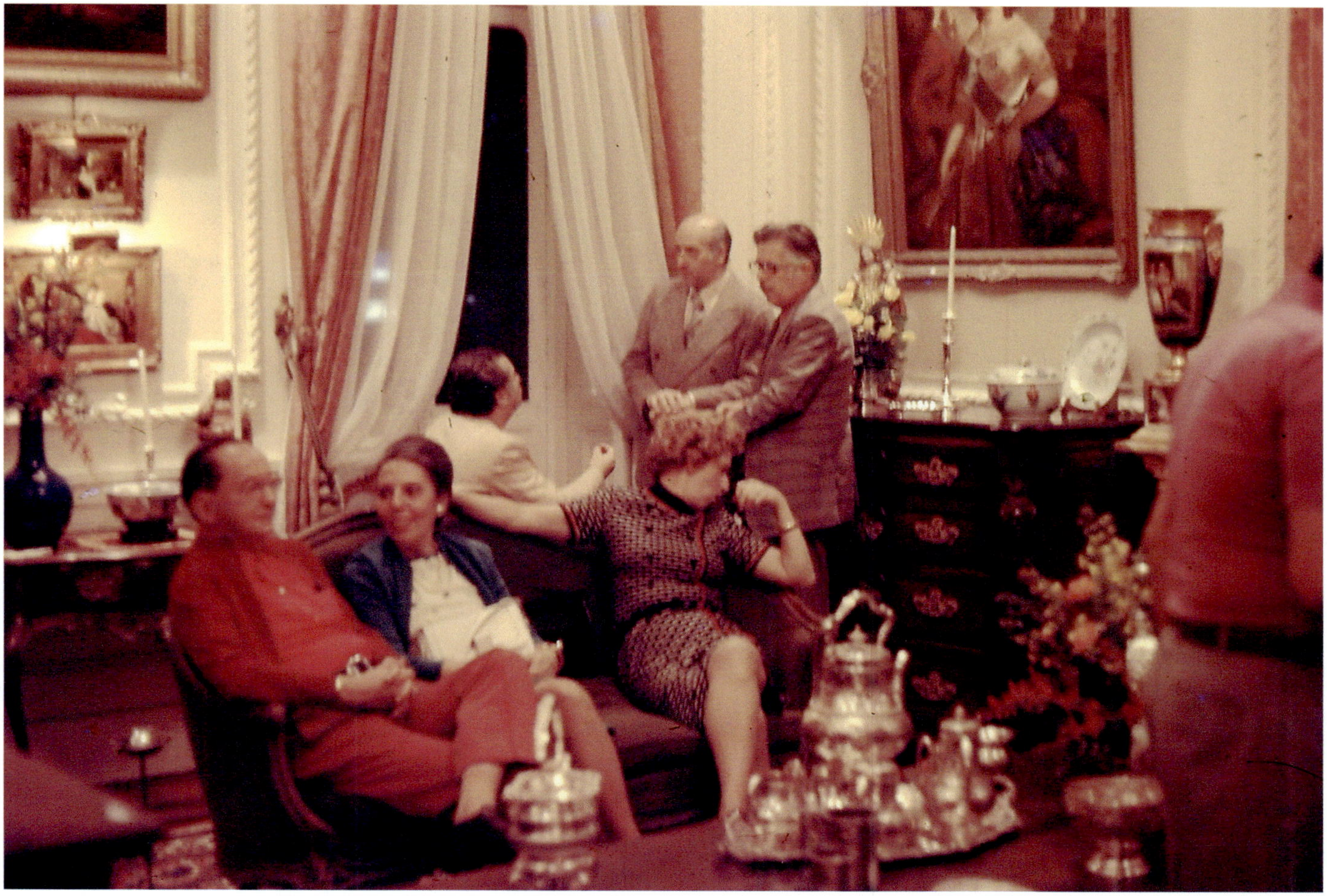

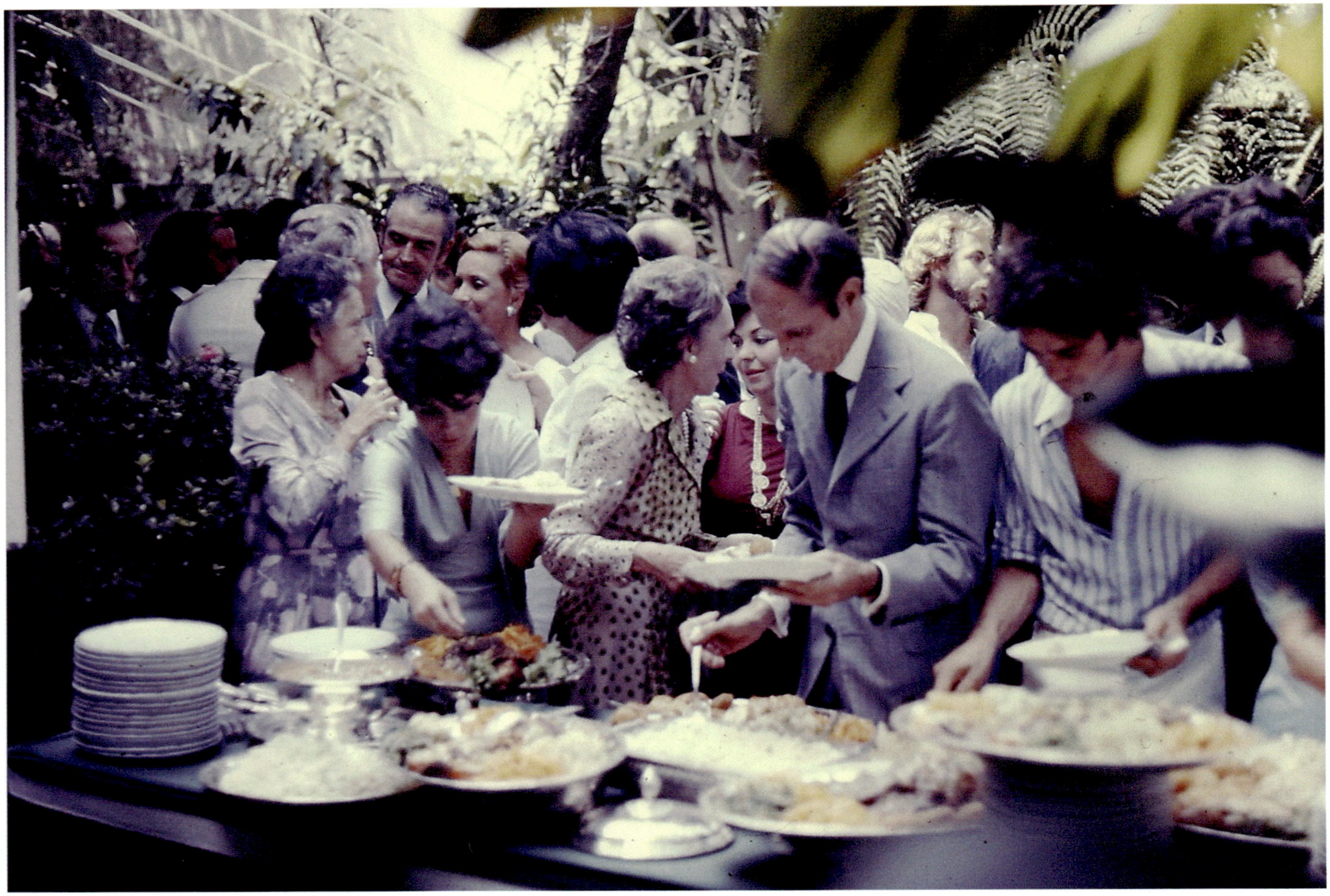

masculine-looking women, and the obsessive cashew fruits—to name a few of the recurring elements in his drawings might struck us as an exaltation of banality, as some have deemed Andy Warhol's canvases and drawings. And Forman, no doubt, engaged in a discreet but profound dialogue with pop art, and especially with Warhol, a descendant of Eastern European immigrants, like him. This dialogue was not, to be sure, with the anonymous and impactful pop aesthetics borrowed from advertising. In comparison, Emil's work would be the opposite of this aesthetics: intimate, silent, self-referential. His identification with that movement comes through in the disenchanted attitude that pop art reveals. Certainly, Forman's works have nothing banal about them, but they point, as pop art does, to the banality of the world and its immediate surface.

As in the photographs, the characters in Forman's drawings are also caricatures, masks, surface, conveyed in a light and refined line. Paradoxically, these humorous drawings carry equal doses of purity and consciousness: the humor and fertile imagination of fairy tales contrasted with the realization of a lack of meanings in our contemporary world.[13]

Photography and drawing accompanied Forman's career from the beginning, practices that he maintained even after leaving Brazil. After presenting his exhibition at MAM-RJ in 1975, he returned to Europe, where he stayed until the end of 1978, dividing his time between Paris and London. During his stay in Europe, he produced numerous drawings, including a series of posters for a musical in 1977 as well as several photographic series, many registering shop windows. In 1976 he participated in *The Venetian Tools Project*, which was organized by the Swiss Écart Group (cofounded in Geneva by John Armleder, Patrick Lucchini and Claude Rychner) and presented at the 37th Venice Biennale. Also in 1976, he published in the Brazilian magazine *GAM* (issue no. 38) four photographs from the series *Marriage Lunch*, and the following year he was part of the traveling exhibition *Salon Magazine*, presented at the Folkwang Museum in Essen, Germany, and at the t'Venster in Rotterdam.

In 1979 Forman relocated to New York and participated in the audiovisual exhibition *Life Styles—ICA Films* at the ICA Arts Center Cinema, where he presented *Films and Slides of Family and Friends in Brazil*, a selection of images from his series on social rituals. In New York, he dedicated more time to drawing, producing numerous small works of great wit and irony in which subtle word play was matched with surreal imagery. With little interest in the mainstream art system, he sought work in parallel areas. To make a living, he worked as assistant to Fabiano Canosa, then film programmer at the Public Theater, helping him organize his film archive. He also assisted the Museum of Modern Art curator Kynneston McShine on a book about Joseph Cornell, whose collages and assemblages of objects had impacted Forman's work.

The series of drawings made in the final years of his life in New York, a commentary of sorts on his daily activities, address the unstable game between word and image. The drawings are packed with cultural references, and strangely enough, they seem to emerge from the artist's immediate moment. It's as if the frantic New York City, with its excess of information, and the oppressive presence of advertisement, had swept Emil away from a nostalgic Parisian-like atmosphere and dropped him, not without violence, in the actuality of the present.

In terms of art, this *present* means the resurgence of painting in the early 1980s, which with its hedonistic discourse challenged the conceptual rigor and experimental taste of the previous two decades. It also meant, in sociological terms, the rise of the Yuppie generation, which, with its conservative mentality and dubious taste, helped create market value, through capital investments, for the new pictorial production.[14]

In 1983, at age twenty-nine, Forman was found dead of unknown causes at Playhouse by the River, a theater in Pennsylvania. The following year, artists Antonio Manuel and Luiz Ferreira, together with Forman's sister Dora Forman, organized a retrospective of his work at the Museum of Modern Art in Rio. Like most artists of his generation, Forman sought to stay away from the commercial art system that was emerging in Brazil in the 1970s, refusing to sell his works. Perhaps this, coupled with the fact that he had moved out of Brazil shortly after his first solo shows, made his work stand at the margin of our recent art history, little seen by both artists of later generations and researchers and art critics.

Ironically, the topics that he was devoted to and that informed his work such as memory, autobiography, inventories, and inquiries about the nature of the image are gaining more and more attention among today's young generation. This presents a propitious context to bring to the public the formidable production of Emil Forman almost half a century after he first appeared on the scene. Showing his work now would contribute, above all, to make our universe of references more complex and diversified and fundamental for our understanding and critical rereading of artistic production in Brazil in the last decades.

Notes

1 / Jozias Benedicto, "Lembrando Emil Forman," blog post, August 23, 2009, http://joziasbenedicto.blogspot.com.br/2009/08/lembrando-emil-forman.html.

2 / Ileana Pradilla Cerón, *Emil Forman: Inventário* (Recife: Museum of Modern Art Aloisio Magalhães, 2006). Catalog for the exhibition held at Aloisio Magalhães Modern Art Museum, from May 11 to July 9, 2006.

3 / Artist statement published in the exhibition's brochure.

4 / Roberto Pontual, "Bienal de Paris—Brasileiros," in *Jornal do Brasil*, Caderno B, 1, September 18, 1975.

5 / In Antonio Manuel and Luis Ferreira, eds., *Emil Forman: Retrospectiva* (Rio de Janeiro: Funarte, 1984). The publication cataloged the traveling exhibition organized by the Museum of Modern Art of Rio de Janeiro and Espaço Arte Brasileira Contemporânea from September 27 to October 28, 1984. The exhibition was also presented at the Universidade de São Paulo Contemporary Art Museum in São Paulo, from November 5 to December 8, 1984.

6 / For more information on this subject see Fernanda Lopes, *Área experimental: Lugar, espaço e dimensão do experimental na arte brasileira dos anos 1970* (Rio de Janeiro: Figo Editora, 2013).

7 / All quotes from editions of the *MAM Bulletin* published between 1975 and 1976. Original editions available at the Center for Research and Documentation of the Museum of Modern Art of Rio de Janeiro.

8 / Between 1975 and 1978, the *Área experimental* presented works by thirty-four artists and one group exhibition: Emil Forman, Sérgio de Campos Mello, Margareth Maciel, Bia Wouk, Ivens Machado, Cildo Meireles, Gastão de Magalhães, Anna Bella Geiger, Tunga, Paulo Herkenhoff, Carlos Zilio, Mauro Kleiman (two shows), Lygia Pape, Yolanda Freire (two shows), Fernando Cocchiarale, Regina Vater, Waltercio Caldas, Sonia Andrade (two shows), Amelia Toledo, João Ricardo Moderno, Ricardo de Souza, Luiz Alphonsus, Reinaldo Cotia Braga, Jayme Bastian Pinto Junior, Dinah Guimaraens, Reinaldo Leitão, Lauro Cavalcanti, Dimitri Ribeiro, Orlando Mollica and Essila Burello Paraíso, as well as Beatriz and Paulo Emílio Lemos, Murilo Antunes and Biiça, Luis Alberto Sartori, Jorge Helt, and Maurício Andrés who participated in the group exhibition *Audiovisuais mineiros*.

9 / Interview with Waltércio Caldas, in Lopes, *Área experimental*.

10 / Cerón, *Emil Forman: Inventário*, 12–14.

11 / In 1943 Jorge de Lima (1893–1953), a poet from Alagoas, published in Rio de Janeiro *A Pintura em Pânico* (Painting in panic), featuring forty-one photomontages, each accompanied by a sentence or verse. The lack of page numbers allows the reader to freely peruse the sequence in a nonlinear manner. In the preface, poet Murilo Mendes (1901–1975) connects Lima's work to surrealism, particularly to Max Ernst.

12 / Cerón, *Emil Forman: Retrospectiva*, 9–11.

13 / Cerón, 12–14.

14 / Cerón, 12–14.

THE FUNERAL OF BRAZILIAN MODERNISM

11

Glauber Rocha and the Death of Di Cavalcanti

Marcos Augusto Gonçalves

On October 27, 1976, film director Glauber Rocha stormed into the lobby of the Museu de Arte Moderna (MAM) in Rio de Janeiro as an open-casket ceremony was underway to pay homage to Emilio di Cavalcanti, a central player in Brazilian modernism who had died the night before from liver complications. An article in *Jornal do Brasil* describes Rocha breaking into the scene "disheveled in navy blue sports pants, light blue jacket, gingham shirt and brown shoes." Accompanied by photographer Mário Carneiro he approached the coffin and commanded: "One, two, three, four, five, six, seven, eight, nine, ten, eleven, twelve . . . Cut! Now get me a close up on his face."

According to the news coverage published on the following day, Rocha's intervention—"to everyone's shock, and revulsion from family and friends"—would only come to an end one hour and twenty-three minutes later, at the São João Batista Cemetery in the Botafogo neighborhood. Asked by a reporter about his motivation for filming the funeral, Rocha answered that the same way the press was covering the event, he also felt obliged to register it. And who would the audience be? "For no one," he replied. "For the museum to have a documentary of Di Cavalcanti's funeral. It is a documentary. I am not sure if it will work out. It is for myself."

The eighteen-minute film *Di Cavalcanti* was shown to the public for the first time on March 11, 1977, at the MAM Cinémathèque, and it won the Jury Special Prize at the Cannes Festival that same year. In 1979, the painter's daughter Elizabeth Di

Cavalcanti obtained a legal injunction prohibiting any further screenings. The court order is still in place, however innocuous as bootleg copies of the work can be easily screened on YouTube. The documentary starts with a traveling shot of the museum's façade that immediately takes the viewer back to the stifling military era of Brazil in the 1970s under General Ernesto Geisel. Two years prior, the moviemaker had surprised the country's political left by vouching for the "gradual and sure" process of political disengagement promised by Geisel and General Golbery do Couto e Silva, the junta's strategist whom Rocha nominated the "genius of the breed." The question "Is the moviemaker mad?" resonated in the left-leaning intellectual and cultural circles at the time, many answering with "yes," others denying it. To make things worse, his performance at the funeral ceremony for Di Cavalcanti just provided more fodder for the polemics.

By 1976, despite his remarkable role as a formal innovator during the first half of the twentieth century, Di Cavalcanti's work was no longer indicative of the "evolutionary line" of Brazilian modernist movement, which had prompted the careers of Tarsila do Amaral, Heitor Villa-Lobos, Mário de Andrade, and Oswald de Andrade. Bohemian and affable, he had remained an admired figure whose work had grown stale (colorful paintings of mulatto women) amid a new environment ruled by geometric abstraction. His name was often associated with a cultural-political faction known as "national-popular" that had projected itself decades earlier under the ideology of the Communist Party, considered with caution by the younger left because of its conciliatory politics, antiquated codes, and narrow nationalism.

Throughout the 1950s and 1960s, Brazil underwent a cultural revolution of sorts as a constructivist bent in the areas of the visual arts and poetry culminated in the concrete and neo-concrete movements. The architecture and urban planning of Brasilia had become recognized worldwide, and following the international explosion of bossa nova, new talents such as Caetano Veloso and Gilberto Gil were proposing Tropicália. In the area of cinema, a new generation of "marginals" was fast replacing the aesthetics of Rocha's Cinema Novo. Whatever remained in scene from the 1920s wave of modernism, derived more vitally from the ideas and works of Oswald de Andrade, author of the 1928 "Manifesto Antropófago."

After a period of ostracism, in the early 1950s, the São Paulo concrete poets reclaimed Andrade's work and presented it to a younger audience now informed by Tropicália. The Teatro Oficina presentation of Andrade's play *O rei da vela* (The candle king) in 1967, under the direction of José Celso Martinez Corrêa, was a landmark event. Andrade's work also became a point of reference in the work of young *tropicalistas* such as Veloso and Gil, moviemakers such as Julio Bressane and Joaquim Pedro de Andrade, and Hélio Oiticica. In the charged post-1964 cultural landscape, the figures of Oswald de Andrade together with Villa-Lobos and Mário de Andrade represented the energy and dare of early modernism in Brazil, as their works were eagerly debated in academic circles as great cultural treasures of the twentieth century.

The 1922 Week of Modern Art in São Paulo was an event organized by a group of artists, journalists, critics, and polemicists with the full support of the elite's progressive sector who sought to capitalize on the event as a modern *carte de visite* of the city to be presented to the rest of the country. They wished to show São Paulo as a city in the quick process of expansion because of the wealth accumulated by the coffee cycle and its financial, commercial, and industrial ramifications. For although São Paulo's economy was the most powerful engine in the country, Rio de Janeiro, the capital, had over one million inhabitants, double the population of São Paulo, and was seen as the most important intellectual and cultural center. It was in opposition to this hegemony that the São Paulo elite presented themselves as the purveyors of futurism and of the new art of the twentieth century.

In the 1910s, the traditional society of coffee farms—previously developed through slave labor but since the turn of the century a magnet for immigrant workers from Europe—was about to acquire an urban interface. Families from the countryside were moving to the capital where old estates were being replaced by elegant buildings following an eclectic fashion that mixed Swiss chalets with Brittany and Italianate vernaculars. In tandem, the fast-paced rhythm of foreign migration was transforming São Paulo into a new Babel of dialects and idioms.

In contrast to Rio, once the center of the royal court where artistic production was already organized among institutions and with advanced means of dissemination, the cultural ambient in São Paulo still lacked structure and demanded private initiative to come to the scene. That is what happened at the turn of the century. In association with local government, or in its name, the so-called coffee barons dedicated themselves to the creation of educational, scientific and artistic institutions. In this scenario, either directly or indirectly, through private sponsorship, or by state subvention, the "green gold" financed the realization of concerts, exhibitions, and theater productions, besides expanding the movie house circuit. In what relates to the visual arts despite the lack of commercial galleries, premodernist São Paulo kept a relatively active calendar as it relates to production, exhibitions, and active market. Throughout the 1910s, there were over two hundred exhibitions in town. With only one museum in the city, the Pinacoteca do Estado, artists organized exhibitions in commercial shops and the salons of private mansions.

It was in one of these mansions in 1917 that Anita Malfatti, who had spent the last few years studying in Germany and the United States, organized a much talked about exhibition. Titled *Exposição de pintura moderna*, it displayed expressionist-leaning works that Malfatti produced while studying under Lovis Corinth in Berlin and Homer Boss in New York and Maine. The polemic exhibition was nevertheless successful in enticing young São Paulo artists unsatisfied with the traditional, academic character that dominated the local scene.

Born in Rio de Janeiro in 1897, Emiliano Di Cavalcanti was a journalist when he moved to São Paulo in 1917, where he had many family connections. Interested in art, he befriended Malfatti and encouraged her to exhibit her work. Opening to the public in December of that year, Malfatti's exhibition caused quite a stir and paved the way for the city's modernist movement. Five years later, *Semana de arte moderna* would take place at the Theatro Municipal, featuring the work of writers, musicians, architects, painters, and sculptors. Again, Di Cavalcanti played an important role, as it was his idea to organize this "futurist" festival, as the press referred to it. Cavalcanti suggested the idea to Paulo Prado, a cultivated, cosmopolitan man and heir to the state's wealthiest family.

The modernist group, which Malfatti joined shortly after the events of the *Semana*, kept active and prominent until the end of the decade, despite the frequent trips of its members to Paris. With the 1929 Wall Street crisis that impacted the coffee trade, Brazil's standing as a thriving nation would change drastically in the following decade. That was the Getúlio Vargas era, the great populist who, at once a political reactionary and a modernizer in many aspects, became known as the "father of the poor" for his role in implementing labor reforms that protected a fast-growing working class. The 1930s was a period marked by political antagonisms in which social issues with nationalist tinges became apparent in the cultural scene. Among the modernists, there was an emphasis on works devoted to popular culture that depicted the "Brazilian man" in his struggles and aspirations. Particularly in painting, one would notice the influence of Mexican revolutionary art in the work of Di Cavalcanti and Candido Portinari, who in the mid-1950s would contribute two murals for the United Nations headquarters in New York.

In the aftermath of World War II, new artistic developments would culminate in the creative explosion of the 1950s, when a new wave of modernism seems to have picked up where the 1920s avant-garde had left off. The strong focus on form that is predominant in that era was developed in an atmosphere charged by an intense political process. Despite the utopian, egalitarian-leaning spirit that prevailed on the scene, there was disagreement about up to what point our populist heritage, with all its good intentions, should be tolerated. In many areas, there was a proliferation of art inspired by narratives of pronounced nationalist and sentimental character that, echoing clichés of the era, explicitly called for the emancipation of the masses from the grip of capitalism and imperialism. Di Cavalcanti was a sympathizer of this segment, as the debate about "form versus content" progressed and attained more focus after the military coup of 1964.

Glauber Rocha entered the scene in the most original and creative manner, through radically engaging with politics and language. Politically speaking, Rocha was a leftist intellectual, a Third World anti-imperialist thinker motivated by the visionary perspective that Brazil, the only Portuguese-speaking country in the Americas, had the potential to stir a popular and creative revolution that would change the course of world history. Such a project would require specific characteristics related to his own choice of medium, for cinema was not made with a typewriter or canvases and paintbrushes. By definition, cinema is an industrial art that entails complex operations, specialized labor, distribution channels, and marketing strategies structured in a context rigged by Hollywood. The task, as Rocha saw it, was not only to defy Hollywood's industrial and commercial apparatus, but its formal artillery as well; its language patterns that were almost universally accepted as the standard for a "well-made" film. It was not enough for Brazilian cinema to merely copy Hollywood's formal and narrative paradigms, as had been attempted with capitalist investments in São Paulo. Nor was it a matter of redressing its models, in a schematic manner, with recognizable national scenes and "social" plots about local lives. It was not a matter of acclimating Hollywood to the tropics; rather it was a matter of fostering a new cinematographic language and setting up a production structure accessible to the Brazilian reality, which had been politically alienated in the face of the hegemony of American cinema: a herculean—and utopian—task for which Rocha fought systematically and methodically for most of his life. A brief consideration in this regard is clearly stated in his 1968 text "O cinema novo e a aventura da criação" (Cinema Novo and the adventure of creativity):

> By refuting the cinema of imitation and choosing another language, Cinema Novo also contested the easy path of an "other language." This other language, typical of the so-called nationalist arts, is "populism." Reflex of a political attitude very much ours. Like the dictator [*caudilho* in the original], the artist sees himself as the father of the people: the call to order is "let's speak simple things that people can understand." I consider disrespectful to our audiences, as underdeveloped they may be, "to make simple things for simple folks." Firstly, people are not simple. Sick, hungry and illiterate, people are complex. The paternalist artist idealizes simple folks as fabulous individuals that even in misery have their philosophy, and poor folks, all they need is "political consciousness" so that, all of a sudden, they can invert the historical process. This disingenuous concept is most harmful than the art of imitation because the art of imitation justifies the industry of artistic taste with the clear aim of profit. Populist art, on the other hand, justify its baseness as "good consciousness." The populist artist often will say: "I am not an intellectual, I am with the people, my art is beautiful because it communicates etc." But communicates what? Generally speaking, it communicates folks' own alienation. It communicates to people its own illiteracy, its own vulgarity born out of a miserable situation that leads us to face life with contempt.[1]

Counter to this strategy, Rocha's Cinema Novo program proposed a tabula rasa approach (*falar do zero*) and called for a cinema "with a different script, different acting, different image, different rhythm, different poetry." To make all this materially viable would allow audiences to see films "technically imperfect, dramatically dissonant, poetic revolting and politically aggressive" while still "unsure like the very political avant-gardes in Brazil."

The six years that followed the publication of Rocha's text, from 1968 to 1974, represented the most terrifying and somber phase of the military government. While radical factions of the Left embraced armed guerrilla fight, the generals' regime closed in on what they deemed the "enemy within." Political persecution, summary executions, torture, and exiles (official or voluntary) marked the era.

The political and cultural disarticulation, and the advance of a cultural industry of fascist overtones for the masses left few paths open, and alternative (also deemed marginal) strategies became an option for the intellectual and artistic milieu. The era was marked by a certain individualist, while also tribal, irrationalism influenced by the American counterculture with its existential, philosophical, and lysergic incursions. Thus, the Cinema Novo program as well as the movements that had appeared in the last two decades came to an end in a brutal fashion.

In 1971, after releasing *O dragão da maldade contra o santo guerreiro*, Rocha left Brazil in an exile that never came to a lasting end. During those lacerating years, he produced a series of difficult films such as *Cabeças cortadas* (1970) and *O leão de sete cabeças* (1970). By the time of Cavalcanti's death in 1976, Rocha no longer fit the part of the prophet of his own utopias, a problem that was certainly not his to own. Cavalcanti's death said something about the longevity of the very project to which the filmmaker had dedicated his life. Made "for no one," as he suggested to the *Jornal do Brasil* reporter, Rocha's *Di Cavalcanti* can be seen as an allegory of the funeral of Brazilian modernism.

Notes

1 / Interview with Zuenir Ventura, "O Cinema novo e a aventura da criação," in Glauber Rocha, *Revolução do cinema novo* [Revolution of Cinema Novo] (Rio de Janeiro: Alhambra/ Embrafilme, 1981), 100.

III

FAVELA NOH Haroldo de Campos and Hélio Oiticica at the Chelsea Hotel

12

Eduardo Jorge de Oliveira

This essay focuses on the historic meeting between poet, scholar, and translator Haroldo de Campos (1929–2003), one of the founders of the concrete poetry movement in Brazil, and Hélio Oiticica (1937–1980), the visual artist whose work has become fundamental to a thorough understanding of the dynamics in effect in Latin America throughout the 1960s and 1970s. The meeting took place in 1971 at the Chelsea Hotel in Lower Manhattan. Earlier that year, Campos had been lecturing at the University of Texas at Austin, and when he heard that Oiticica was awarded a Guggenheim Fellowship, which allowed the artist to settle in New York City for a longer period of time, Campos extended his trip to New York to meet with Oiticica. Since Campos had booked a room at the Chelsea Hotel, Oiticica seized the opportunity to record their meeting in the famed hotel's lobby in a mix of journalism and performance. Their conversation is one of the most important documents about Brazilian culture produced in the 1970s.

The conversation between these two important Brazilian artist-intellectuals took place over a period of two days, from May 27 to 28, and was later published in issues 3 and 4 of the underground periodical *Flor do Mal* (Flower of evil).[1] Campos and Oiticica explored several shared interests, including poetry, translation, and Japanese Noh theater. They discussed the genesis of Campos's book of poetry *Galaxies* (defined by the poet as a "book of essays"), Oiticica's installation *Tropicália* (described as a "critical museum from the tropics"), and even chatted about *The*

Wall Street Inferno, Joaquim de Sousândrade's groundbreaking poem written in New York circa 1870. Their discussion began with the aesthetics of Noh theater and its ritualistic emphasis on wardrobe, most famously the feather mantle in *Hagoromo*, and then continued with Oiticica's nest (*ninhos*) work and his series of performance capes known as *parangolés*. Their encounter represents a point of intersection between the concrete and neoconcrete movements, often seen as polar opposites: whereas concrete and constructivist artists valorized the rational and the formal, the neoconcrete movement emphasized the sensory, the experiential, that which exceeds form. The relationship between these two orientations, however, is much more complex. The conversation at the Chelsea Hotel between a poet often identified with concretism and an artist commonly associated with neoconcretism allows us to spotlight the differences between these two movements and their approaches to artistic practice and better identify their points of interaction, contact, and transfer. Indeed, because of the format of their meeting—a conversation, which inadvertently allows for improvisation and spontaneity—the exchange appears less between two individuals and more between two styles of thought and practice that interrogate each other.

For context, upon arriving in New York in January 1971, Oiticica started working on a series of texts titled *conglomerado newyorkaises* that he considered an interminable task. Indeed, he never managed to finish these projects, which he hoped would become a book drawn from his experience of living in Manhattan (1971–1977). Organized by Frederico Coelho and César Oiticica Filho, the collected texts were finally published in 2013, and a careful reading of this material confirms the importance of his meeting with Campos in the further development of his artistic vision. For example, in "BODYWISE," written between June and October 1973, Oiticica wrote on the masthead: "for BODYWISE following the excerpt by H. Campos *Hagoromo* (last episode)."[2] The text continues with a collage of fragments from Ezra Pound's translation of *Hagoromo*. In another fragment scribbled on the pages of a notebook (May 28, 1974), Oiticica wrote: "Branco sobre branco/White on white." The manuscript references Kasimir Malevitch, Stéphane Mallarmé, Haroldo de Campos, García Lorca, Joaquim de Sousandrade, and Antonin Artaud. And a reference to Noh theater directly connects the artist to the poet: "I-Haroldo/Haroldo-Noh."[3] These texts document Oiticica's exploration of New York, which assumes a prominent character in his writing.[4]

Throughout the 1950s and 1960s, Campos's work seems to have exerted no influence on Oiticica's creative process. In the early 1970s, however, as Campos was working on *Galáxias*—a work that would become a watershed in Brazilian poetry because of its remarkably neo-baroque swerve—a meeting of the minds was bound to happen. The interview conveys the sense that whatever Oiticica absorbed about *Galáxias* during their conversation would have a decisive effect on his own relationship to writing. If we take into consideration the analyses advanced in *Livro ou livro-me*, Coelho's seminal study of Oiticica's writing, we might indeed imagine that Oiticica's relationship with writing was, in his own way, galactic, expansive, nonlinear; and that, after his meeting with Campos, he also drew on the concept of the "bioscriptural drive" that animates *Galáxias*, taking it to the limits of his life experience.[5]

Both Campos and Oiticica shared an affinity for the baroque legacy in Brazilian culture. Many critics noted the baroque inflection of his poetry when Campos published his first book, *Auto do possesso* (1949), describing it as Babylonian writing. Literary critic Fausto Cunha, for example, described the work as a "poetic mimesis that abuses Babylonian motifs," whereas poet Sérgio Milliet remarked that there was an excess that disturbs the transition of emotional power, something he found formally pleasing. In view of that auspicious beginning, one is not entirely surprised to realize that the fifty texts that compose the *Galáxias* constitute a baroque and Babylonian operation par excellence. The same can be said of Oiticica's experiments with writing and his pursuit of excess, mixing Portuguese and English and also incorporating French and Spanish words. "Barnbilônia," for example, a text that is in dialogue with Lorca's poetry while also establishing a dialogue with poetry and rock: "rimbaud-hendrix." Indeed, their mutual interest in Noh theater provided them with a springboard for discussing their common interest in Babylonian and baroque forms.

THE A-SIDE

Campos and Oiticica's conversation starts with a discussion of the Japanese Noh play *Hagoromo* (*The Feather Mantle*),[6] which Campos had translated into Portuguese based on the English translation by Ernest Fenollosa and Ezra Pound, in *"Noh" or Accomplishment: A Study of the Classical Stage of Japan* (1916).[7] Campos mentions a specific image from *Hagoromo* in connection with something he had seen when leaving Oiticica's New York studio: the feather mantle. This image represents the formal link between the importance of wardrobe in Noh plays and Oiticica's *parangolés*, ritualistic cloaks designed for samba dancers that accentuate the rhythms of their movements. In the *Hagoromo*, an angel-woman leaves her feather mantle on a tree where a fisherman finds it and will only return it if she performs the "moon dance." When she gets her mantle back, she returns to the clouds. The ending of *Hagoromo*, the juxtaposition of white (the cloak) on white (the clouds),[8] reminds Campos of the work of Russian suprematist artist Kazimir

On the following pages:

Haroldo de Campos, "Heliotapes" 1, *Flor do Mal*, no. 3.

Haroldo de Campos, "Heliotapes" 2, Flor do Mal, no. 4.

HELIOTAPES

Transcrição: entrevista gravada em Heliotapes: Haroldo de Campos: New York, Chelsea Hotel, May 27/28 1971.

Side A: May 27: 1 10 PM: haroldo de campos acaba de chegar de austin, texas: já vimos hoje dois filmes no new yorker. júlio bressane: haroldo — "eu quero lhe dizer o seguinte: primeiro eu queria aproveitar, nós estávamos falando agora disso, eu estava pensando naquela coisa que nós vimos no seu ateliê noutro dia, os ninhos, eu saí de lá e comecei a pensar numa série de coisas que me interessavam nesse mesmo tipo de idéia sua, e eu estava me lembrando de uma peça do teatro japonês nô, **hagoromo** (o manto de plumas), que é uma das peças que o ezra pound traduziu para o inglês, uma peça curta, lindíssima, e onde justamente a coisa que é o centro da peça é êste manto de plumas que ao mesmo tempo tem uma côr lindíssima e tem uma fragrância, um perfume maravilhoso que naquela altura já é um problema de sinestesia, de correspondência de sons, de côres e êste manto estava largado em cima de uma árvore, o anjo viu que êste manto estava espairecendo e deixou em cima da árvore descuidadamente, o pescador viu o manto, sentiu o aroma, o aroma do brilho, e apanhou o manto e obrigou o anjo, como preço para obter o manto, sem o qual o anjo não poderia voltar ao céu, a dançar para êle a dança da lua que é uma dança belíssima, que traria a felicidade; o anjo coagido, porque êle não queria dançar, dançar, essa dança que não era para isso, como êste manto maravilhoso, e então o pescador com o cumprir da dança, e o manto, êle é branco e vai flutuando no espaço, e se dissolve no céu do céu; justamente o problema do ninho, onde você usou determinados elementos luminosos, brancos, nos brancos mais brancos, você conseguiu assim algo de jôgo do visível e não visível, constante, é uma espécie assim de ninho dentro do céu do céu; então eu achava que havia uma relação, e por isso é que lhe dou e vou ler pra você esta tradução que eu fiz, que é uma tradução do fragmento final, que não fica traduzido de uma determinada maneira, traduzem discursivamente e procuram preencher os buracos da língua tão reduzida que é a linguagem dessa peça, com explicações discursivas, porque o ocidental não resiste à linguagem sintética; mas eu fiz uma tradução hiperpoundiana, superpoundiana, que é assim:

HAGOROMO (O MANTO DE PLUMAS, Peça NÔ)
fragmento final

Muitos são os jogos do Nascente
Muitos são os júbilos do Nascente
Quem se chama Pessoa do Palácio
/da Lua
Na décima-quinta noite culmina:
Plenilúnio
Plenitude
Perfeição
Cumpriram-se os votos circulares:
Espada e alabarda guardam o país
O tesouro das sete benesses
Chove
Profuso
Na terra
Passa-se agora o tempo:
O celeste manto de plumas está no
/vento
Sôbre o pinheiral de Miho
Sôbre as Ilhas Balouçantes
Sôbre o monte Ashitaka
Sôbre o pico do Fuji
flutua
Excelso
Dissolvido no céu do céu
Esfuma-se na névoa
E a vista o perde

hélio — "eu tava agora perguntando a haroldo sôbre o problema de tropicália; bem, eu sempre cito, você sabe, tanto em cartas como em artigos, conferências e tudo êsse negócio que nós conversávamos muito em belém, que você sempre dizia, uma coisa importantíssima, que tropicália não era tropicalismo, e eu acho que na realidade o que acabou sendo foi mais tropicalismo que tropicália; agora, de repente eu senti assim uma necessidade de usar a palavra tropicália outra vez, que eu acho que ela está revestida outra vez de uma pureza, estranha, assim; ela não está carregada assim dessa coisa dissolvente que aconteceu, que a meu ver a idéia de tropicalismo já estaria não só a priori carregada disso, como agora está realmente insuportável de se ouvir, que é que você acha dessa coisa: você acha que eu devo usar tropicália ainda, como meio de informação":

haroldo — "eu acho que no seu trabalho inclusive, essa idéia de tropicália já vem de bastante tempo, está ligada à idéia de labirintos e uma série de experiência suas, e essa coisa do ismo é uma coisa que se passa sempre, tôda vez que os críticos mais conservadores, os artistas que não têem o mesmo, não tentam fazer uma contínua invenção, êles procuram acrescentar a palavra ismo tôda vez que se faz uma coisa nova dentro da arte, porque essa palavra ismo é uma maneira de etiquetar e transformar a coisa em objeto de museu e permitir que não se fale mais do assunto; assim tropicalismo é uma coisa que já está inventada, já tem um ismo, pertence aos dicionários dos ismos, e então permite um campo aberto a tôdas as diluições, é uma maneira com que a própria, o próprio establishment acadêmico reage contra a invenção procurando neutralizá-la através do ismo; nós, por exemplo, nunca aceitamos a idéia de "concretismo"; para nós era a **poesia concreta;** o que nos interessava não era um ismo, mas a idéia da concreção da linguagem, a linguagem como material concreto de trabalho é isso que pra mim, por exemplo, dante é um poeta concreto, é assim pala para muitos poetas concretos internacionais que ficam estupefatos, que pensam que a poesia concreta é um determinado momento; não é, é uma atitude total diante da literatura; o que interessa num poema concreto é a concreção da linguagem, a velha linguagem como material, e a palavra concreto veio disso mesmo, uma concreção da linguagem, visual, sonora e semântica."

hélio — "como surrealismo, por exemplo, é muito melhor usar o têrmo surreal."

haroldo — "Surreal"; agora, hélio, na tropicália eu acho que existe inclusive, um elemento interessante, há uma coisa brasileira mas sem ser provinciana; tropicália dá assim uma idéia de uma coleção de coisas dos trópicos, mas vista de um ponto de vista assim como um **museu crítico do trópico,** museu vivo, né; e um antimuseu também; tropicália tem uma idéia de parafernália; tropicália é uma palavra que termina em **ália** (risos); isso é muito interessante: ao que parece, dá uma impressão de que como tal é válido; embora que o tropicalismo já é uma etiquêta, coisa que nada tem a ver com a idéia de tropicália; o melhor que você fazia, neo-canibalismo oswaldiano, uma verificação crítica do museu brasileiro, isso é que é tropicália; isso não temos aqui."

hélio — "é, isso é importante; no contexto internacional, o importante é informar; é muito fácil; eu senti que havia uma facilidade incrível informar o que fôsse tropicália, de imediato; no brasil acabaram por transformar assim, numa coisa folclórica; folclore de tropicalismo que é uma coisa insuportável."

haroldo — "como é insuportável todo tipo de diluição, né; mas é inevitável, também; é inevitável; há certo momento em que a gente encontra no cubismo, um momento em que há uma série de diluições do cubismo, o que não interessa mais; e assim por diante: surrealismo."

. . . .

(mesmo dia depois do almôço, mesmo lugar)

haroldo — "eu quero dizer aqui uma coisa pro hélio, sôbre o trabalho que estou fazendo há alguns anos, desde 63, e cuja primeira parte já foi publicada, na revista invenção nos números 4 e 5, 64/65, que tem êsse título, **livro de ensaios: galáxias,** e que é um texto que está previsto, em elaboração, que eu já tenho umas 50 páginas escritas, e cada página pra ser lida, numa audição que farei oportunamente, vou fazer um projeto gráfico, e você então recebe aquelas páginas como estão ligadas, juntas, não é um livro comum, mas elas estão juntas e organizadas de uma certa maneira e o leitor pode começar a leitura do ponto que queira, pode ler o pedaço que quer, e cada página tem uma vértebra semântica, que é a idéia da viagem, que no livro diriam-se viagens, e em tôrno disso se constelam exemplos da vida cotidiana, coisa lida, fragmentos de leitura, em total liberdade; é um trabalho muito constante, muito intenso sôbre o problema da linguagem; cada palavra do texto é trabalhada assim, do ponto de vista sonoro, do entrechoque de sons, da paródia, do uso de vários idiomas, lentamente trabalhado, de modo que cada página dessas equivale a um verdadeiro poema; e justamente tenho aqui um fragmento que está inédito, meu, que escrevi em 69, e que tem a ver com o problema do manto de plumas do **hagoromo;** eu quero então ler um dos fragmentos que eu quero inclusive dedicar ao hélio, que parece que tem uma relação com o trabalho dêle:

tudo isto tem que ver com um suplício chinês que revesa seus quadros em disposições geométricas pode não parecer mas cada palavra pratica uma acupunctura com agulhas de prata especialmente afiladas e que penetram um preciso ponto nesse tecido conjuntivo quando se lê não se tem a impressão dessa ordem regendo a subcutânea presença das agulhas mas ela existe e estabelece um sistema simpático de linfas ninfas que se querem perpetuar por um simples contágio de significantes essa torsão de significados no instante êsse deslizamento de superfícies fônicas que por mínimos desvão criam figuras de rociado rosicler et volucres veneris mea turba columbae mas é também um suplício chinês a vítima entre lâminas eróticas que cortam sem cortar tão finas como plumas passando entre rodízios tinguunt gorgoneo de vento o sangue não aflora contido em capilares prêso sem paredes venosas cuja textura punica rostra lacu não foi afetada ou foi mas se mantém tacta e intangida intangida depois um impulso um sôpro um alento um descolar de coluna de ar e a cabeça rola rompido seu instável equilíbrio por uma exígüa navalha de éter mas é você lapso e relapso você quem move os gonzos dêsse acaso os ábacos dêsse jôgo de avelórios um homem-pena como diria summes juice me poenitet hopluma êle está sentado ratoneiro de ratoletras e não se menos de seu estêrco dourado uma sopa de letrias que baba como bulha-à-beça alhos migalhas bugalhos o argueiro ôlho alheio a trave no ôlho nosso a carocha o caroço o osso o caruncho tudo isso e mais chicória alfavaca alperche alquequenje alitis aliter fervem nesse caldo de nostrademo futurando o postrêmio assim quando êle tem cólica de rins vai-se ver e é uma cólica de runas uma melancólica de belasletras deletreadas em tritos detritos a ourina pelos ureteres calcificou em calcário de ur e pelos cânulos ouripingou um ouro-pigmento mais venimoso que sulfurgueto de armêni vademecum vaderetro sassafrásio êle esta personagem no grata tendo o livro por menagem se compraz em crisoprásio atende pelo vulgo de bocadouro e pelo invulgo de crisóstomo enquanto excreta crispando-se seus crisditos crisográficos ninguém se espante porém com tais crocidismos crocodilares quando estiver deveras extremungido e limpo de letras e lastros vai fazer o morto mudo e mouco feito um ôco então nostrademo cacofante descriptará os renogramas pétreos cacata carta na frase de catúlio bat-face e se ouvirá o seu testamento acolhido por uma palma de salvas fiat jus era uma vez o entremez do último céu que vem a ser o céu do céu caem êsses fios de luz que se prendem entre o visível e o invisível poderia ser hagoromo o manto de penas urdindo-se da luz dançado pelo anjo ou um vento que deixasse congelar suas arestas seus vértices seus vórtices em profilaturas provocadas por um desgarre súbito de pontos migratórios depois não se vê mais nada porque a vista pára num poro entre visto e invisto onde o visível gesto vai daí a cabeça rompido o equilíbrio descabeça e cai.

1

HELIOTAPES ②

Haroldo — "Êsse é um fragmento justamente das **galáxias**, no qual eu vejo uma carta-relação, em tôrno da linguagem, com um tipo de visão que eu encontro nos trabalhos do Hélio; é uma busca de alguma coisa, de alguma coisa "entre", de uma coisa que fica entre o visível e o invisível, alguma coisa que fica "entre", não é isso nem aquilo, está entre os dois, né".

Hélio — "É, isso eu sinto muito em relação a tôdas as coisas, como se fôssem as coisas assim pelas frestas, pelos perfis".

Haroldo — "Pelos perfis? Sim, muito bonito".

Hélio — "Meu trabalho tem muito isso".

Haroldo — "Frestas; são frestas".

Hélio — "Sabe o que estou fazendo? Estou anotando aqui pra saber as coisas: que dia, que hora; que horas são agora"?

Haroldo — "São 3 horas".

Hélio — "Você sabe, tinha um negócio que eu estava lhe querendo falar; se lembra que no **Inferno de Wall Street** tem um negócio que diz assim: "Templo de Kun, 666" que era difícil de descobrir; olha, eu sei o que existia, qual era a parte de Nova Iorque; você sabe que o 666 que existe agora é um dos edifícios mais famosos; na época êsse edifício não existia, mas o lugar já devia existir, que é 5ª avenida com a rua 53, é chamado "top of the sixes", que é 666, 5ª avenida; chama-se Tishman Building, mas é mais conhecido como 666; tenho impressão que anteriormente deveria existir ali, alguma coisa assim como um clube de **businessmen** que agora se chama 666 ou "top of the sixes", apesar do edifício ter outro nome; quer dizer, ficou um apelido que havia; então eu estava pensando em consultar uma amiga minha, Dore Ashton, crítica de arte, que escreveu um livro sôbre Nova Iorque, e fêz uma pesquisa enorme, e eu tinha pensado em uma consulta sôbre isso; ela tem uma bibliografia enorme sôbre Nova Iorque; o que existiria nessa época naquele lugar, entende"?

Haroldo — "Êsse número, 666, faz lembrar da bêsta do apocalipse, né, tem uma ligação, mas deve ter uma referência concreta, como êle faz constantemente, com palavras e tudo; êle pega o "urso", que na bôlsa significa invasão da bôlsa, aquêle sujeito que vende a série de bilhetes antes de ter ganho, o "urso", que era o especulador, êle usa o urso como símbolo da constelação das ursas. Como símbolo de Nova Iorque, etc., em vários sentidos; tenho a impressão que você pode ter razão".

Hélio — "Agora, o que eu não sei é se aquela parte, na rua 53 onde tem o Museu de Arte Moderna, não sei, mas já deveria existir alguma coisa lá".

Haroldo — "Êle fala na 5ª avenida tôda hora, né".

Hélio — "5ª avenida começa da Washigton Square pra cima; a região de Wall St. existia antes, mas isso era muito antes; por ali não existia nada, era muito antes; por ali não existia nada, era um alagadiço, depois é que . . .; sabe, quando no museu eu estava fazendo os ninhos, alguém falou assim: é logo ali, no 666, eu disse: six, six, six, então é Sousândrade, foi aí que eu pesquei".

Haroldo — "É bem provável, bem provável".

Hélio — "Então disseram, aquêle edifício é chamado "ton of the sixes!" é um edifício enorme, nôvo, deve ter sido construído depois dos anos 40; de modo que eu queria saber o que é que existia antes naquele lugar.

Haroldo — "Isso é interessante, fazer essa pesquisa; o que me mostra isso, é que a pessoa vive em Nova Iorque, o Sousândrade é um poeta que quase significa assim algo que vive; eu me lembro que quando visitei a Itália pela primeira vez, eu ia à cidade e via os cantos de Ezra Pound nas coisas, na vida, na Tôrre de Pisa; justamente isso em Nova Iorque sente-se a presença de Sousândrade, inclusive no estilo montagem, porque Nova Iorque é a cidade da montagem".

Hélio — "É; sabe de uma outra coisa, p. ex, tem uma hora que êle fala **pear-soap**, não é **pear** (pêra; pronúncia "pér") mas **pear** (pronúncia "pier"), que é uma marca de sabão".

Haroldo — "É um sabão de pêra".

Hélio — 'Mas não é: é um sabão que parece phebo; é um sabão marrom transparente que antigamente usavam pra lavar roupa, êle relaciona isso com **washing-women** (lavadeiras) ou uma coias assim; então achei engraçado isso, pois talvez se relacionasse com pêra, mas talvez fôsse com **pear**, que é inclusive um nome judaico".

Haroldo — "É muito provável".

Hélio — "Êsse sabão vende muito no Village; tem assim um floreado, como sabão antigo brasileiro".

Haroldo — "Tem um outro nome que aparece lá, que uma amiga aqui em Nova Iorque me elucidou, que é mais ou menos nesse sentido: **liederkranz**, que nós não sabíamos o que que era, e ela vivia passando por uma mercearia e viu um queijo que tem a marca "liederkranz", que é dos mais antigos que êles faziam, e cuja fábrica era de uma família das mais antigas de Nova Iorque; de modo que quando êle falava em "liederkranz", êle se referia àquela família, ou ao tipo de queijo".

Hélio — "O que pròvàvelmente era às duas coisas".

Haroldo — "Eu vi a marca, tôda floreada; marca de queijo".

Hélio — "O que pròvàvelmente era as duas coisas".

Haroldo — "Eu vi a marca, tôda floreada; marca de queijo".

Hélio — "Por isso é que quando vi, êle dizia **washing-women**, nem **pear-soap** pode tirar a marca do dólar, pensei nisso".

Haroldo — "O problema do Sousândrade muito importante (e nesse particular êle foi um antecipador da poesia moderna): da técnica de montagem do Pound, e até do próprio Mallarmé, que dizia que via num jornal cotidiano, que a maioria dos enciclopédicos devem ter ali o grande livro dêles; o Sousândrade quando escreveu **O Guesa**, a sessão justamente de **Wall St.**, êle se inspirava no dia; fantástico, êle dizia: "estou escrevendo êste capítulo sob a impressão que causam os jornais de Nova Iorque"; os acontecimentos não eram uma coisa arbitrária, êle próprio sabia o que estava fazendo; e êle fêz um processo elementar; Rainha Vitória, a vinda de Pedro II aos Estados Unidos, o que êle via em jornais: as notícias, de um determinado crime acontecido no parque, êle tirava com citações dos acontecimentos da época, e as envolvia em citações históricas, mitológicas; é o processo com que aparecem as notícias nesse mosaico constelar que é um jornal moderno; o maior exemplo de poema surrealista é o jornal moderno; os jornais numa banca de jornal, uma loucura! A grande modernidade de Sousândrade é que êle sentia essa sintaxe de linguagem em 1870. **O Inferno de Wall St.** é tão moderno que não parece um poema, parece uma visão; o cotidiano é aí tão fantástico que não precisa inventar nada; ao expor o cotidiano em têrmos de poesia, a genialidade dêle foi compreender a sintaxe dêsse cotidiano, na época do romantismo brasileiro, onde os poetas escreviam peças retóricas, oratórias, a linguagem dêle era ininteligível para os mesmos, signo nôvo".

Hélio — "No contexto internacional, êle fazia coisas que ninguém havia feito".

Haroldo — "Mallarmé escreveu o **Lance de Dados**, em que êle se inspirou na partitura e na disposição tipográfica dos jornais, 20 anos depois da sessão de **Wall St.**, 1897".

Hélio — "Mallarmé tem uma coisa: é assim como se fôsse a culminância de um processo clássico de criação; êle foi chegando a uma coisa, num processo diferente: Sousândrade é como se fôsse uma explosão, como você diz".

Haroldo — "Sousândrade é brutal, fantástico; Mallarmé é um intelectual, como Débussy em música; Sousândrade é como música americana de John Cage, montagem brutal de pedaços macro-crus da realidade".

Hélio — "Pensando também em Godard, e a relação com experiências como as de Julinho Bressane, Godard fica assim como a culminância de um refinamento intelectual, no que difere muito de coisa que acontecem no Brasil, que são como se fôssem descobertas pela primeira vez: ao passo que em coisas européias, há culminância de processos, é diferente".

Haroldo — "É; eu acho muito boa nesse particular uma coisa do Décio (Pignatari) sôbre a poesia do Oswald (de Andrade), quando diz que a poesia do Oswald é uma poesia da posse contra a propriedade", que a poesia tem contacto direto; passo que o europeu é uma poesia do decantamento de tôda uma tradição; a poesia do brasileiro é uma apropriação total da poesia num contacto direto por processos relativos diretos; daí a importância do conceito de **antropofagia** em têrmos culturais: uma devoração cultural, uma maneira de devorar os outros valôres, mas do ponto de vista de uma cultura brasileira; isso é que é importante: modificando as relações: dando uma nova ordem nas coisas; isso é muito importante, isto é, não é uma transposição, mas uma renovação das ligações; como dizia o Oswald na prosa dêle **Sócrates e Tarzan e Odaliscas do Catumbi**, são tipos de revelação que são feitos num contexto que é completamente diferente do contexto europeu".

Hélio — "Nós falávamos no carro sôbre o programa de televisão do Chacrinha; quer dizer, quando você compara a tv brasileira com a americana, em programas de auditório, em grandes **shows**, o Chacrinha é o grande palhaço da televisão, é o sujeito que levou a idéia de circo para a televisão, e isso tudo nasceu de um programa de rádio dêle, que êle sòzinho fazia: a discoteca do Chacrinha; êle tinha uma versatilidade, a ausência de meios o obrigava a inventar tudo; então quando mudaram para a televisão, êle percebe que a televisão é uma linguagem de fragmento; é o que se chama tècnicamente uma **linguagem metonímica**, isto é, a parte pelo todo; então êle usa um **dial** de telefone, como fantasia dêle, êle usa o gesto, não é? O gesto como indicador de todo um processo; por isso o Chacrinha tem uma inteligência de **media**; êle compreendeu a televisão e levou a idéia de circo, que era admirada pelo Oswald, pelo Maiacovsky, uma coisa que para arte moderna tem uma enorme importância, a idéia do circo, não apenas como inspiração mas como momentos de improvisação e impressão; pode-se ver como, nas memórias de Maiacovsky e Oswald, o circo como adoração infantil, foi poderoso na arte dêles; o Chacrinha tem essa inteligência, pegando o **media** de televisão, que é fragmentário, levando o circo para a televisão; e fazendo uma arte de vanguarda assim num nível de cultura popular; uma espécie de **brutalismo de vanguarda**; nêle não há primitivismo, que é ingenuidade, mas um brutalismo, uma utilização constante e brutal do meio".

Hélio — "Nesse sentido, as coisas feitas no Brasil, já têm um caráter **a priori underground**, no sentido em que o **underground** americano quer contrapor-se à cultura profissionalizada; foi uma coisa que nasceu para demolir o que Hollywood era: profissionalismo condicionado ao gôsto do consumo; de repente foi preciso aparecer o **underground**, para outra vez as pessoas fazerem as coisas mais livres; por isso não tem sentido dizer **underground** brasileiro, pois em relação à cultura de consumo americano-européia, a coisa já é automàticamente, aqui, **underground.**

Malevich. In his own work, Campos also pursues white, but of another nature, one that eschews references to suprematism. For Campos, the translator-poet struggles between two kinds of *white* and ends up developing one that cannot be considered as pure color but rather evokes the body and its fluids, which are viscous or sperm-like. Even the white of the paper is described as losing its purity: the "carcass-paper smells of bone white" ("*papel-carcaça fede-branco osso*"),[9] as he wrote in *Galáxias*. Campos sees this chromatic impurity at work in Oiticica's *parangolés*, which he thereby differentiates from the Noh play he had first compared them to.

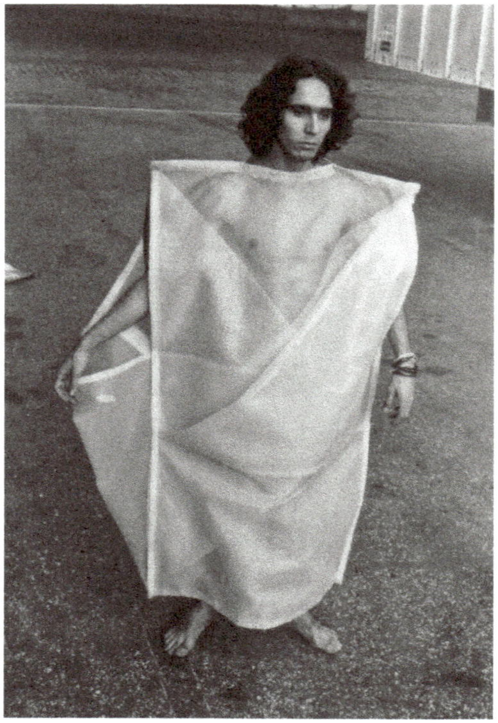

Fernando Luis Guimarães wearing Hélio Oiticica's *Parangolé Cape 23*, M'Way Ke, New York, 1972. Photograph by Hélio Oiticica. Courtesy Projeto HO.

The question of impure color would become important in Campos's *Galáxias*, which was in gestation around the time of the Chelsea meeting. As diverse passages in the book demonstrate, colors convey the various states of decomposition of matter, be that of the body, places, or objects. Indeed, chromatic stimuli in *Galáxias* are very important, producing not only synesthesia, far from Baudelairean correspondences, but also the symptoms of the sick body. For example, the most recurrent color in *Galáxias* is yellow, the yellow of bile and urine, denoting how Campos corrupts the purity of yellow as a pigment.

Having subverted the abstract *whiteness* of suprematism, Campos will then start a movement in the reverse direction, in a manner similar to Oiticica's *parangolés*, in which he takes the impure colors of Oiticica's work as a point of departure to elevate color but without any suprematist aspirations. Indeed, in his subsequent work, the nature of yellow becomes not so much the color of sickness but of the sun. This is the case in the 1985 poem he dedicated to Oiticica, entitled "Parafernália para Hélio Oiticica" ("Paraphernalia for Hélio Oiticica"):

1.
reticles
nets unnets
reticulairs airs areas
snares resnares nets
areas
reticulairs
reticularia
necklaces of small squares
beads cubicles
areas airs
snares resnares
disarticularia
of real areas
the face implodes
kaleidoscopichamelon

2.
yellow
the bellow of yellow
red
the reflections of red
green
the resonance of green
blue
the nudes of blue
the meadows of yellow
the roads of red
the schemes of green
the nude zulus of blue
the white elephants of white

3.
helios, the sun, does not exceed

4.
(cinetheater noh: piscoset-designed by sousândrade
                    with ideogramic script by eisenstein):
        where you read *Hagoromo*, read instead parangolé
        where you see mount fuji, see instead hillside of mangueira
              the parangonome
                          pluriplumes
heliexcels
helliphant
cellucinary
until
dissolskying itself
in the sky
of skies

5.
helio mounts the zeppelin of colors
powered by parangol'helium
and dissolves in the sky's sun[10]

In the poem, Campos describes the artist experiencing different colors until eventually disappearing into the sun (helios is a play on Oiticica's first name). Oiticica here seems to occupy the place of the angel-woman who ascends into the sky in *Hagoromo*, but in Campos's formulation this ascension no longer operates in order to affirm total power but rather serves to make the individual disappear, becoming color itself.

Campos's poem also registers Oiticica moving away from painting and representation and his growing investment in a corporal and spatial experience of color. Indeed, this poem describes with remarkable precision the experience of color in Oiticica's work, in which light acts to create and dissolve color. Oiticica's approach to body and space led him not only to create wearable artworks (the *parangolés*) but also to rethink how we inhabit space on different levels. Even though the *parangolés* can be seen as new forms of clothing, it is the dance to be performed while wearing these clothes that truly matters.[11] On another level, however, Oiticica also developed architectural follies (the *penetráveis* [penetrables]) inspired by vernacular forms such as we find in the favelas. While these works can be seen as praising the do-it-yourself spirit of survival necessary to live in the hills around Rio, they also seem to explore the liminal space that the favela marks between the urban and the rural.

At some point in their conversation, Oiticica confesses his disappointment with how his idea of *Tropicália* (an installation he developed in 1967) had been diluted by a group of musicians who appropriated the term to promote a pop movement named Tropicalism. Nevertheless, Campos argues that the term *Tropicália* remains a useful critical tool, and merits development in and of itself. He suggests that the term *Tropicália* be used instead of Tropicalism, because the suffix (*-ism*) transforms the term into a dictionary form to be catalogued by encyclopedias, universities, and museums. By dropping the suffix, *Tropicália* sides with spaces outside institutions. Their discussion about *Tropicália* is extremely relevant as it leads Campos to imagine environments in terms of mazes, places that might constitute a "critical museum of the tropics," a "live museum" or even an "anti-museum."[12] He also says the term *Tropicália* better renders the idea of "paraphernalia."

After their discussion of *Tropicália*, Campos brings up his work on *Galáxias*, a project he sees as the result of a number of positions he had adopted concerning language, poetry, and art more generally. In his opinion, after Joyce, epic poetry is no longer possible. Epiphanies are the only ones that can now be used.[13] The notion of epiphany allows Campos to overcome the opposition between prose and poetry, a subject gleaned from his close readings of Mallarmé's *Un coup de dés*, which he had translated. In *Galáxias*, he also abandoned the subject of poetry in order to take writing as the subject itself. Another motif that he stakes in *Galáxias* is the importance of travels. He takes this idea from Goethe's notion of *Bildung*. In German, the term means "education" and "formation." It is a key term in Campos's vocabulary, as we find discussions about form in movement in his work which is always in progress.

In their conversation, Campos provides an outline of his process in *Galáxias*: (1) the creation of paratactic constellations of daily life events; (2) exploring sounds produced when different words are brought together in order to create new effects; (3) parody; and (4) the deliberate use of other languages, such as German, Italian, French, and English, in addition to Portuguese. These strategies, explored in *Galáxias*, are still being used by poets today,[14] and we can see them in use in this reference to the *Hagoromo* image of the feather mantle in fragment 41: "the erotic blades that cut without cutting, thin as feathers." In this line, a tension is created between two different materials: a blade and a feather. In fact, the text begins with references to needles and blades before the cut to the feather. Puncturing occurs on two levels: the text describes needles and blades which cut the skin like the Chinese martyr's, an operation that is also performed by the text, which cuts and pierces the words used. Campos reads this fragment aloud to Oiticica and mentions he would dedicate it to him, but he did not; the poem he actually dedicated to Hélio was "Paraphernalia to Hélio Oiticica." The tape's A-side ends with Campos reading fragment 41.

INTERLUDE: EPIPHANY AS METHOD IN *GALÁXIAS*

Galáxias is a book of fifty fragments (or formants) written between 1963 and 1976 and published in its entirety in 1984. Some fragments were published previously in journals and magazines and a small selection was included in Campos's 1976 anthology *Xadrez de Estrelas: Percurso Textual*, 1949–1974 (Star Chess: Textual Pathway). In a statement about the book's innovative mixing of prose and poetry, Campos affirmed: "I wanted to experiment with poetic form, to abolish the limits between poetry and prose, to make it more porous, not exactly in the epic (narrative) sense but in the sense of an epiphany (a vision). In what relates to the microstructure of each of the fifty galactic texts, I made use of composition techniques such as paronomasia, permutation, phonic proliferations, proper of concrete poetry."[15] From that ensues that concrete poetry ought to be considered as the prescription of techniques for the renewal of poetry, criticism, and translation. Campos himself seized that moment in which concrete poetry inserted itself in Brazilian literary history to push the boundaries with his *Galáxias* despite the fact that it was only published as a whole after the heroic phase of concretism. With *Galáxias*, Campos complicated the legacy of concrete poetry by adopting procedures such as the use of "formants," a term borrowed from the composer and conductor Pierre Boulez that indicates the linguistic and acoustic tonic sound of each word (also understood as a semantic vertebra around which words align in an autonomous process). Through paronomasia, Campos creates simultaneously a flow and friction between each separate word (each word a *vertebra*), and yet, through this friction, the poet recreates a flow (the text as a *spinal column*). Campos defines this flow as "bioscriptural drive in galactic expansion," made possible by *action writing*, which allows the poem to abandon historical poetic conventions, be they epic poetry or epiphanies. In contrast, *action writing* organizes images of daily life into immanent constellations.[16]

After the first page, which weaves various endorsements together like a map, comes the title page, followed by a frontispiece that features a line from Mallarmé: *La fiction affleura et se dissipera, vite, d'après la mobilité de l'écrit* (Fiction will brush up and dissolve, quickly, following writing's mobility). Likewise, in *Galáxias*, the "fictus," the "fingere" ("pretense") of poetry loses its allegorical, mythical, and even imaginary quality, transforming writing into an approximation of the "real," in the Lacanian sense of the term, that is, the unattainable that gives writing its energy in movement. Writing therefore leaps from one kind of meaningfulness to another, scrutinizing its objects, emptying them of meaning until the "concretion" of language acquires another status, one that allows language to accompany the real. What is at stake here is the *Prägnanz*, the meaningfulness (or significance) of a sign. It is from this perspective that the poet calls *Galáxias* a "book of essays"— the poem solicits historical, circumstantial forms, while the essay uses the poetic imagination, critically participating in the real or in the writing of the real. In this sense, his analysis of Sousândrade may be applied to all the formants of *Galáxias*: "After the denotative function is atomized, minimized and crumbled, all happens now in the region of the meanings, in whose chain, as Lacan said, the sense insists, although none of its elements consist in the sense of what it is capable of in the given moment."[17] Indeed, the effect of bioscriptural drive is to break with the "*fingere*" (pretense). Fiction loses its referentiality and writing occupies, in turn, a space cut off from subject and object, a space in which generic distinctions no longer hold. In other words, *Galáxias* has no subject and it is not a book of poetry. Rather "the whole book is an essay book of book trials . . . the grasping story doesn't eat me doesn't consume me doesn't bell jar me."[18] Fiction disappears, and even the notions of the "book" and of "travel," which might seem at first glance to be the possible themes, dissolve into necessary, pulsating forces, in order to obtain the plasticity of writing that so amazes Oiticica.

Oiticica nevertheless finds this plasticity of consciousness linked to historical knowledge in Campos's writing, because there's a history of art in the poet's work, albeit of a very singular kind. His way of telling art history is marked by anecdotes and recycled signifiers in order to invest these artistic references with particular meanings. In *Galáxias*, we find Cranach's Lucrecia's dagger in fragment 6, the anonymous graffiti of Pompeii appears in fragment 11, Giacometti and Etruscan art figure in fragment 14, Brancusi and the infinite column in fragment 21, Yves Klein's anthropophagy in fragment 30, and Monet's water lilies in fragment 39, to mention only the most obvious references. These references are allusive, there is no ekphrasis, and the connotations of the art works' titles or motifs are foregrounded. For instance, Lucrecia's dagger is doubled up by a brief news story that refers to the death of a young Brazilian prostitute that made the headlines of a Geneva newspaper. This doubling effect gives the fragment a real sense of the *quotidian* ("daily coitus"), denoting the fact that anecdotes construct a very sensual galaxy of art history.

This sensual galaxy also has aspects of parody. Campos develops his conception of parody as a parallel chant (from the Greek *pára odé*) in *Deus e o Diabo no Fausto de Goethe* ("God and the Devil in Goethe's Faust"). Hence his use of anecdotes, and various versions of stories: the more they proliferate the less a story is fixed. In *Galáxias*, a group of anecdotes mixes well-known historical figures with unknown folk artists. Thus we find Schiller's joke on the word *red*, taken from Hölderlin's translation of Sophocles's *Antigone* (which he calls a "pigment-joke") and Brancusi kicking the *femme folle* out of his atelier, alongside the music sung "in the gut of poverty," a music that Campos claims to have heard at a countryside fair, in the Brazilian northeast.[19] This gesture also reconnects with the German Romantic's interest in folk culture. By juxtaposing well-known and unknown creators on the page without hierarchy, Campos uses the text as a kind of surface that balances out heterogeneous elements.

This notion of the *surface of the text* leads us to consider another attribute in Campos's notion of "bioscriptural drive," mainly his references to "skin" throughout *Galáxias* in images such as: "mar pele de fera" (beast skin sea), "cetim de fera" (beast satin), "mar polipantera" (poly-panther sea), "twisting sensual muscles under the stars," "fruit skin," "pelepregas" (skin folds), "words like skin under deep water," a "book that is skin." In this regard, *Galáxias* is a conjunctive, epidermal set. Didier Anzieu defines skin most acutely as a peripheral brain.[20] It is in this skin tissue that we find the poem's *katabasis* and its *anabasis*. The poem goes up and down, and we can hear the rhythm of the things in the world through the surface of the skin, such that, in Fernando Pessoa's terms: "what in me feels is thinking." *Galáxias* therefore has a sensual, heterogeneous materialism. It absorbs what was possible until it was itself absorbed by the homogeneous world of literary systems and typologies.

When Campos goes into the details of the skin and the sensuality of the body, his work gives rise to an abject constellation, in which the skin is punctured and traversed as well as being a continuous surface. He thereby brings together raw, viscous, sperm-like matter, the strong smell of urine, blood, vomit, rheum, aureate anus, venereal nests, molds of pubes, gangrenous legs, and all the odors emanating from sewers. *Galáxias* evokes these odors as excess and suffering (as in the example of *circuladô de fulô*). Through the poet's mobile exploration of skin and the abject, *Galáxias* entails an "education of the five senses," to paraphrase the title of the book that Campos published in 1985, the year after *Galáxias* came out. History itself, says Campos, a reader of Walter Benjamin, becomes the malleable matter of desire. This plasticity is to be understood in the sense Nietzsche gave to the term Hegel invented.[21]

To conclude, I would suggest that Campos's reflections on *skin* undermined the distinction between the rational and the emotional (or sensorial) that underpins the concrete and neoconcrete divide. *Skin* thereby is the meeting point between the two movements, for it is malleable, mobile, and material in nature. This notion of plasticity allows us to read in the "feather mantle" another version of the *skin*, a locus in which the concrete and neoconcrete are not opposites but, once again, find a meeting point. For indeed, Campos and Oiticica's encounter at the Chelsea Hotel transforms the way we consider the relationship between the concrete and neoconcrete movements, allowing us to take a certain distance from museum discourse and diachronic literary history.

THE B-SIDE

On the tape's B-side the conversation between Campos and Oiticica ranges from *Galáxias* to a discussion of Joaquim de Sousândrade's poem *O Guesa errante* (The wandering Guesa), in particular, the section titled "Inferno de Wall Street." Long before Lorca or Mayakovski, while residing in New York in the last quarter of the nineteenth century, the Brazilian poet and journalist Sousândrade saw the hectic city in terms of a collage of the news he read in local papers, and in the section about Wall Street he created what is possibly the first collage poem, built entirely of references cued from the newspapers of the time. The collage aspect of Sousândrade's poetry was inspiring to both Campos and Oiticica. More importantly, Campos and his brother Augusto were among the first poets to call for a reenvisioning/revision (*re-visão*) of Sousândrade's heritage in a volume published in 1964. Campos and Oiticica also drew on Sousândrade's poetry as a source of inspiration for their own work. In his 1971 conversation with Oiticica, Campos describes Sousândrade's practice in the following terms: "What he saw in newspapers, such as the news of a certain crime that took place in the park, he took quotes of the events of that time and involved them with historical, mythological quotes. Such a process places the news in the constellate mosaic that is the modern newspaper." Both Oiticica and Campos adopt a comparable relationship to *fait divers*, taking events or images read in newspapers as the raw material for poetic creation. Consider, for example, Oiticica's *Bólide caixa 18,*

"Homenagem a cara de cavalo" (1966), which juxtaposes a newspaper photograph and a text memorializing the death of an infamous criminal (Cara de cavalo [Horse face]). Consider also that in 1964, Campos used a similar strategy in fragment 8 of the *Galáxias*, about the death of a prostitute from Paraiba (in the Brazilian northeast) making the headlines in Geneva: "il mondo signorina stromboli or the little prostitute from Paraíba opening the headlines in Geneva's newspapers like the blood spilled from an open throat in a cubicle smelling of urine. And this one is that one and that one is this one." In their conversation, Campos describes the journalistic collage procedure pioneered by "Inferno de Wall Street," which he used in the aforementioned fragment, as a "brutal montage of macro-raw pieces of reality." In this collage, the new organization of material invites us to use not so much the term "transposition" to describe the relationship between the newspaper and the poem, but rather that of "renewing connections."

Another way of thinking about literary history and the relationship to be established with other artistic movements is expressed in terms of a seismic metaphor: during their conversation, Campos describes historiography "as the seismic graph of subversive fragmentation rather than the tautological homologation of the homogeneous."[22] But all forms of fragmentation in these artistic projects are counterbalanced by a movement of construction. This movement of construction can be understood as a dynamic morphology, in which forms are constantly becoming other, taking the risk of building up as well as breaking down. For both Campos and Oiticica, the backdrop for all their work is a complex tradition drawing on historical art practiced in Europe and what Campos refers to as the codes of "professionalism conditioned by the gesture of consumption" in America. Their practices of decomposition and recomposition are to be set in relation to this backdrop.

Their conversation itself also enacts the dynamics of their relationship. Consider, for example, their mutual interest in *Hagoromo*: attributed to Motokiyo Zeami (1363–1443), the play was a source of fascination to poets like William Butler Yeats and Ezra Pound before coming to Campos's and Oiticica's attention. Their idiosyncratic appropriation of this play during their conversation might be understood as concocting a "paran-galactic" axis that merged Oiticica's production of *parangolés* with Campos's ongoing work on *Galáxias*. We see in this merging the simplicity of a Japanese aesthetic meeting the precariousness of life in the hills in a Brazilian slum, the Japanese moon dance merging with the Brazilian samba, each form opening onto new forms. The movement of the samba brings with it the idea of performance set in a particular landscape, which in turn conjures up the question of environmental art, which then interrogates the experience of the ordinary, the everyday. In this fashion, the morphology of forms brings us back to the question of experience, to the nexus between the formal and the experiential. Where Campos emphasizes form, Oiticica emphasizes lived experience. Ultimately, what united them is what Campos refers to as a common "underground," simultaneously constructivist and experimental.

This tension between the construction and fragmentation of forms in art and life adds to the reflection on "formation"—the construction of one's self—that is characteristic of Brazilian political, social, and poetic thought. In "Anatomia da formação" (Anatomy of formation)—published in *Folha de São Paulo* on September 7, 2014—Silviano Santiago traced the history of the term from Joaquim Nabuco's *Minha formação* (My Formation, 1900), in which the formation of individual intellectuals could not be transmitted to others, rather their education was a fundamental and exclusively individual process. In the 1950s, the term *formation* evolved and acquired an economic connotation, with the publication of Celso Furtado's *Formação econômica do Brasil.*[23] By the end of the 1950s, Antonio Cândido had published *Formação da literatura brasileira: momentos decisivos* (Formation of Brazilian literature: Decisive moments). This is the context in which the relationship between life and form comes up in the conversation between Campos and Oiticica, two intellectual artists who had traveled and sought to deconstruct their own positions in relationship to their work and their sociohistorical moment.[24]

In the case of Campos and Oiticica—as with many writers, intellectuals, and artists—engagements with form took place outside institutions such as universities and museums. In these extra-institutional locations, the work of formation never ends. Even when works come into being, they are still in formation. In "Brasil diarréia" (1973), Oiticica wrote: "Personal experience: my formation, the meaning of everything I've tried and try, took me in one direction: the Brazilian condition, more than merely marginal within the world, is underground, i.e., splits and must rise up as something specific still in formation"[25]—"still in formation": it is shapeless, in metamorphosis. The experimental as it is imagined in their work is simultaneously sensual and constructive.

A RIGOROUS ANARCHOPEDIA

After Campos and Oiticica's meeting at the Chelsea Hotel, the clash between concretism and neoconcretism ought to be seen as an overly simplistic categorization masking a rather more complex reality of Brazilian literary and artistic production, in which the points of correspondence and transfer between the supposedly opposing approaches to art run much deeper. If we examine the works together, the points of friction are not where academic, institutional distinctions might have us believe. The experiments of Campos and Oiticica do not amount to a systematic encyclopedia of contemporary Brazilian socio-politico-cultural life, which would allow for classification, but rather to an "anarcopedia of forms" (Galáxias, fragment 36), from which, nevertheless we can learn a thing or two.

Likewise, the 1971 meeting between Haroldo de Campos and Hélio Oiticica might be described as an "anarcopedia." Both form (which concretism foregrounds) and feeling (which neoconcretism insists upon) are enacted in their conversation, giving rise to a new "education of the five senses." The work of each artist thereby continues to interrogate that of the other.

Notes

1 / *Flor do Mal* was a tabloid-format periodical published by the journalist Luiz Carlos Maciel in the late 1960s. It folded after five issues. I thank the Núcleo de Estudos Literários & Culturais (NELIC) at Universidade Federal de Santa Catarina (UFSC) for allowing me access to magazine archives.

2 / César Oititica Filho and Frederico Coelho, eds., *Helio Oiticica: Conglomerado Newyorkkaises* (Rio de Janeiro: Azougue, 2013), 27.

3 / Oiticica, 69.

4 / Oiticica's experience of New York was influenced by the fact that the city seemed to literally overlap art with a literary dimension. In that sense, Lorca and Sousândrade represent two distinct poetic sensibilities that find a common motif in Wall Street. See Frederico García Lorca, *Poesía completa* (New York: Random House, 2012), 412: "Lo impresionante por frío y por cruel es Wall Street. Llega el oro en ríos de todas las partes de la tierra y la muerte llega con él. En ningún sitio del mundo se siente como allí la ausencia total del espíritu: manadas de hombres que no pueden pasar del seis, desprecio de la ciencia pura y valor demoníaco del presente. Y lo terrible es que toda la multitud que lo llena cree que el mundo será siempre igual, y que su deber consiste en mover aquella gran máquina día y noche y siempre." As for Sousândrade, an entire canto of his *Guesa* was composed of news cued from the local newspapers related to the New York Stock Exchange. The literary constellation shared by Campos and Oiticica during their meeting at the Chelsea Hotel would be the basis for Oiticica's 1972, *Agrippina é Roma Manhattan*, a sixteen-minute film was shot in Super 8 on location at the steps of the New York Stock Exchange. The scenario mixes references to Sousândrade (the title is taken from his poem *Guesa errante*) and Mallarmé in a scene in which Brazilian visual artist Antonio Dias plays dice with Andy Warhol superstar Mario Montez.

5 / The expression "bioscriptural drive" (*pulsão bioescritural*) appears at the end of *Galáxias*: "pulsão bioescritural em expansão galática entre esses dois formantes cambiáveis e cambiantes (tendo por ímã temático a viagem como livro ou o livro como viagem, e por isso mesmo entendido também como um 'livro de ensaios') [bioscriptural drive in galactic expansion between these two exchangeable and exchanging formants (having as thematic compass the voyage as a book or the book as a voyage, hence understood as a 'book of essays')]." Haroldo de Campos, *Galáxias* (São Paulo: Ex-Libris, 1984), n.p. For more about this concept, see Eduardo Jorge de Oliveira, "A pulsão bioescritural como método: as *Galáxias* de Haroldo de Campos," in *Bioescritas/Biopoéticas: Corpo, memória e arquivos* (Biowriting/Biopoetics: the body, memory and archives), ed. Ana Chiara, André Masseno, Daniele Ribeiro Fortuna, and Marcelo dos Santos (Porto Alegre: Editora Sulina, 2018), 43–61.

6 / Campos produced a performance of *Hagoromo—o manto de plumas* in 1994 at Centro Cultural São Paulo. The play was directed by Alice K., who also played the role of Tennin. According to the performer, the use of Oiticica's *parangolés* (*Hagoromo*) was made impossible because of the two-month run of the spectacle. From a private e-mail exchange with the performer on January 24, 2016.

7 / *"Noh" or Accomplishment* was republished in 2004 under a new title: *The Noh Theatre of Japan: With Complete Texts of 15 Classic Plays*. The introduction includes two remarks about Japanese theater aesthetics that so fascinated Campos and Oiticica: "The art of allusion, or this love of allusion in art, is at the root of the Noh. These plays, or eclogues, were made only for the few; for the nobles; for those trained to catch the allusion. In the Noh we find an art built upon the god-dance, or upon some local legend of spiritual apparition, or later, on gestes of war and feats of history; an art of splendid posture, of dancing and chanting, and of acting that is not mimetic." The second citation entails a synthesis concocted by Pound: "As the tradition of Noh is unbroken, we find in the complete performance numerous elements which have disappeared from our Western stage; that is, morality plays, religious mysteries, and even dances—like those of the mass—which have lost what we might call their dramatic significance." Ezra Pound and Ernest Fenollosa, *The Noh Theatre of Japan: With Complete Texts of 15 Classic Plays* (New York: Dover, 2004), 5, 18.

8 / Gonzalo Aguilar, *Hélio Oititica: A asa branca do extase—Arte brasileira 1964–1980*, trans. Genese Andrade (São Paulo: Anfiteatro, 2016).

9 / See fragment 48 in Campos, *Galáxias*.

10 / Haroldo de Campos, *Novas: Selected Writings*, ed. Antonio Sergio Bessa and Odile Cisneros (Evanston, IL: Northwestern University Press, 2007), 119–120; translated by Micaela Kramer.

11 / In *Conglomerado Newyorkaises*, written between July 26 and December 26, 1972, Oiticica seems to hint at a new definition of his practice in "*Parangolé-síntese*." He wrote: "Inventions are extensions of man's energy" and "perform doesn't become preform," which seem to denote a new position concerning the *Parangolés*. Here he suggests that the *Parangolé* is a "concretion" (*concreção*). Concretion here is to be read neither in the concrete nor in the neoconcrete acceptance of the word but in reference to a form that seeks to create an inversion of the myth. In the words of the artist: it is "*play-concreção*." See

Oititica, *Conglomerado Newyorkaises*, 21–25, in passim.

12 / In a 1987 interview with Lenora de Barros, Campos described Oiticica's work as "organized delirium." He also addressed Oiticica's mazes: "What are Hélio's mazes? They are scopes he constructs and deconstructs, in which his particular inventions find their natural home ground, such as in a Japanese house, entirely planned and looking like some sort of reverberation of a Mondrian painting: an essential home from the tatami to the floor mat, passing through the objects, the vase to drink water, the bowl to eat, the chopsticks to grab the food, everything oriented to obey the same general project of beauty. In Hélio's case, the maze is the scope where his birdless 'nests' hover naturally, while, due to the bird's absence, simultaneously call for a flight he would later restitute to the nests through the *parangolé*; a place where the absent bird gains wings to disembarrass its flight; ultimately, the several types of objects or deconstructions he used to make, which required palpation from the observer or visitor of this space, are then present one way or another, at times even in metamorphic variants, such as a given floor you need to move through barefoot in order to feel a certain kind of tactual sensation; a wet surface you need to cross to reach through another space, where you get sensitized by the presence of nearly arachnoid threads hanging in the air. He created actual environments, actual galactic dwellings where these objects—in-between objects, trans-spatial inventions—could find shelter and be enjoyed, used, and savored, so to speak, because the spectator could also find a pleasurable element in this artistic practice, thus becoming a partaker of this apparently inconclusive elaboration and initiative, the completion of which, i.e., its unwinding, assumed the presence and the desire of the other: it assumed the alterity, the participation of a manipulator as a pleasurable enjoyer of these inventions, this faery plasticity which Hélio's imagination was ever capable of configuring in kaleidoscopically different manners." See Haroldo de Campos, "Hang-glider of Ecstasy," in *Hélio Oiticica* (Minneapolis: Walker Art Center, 1993), 217.

13 / It is worth noting that this movement is the opposite of the one Joyce's work follows. See, for example, Jean-Michel Rabaté, *James Joyce* (Paris: Hachette, 1993), 11–17.

14 / In the 1970s, many young poets in Brazil found in the aesthetic paths opened up by *Galáxias* new possibilities to experiment. Leaving aside the prickly issue of influence, I propose to see these new developments as a constellation that connects the counterculture of the 1970s with the work developed by the concrete poets since the early 1950s. We can include in this network Paulo Leminsky's *Catatau* (1975) and Waly Salomão's *Me segura que eu vou dar um troço* (1972), as well as works by Josely Vianna Baptista and Ricardo Aleixo, among others.

15 / Haroldo de Campos, *Depoimentos de oficina* (São Paulo: Unimarco, 2002), 49.

16 / Curiously, one such constellation is found in the series of blurbs praising the book (by Guimarães Rosa, Caetano Veloso, Octavio Paz, Severo Sarduy, Benedito Nunes, Andrés Sánchez Robayna, João Alexandre Barbosa). Each individual blurb is also a cut, an opening in time, an eye from another text, imposing a reading tempo that invites us to consider tradition not as static but as ecstatic, bringing two or more different texts into neighborly relation (*punti luminosi*).

17 / The complete quote in Portuguese is: "Atomizada, minimizada, esfarelada a função denotative, tudo se passa agora na região dos significantes, em cuja cadeia, como diz Lacan, o sentido insiste, embora nenhum dos elementos dela consista no sentido de que é capaz no instante." Campos refers to Lacan's "L'instance de la letter dans l'inconscient ou la raison depuis Freud," published in *Écrits*. See Augusto de Campos and Haroldo de Campos, *Re visão de Sousândrade* [Revision of Sousândrade] (São Paulo: Perspectiva, 2002), 526.

18 / In the original: "todo livro é um livro de ensaio de ensaios do livro", "a unha-de-fome da estória não me come não me consome não me redoma." Excerpts from the first fragment of *Galáxias*, n.p. I thank Hellen Guareschi for her translation.

19 / This episode is narrated in fragment 15, often referred to as "circuladô de fulô," which became a popular hit recorded by Caetano Veloso and best illustrates the close relationship between music and poetry after *Tropicália*.

20 / Didier Anzieu, *Le moi-peau* (Paris: Dunod, 1995).

21 / Catherine Malabou draws the neologism *plasticity* from the preface of Hegel's *The Phenomenology of Spirit*. This word is officially incorporated into the German lexicon during the transition from the eighteenth to the nineteenth century. According to Malabou, it is rooted in the Greek etymon *plassein*, "shape, fashion, form" and has two meanings: to receive and to give shape. However, the term can also refer to the power to void the shape of its contents. For Hegel, plasticity describes a movement in formation. Textually, plasticity implies the structure of a phrase that can be split into subject, verb, and predicate, which we can call object. That is what Catherine Malabou describes in the "plasticity" entry of the *Dictionary of Untranslatables: A Philosophical Lexicon*. In his second *Untimely Medidation*, Nietzsche evokes a "plastic power" of regenerative nature (hence, of healing potential, the same term employed by Hegel)

not only for the individual but for people in general and for civilization as a whole, thus also allowing the transformation of past and foreign things. For the complete text see Catherine Malabou "Plasticity," in *Dictionary of Untranslatables: A Philosophical Lexicon*, ed. Barbara Cassin (Princeton, NJ: Princeton University Press, 2014), 788.

22 / Malabou, 162.

23 / Celso Furtado, *The Economic Growth of Brazil: A Survey from Colonial to Modern Times* (Berkeley: University of California Press, 1971).

24 / One important aspect of this deconstruction is the recuperation of the baroque from the place Cândido had relegated it to, that of the invisible margins of Brazilian literary history. Indeed, Cândido excluded the baroque from the Brazilian literary tradition, which, in his narration of this history, begins with Romanticism. Campos takes issue with this reading and attempts to rehabilitate this silenced aspect of Brazilian heritage. The dynamic morphology so important to Campos's own aesthetic obviously plays a critical role in this project of rehabilitation. Both Campos and Oiticica's work represents a kind of morphological persistence of the baroque at a time in which other artists were turning their backs on the baroque. Their exploration of bioscriptural motifs is part of this project, which also understands literary history not so much in terms of linear evolution or progress but rather as a place where a baroque background can resurge, irrupting into the present without continuity or systemic development. This position therefore informs the relationship each of the two artists maintain with history: history is what emerges through experiments with form, understood in both social and poetic terms. We could visualize a "meta scheme," to use Oiticica's term, of a baroque underground in Brazilian literature, one that emerges on the surface in an irregular and unpredictable fashion. In this underground, a battle is waged between different forms of experience that do not depend on Cândido's author-reader-producer circuit as the regulatory force in a national literature. Even though it was published later, Campos's *O sequestro do barroco na formação da literatura brasileira: o caso Gregório de Matos* (*Disappearance of the Baroque in Brazilian Literature: The Case Gregório de Matos*), through the use of poetic and metalinguistic functions of language, argues for the reappropriation of this latent baroque undercurrent in Brazilian history in order to break with the idea of the concept as substance and with the biological-evolutional movement of historiography that underpins Cândido's method. Nevertheless, in spite of the polemical opposition over the status of Brazilian literary history that arose between Cândido and Campos, Cândido's publication of a seminal text on Brazilian literature "Dialética da malandragem" (The dialectics of roguery, 1970)—in which he identifies the figure of the rogue as a central character in the Brazilian literary imagination—remains very important. This text provides us with a useful prism through which to read Oiticica's work. Indeed, Campos recognizes and appreciates the pertinence of Cândido's idea of the rogue for analysis of Brazilian literature.

25 / Hélio Oititica, "Brasil diarréia," in *Arte brasileira hoje*, ed. Ferreira Gullar (Rio de Janeiro: Paz e Terra, 1973), 151.

RETRIEVING THE UNREADABLE Arno Holz and Sousândrade Revisited by Augusto and Haroldo de Campos

Simone Homem de Mello

One intriguing aspect of Brazilian concrete poetry spearheaded by the Noigandres group is the discrepancy between its search for the most immediate visual-textual directness, clearness, and pithiness and its founders' seemingly anachronistic interest in reassessing authors whose works were excluded from the literary mainstream for being considered illegible. By doing so, Noigandres endeavored to retrieve the lineage of *trobar clus* ("closed form" in Occitan), the obscure, highly ciphered and nontransparent form championed by Provençal poets. This discrepancy not only provides important clues as to the different paths the founders of concrete poetry would take after the programmatic phase of the movement, but it also reinforces their concept of reading as an active practice of deciphering, as if the text would be a *gestalt*, a foreground figure to be recognized on a background of semantic noise. In this context, I will focus on the reevaluation of the work of the Brazilian poet Joaquim de Sousândrade (1833–1902) and the German poet Arno Holz (1863–1929) by the poets Augusto de Campos and Haroldo de Campos.

It is remarkable that the literary paradigm that the Noigandres group—founded by the Campos brothers and Décio Pignatari in 1952—referred to was not, in its first manifestos, the tradition of figural poetry, which inadvertently could be considered to correspond to their programmatic proposal of a "verbivocovisual" approach to poetic language. In the manifestos published from the mid-1950s on, they were pleading for a poetry that would cope with the short attention span of newspaper headline's readers.[1] One of the virtues of the concrete poem would be to "establish a quick communication";[2] more specifically, the poem should be organized "in precise consonance with the urgency for a more rapid, direct, and economic communication . . . which characterizes the antidiscursive and objective contemporary mind."[3] According to them, concrete poetry should "place itself in position of absolute realism."[4] This new form would "prefigure the reintegration of the poem into daily life—analogously to what Bauhaus had proposed for the visual arts: as a vehicle for commercial advertising (newspapers, billboards, TV, movies, etc.), as an object for pure fruition . . . and with an array of possibilities analogous to the art object—and so it would substitute the magical, the mystical, and the *maudit* for the USEFUL."[5]

However, all these postulates would not lead the Noigandres poets to acknowledge without reservation certain poetic traditions of visual immediacy and easy apprehension as a decisive reference to their works. They scarcely mention figural poetry,[6] probably because they tend to dismiss the figurative representation of objects through a certain typographic disposition—including Apollinaire's *Calligrammes*—as merely ornamental. In concrete poetry, the "word should be used in its integrity and not mutilated by a biased reduction to descriptive music (Lettrism) or to decorative pictography (*calligrammes* or any other graphic-hedonistic arrangement)."[7] Apollinaire's *Calligrammes* as well as Dadaist and Futurist poetry were recognized with a certain reserve only as secondary references to the new procedures.[8] Apollinaire has been taken into consideration for his statement about the "ideographic poem," according to which "it would be necessary that our intelligence become accustomed to read synthetically-ideographically instead of analytically-discursively."[9] In fact, the French poet was more appreciated for his early insight on language as ideogram than for the realization of his *calligrammes* properly, which were considered to be "a mere figurative representation of the concept,"[10] or "pointless *décor*"[11] As far as the works of the Futurists and Dadaists are concerned, some of their procedures could be reappraised by concrete poets, such as "neo-typography," "*parole in libertà*" (Marinetti's "words-in-freedom"), "imagination without strings," "simultaneism," and "sonorism"—albeit exclusively "in function of an OBJECTIVE or CONCRETE poetic expression," "in function of a phenomenology of composition (and not only a psychology of composition)."[12] Futurists and Dadaists were criticized for their "descriptive kinematics," for their "frenetic subjectivism," and for "hypostatizing [a kind of] ultra-romanticism"; but above all, the Noigandres poets felt the lack of a "constructive organization" in most Futurist and Dadaist works.[13] So it is the destructive impetus of modernist avant-garde poetry or—to use an expression of Augusto de Campos—"the early [twentieth] century's various pugil/isms" which is pointed out as problematic, especially because it "overshadowed the importance" of Stéphane Mallarmé's "great typographic and cosmogonic poem," *Un coup de dés*.

Instead of associating concrete poetry with a modern tradition of poetic immediacy, the Noigandres poets included in their canon authors who notoriously played with readability, indirectness, and extensiveness, being sometimes considered even inscrutable (such as Mallarmé, Ezra Pound, and James Joyce). As translators and introducers of a new poetry translation concept, Augusto de Campos, Décio Pignatari, and Haroldo de Campos "recreated" some poets of this tradition in Portuguese. One of their main references was Ezra Pound, with his call to continually update the world literature tradition by means of poetry and to constantly renew the literary language by continuing to write. In 1955, Haroldo de Campos synthetized their adhesion to the Poundian *make-it-new* principle as follows: "the art of poetry has no experiential value as a function of history and is founded rather on a metahistorical continuum that makes Homer and Pound, Dante and Eliot, Góngora and Mallarmé contemporaries—not in the sense of a world hierarchy but rather as a vectoral metamorphosis, a qualitative transformation, a cultural morphology."[14]

Their understanding of literary tradition as a network of nonlinear and nonhierarchical relationships between authors from different cultures and periods to whom contemporary literary production shows affinities allowed the Noigandres poets to reassess writers that had been dismissed by mainstream historiography as well as to identify similarities between authors who were not connected historically or through mutual influence. This is the case for the Brazilian poet Joaquim de Sousândrade, widely considered to belong to the second Romantic generation in Brazilian literature, and of the German poet Arno Holz, founder of naturalism and a pioneer of modern avant-garde poetry in Germany.

Both poets had dedicated over three decades to the production of one long poem, which came to be their life's work—*O Guesa errante* (1858–1888) and *Phantasus* (1885–1929). Both poets had their work ignored by their contemporaries, who dismissed them at best as having written for the future.[15] Both Sousândrade and Holz dedicated themselves to the genre of the long poem and anticipated concepts and poetic procedures that would be fundamental in later movements such as imagism. What attracted the attention of the Campos brothers was primarily the poets' affinity to literary procedures that focus on the materiality and concreteness of language and their search for poetic innovations, which on occasions have been considered pathological by some critics. In some of their articles published between 1957 and 1962,[16] the Campos brothers would reevaluate Arno Holz not only because of his penchant for neologisms and of his significant use of typographic resources (at the same time as Mallarmé in France) but also because of his affinity with the baroque. They would also recognize and emphasize both of these tendencies in Sousândrade's work, which they rescued from obscurity with their 1964 critical anthology *Re visão de sousândrade*, which they would continue to expand in subsequent editions until

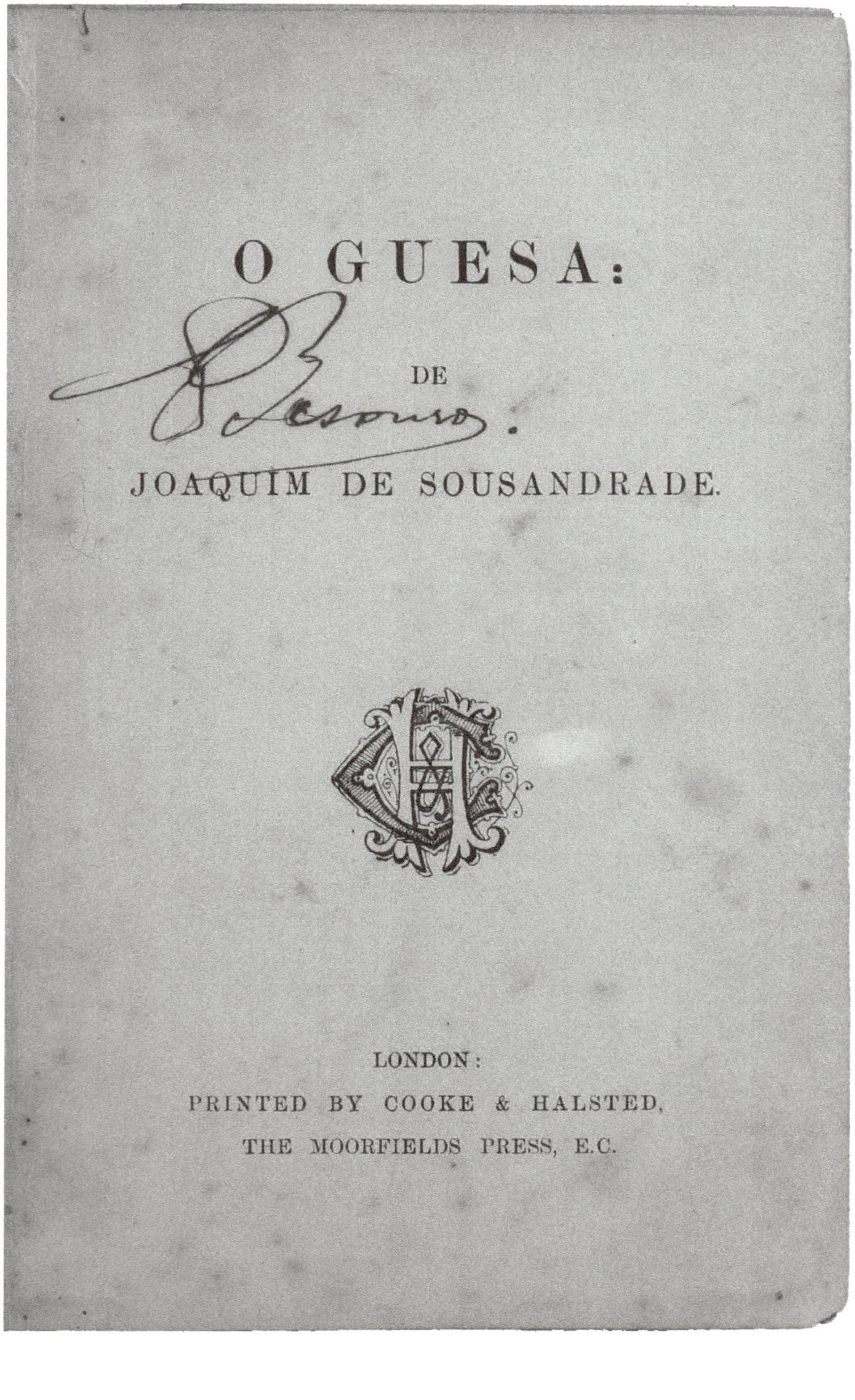

Joaquim de Sousandrade, *O Guesa*. Frontispiece of the Cooke and Halsted edition, n.d. Courtesy Biblioteca Brasiliana Guita e José Mindlin—PRCEU/USP.

2002 to include articles the authors had published after 1964. In recontextualizing Sousândrade's poetry, they associated it with daring techniques and procedures of the modern avant-garde while also identifying a certain "baroquism" in the sense of an abstract style designated as "trans-epochal."[17]

In "Arno Holz: Da revolução da lírica à elefantíase do projeto" (Arno Holz: From lyrical revolution to project elephantiasis, 1962), Augusto and Haroldo de Campos introduced the German poet to the Brazilian readers through two translations from the 1925 version of *Phantasus*: "Mondabend"/"Noite de Lua" (by Haroldo de Campos) and "Barocke Marine"/"Marinha Barroca" (by Augusto and Haroldo de Campos). Their translations succeed in recreating the most innovative aspects of Holz's poetry, above all his neologisms, which are frequently depicted as periphrastic expressions in other translations.[18] The essay—as well as a second text on Holz which the brothers wrote two years later, "De Holz a Sousândrade" (From Holz to Sousândrade)—outlines the position of Holz as an avant-garde poet who had been rediscovered by the youngest German-speaking authors involved in the concrete poetry or visual poetry movements in the 1950s and 1960s. Indeed, authors such as Eugen Gomringer, Franz Mon, and Ferdinand Kriwet were interested in Holz mainly because of the lexical transformations implied in the neologisms of *Phantasus* and because of his proposal of a poetry conceived in terms of spatiality.[19] The latter aspect led the Brazilian poets to see a striking parallel between the position of Arno Holz's *Phantasus* in German modern poetry and the position of Mallarmé's *Un coup de dés* in modern French poetry.[20] What evidently interested the Campos brothers, as cofounders of concrete poetry, was Holz's contribution to a certain lineage of literary avant-garde as well as his ideas toward a synthetic codification in poetry, such as his conception of the poem as a typographical music score. At the same time, they stressed the baroque aspect of *Phantasus*, choosing to translate one of the most inventive fragments of the 1925 edition—"Barocke Marine"—which plays with the baroque opulence of imagery and verbal profusion and contains complex portmanteau words, as the first two strophes of the poem show:

Barocke Marine

See,
See, sonnigste See,
soweit
du . . . siehst!
Über die rollenden Wasser hin,
lärmend, jauchzjolend, wonnejubelnd, lustlachend, schwärmend,
sich grunzwölternd, sich wälzwerfend, sich
rückenschleidernd,
sich
wärmend,
sich hohlhandzurufend, sich hohlhandzuschreiend, sich

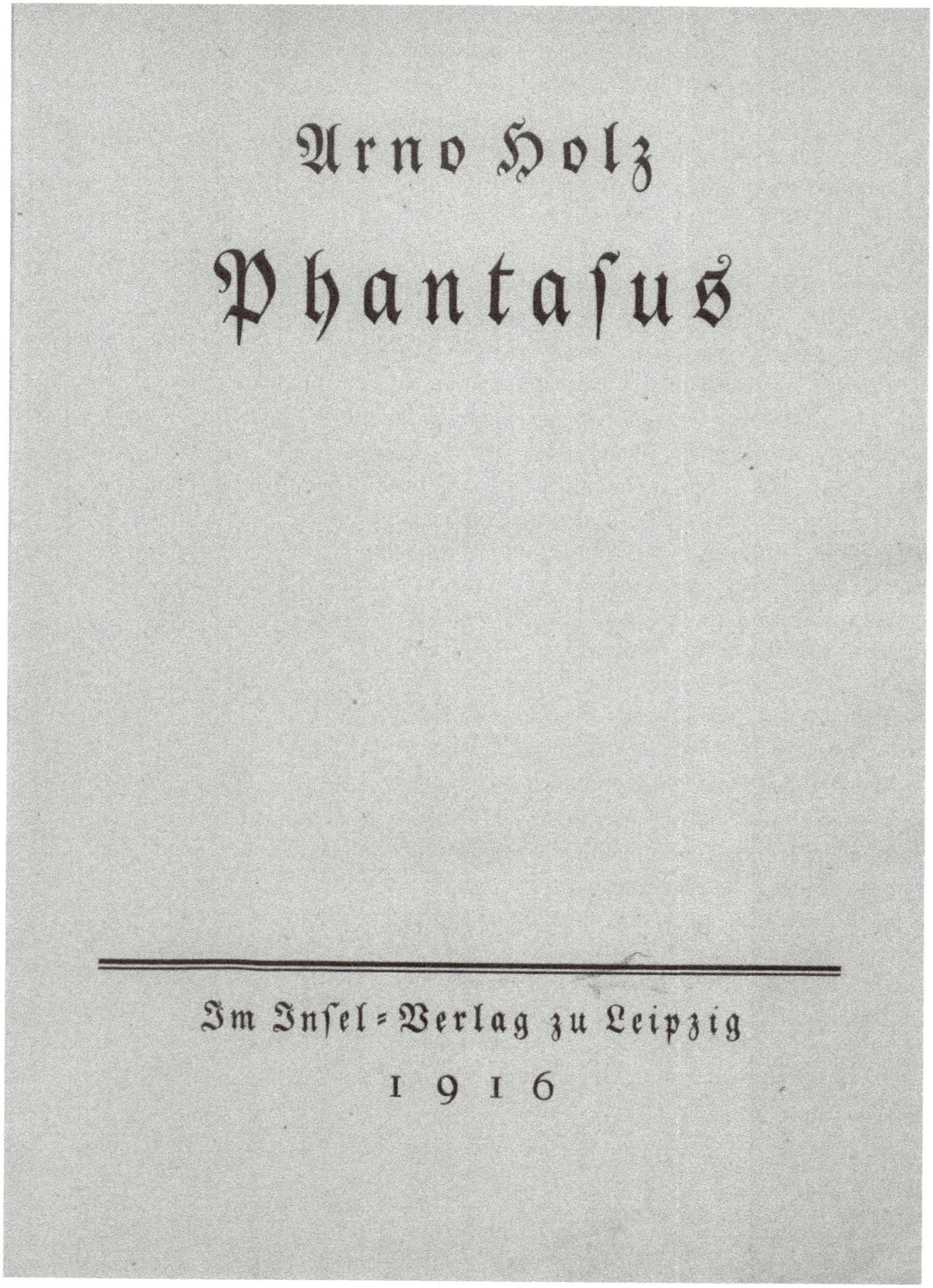

Arno Holz

Phantasus

Im Insel-Verlag zu Leipzig

1916

Arno Holz, *Phantasus*.
Frontispiece of the 1916 edition published by Im Insel Verlag zu Leipzig, 1916.

hohlhandzugröhlend,
tanggrünhaarig, schuppenglitzleiberig, störschwanzflossig,
schwimmtauchblinkend, schwimmfauchflinkend,
schwimmpustpfasend
wie
rasend, Drommetenschneckenhörner blasend,
tausend . . . Tritonen!
[. . .]
Mar,
mar, o mais solar,
mirar o
mar!
Sobre águas rolantes, eis
bramantes, jubilogritantes, alacreberrrantes, lubrigargalhantes,
estuantes, grunhesponjando-se, voltevolteando-se,
retrolançando,
se
ensolarando,
mãos-em-concha-rugindo, mãos-em-concha-clamando,
mãos-em-concha-ululando,
algaverdecomados, escamiventreprateados, esturjãocaudulantes,
nadimergulímpidos, nadirresfolfúlgidos,
nadibufsoprando
como
loucos, soando buziocôncavastrompas,
trilhões de tritões![21]

In reference to this poem, Augusto and Haroldo de Campos identified an "appeal for the hypertrophic exploration of the ornamental" and a tendency to the "baroque farce."[22] Holz's *Phantasus*, as a work-in-progress that combines lexical compression with syntactical expansion—in both tendencies toward condensation and prolixity—questions our ability to read, an issue also problematized by the Brazilian founders of concrete poetry in their programmatic poems.

In their appreciation of Sousândrade's poetry, Augusto and Haroldo de Campos attributed the historiographical undervaluation of his work to the prejudice of Brazilian literary critics against baroque literature, which has been dismissed as extraneous to the Brazilian literary tradition.[23] The "baroquizing manifestations" in Sousândrade's work were misunderstood as mere "preciosity,"[24] and his rupture with the Romantic canon has not been grasped as it should, that is, as an anticipation of central modernist issues, such as "the rupture with the genius of the Portuguese language (disturbed by his syntactical and lexical innovations) and with the linearity and discursivity of the Western pattern of logical thinking."[25] Besides analyzing Sousândrade's work as part of concrete poetry's *paideuma*, Augusto and Haroldo de Campos have contributed greatly to make him accessible to the contemporary Brazilian reading public, for it is because of their anthology that this unclassifiable author has come again into circulation.

The title of Sousândrade's long poem refers to a pre-Columbian legend about an Incan ritual in which a kidnapped child is brought up under strict priestly protection. After a period of pilgrimage, the priests eventually sacrifice the youth at the age of fifteen. In Sousândrade's poem, the tale of the *guesa* becomes an image of the poet as a nomad displaced in the contemporary industrial and capitalistic world. The tale is also an image of the destiny of all pre-Columbian Pan-American populations after the arrival of Europeans in America. In its criticism of capitalism and colonialism, *O Guesa errante* mingles myth and history, denoting the clash of both narrative modes. This clash also implies an upheaval of language, to which some poem's episodes culminate. In the section of Canto Tenth, often referred to as "The Wall Street Inferno," the world of finances is configured in a sequence of limerick stanzas in which information taken from New York newspapers is gathered in a montage of rapid cuts; its accelerated and elliptical language sounds mantric and ritualistic. The same montage technique happens in the episode "Tatuturema," in Canto Second, in which Portuguese is mixed with Brazilian indigenous languages and Latin phrases into a complex hybrid. Through these and other means, *O Guesa errante* imposes upon the reader an unusually cryptic language and the question of reading as an act of decoding.

O Guesa errante (1876)

Canto X: "O Inferno de Wall Street"
(O Guesa, tendo atravessado as Antilhas, crê-se livre dos Xeques e
penetra em New-York-Stock-Exchange; a Voz dos desertos:)
—Orfeu, Dante, Æneas, ao inferno
Desceram; o Inca há de subir . . .
= Ogni sp'ranza lasciate,
Che entrate . . .
—Swedenborg, há mundo porvir?
(Xeques surgindo risonhos e disfarçados em Railroad-*managers*,
Stockjobbers, Pimpbrokers, etc., etc., apregoando:)
—Harlem! Erie! Central! Pennsylvania!
= Milhão! cem milhões!! mil milhões!!!
—Young é Grant! Jackson,
Atkinson!
Vanderbilts, Jay Goulds, anões!
(A Voz mal ouvida dentre a trovoada:)
—Fulton's *Folly*; Codezo's *Forgery* . . .
Fraude é o clamor da nação!
Não entendem odes
Railroads;
Paralela Wall-Street à Chattám . . .
(Corretores continuando:)
—Pigmeus, Brown Brothers! Bennet! Stewart!
Rotschild e o ruivalho d'Astor!!
= Gigantes, escravos
Se os cravos
Jorram luz, se finda-se a dor![26]

Analogously to Sousândrade's *Guesa*, Holz's *Phantasus* conveys a similar view of modernity and the difficulty in grasping the multiple and simultaneous phenomena in modern life, putting into question our ability of representing the complexity of the world by means of communicative language. Derived from Greek mythology, the title *Phantasus* refers to one of Hypno's sons, one of the three gods of dreams (Morpheus and Phobetor being the other two), capable of transforming himself into inanimate things. The whole poem—which in its last (and still unfinished) version (Holz had been working on it up to his death in 1929 and the poem was published posthumously not until the early 1960s) has around forty-five thousand verses—also addresses the poet's feeling of displacement and his search for a refuge in language. Written under the influence of the newest scientific developments such as Charles Darwin's evolution theory, *Phantasus* enacts the progress of the human being along the evolution of species, throughout history, throughout the individual life phases and the seasons of the year. The following *Phantasus* strophe, for instance, depicts one of the stages of evolution as a metamorphosis of the self:

Als mißgestalteter Schuppenlurch,
mit eklem, breitrund zähnebespicktem Kaulquappenmaul,
plattem, stumpfem Ruderschwanz und fetten, quabbligen Fünffingerzehen,
halb noch aus Kiemen, halb schon aus Lungen atmend,
jagte ich,
unter cylindrisch storren, besenbüschligen Sigillarien, gigantischst kandelaberartig sich
verästelnden Bärlappbäumen
und steilen, kirchturmhohen Schachtelhalmen,
zwischen schwimmenden Algen und Kletterfarnen,
in einem ewig nebelheiß brodelnden,
fast ununterbrochen von prasselnden, peitschenden, wirbelnden
Regensturmgüssen, rollenden, krachenden Donnerschlägen und zuckend wolkenzerreißenden
Blitzen durchtobten,
beständigst triefendsten Steinkohlenwald,
nach Schaben, Grillen, Tausendfüßern, Skorpionen, Spinnen, Gespensterheuschrecken
und meinesgleichen![27]

Beginning with the 1916 edition, the poem was conceived as an encyclopedic text which—by means of intense word enumeration, neologisms, and labyrinthine syntax—tracks the history of mankind as a sequence of power struggles, wars, and slaughters. The all-encompassing movement of the poem, which grows significantly along the years, culminates with the collapse of representation rendering its enormous fragmentary text almost unreadable in its totality.

Establishing similarities between Sousândrade and Holz was a most unexpected and sagacious insight in the Campos brothers' project to remap literary history. In addition to identifying parallels in their early essay "Arno Holz: Da revolução da lírica à elefantíase do projeto" (1962), they also uncovered elements about the Brazilian poet in *Re visão de sousândrade* that could also be applied to

Holz. They asserted, on one hand, that Sousândrade had recovered elements of a baroque tradition (notably in his use of "lexical and syntactical cultisms," in "the metaphorical process," in the extensive use of "figures of rhetoric" and "sound texture," as well as in "idiomatic hybridisms"), while, on the other hand, prefiguring the conciseness and transparency in poetic images that its clarity and pithiness brought to mind Pound's idea of *phanopoeia*.[28] This convergence of traditions of verbal proliferation and conciseness also occurs in Holz's *Phantasus* project. Having published in 1904 a parody of baroque poetry, *Dafnis—Lyrisches Portrait aus dem 17. Jahrhundert* (Dafnis—A lyrical portrait from the 17th century), Holz is one of the very few German poets to whom baroque and modernism are not in contradiction. His *Phantasus* version published in 1916—mocked as "Elephantasus" by his contemporaries because of the book format (44cm x 33cm) and the poem's length (336 pages)—combines prolixity with uttermost lexical condensation.

Even though his concept of modern literature did not shun overflowing discursive excesses, Holz was perceptive to the propagation of Japanese aesthetics in the European art scene at the end of the nineteenth century and its clear tendency toward reductive media and forms. His interest in Japanese woodcuts and haiku dates back to the turn of the century, when the first version of *Phantasus* was released in two booklets (1898/99).

Phantasus

In meinem schwarzen Taxuswald
singt ein Märchenvogel—
die ganze Nacht.
Blumen blinken.
Unter Sternen, die sich spiegeln,
treibt mein Boot.
Meine träumenden Hände
tauchen in schwimmende Wasserrosen.
Unten,
lautlos, die Tiefe.
Fern die Ufer! Das Lied . . .[29]

Even in subsequent extended versions of these poems, Holz keeps the paratactic superposition of clearly delineated scenes and imagery insights that characterize this genre of Japanese poetry.

In Sousândrade's *Guesa*, Augusto and Haroldo de Campos also reveal a kind of "imagism of movie shots that operate with the immediacy of a haiku."[30]

. . . vede a tremente
Ondulação das malhas luminosas
Num relâmpago, o tigre atrás da corça.[31]

At the same time, they characterize the "Tatuturema" episode in the *Guesa* as a Faustian Walpurgisnacht: a "burlesque timeless masquerade, in which fictitious characters and historical or mythological events alternate and superimpose, not in a logical narrative but according to an "analogical, synthetic-ideogrammatic order"—recalling Apollinaire's quote included in the concrete poetry manifesto.[32] As a matter of fact, the Walpurgisnacht in Goethe's *Faust II* (a work into which Haroldo de Campos read baroque features in a "transepochal" sense[33]) was also a point of reference in Holz's "Moderne Walpurgisnacht—Kein Misterium" (1899),[34] later incorporated in his play *Die Blechschmiede* (1902–1921), a work-in-progress that, along with *Phantasus*, could be considered his most innovative and radically modern creation.

Sousândrade's *O Guesa errante* and Holz's *Phantasus* share other common traits and thematic correspondences, such as the conception of the long poem as a transcontinental *periplus* or a transformation process, presented by the Brazilian poet as an initiation rite and by the German author as a manifestation of evolutionism and transmigration. Another aspect common to them both is the concept of the poem as discourse in metamorphic process, in which the act of (re)writing leaves its marks. Moreover, they seemed equally concerned with the formal aspect of poetic language, a topic that the Noigandres poets recognized as intrinsic to their own *verbivocovisual* project: "We could say that Sousândrade succeeded in finding the difficult balance between revolutionary content and revolutionary form, achieving at his time the ideal Mayakovsky would plead for, in our days, for the sake of a committed avant-garde poetry: 'without revolutionary form there is no revolutionary art.'"[35] Mayakovsky's motto, taken from a letter written on September 1, 1922,[36] echoes Arno Holz's claim for the language renovation in German poetry thirty-six years earlier: "Without form, the best ideas have no use in art."[37]

In their long poems-in-progress, which were left unfinished after a period of at least thirty years, both Sousândrade and Holz laid bare the clash of discourses, oscillating between myth, historiography, and science. By means of extensive writing, they endeavored a poetic form able to encompass all discursive discrepancies, ranging from the conversational register to the highly artificial. And out of the noise of the many voices—which manifests itself in techniques such as text collage, multilingual strategies, hybrid composite words, among others—the authors searched for form through writing, in a process that eventually turned out to be endless, the remaining text-form as a trace of the impossibility to find a definite form. This never-ending search for form also turns out to be the reader's search. The fruition of poems such as *O Guesa errante* and *Phantasus* has primarily to do with deciphering or decoding; with finding the figure in the midst of mixed discourses and messages, so that misreading/misunderstanding turns to be an essential part of the aesthetic experience.

In reference to Sousândrade's later poem *Harpa de oiro* (1889–1899), finished in the same year Holz published the second booklet of his first *Phantasus* edition, Haroldo de Campos commented on unreadability as a link to modernity:

> We feel confronted with an Icarus protocol that registers the characteristics of falling rather than those of the flight. That does not prevent us from recognizing the radical tenure of Sousândrades's gesture, whose accomplishment had already stood out in its exuberance in previous poems. This gesture consists of systematically disrupting the discursive representation order; of weaving a synthetic, hieroglyphic, cryptic language across the grain of discourse, undermining it deeply; of introducing unreadability where once prevailed the legible platitude of Romantic and Parnassian poetic discourse (the unreadability that would be proposed again later, in the modern era, as the only possibility of the readable, as far as that previous effortless readability of our Romanticism and of our Parnassianism eventually expired and lapsed). . . . The "falling outs" (the loss of control over the productive activity released by the violence of the destructive movement) correspond to silence or to its compensation figure, chaos, entropic and indifferent disorder of elements, like in the "white noise" of experimental music, a sort of background noise that follows the placental displacement of language.[38]

That is also the question of readability that interests concrete poetry in its proposal of a new poetic form in mixed media. The most programmatic concrete poems asked that the reader find—even at the most primary optic level—his/her way in a multidirectional text. If linearity is chosen as a constitutive element of the poem, it is often in order to show how linear order can also lead to semantic misconstruction. Since the emphasis of concrete poetry falls on the materiality of language, so that letters are treated as images, sometimes the poem plays with the variable distance between the reader and the text, often in order to explore possible ambiguities in the process of reading.

Other strategies for creating ambiguity relate to the discrepancies (or the clash) between the acoustic and the visual aspects of language, as well as the framing of the text and the distribution of words on the page—the way we splice language together to create other levels of reading. Sometimes, the configuration of letters and words has also the function of composing a scenic scheme, so that the text is read not only as a discourse flow but also as a diagram in which the order of words suggests a certain distribution of things in space. The concrete poem is often conceived as a constellation of words that sometimes reveals a regular pattern, with symmetrical or mirrored structures, and at other times grows irregularly into more unstable forms. Other procedures (such as permutation, anagrammatic variation, superimposition of text layers) and the use of borrowed arrangements (as crossword puzzle, emblems or logograms, among others) lead to the central question of reading as an active and continuous decoding process.

All these textual practices date back to the programmatic phase of concrete poetry in the 1950s and 1960s. From the 1970s on, the Campos brothers followed different paths, but the question of decoding and readability has remained an underlying poetic concern until their later work. Augusto de Campos has never abandoned the core tenets of concrete poetry—such as emphasis on the visual property of language, brevity, and condensation—and he has gone even further in this direction since the 1990s, as he started to use digital technology in conceiving or producing poems. One might say that concrete poetry anticipated—with by today's standards low-tech means—a kind of hypertextuality that would become more easily achievable half a century later through electronic media. The limited resources with which authors of concrete poetry had to cope with sixty years ago led them to create highly inventive effects of textual spatiality and multidirectionality, in order to release the poem from the restraints imposed by the book format. The access to digital technology, on the one hand, has opened the way to several new resources, but, on the other hand, it has facilitated the merely decorative employment of visual effects, which the Brazilian inventors of concrete poetry resolutely rejected. However, in adhering to digital technology, Augusto de Campos has not neglected his poetic roots, including the conception of the poem's spatiality as a function of the temporality of reading and as a problematization of readability.

As far as Haroldo de Campos is concerned, the "verbivocovisual" approach of his poetry changed radically starting in the late 1960s. In comparison to his early concrete poems from the 1950s, his book *Signantia Quasi Coelum—Signância Quase Céu* (1979) shows a less strictly functional use of spatiality; the sparse distribution of words in this book's poems is less diagrammatic than rhythmic, suggesting a more subtle presence of silence in the text. From the 1980s on, Haroldo de Campos has definitely reduced the emphasis on graphic layout, keeping, however, the highly elaborated melopoeia of his earliest poems. Although important issues of concrete poetry still underline his later works, especially the ambiguities promoted by textual segmentation and textual accumulation, his affinity to baroque logopoeia has increasingly shaped his diction from *Galáxias* (1964–1984) until *A Máquina do Mundo Repensada* (2000), just to mention his more extensive book projects. Along with the change of Haroldo de Campos's approach to "verbivocovisuality," it is possible to notice that the focus on textual density—constitutive of concrete poetics, in affinity to Ezra Pound's definition of "great literature [as] language charged with meaning to the utmost degree"—has changed from formal reduction to verbal expansiveness coupled with referential stratification. It is this kind of poetic intensity—inseparable from Haroldo de Campos's role as a translator and theoretician—that reposes the question of readability in his later works.

To investigate the question of readability in the work of the Campos brothers can be a relevant key to understanding the apparent contradiction between the programmatic concrete poetics of the Noigandres poets, with their call for perceptual immediacy and direct textual apprehensibility, and their tendency to include in their "paideuma" authors of remarkable literary opacity, among whom Holz and Sousândrade could be considered especially radical and displaced in their lifetimes. Moreover, it can offer a broader view of the development of concrete poetics into very different literary lineages and help to investigate the connection between the baroque and modernist avant-garde which seems to be especially familiar to Latin American literature. Finally, it can lead to the perception of lines of continuity in the history and legacy of the concrete avant-garde, which tends to be characterized as an isolated moment of rupture.

The word *Noigandres*—which Augusto de Campos, Décio Pignatari, and Haroldo de Campos chose to name their group and their first literary magazine in the early 1950s—is already an undeciphered sign. Taken from a poem by the Provençal troubadour Arnaut Daniel (1150–1200), the word, whose meaning was supposedly long disputed by philologists, is mentioned in Ezra Pound's "Canto XX" in the context of a conversation with the German scholar Emil Lévy, who ends up saying, "Noigandres! NOIgandres! / You know for seex mon's of my life / Effery night when I go to bett, I say to myself: / Noigandres, eh, noigandres, Now what the DEFFIL can that mean!"[39]

Notes

1 / Décio Pignatari, "Nova Poesia: Concreta (manifesto)," in *Teoria da poesia concreta: Textos críticos e manifestos 1950–1960*, ed. Augusto de Campos, Decio Pignatari, and Haroldo de Campos (Cotia: Ateliê Editorial, 2006), 56. Originally published in *Ad: Arquitetura e Decoração*, no. 20 (November–December 1956). Translations are mine unless otherwise noted.

2 / Haroldo de Campos, "Poesia concreta—linguagem—comunicação" [1957], in Campos, Pignatari, and Campos, *Teoria da poesia concreta*, 119. Originally published in "Suplemento Dominical," *Jornal do Brasil*, April 28, 1957.

3 / Haroldo de Campos, "Aspectos da poesia concreta" [1957], in Campos, Pignatari, and Campos, *Teoria da poesia concreta*, 142. Originally published in *Diálogo*, no. 7, São Paulo, July 1957.

4 / Augusto de Campos, "Poesia Concreta (manifesto)" [1956], in Campos, Pignatari, and Campos, *Teoria da Poesia Concreta*, 71. Originally published in *Ad: Arquitetura e Decoração*, no. 20 (November–December 1956).

5 / Haroldo de Campos, "Olho por Olho a Olho Nu (manifesto)" [1956], in Campos, Pignatari, and Campos, *Teoria da poesia concreta*, 76. Originally published in *Ad: Arquitetura e Decoração*, no. 20 (November–December 1956).

6 / In "Ovo Novo No Velho," Décio Pignatari traces a parallel between Augusto de Campos's poem "Ovo Novelo" and a poem by Symmias of Rhodes, referring to the contributions of the Greek Anthology (Antologia Graeca) to the optic poetry.

7 / H. de Campos, "Poesia concreta," in Campos, Pignatari, and Campos, *Teoria da poesia concreta*, 110.

8 / A. de Campos, "Poesia concreta (manifesto)," in Campos, Pignatari, and Campos, *Teoria da poesia concreta*, 71.

9 / Augusto de Campos. "Pontos—Periferia—Poesia Concreta" [1956], in Campos, Pignatari, and Campos, *Teoria da poesia concreta*, 37. Originally published in "Suplemento Dominical," *Jornal do Brasil*, November 11, 1956.

10 / A. de Campos, 38.

11 / A. de Campos, 38. Décio Pignatari, "Poesia concreta: Pequena marcação histórico-formal" [1957], in Campos, Pignatari, and Campos, *Teoria da poesia concreta*, 97. Originally published in *Ad: Arquitetura e Decoração* 4, no. 2 (March–April 1957).

12 / H. de Campos, "Olho por Olho," in Campos, Pignatari, and Campos, *Teoria da poesia concreta*, 75.

13 / H. de Campos, "Aspectos da poesia concreta," in Campos, Pignatari, and Campos, *Teoria da poesia concreta*, 139.

14 / H. de Campos, 43.

15 / In "Memorabilia" (1877), introduction to the seventh Canto of the New York edition of his *Guesa*, Sousândrade affirms he got sad as he heard twice that his book would just be read fifty years later, declaring himself upset for having written it fifty years too early. See Augusto de Campos and Haroldo de Campos, *Re-visão de Sousândrade* (São Paulo: Editora Perspectiva, 2002), 24. Analogously, in a letter to Prof. Liebmann dated January 17, 1916, Arno Holz shows himself convinced of his role as an avant-garde poet, considering himself "ahead of his time" and misunderstood by his contemporaries, because of his "aberrant achievements." Arno Holz, *Briefe* (Munich: Piper Verlag, 1948), 211. To this day, Sousândrade and Holz are not part of the mainstream literary canon in their respective countries. Holz is scarcely translated into other languages: English translations were published in some avant-garde magazines in the 1910s and 1920s—as *The Egoist* (London) and *Poetry* (Chicago)—and in anthologies for contemporary poetry in the same period; complete translations of the first *Phantasus* version (1898) were published in the last fifteen years in French (by Éd. Comp'act in 2003, translated by Huguette Radrizzani and René Radrizzani) and in Italian (by Campanotto Editore, Udine, 2008, translated by Donatella Casarini and Enzo Minarelli); from the subsequent *Phantasus* versions, which are poetically much more radical and challenging, some fragments were published in English (1961 postumous edition, translated by David Dodd in 1996 and revised in 1999), in Italian (1925 edition, translated by Donatella Casarini and Enzo Minarelli and published in 2015), Portuguese (1916 and 1925 editions, translated by Augusto de Campos and Haroldo de Campos in the 1960s and 1990s). There is also a Polish translation by Krzysztof D. Szatrawski, which was published in 2013. As far as Sousândrade is concerned, the *Guesa errante* episode "The Inferno of Wall Street" was translated into into Spanish by the Peruvian poet Reynaldo Jimenez (libros de la resistencia, 2015) and into English by Robert E. Brown. Campos and Campos, *Re-visão de Sousândrade*, 583–624.

16 / Haroldo de Campos: "Avolução das formas: Poesia concreta" (1957); Haroldo de Campos, "Contexto de uma vanguarda" (1960); Augusto de Campos and Haroldo de Campos, "Arno Holz: Da revolução da lírica à elefantíase do projeto" (1962; the article includes the translation of Arno Holz's "Barocke Marine"); and Augusto de Campos and Haroldo de Campos, "De Holz a Sousândrade" (1962).

17 / Haroldo de Campos, *Deus e o diabo* no Fausto *de Goethe* (São Paulo: Editora Perspectiva, 1981), 128. On the certain abstract style, see Campos and Campos, *Re-visão de Sousândrade*, 32.

18 / See David Dodd's

tendency to substitute neologisms by periphrases in his translation of a fragment of the posthumous *Phantasus* edition, http://artsites.ucsc.edu/GDead/agdl/holz.html.

19 / Haroldo de Campos, "Arno Holz: Da revolução da lírica à elefantíase do projeto," in *O arco-íris branco* (Rio de Janeiro: Imago, 1997), 76–77.

20 / H. de Campos, 76–77.

21 / H. de Campos, 87, 90.

22 / Campos and Campos, *Re-visão de Sousândrade*, 509.

23 / In the 2001 article "A Peregrinação Transamericana do *Guesa* de Sousândrade" about the influence of Alexander von Humboldt's naturalistic studies on Sousândrade's *Guesa*, Haroldo de Campos restates his disapproval of the sociohistorical literary criticism in Brazil, which used to exclude the baroque from its historiographical view because this movement, having preceded the Brazilian independence from Portugal, could not be said to have contributed to the constitution of the local literary system as an expression of the "national spirit." Campos's *O sequestro do barroco na formação da literatura brasileira* already argues against the dismissal of the baroque in the literary criticism tradition represented by Antonio Candido de Mello e Souza and his followers. The essay was translated to English as "Disappearence of Baroque in Brazilian Literature," in *Novas: Selected Writings of Haroldo de Campos* (Evenston, IL: Northwestern University Press, 2007).

24 / Campos and Campos, *Re-visão de Sousândrade*, 536.

25 / Campos and Campos, 522.

26 / Campos and Campos, 343–344.

27 / Arno Holz, *Phantasus* (Leipzig: Insel Verlag, 1916), 22.

28 / Campos and Campos, *Re-visão de Sousândrade*, 33.

29 / Arno Holz, *Phantasus* (Berlin: Sassenbach, 1898), n.p. (34).

30 / Campos and Campos, *Re-visão de Sousândrade*, 35.

31 / Campos and Campos, 35.

32 / Campos and Campos, 56–57.

33 / H. de Campos, *Deus e o Diabo*, 128.

34 / Arno Holz, "Moderne Walpurgisnacht," *Pan*1 (November 1899), http://bluemountain.princeton.edu/bluemtn/cgi-bin/bluemtn?a=d&d=bmtnabe189911-01.2.14&e=-------en-20--1--txt-txIN-------#.

35 / Campos and Campos, *Re-visão de Sousândrade*, 123.

36 / Campos and Campos, 124.

37 / Holz, *Briefe*, 72.

38 / Campos and Campos, *Re-visão de Sousândrade*, 528–529.

39 / "And I went to old Lévy, and it was by then 6:30/in the evening, and he trailed half way across Freiburg/before dinner, to see the two strips of copy, /Arnaut's, settant'uno R. superiore (Ambrosiana)/Not that I could sing him the music./And he said: 'Now is there anything I can tell you?'/And I said: I dunno, sir, or 'Yes, Doctor, what do they mean by noigandres?/And he said: 'Noigandres! NOIgandres!/'You know for seex mon's of my life / 'Effery night when I go to bett, I say to myself:/'Noigandres, eh, noigandres, 'Now what the DEFFIL can that mean!" See Ezra Pound, "Canto XX," in *The Cantos* (London: Faber and Faber, 1994), 89.

THE WANDERER, THE EARTH Nature and History in the Work of Sousândrade and Paulo Nazareth

14

Eduardo Sterzi

Sousândrade opens his great poem *O Guesa* (written between 1858 and 1888) with what would look like a quintessentially Romantic invocation, an exclamation that determines and immediately marks, already in the poem's first line, an interruption—a decasyllable cut in two quasi-verses.

> Eia, imaginação divina!
>   Os Andes

And the strophe continues:

>   Volcanicos elevam cumes calvos,
>   Circumdados de gelos, mudos, alvos,
>   Nuvens fluctuando—que espetac'los grandes!
> Lá, onde o poncto do kondor negreja,
>   Scintillando no espaço como brilhos
>   D'olhos, e cae a prumo sobre os filhos
>   Do lhama descuidado; onde lampeja
> Da tempestade o raio; onde deserto,
>   O azul sertão formoso e deslumbrante,
>   Arde do sol o incendio, delirante
>   Coração vivo em céu profundo aberto![1]
>
> [Eia, divine imagination!
>   The volcanic Andes,
>   bald peaks raising,

Surrounded of ice, silent, blank,
Fluttering clouds—what a great spectacle!
There, where the condor is a black point,
Scintillating in space like sparkles
of eyes, preying on the offspring
Of the inattentive llama; Where flashes
Lightning amid the storm; Where deserted,
The blue hinterland handsome and dazzling,
Burning the delirious, fire of the sun,
Living heart in deep open sky!]

The internal rupture of the first verse anticipates a deeper scission between the poem's first strophe—the sublime vision of nature—and the one that follows. For if it was necessary, in the poet's eyes, for a "divine imagination" to conceive of the Andes in all its grandeur, only an earthly imagination would account for what follows as the poem progresses: the remembering of the massacre of natives by the Spanish conquerors. And it will be *earthly imagination* at work that we will witness along the entire poem, in constant oscillation with what has been named here "divine imagination." Augusto de Campos called attention to the "semantic unraveling" (*esgarçada semântica*) in *O Guesa*, resulting from its "fragmentary style" that alternates "images of nature with lyrical-biographical experiences."[2] As a matter of fact, Sousândrade does not discern between the two approaches, as *O Guesa* proposes an unsettled and unsettling experience of a nature hopelessly submitted to the ills of colonization. In the poem, images of an untouched primeval nature appear only in contrast with the ubiquitous destruction; and even those images of pure nature seem abated by the earthly imagination that produces allegories of horror—note in the previous excerpt the stress given to the scene of a condor menacing a llama offspring at the same time that the "living heart open in the deep sky" (an extraordinary image of the sun) refers to the extricated heart of the *guesa* mentioned in the poem's epigraph. Nature, for Sousândrade, is history. Hence the poet often refers to natural landscapes as human construction, or architecture.

Guesa is the one who listens not only to the echoes of extinguished tribes, but to nature as a whole. And he not only listens but invites us to listen together with him, and pay attention to that endangered universe:

Oiçamos . . . o fervor de extranha prece,
Que no silencio a natureza imita
De nossos corações . . . aquem palpita . . .
Além suspira . . . além, no amor floresce . . .
Porque eu venho, do mundo fugitivo,
No deserto escutar a voz da terra:
—Eu sou qual este lírio, triste, esquivo,
Qual esta brisa que nos ares erra.[3]

[Let us listen . . . The fervor of strange prayer,
    That in silence nature imitates
    From our hearts . . . palpitating . . .
    sighing . . . and, blossoming in love . . .
For I come from the furtive world,
    to hear the voice of the earth in the desert:
    —I am like this lily, dismal, elusive,
    Like this breeze that err in the air?"]

Therefore, the poet is the one who "listens to the voice of the earth": earthly imagination is, above all else, the imagination of earth (*imaginação da terra*). And rhyme is no minor matter here for in *O Guesa erra* is the preferential rhyme for *terra*; which strikes me as an indicator that *terra* (earth) evokes, for Sousândrade, above all else, *errância* (wandering) and not belonging (or, at least, not any simple kind of belonging). This wandering—this non-belonging—inscribes itself in the *guesa*'s very identity. Although the *guesa* originates from the Muisca people, Sousândrade conceives of him as a composite figure with elements borrowed from the Inca and others from Amazonian natives. Furthermore, he gives to his character his own history to some extent, although as the *guesa* tours throughout America, his identity becomes fluid. Sousândrade is a propitious author to those who, like Marília Librandi-Rocha, propose to "examine all that in Brazil extrapolates its boundaries, crosses frontiers and leave territorial borders."[5] That which does not shy away from an "ex-centric" position. It's a matter of "thinking in terms of a multiplicity of relationships rather than of a plurality of identities."[6]

In Sousândrade's poem, the *guesa*, besides Muisca, "is at the same time Inca, Tupi, Araucano, Timbira, Sioux, and is himself Sousândrade, a wanderer, homeless, and thus, without a nation."[7] In sum, "a metamorphic character, multiethnic, transcontinental, American."[8] *Guesa* is "not a dead ancestral Indian, transformed into original hero of the Brazilian nation, but rather a living anti-hero made symbol of a Pan-American world." In other words, a *survivor* anti-hero, a *resistant* character defying the avowedly inevitable extinction of the tribes; defying the massacre of the indigenous people.[9]

By taking his concept of Pan-Americanism to the extreme, Sousândrade unveils, as few other Brazilian authors and thinkers, the global dimension of any action after the consolidation of capitalism.[10] The imaging of earth both as element and ground, which ends up being the *imagination of Earth* as planet and dwelling, is political imaging par excellence. Which does not eliminate the municipal or provincial dimensions of its reach, but rather sets up a new, broader perspective: not by accident, in returning to Brazil after a decade abroad, Sousândrade became the mayor in his native São Luis do Maranhão; he also worked on a plan to open a university, which he would name Atlantis or New Athens and that would have a chair of Indian

Law. The connection between local spheres and *O Guesa*'s all-encompassing master plan is evident in sequences of infernal moments that speak of the degradation of indigenous cultures through colonial exploration (in the "Tatuturema" sequence in Canto Second), or that outline the risks of financial capitalism through the submission to the god Mamon (in "The Wall Street Inferno" section of Canto Tenth)—an intuition that we find updated in a recent claim by Giorgio Agamben who said "God is not dead, he became Money."[11]

After the torture and killings at Escuela Superior de Mecánica de la Armada, (Buenos Aires) after the massacres at Candelária (Rio de Janeiro), Carandiru (São Paulo), and Eldorado dos Carajás (Pará), after Ciudad Juarez (Mexico), after the endless massacres whose names form a dark constellation in the sky of modernity—we can see that the anticipatory aspect of Sousândrade's oeuvre surpasses any of the formal strategies that announced the avant-gardes. Indeed, his work diverts such strategies (born from his singular assimilation of Brazilian and English Romanticism) toward a new reading of modern history as the intersection of capitalism and massacre. It is a matter of *vision*, as Luis Costa Lima first noted.[12] Lima points out that, in contrast to the "nature-devouring" characteristic in Brazilian Romanticism—the conversion of "experiencing the world" into an experience of consumption, through which "all reality, nature, the elements, the stars was sacrificed in favor of the I"—Sousândrade initiated a "poetics of concreteness, open to the world."[13] Against the "description . . . of emotional states" of conventional Romanticism, he proposes to open poetry to "an ontological dimension."[14] Opening up to the world entails that *voyage* becomes a form of poetry, instead of merely its subject. Costa Lima stresses in Sousândrade the importance of physical contact with reality for the kind of expression that he is after, which would become clear in comparing the artistic achievements of "The Wall Street Inferno" to the supposed failure of *Harpas de oiro*: "the visualization of reality is the *a priori* condition for the artist's discovery of the aesthetic correspondent."[15] Hence, the voyages of the *guesa* are also Sousândrade's voyages, albeit reconfigured.

Not by chance, Sousândrade, in his epigraph extracted from Stanislas Marie César Famin, sees himself as the "Guesa, or the wanderer, i.e., the homeless being"[16]—as some kind of indigenous version of the *homo sacer* (sacred man), to refer to that obscure figure of Roman jurisprudence in which Agamben found the paradigm of modern and contemporary political life.[17] Which means that from the very start—through his epigraphs—Sousândrade places the poem under the sign of sacrifice, or more importantly, under the sign of extermination. This is, however, a poem of resistance to sacrifice—self-sacrifice as well as sacrifice of the other—personal and collective, dedicated to any god, including the god of money, Mamon. He who listens to the voice of earth will inevitably end up listening to the voices of those whose bodies, many never identified, never duly memorialized, lie on earth. And will strive to become one with this voice—as the Portuguese poet Ruy Belo wrote:

> My supreme ambition, my ideal—unattainable as any ideal, but always present as limit— . . . is to become mineral, impassive in its adherence to the earth, to which I will return not only by condition but by a profound, ever felt desire that will only be satisfied the day my voice becomes one with the voice of earth, more important than all the words that I have been allowed to proffer on its surface throughout my more or less short life, but ultimately always short, if seen from the perspective of man's destiny as species and the life of the planet as his ambient as ever and forever.[18]

Sousândrade sets off the *guesa*'s voyage following the death of the parents, that is to say, upon the erasure of origin, as well as on the infinite regret of this erased origin that is made into absence and, above all, a phantom (and this will be all along, a poem of phantoms):

Passa uma sombra diaphana e tão pura
A extinguir-se através da noite etherea,
Das grandes sombras na distancia obscura . . .
Passa outra sombra, longe da primeira.
—Ora, de terra em terra o sempre ausente,
Sem mais vêr patria alguma que o contente,
Ledo incanta-se aos mimos da belleza
E d'elles desincanta-se—ai do Guesa!
Ai quem do mundo assim, e seu mau grado,
Correndo as zonas for, qual em procura
D'outro amor, d'outros homens, d'outro estado,
Ou d'outro sol, ou d'outra sepultura![19]

[A shadow diaphanous and pure passes
And extinguishes into the ethereal night,
From the great shadows in the obscure distance . . .
Another shadow passes, far from the first.
—Now, from land to land, the ever absent,
Without devising his country any more than the content,
Foolishly in love with beauty's snares
Only to reject them—poor Guesa!
Woe those who run the ends of this world
Against all odds, crossing all zones
In search of other love, other men, other state
Or of other sun, or another tomb.]

In Sousândrade's cosmic-political imagination, dawn means the awakening of earth itself, which he contrasts with the melancholy of the native robbed of a future by the colonizer's violence:

Acorda a terra; as flores da alegria
Abrem, fazem do leito de seus ramos
Sua glória infantil; Alcyon em clamos

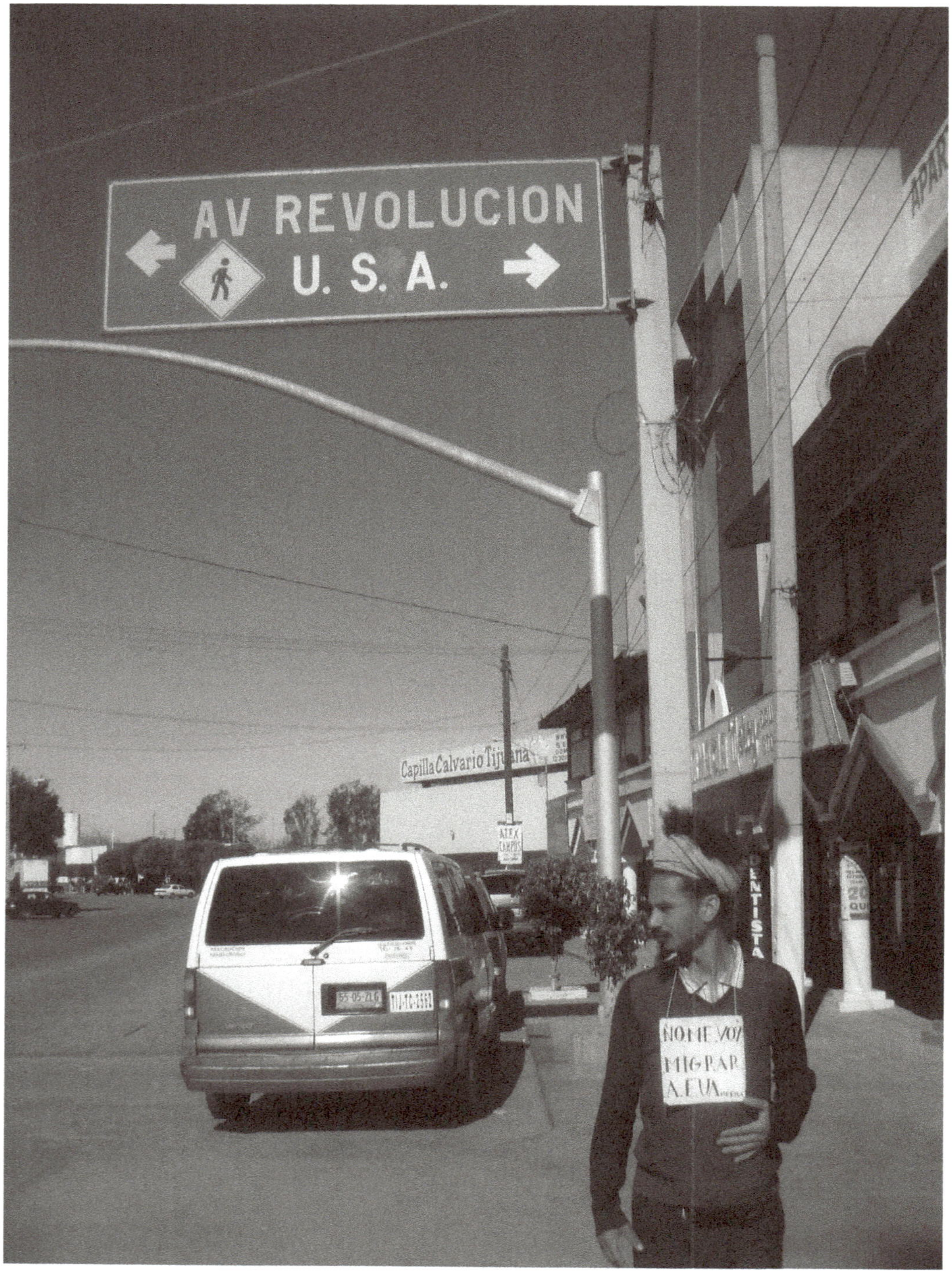

Paulo Nazareth, *Untitled*. From the series *Notícias de América*, 2012. Photo printing on cotton paper. Courtesy Mendes Wood DM.

Passa cantando sobre o cedro ao dia
Lindas loas boyantes; o selvagem
Cala-se, evoca d'outro tempo um sonho,
E curva a fronte . . . Deus, como é tristonho
Seu vulto sem porvir, em pé na margem![20]

[The earth awakens; the joyful flowers
open, and make from the bed of their branches
Her puerile glory; Alcyon in flames
Singing by the cedar to no one
Beautiful fluid songs; The native
Becomes mute, and recalls a dream from another time,
And bows the forehead . . . God, how depressing
His figure without future, standing on the bank!]

Sousândrade is ambiguous about the dances performed by natives that, even though already in process of "degradation," keep the "memory of grander times;" the horizon here, is the *destruction of the peoples*, more specifically, the *minor peoples*:

Selvagens—mas tão bellos, que se sente
Um barbaro prazer n'essa memoria
Dos grandes tempos, recordando a historia
dos formosos guerreiros reluzentes:
Em cruentos festins, na vária festa,
Nas ledas caças ao romper da aurora;
E à voz profunda que a ribeira chora
Enlanguecer, dormir saudosa sesta . . .
A voz das fontes celebrava amores!
As aves em fagueira direcção
Alevantando os voos, trovadores
Cantavam a partir o coração!
Selvagens, sim; porém tendo uma crença;
De erros ou bôa, acreditando n'ella:
Hoje, se riem com fatal descrença
E a luz apagam de Tupana-estrella.

Destino das nações! um povo erguido
Dos virgens seios d'esta natureza,
Antes de haver coberto da nudeza
O cincto e o coração, foi destruído:
E nem pelos combates tão feridos,
Tão sanguinarias, barbaras usanças;
Por esta religião falsa d'esperanças
Nos apostolos seus, falsos, mentidos
Ai! vinde ver a transição dolente
Do passado ao porvir, n'este presente!
Vinde ver do Amazonas o thesoiro,
A onda vasta, os grandes valles de oiro!
Immensa solidão vedada ao mundo,
Nas chammas do equador, longe da luz!
Donde fugiu o tabernac'lo immundo,
Mas onde ainda não abre o braço a cruz![21]

[Wild natives—but so beautiful, that one feels
a barbaric pleasure in the memory
of great times, remembering the history
of galant gleaming warriors:
In bloody feasts, in various feasts,
In lazy hunts at the breaking of dawn;
And with the deep cry of the river voice
To languish, to sleep forgetful naps . . .
The voice of the fountains celebrated loves!
The birds in friendly direction
taking flights, troubadours
singing from the heart!
Savages, yes; but with faith;
rights or wrong, believing in her:
Today, one laughs with fatal disbelief
and the light goes out in Tupana-star.

Fate of nations! A people borne
of nature's virgin entrails,
Before having covered from nudity
The girdle and the heart were destroyed:
And neither by the fighting so wounded,
So sanguinary, barbaric uses;
For this false religion of hopes
In its apostles, false, lying
Aye! Come see the slow transition
From the past to come, in this present!
Come and see from Amazonas the treasure,
The vast wave, the great valleys of gold!
Immense solitude blind to the world,
In the flames of the equator, away from the light!
From where the unclean tabernacle fled,
But where the arm does not yet open the cross.]

According to Sousândrade, the destitute native is the remnant of a natural world,[22] and in "Tatuturema," we hear the *guesa* speak:

—Eu nasci no deserto,
Sob o sol do equador:
As saudades do mundo,
Do mundo . . .
Diabos levem tal dor![23]

[I was born in the desert,
Under the equatorial sun:
Nostalgias of the world,
Of the world . . .
The devils take this pain!]

The expression "nostalgia of the world" (*saudades do mundo*) can be read in two ways, and neither invalidates the other: initially it is an allusion to the natural world from which the *guesa* originates, referred to in the first two verses (the equatorial desert); but we can also read *world* in a broader sense without losing sight of its strict meaning, whereas "nostalgia of the world" becomes the very propeller for the hero in his voyages; the object of his search is nothing less than the world itself, perceived as lost at that very moment. He goes out in search of the world from which he himself is a survivor.

The survivors of a disappearing world are called "witness people" by Brazilian anthropologist Darcy Ribeiro.[24] Notions of survival and witnessing,[25] however, acquire thoroughly critical and political values only when read under the perspective provided by anthropologist Eduardo Viveros de Castro in an interview to poet and law scholar Pádua Fernandes: "native-hood is a project for the future, not a memory of the past"; or "being a native is not a concept that remits us only and mainly to the past—we are natives because we were natives—but rather a concept that also remits us to the future—it is possible to become a native again."[26] In short, as Viveiros de Castro and Déborah Danowski propose elsewhere, natives are a "figuration of the future" not a "remnant of the past."[27]

Literature plays a decisive role in this project that attempts to exact revenge for the *vanquished tribes*—a term coined by Machado de Assis in an essay on the *instinct of nationality*, published in the New York Republican newspaper *O Novo Mundo*, for which Sousândrade served as secretary and contributor. Assis wrote: "Certainly Brazilian civilization is not connected to the indigenous element nor has it been influenced by it; and that suffices to prevent us from searching amid the vanquished tribes the titles of our literary personality."[28] A few lines later in the same text, however, overwhelmed by the diagnostic of a total massacre, Assis attempts to base poetry on a sentiment of piety for the supposedly disappeared natives, now merely traces on the brink of erasure from a tradition that confuses itself with antiquity, thus isolating itself in a past that cannot be retrieved:

> The native tribes, whose traditions and mores João Francisco Lisboa found similar to those of the ancient Germanic people related in Tacitus book, certainly disappeared from the region that for long belonged to them; but the conqueror that surveyed the area collected precious information and transmitted them to us as veritable poetic elements. Piety, as other arguments of greater value diminish, should at least incline the poets' imagination toward the people that first absorbed the airs from these regions, rescuing in literature those killed by the fatality of history.[29]

If the fatality of history generates piety, the acknowledgment of survival and the determination of resistance—against everything and against all—take the shape of vengeance as an affirmation of life where only desolation was expected (*vengeance* not only as retribution but also as an act of resistance against any adverse expectation). This kind of revenge is active not only in Sousândrade but also in some of

Paulo Nazareth, *Untitled*. From the series *Notícias de América*, 2011/2012. Photo printing on cotton paper. Courtesy Mendes Wood DM.

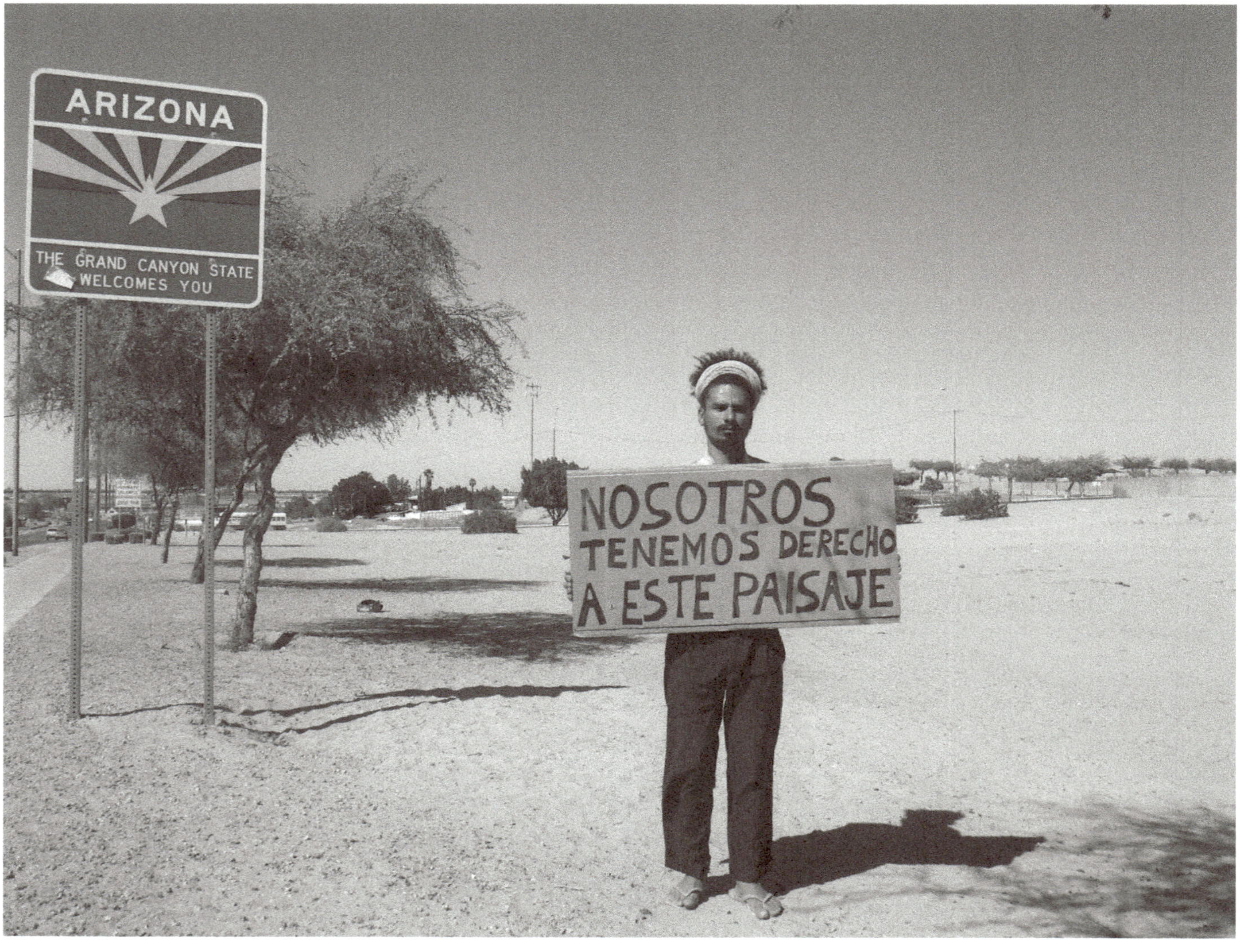

the best moments of our Romantic literature dedicated to the figuration of the native, as well as in Mario de Andrade's *Macunaíma*; in the cannibalism (anthropophagia) of Oswald de Andrade and Raul Bopp; in a few poems by Carlos Drummond de Andrade such as "Pranto geral dos índios" (The natives' general plaint), "Kreen-Akarore," and "Adeus a Sete Quedas" (Goodbye to seven falls); and more recently in Alberto Mussa's *Meu destino é ser onça* (My destiny is to become a panther), Josely Vianna Baptista's *Roça barroca* (Baroque orchard), and André Vallias's *Totem*, among others.

What is the meaning of Sousândrade making himself into *guesa*, making himself a native? As Gilles Deleuze and Félix Guattari observed in regard to Martin Heidegger,[30] in poetry, a "people to come" is always in question.

> For the race summoned forth by art or philosophy is not the one that claims to be pure but rather an oppressed, bastard, lower, anarchical, nomadic, and irremediably minor race—the very ones that Kant excluded from the paths of the new *Critique*. Artaud said: to write *for* the illiterate—to speak for the aphasic, to think for the acephalous. But what does "for" mean? It is not "for their benefit," or yet "in their place." It is "before." It is a question of becoming. The thinker is not acephalic, aphasic, or illiterate, but becomes so. He becomes Indian, and never stops becoming so—perhaps "so that" the Indian who is himself Indian becomes something else and tears himself away from his own agony. Becoming is always double, and it is this double becoming that constitutes the people to come and the new earth.[31]

In this passage, Deleuze and Guattari evoke a short text that Kafka included in his first book, *Contemplation*. The story is titled "The Wish to Be a Red Indian" ("Wunsch, Indianer zu werden"): "If we were only Indians, instantly alert, on the racing horse, leaning into the wind, always jerking with brief quivers on the quivering ground, until the spurs are shed, for there are no spurs, until the reins are thrown away, for there are no reins, and the land unfolding before one's sight is shorn heath, already without horse's neck and horse's head."[32] If this desire to become native, this pursuit of the savage as singularity and not identity, bridges the distance by means of images of literature or of cinema, in a Brazilian such as Sousândrade (or later, Oswald de Andrade), the question becomes immediately political. Consider, for example, Andrade's short essay titled "To Become Indian":

> The professor closed the book, scratched his head and appallingly announced to his family:
>
> —Today I'll buy a bow and arrow and board the train to Sorocabana. At least for this plan Brazil might work my way. I will lose myself in the great jungle and shall never return. I bought life insurance of which you are all beneficiaries. You don't need me anymore. And I cannot take this any longer! Philosophers, politicians, and sociologists all agree that this is the fall of a class, the debacle of the bourgeoisie. What about the Nuremberg trial? Did the bourgeois act as Hitler's obedient dogs in Buchenwald's gas chambers? Those were common folks! The human race is decomposing, carrying with it all the social classes! Pay attention to what is going on in high society.

. . .

And what about politics? Have you noticed what happened in our paradisiacal corner? What about free and honest elections? Our cities are inundated by stupefying propaganda, while in the countryside electors are hounded by campaign managers like inmates marching to a concentration camp; locked up in warehouses and fired from their farm jobs the next day for disobeying directions and changing party. And how do these people live, in shanty towns with no furniture, eating unsalted beans, manioc, and porridge; debilitated elders dying, children's bellies infested with vermin. In the prosperous areas, where to find schools and hospitals? Almsgiving still prevails in its most humiliating semblance. And as for the idealists, they are selling their consciousness by the pound! I am out of here. Radars already established contact with the moon, sparkling the lightest hope that soon man will be leaving this planet. Until that day comes, until I am able to board on the first rocket to the moon, like Lucian de Samosata envisioned in the first century, leaving behind the tragic roofless homes—I am becoming an Indian.[33]

Impossible not to recall here the idea of a flight to the interior, proposed on several occasions by Eduardo Viveiros de Castro:

I embraced ethnology to run away from Brazilian society, the purportedly compulsory subject of any social scientist in Brazil. Running away from Brazil was a method to arrive in Brazil by detour. Circumnavigation. It's important that the Brazil where we would arrive was the other, the other side of the Brazil we departed from. Certainly, it was not about running away from Brazil to vacation in Europe. It was about running away from Brazil, but to arrive in another more interesting place that had not been weighted, counted, and measured by these European categories, as Jorge Luis Borges noted—a place more interesting than the "Brazil" of the powerful. The indigenous as an antidote to the idea of Brazil.[34]

Equally important is the heuristic excess proposed by Viveiros de Castro when he maintains "in Brazil, everybody is indigenous, except those who are not." The problem is, he suggests, "who is *not* Indian":[35] "Darcy Ribeiro insisted on the fact that 'Brazilian people' is much more indigenous than one suspects or supposes. The man freed from slavery, to use the language of Maria Silvia Carvalho Franco, is an Indian. The hillbilly is an Indian, the coastal man (*caiçara*) is an Indian, the mixed-race (*caboclo*) is an Indian, the peasant from the Northeast hinterland is an Indian. In what sense? For starters, they are genetically Indian, although that is irrelevant."[36] Irrelevant because more than genetics, it is the *political Indian* that matters: "I maintain that the groups of coastal peoples, mixed-races, peasants and *Indians* are Indians (and not 33 percent Indian) in that they are the product of a history of a systematic process of cultural destruction, of political subjugation, of 'social exclusion' (or worse, of 'social inclusion'), a process that is obviously endless."[37] To become Indian is to incorporate in oneself—in the body and in the culture—*resistance* (life, and not only survival) as well as an image of desire:

> However successful the process of acculturation (set forth by catechesis, missionary zeal, modernization, and nationalization) was or has been, it is impossible to annul history and suppress all memory. Human collectives exist crucially and eminently at the moment of their reproduction, in the intergenerational passage from that relational mode, which is the collective, and unless those communities are physically exterminated, expatriated, deported, it is extremely hard to to entirely destroy them. And even when they are destroyed, or reduced to their individual components, apart from the relations that constituted them, as it happened to the African slaves, these components reinvent a culture and a way of life—a relational world that, however constrained by local adverse conditions, is as valid an expression of human life as any other. There are no unauthentic cultures, for there are no authentic cultures. There are, by the way, no authentic Indians. Indians, Caucasians, Afro-descendants, or whoever—for authenticity is not a prerogative of humankind. Or perhaps it is something that only whites can be (to their detriment).[38]

Viveiros de Castro positions himself firmly against the identity-obsessed posture that characterize the Westernized reaction to our endlessly mutable world in which everything and everybody always seem to be on the verge of becoming something other, even another humanity. "Very badly comparing—and I say badly because the comparison risks rekindling old and grotesque stereotypes, it can be said that being Indian is like what Lacan said about being crazy: it is not who wants to be. Nor who just says it so. For only an Indian is granted to be so."[39] An endless metamorphic transitivity without limits, neither internal nor external.

> Our theoretical and political goal, as anthropologists, was to establish once and for all that to be an *Indian* is not a matter of adorning oneself with feathers and body paint, carrying a bow and arrow; not some stereotypical visual signifier but rather a matter of a "spiritual state." Not only a look but a way of being. Indeed, something more (or less) than a way of being: Indianhood meant to us a certain mode of becoming, something essentially invisible, but no less effective: an infinitely continuous movement of differentiation, and not a massive state of preestablished "difference," that is, an identity. Our struggle, therefore, was for a conceptual fight: to make the word *still* in construction such as "these people are *still* Indian" (or, "are no longer Indian") lose its meaning as "state of transition," or "phase to be overcome." The idea being that Indians *still* have not been defeated, nor will they ever be. They (will) never cease to be Indian. In short, the idea was that the Indian could not be seen as a phase in the progressive march to the enviable state of becoming "white" or "civilized." We haven't succeeded but I believe one day we'll get there.[40]

Those who walk across the world in search of a *world*, recognizing themselves in a process of becoming, cannot aspire for a direct route. The feeling of *regrets*—in the plural, as we find in Darius Milhaud's *Saudades do Brasil*, and later in Claude Lévi-Strauss's photographic memoir—are not merely the nostalgia that takes us back (to that which no longer exists) but rather something that propels us forward and outward (toward that which still does not exist). Otherwise, what's been put into question is precisely an integral disassembling of the philosophical categories that in the past organized our experience of the world, beginning with the idea of linearity of time, and of history:

Paulo Nazareth, *Untitled*. From the series *Notícias de América*, 2012. Photo printing on cotton paper. Courtesy Mendes Wood DM.

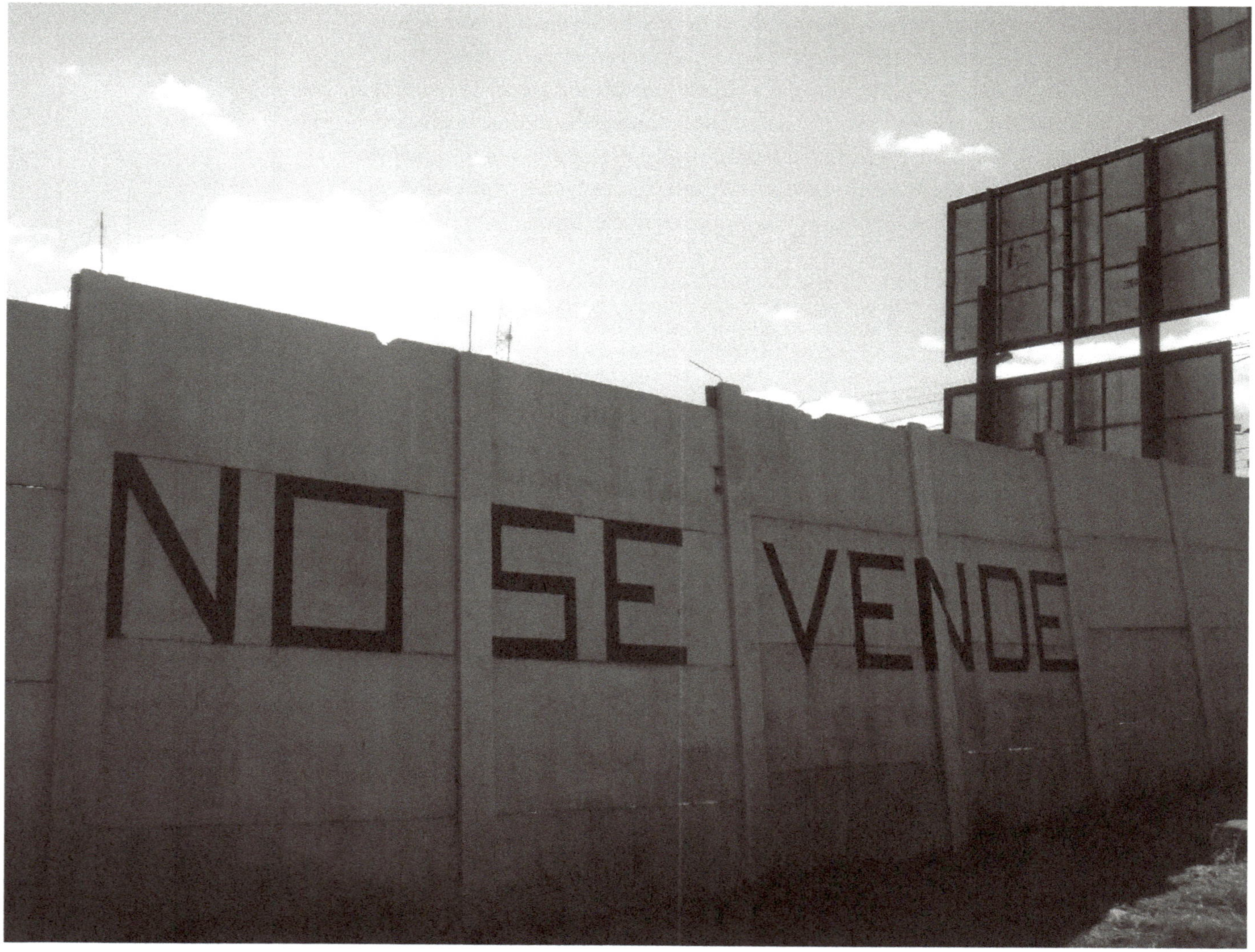

Just as we once had a horror of the vacuum, today we are disgusted at the thought of deceleration, regression, retreat, limitation, braking, decay, descent-sufficiency. Anything that reminds one of these movements in search of an intensive world-sufficiency (rather than an epic "limit" overhaul of a hyper-world) is readily accused of naive localism, primitivism, irrationalism, bad conscience, guilty feeling, or even, without flair, of fascination. For almost all the forms assumed by today's dominant thought among "we," only one direction is thinkable and desirable, that which leads from the "negative" to the "positive": from less to more, from little ownership to ownership of much, "subsistence technique" to "state-of-the-art technology," from the Paleolithic nomad to the modern cosmopolitan citizen, from the savage Indian to the civilized worker. Thus, when peasant communities "in the process of modernization" decide to return to being indigenous, demonstrating in court their historical continuity with officially extinct native peoples, as so many rural settlements have been doing in Brazil since the promulgation of the 1988 Constitution—which gave collective rights of possession of the land to the Indians and descendants of slaves implanted in the countryside—the shocked and furious reaction of the ruling classes has been a spectacle not to be missed. Unfortunately, one cannot find grace for a long time from those who continue with the whip in their hands; the fury, along with greed, of those who need the inexistence of otherness is translated into a concerted offensive, by legal and illegal means, legislative and criminal, of the great landowners—and their partners, and their clients, and their bosses—against the Indians and other traditional peoples of the country. Thus, it is only possible (and desirable) that an individual or community cease to be an Indian, it is impossible (and repulsive) to be an Indian again: how can one wish for a future as a backwardness? Well, maybe the scandal has its reason: maybe it's impossible to go back historically to be an Indian. But it is quite possible, more than that, that an Indian-local, a local as a global, a particular as a general, an incessant becoming-again-Indian is taking over important sectors of the Brazilian "population" in a completely unexpected way. This is one of the most important political events that we witness in Brazil today and that is gradually contaminating many other Brazilian peoples besides indigenous peoples.[41]

Above all, the main change is in discerning the placement for each creature and each object (thing) in this world (or more radically, the discernment of different worlds coexisting, not often peacefully, in the same places).

J. M. G. Le Clézio's *Haï*—translated in Portuguse as *Índio branco* (White Indian)—stresses the modernity of the encounter with the Indian world, while also correctly interpreting it as a matter of survival: "Today, the encounter with the Indian world is not a luxury. It has become a necessity for those who wish to understand what is going on in the modern world. It's not enough, however, to merely try to understand it; but rather of trying to go to the end of all obscure galleries, of opening some of its doors—ultimately, of trying to survive."[42]

The *guesa*'s journey has been mapped out by Augusto de Campos thus:

Cantos I to III: the descent from the Andes until the source of the Amazonas River; Cantos IV and V: interludes in Maranhão; Canto VI: trip to Rio de Janeiro; Canto VII: studies in Europe and trips to Africa (incomplete Canto); Canto VIII: new interlude in Maranhão; Canto IX: travels through Antilhas, América Central, Golfo do México, and to the United States; Canto X: Guesa arrives in New York and travels across the United States; Canto XI: Pacific Ocean, Panama, Colombia, Venezuela, Peru; Canto XII: along the Pacific Ocean and toward

> Argentina, the Andean cordilleras, with incursions into Bolivia and Chile; Canto XIII: returns to Maranhão (incomplete Canto).[43]

Sousândrade's many travels, accomplished at different times, intertwine in *O Guesa* as one atemporal journey. If these episodes lack a center, as the Campos brothers have noted, their structure nevertheless display a shifting axis, like a hurricane destroying everything in its path. The New York episode is therefore fundamental, as it informs the poem with the extreme actuality of financial capitalism as the most recent avatar of colonialism. "Which other poet of his time," asked the Campos in 1964, "could have traced the Dantesque vision of the New York Stock Exchange—the epicenter of the capitalist world—as an infernal circle?"[44] Inferno's most terrifying aspect is its eternal duration, and it is thus understandable that Sousândrade would construct his vision of hell through an asynchronous collection in which different eras intersperse and collide. As he starts the episode, Sousândrade notes that the wall that names the street was erected as a "defense against the Indians."[45]

The notion of dislocation defines the *guesa* and the poet Sousândrade, as well as his poetry overall, especially as it is presented in this poem. Character, poet, and poem enact an *art of constant dislocation*, through which they question any feeling of belonging exclusively to a territory, and to a language. Sousândrade is an odd romantic, for whom there is not *one* language, but languages; not one (national) territory, but first and foremost, the earth: limitless and without frontiers; element, hearth, and planet; the lands where one wanders, imbued with a deeper feeling of belonging (because the being is grounded on earth) and yet, extremely superficial (because the being is nomad, fleeting, never reducible to a stable essence, to an identity). In the figure of his cosmopolitan Indian, Sousândrade seems to have synthesized an understanding of Amerindian thought that would only be articulated by Oswald de Andrade's anthropophagia half a century later.

Like a *guesa*, Paulo Nazareth became a wandering artist who made of his own sense of dislocation the very issue of his art practice. Art critic Kiki Mazzuchelli noted that from the beginning, drifting away has been a characteristic of his process. *News from America*, his best-known project, represents the moment in which his drifting took on epic proportions, allowing for previously local concerns, to gain wider scope.[46] Indeed, Mazzuchelli refers to *News from America* in terms of an "American epic."

News from America consisted of a series of nonlinear trips starting in Brazil and through various countries in Latin America until its final destination in the United States. Throughout his journey Nazareth wore the same pair of plastic sandals, never washing his feet and accumulating dust gathered on Latin America soil. The project ended in New York, as he washed his feet in the Hudson river. Throughout his pilgrimage, Nazareth was attuned to both the public reaction to his ethnicity (he is a descendent of Krenak Indians mixed in with black and Italian), and to the recent historical trauma related to political strife in the Americas. The strength of *News from America* resides in the intertwining of these three threads: pilgrimage, mixed ethnicity, and political upheaval.

News from America, which started in March 2011 and lasted for one year, was a hybrid of itinerant residency and field study. The pamphlet titled *Lo que llevo en mi memoria*, issued by the artist during the journey, opens with a reflection on the recent dictatorship in Brazil: "In Guatemala, I am aware that by digging in the ground, just like in any place in Latin America, there's a possibility of coming across bones by chance. At the moment I am in the Memory Site Campo La Ribera (Córdoba, Argentina), I dig like a dog, sensing that I might come across fragments of memories . . . in Brazil my memory is erased, the people do not seem to remember the wounds of the past, either from the military dictatorship, or slavery"[47] Kiki Mazzuchelli notes: "In this short fragment, Nazareth makes explicit his search for erased memory and suggests the possibility of discovering it in another land, a different culture but perhaps analogous, that in some way might share common traits with his native land."[48]

Nazareth's wanderlust, his need to meet different people and cultures, aims to foster "unsuspected links in an attempt to reconstruct histories never told or deliberately erased."[49]

> When I invited him to participate in a group show in Paris in 2011, he replied that he would like to participate but that unfortunately he could not be present for he would only arrive in Europe after exploring Africa, the same way that he got to the United States through Latin America. In one of our last conversations, when he was about to end his American journey, he told me:
>
> "I become myself in my mixed ethnicity
>
> I am indian and black
>
> It's incredible"[50]

"His mestizo origin allows him to play with his own image, becoming black, Indian or simply exotic according to the situation," Mazzuchelli writes. One of the performances produced during *News from America* consisted of the artist carrying a poster with the phrase: "Vendo mi imagen de hombre exótico" (Exotic Man Image For Sale). In yet another project, *Cara de índio* (Indian Face), he photographed himself with "city-dwelling indigenous persons from the extreme south to the extreme north of the Americas," comparing his mestizo face to the face of the other.[51]

At the end of his Trans-American itinerary, Nazareth seems to revert and disassemble the art of the conqueror; as Sousândrade described in *O Guesa*: "e os fanfarrões d'Hespanha,/Em sangue edêneo os pés lavando, passam" (and the Spaniards, with their braggadocio/washing their feet in Edenic blood, they go).[52] Marília Librandi-Rocha invites us to consider *O Guesa*—above all the episodes known as "Tatuturema," and "O inferno de Wall Street"—as "performance poems,"[53] as body poems, with their share of "dance" and "pandemonium."[54] In some of his works, Nazareth actually seems to perform what in *O Guesa* was given as virtual.

Walter Benjamin wrote "Origin is a whirlpool in the river of becoming and swallows up the genetic material in its rhythm." When Paulo Nazareth at last dips his feet in the Hudson River, near Wall Street, he proposes something like a counter-origin—returning to the waters the dust of all that apparently is no longer there but that in fact has always been there, a land with an improper name "America" that goes beyond the United States. He adds flux (walking, erring, trailing) to the flux (the river). If *experience* is wandering, dust is experience materialized as residue, relics.

Earth, in this context, contradicts territory; it is the refusal of territoriality, stuck to the body; it creates something like a minimal trans-territorial space, extraterritorial, subterritorial (underground) rather than supraterritorial (celestial). Dissolved in the waters of another territory, it stands as an inscription, like a tattoo, even though a mobile one; an inscription that takes its strength from its immediate dissipation (standing there, yet, putting in question the stability of *there*).

Paulo Nazareth teaches us that, contrary to what we read in Sousândrade's poem, there is no such thing as the *last guesa*. Every *guesa*, albeit a figuration of dubious and mutable identity (which is the Latin-American identity, and, more broadly, post-Western identity) is always the *penultimate*: because there will always be another to testify and to sing "De tudo resta um pouco" (A residue remains from everything), wrote Carlos Drummond de Andrade. And perhaps literature will always be the *residue* that *remains* from *everything* that we call history. The posthumous condition, hinted at by Sousândrade's *last guesa*, is tantamount to surviving; and to survive is to witness, that is, to *insist in the word*. Perhaps the unfinished character of *O Guesa* (a modernist trait present in the oeuvres of Flaubert, Proust, Kafka, Musil, and even Bolaño[55]) can be considered as an attempt to assume this penultimate condition. The ultimate word never arrives. If there is still a word, it is because another will come. Besides the apocalyptical moments in *O Guesa*, Sousândrade seems less interested in the *end of the world* than in what he himself deems as the "world of the end":

> —São d'electricidade
> Tempos, mundo do fim;
> = São as manchas solares,
>   Dos ares
> A alumiar tudo *assim*![56]

Perhaps the same can be said of Paulo Nazareth. Instead of the paralyzing fear in face of the world (space closure by time), Sousândrade and Nazareth opt for a poetic mapping of the *world of the end* (time opening up through space). By facing the world's evil head on, and revealing it in their own time, the poet and the artist kept the possibility of utopia alive.

> Lá está íris!—ha de haver abysmo . . .
> Onde o arco vê-se da visão formosa
> Dobrar-se luminoso, um cataclysmo
> Se deu, ou s'está dando.[57]

We must not forget that it is precisely when Guesa enters into the "Wall Street inferno" and is summoned to leave behind all hope, that "a Voice from the deserts" asks: "Swedenborg, is there a world to come?"[58] Swedenborg's answer comes a few stanzas later, and this postponing of the reply is graphically marked by the poet:

> (SWEDENBORG respondendo *depois*:)
> —Ha mundos futuros: república,
> Christianismo, céus, Lohengrin.
> São mundos presentes:
> Patentes,
> Vanderbilt-North, Sul-Seraphim.[59]

It is from the horror and degradation of "present worlds" that "future worlds" are born. Those who "mourn the world" and go after the world to quench their longing do not mourn the world that was but also the world to come.

Notes

I thank the Fundação de Amparo à Pesquisa do Estado de São Paulo (FAPESP) for their support of my research for this essay. Translation from *O Guesa* by Antonio Sergio Bessa.

1 / Joaquim de Sousândrade, *O Guesa* (São Paulo: Demônio Negro, 2009), 19.

2 / Augusto de Campos, "Errâncias de Sousândrade," in Sousândrade, *O Guesa*, 7.

3 / Sousândrade, *O Guesa*, 60.

4 / See Sousândrade, *O Guesa*, 22, 29, 60, 84.

5 / Marília Librandi-Rocha, "Maranhão-Manhattan: uma ponte entre nós. Uma visão dissonante da literatura e da cultura brasileiras" [2008], in *Maranhão-Manhattan: Ensaios de literatura brasileira* (Rio de Janeiro: 7Letras, 2009), 23.

6 / Librandi-Rocha, 23.

7 / Librandi-Rocha, 24.

8 / Librandi-Rocha, 24.

9 / Librandi-Rocha, 23.

10 / Francisco Foot Hardman, "A Panamérica utópica de Sousândrade", in *A vingança da Hileia: Euclides da Cunha, a Amazônia e a literatura moderna* (São Paulo: Editora UNESP, 2009), 213–224.

11 / Giorgio Agamben, "Giorgio Agamben, intervista a Peppe Savà: Amo Scicli e Guccione," interview with Giuseppe Savà, RagusaNews.com, August 16, 2012, http://www.ragusanews.com/articolo/28021/giorgio-agamben-intervista-a-peppe-sava-amo-scicli-e-guccione.

12 / Luiz Costa Lima, "O campo visual de uma experiência antecipadora: Sousândrade," [The visual field of an anticipatory experience: Sousândrade], in *ReVisão de Sousândrade*, ed. Augusto de Campos and Haroldo de Campos, 2nd ed. (Rio de Janeiro: Nova Fronteira, 1982), 395–434.

13 / Lima, 399–400 and 407.

14 / Lima, 407.

15 / Lima, 410.

16 / "C'était le GUESA, ou l'errant, c'est-à-dire la créature sans asile." Quoted from the encyclopedia *L'Univers, ou histoire et description de tout les peuples, de leurs religions, moeurs, coutumes, etc.—Colombie et Guyanes*, by M. C, Famin, in Sousândrade, O Guesa, 17.

17 / See Giorgio Agamben, *Homo sacer: Il potere sovrano e la nuda vita* (Turim: Einaudi, 2008 [1995]).

18 / Ruy Belo, "Explicação que o autor houve por indispensável antepor a esta segunda edição" [Explanation the author felt indispensible to include in this second edition], in *Aquele grande rio Eufrates* [That great river Euphrates] (1961, 2nd ed. rev. 1972), included in *Todos os poemas* [All the poems] (Lisboa: Assírio & Alvim, 2000), 15. See also Eduardo Sterzi, "A voz da terra," in *Transporte no tempo* [Transported in time], ed. Ruy Belo (Rio de Janeiro: 7Letras, 2014), 7–13.

19 / Sousândrade, *O Guesa*, 291–293.

20 / Sousândrade, 35.

21 / Sousândrade, 38–39.

22 / Sousândrade, 37.

23 / Sousândrade, 47.

24 / Darcy Ribeiro, *Testemunho* (São Paulo: Siciliano, 1991), 94: "Com a expressão, refere-se especificamente aos 'remanescentes atuais de altas civilizações originais contra as quais se chocou a expansão europeia,' isto é, aos sobreviventes das grandes civilizações pré-colombianas, como incas e maias." (The expression refers specifically to the "remnants of the original high civilizations against which European expansion has collided," that is, the survivors of the great pre-Columbian civilizations, such as the Incas and the Maya.)

25 / In *Quel che resta di Auschwitz*, Giorgio Agamben thought "witness" precisely in relation with the remnant, more specifically the notion of the people that remains (*povo que resta*). Giorgio Agamben, *Quel che resta di Auschwitz: L'archivio e il testimone* (Torino: Bollati Boringhieri, 1998).

26 / Eduardo Viveiros de Castro, "A indianidade é um projeto de futuro, não uma memória do passado," interview with Pádua Fernandes, *Prisma Jurídico* 10, no. 2 (July–December 2011): 265.

27 / Déborah Danowski and Eduardo Viveiros de Castro, *Há mundo por vir? Ensaio sobre os medos e os fins* (São Paulo: Instituto Socioambiental, 2014), 158.

28 / See Machado de Assis "[Notícia atual da] Literatura brazileira—Instincto de nacionalidade" [1873], in *Critica litteraria* (Rio de Janeiro: W. M. Jackson, 1944), 136.

29 / Assis, 137.

30 / See "He got the wrong people, earth and blood," in Gilles Deleuze and Félix Guattari, *What Is Philosophy?*, trans. Hugh Tomlinson and Graham Burchell (New York: Columbia University Press, 1994), 109.

31 / Deleuze and Guattari, 109.

32 / Franz Kafka, "The Wish to Be a Red Indian," trans. Alessandro Baruffi, in *The Tales of Franz Kafka: English Translations with Original Text in German* (Philadelphia: Literary Joint Press, 2016), 11.

33 / Oswald de Andrade, "Virar índio" [1946], in *Telefonema*, ed. Vera Maria Chalmers (São Paulo: Globo, 1996), 135–136.

34 / Oswald de Andrade, "O chocalho do xamã é um acelerador de partículas" [1999], interview with Renato Sztutman, Silvana Nascimento, and Stelio

Marras, in *Eduardo Viveiros de Castro*, ed. Renato Sztutman (Rio de Janeiro: Azougue, 2007), 47. Oswald de Andrade, "Uma boa política é aquela que multiplica os possíveis," interview with Renato Sztutman and Stelio Marras, in *Eduardo Viveiros de Castro*, 249.

35 / Eduardo Viveiros de Castro, "No Brasil todo mundo é índio, exceto quem não é," (In Brazil, everyone is Indian except for those who aren't), interview with Carlos Dias Jr., Fany Ricardo, Lívia Chede Almendary, Renato Sztutman, Rogério Duarte do Pateo and Uirá Felippe Garcia, in *Eduardo Viveiros de Castro*, 146.

36 / Castro, 146–147.

37 / Castro, 147.

38 / Castro, 147–148.

39 / Castro, 142.

40 / Castro, 135–137.

41 / Déborah Danowski and Eduardo Viveiros de Castro, *Há mundo por vir? Ensaio sobre os medos e os fins* (São Paulo: Instituto Socioambiental, 2014), 156–157.

42 / J. M. G. Le Clézio, *Índio branco* [1971], trans. Júlio Henriques, (Lisboa: Fenda, 1989), 13.

43 / Augusto de Campos, "Errâncias de Sousândrade" [Sousândrade's wanderings], in Sousândrade, *O Guesa*, 8–9.

44 / Campos and Campos, 109.

45 / Sousândrade, *O Guesa*, 247.

46 / Kiki Mazzucchelli, "Sobre marfins, dentes e ossos: uma breve introdução ao trabalho de Paulo Nazareth" [About ivory, teeth, bones: A brief introduction to the work of Paulo Nazareth], in *Paulo Nazareth: Arte contemporânea/LTDA* (Contemporary Art Inc.), ed. Paulo Nazareth (Rio de Janeiro: Cobogó, 2012), 11–21.

47 / Mazzucchelli, 20–21.

48 / Mazzucchelli, 20.

49 / Mazzucchelli, 20.

50 / Mazzucchelli, 20.

51 / Mazzucchelli, 18.

52 / Sousândrade, *O Guesa*, 20.

53 / Librandi-Rocha, "Maranhão-Manhattan," 49.

54 / Librandi-Rocha, 49.

55 / See also Jorge Herralde, "Respuestas a un cuestionario de la revista *Qué pasa* de Santiago de Chile," in *Para Roberto Bolaño* (Buenos Aires: Adriana Hidalgo, 2005), 65.

56 / Sousândrade, *O Guesa*, 50.

57 / Sousândrade, 284.

58 / Sousândrade, 247. From this verse, Danowski and Castro extracted the title of their volume *Há mundo por vir?*.

59 / Sousândrade, *O Guesa*, 264.

ACKNOWLEDGMENTS

Form and Feeling is the culmination of a conference sponsored by a generous research grant from the Andy Warhol Foundation and presented at the Graduate Center at the City University of New York (CUNY) in 2016. Additional funding for this publication was provided by the Consulate General of Brazil in New York. I am deeply indebted to my colleague Julieta Gonzalez for her valuable input in the initial phase of this project during her tenure as adjunct curator at the Bronx Museum. In addition, we counted on the extraordinary talent of Momo Ishiguro, our grants writer at the time, who was able to organize our ideas into a strong proposal. For the conference, art historian Luisa Valle offered extraordinary support not only in securing a date in the Graduate Center's hectic calendar but also in coordinating travel arrangements for all participants. Anna Indych-López, associate professor of art history at the City College of New York and the Graduate Center embraced our idea from the start, facilitating scheduling and, most importantly, introducing the conference and moderating one of the sections.

I would also like to thank all the participants for their generous reception to our proposal and their insightful contributions: Dr. Michael Asbury (University of the Arts, London); Dr. Irene Small (Princeton University); Dr. Frederico Coelho (Pontifical Catholic University of Rio de Janeiro); Dr. José Lira (School of Architecture and Urbanism, São Paulo University); Dr. Rachel Imanishi (Brasilia National University); Dr. Eduardo Jorge de Oliveira (Zurich University); Dr. Claudia Calirman (John Jay College of Criminal Justice/CUNY); Luisa Valle (The Graduate Center of The City University of New York); Dr. Adele Nelson (University of Texas, Austin) and Dr. Martin Mäntele (director of the museum and archives of the Ulm School of Design). When putting together the manuscript for this book, two participants in the conference withdrew their original papers. To present a more nuanced picture of the era, we reached out to four colleagues and asked for specific contributions in their respective areas. I am extremely indebted to Fernanda Lopes (Curator at Museum of Modern Art, Rio de Janeiro), Claudia Saldanha (Director of Paço Imperial, Rio de Janeiro), Marcos Augusto Gonçalves (Journalist at Folha de São Paulo, and author of *1922: A Semana que não terminou*), and Eduardo Sterzi (Campinas University, São Paulo) for their utmost professionalism and spirit of collaboration. Their contributions helped make this collection a valuable resource for those interested in a cultural moment unfolding throughout a turbulent period in Brazilian history.

Finally, I would like to thank the individuals and institutions that collaborated with this project in kindly granting permission to research in their archives. They include: Ginevra Bria and Atto Belolli Ardessi at Istituto Internazionale di Studi sul Futurismo in Milan, Italy, for allowing access to the archives of Mary Vieira; Jakob Bill for granting an interview at Max Bill's residence in Zurich, Switzerland; Martin Mäntele at the Hochschule für Gestaltung in Ulm, Germany, for allowing me to research in the school's archives; Mrs. Sigrid Mavignier for coordinating a meeting with Almir Mavignier in Hamburg, Germany, where I also had the opportunity to visit the artist's studio; Beny Palatnik for coordinating a meeting with Abraham Palatnik in his apartment in Rio de Janeiro, Brazil. In addition, I would like to thank those who granted permission to reproduce images from their archives and collections: Alessandra Clark and Fabiane Moraes at the World of Lygia Clark; Cesar Oiticica and Ariane Figueiredo at Projeto HO; Luciano Figueiredo for images related to Navilouca; the Acervo do Centro de Pesquisa do MASP; the Arquivo Fundação Bienal de São Paulo; Mendes Wood DM; Nara Roesler Gallery; Hugo Segawa for images of Flávio de Carvalho; Anna Maria Maiolino and Livia Gonzaga, at Studio Anna Maria Maiolino; the interlibrary services at the University of Texas at Austin; and Isadora Porfirio at Instituto Bardi—Casa de Vidro.

CONTRIBUTORS

Michael Asbury is a London-based art historian, art critic, and curator. He is Reader of Art History and Theory at Chelsea College of Arts, University of the Arts London (UAL) and founding member of the Research Centre for Transnational Art, Identity and Nation (TrAIN). Over the last twenty years he has written extensively on themes involving modern and contemporary art with a particular emphasis on Brazilian culture. His work has been published internationally by Americas Society, Art in America, Astrup Fearnley, Cisneros Fontanals Art Foundation, Cosac Naify, Documenta Kassel (12), Fundação Calouste Gulbenkian, Flash Art, Fundação Iberê Camargo, Liverpool University Press, MIT Press, Perspectiva, Rodopi, Schirn Kunsthalle Frankfurt, Tate Publishing, Third Text, Turner Contemporary, and Wilhelm/Fink, among others. He has curated a number of exhibitions on artists such as Alfredo Volpi, Anna Maria Maiolino, Antonio Manuel, Cao Guimaraes, Cildo Meireles, Detanico and Lain, Ibere Camargo, Jose Oiticica Filho, José Patricio, and Rosangela Rennó as well as on themes such as Brazilian photography and architecture, concrete and neoconcrete art, and the monochrome in contemporary art.

Antonio Sergio Bessa is chief curator emeritus at the Bronx Museum of the Arts, and used to lead a museum education seminar at Columbia University's Teachers College (2006–2016). A scholar of concrete poetry, he has organized several exhibitions on themes related to text-based art, including *Double Space* (Apex Art, New York, 2000); *Re: La Chinoise* (Baumgartner Gallery, New York, 2002); *Animating Fahlström* (BAWAG Foundation, Vienna, and the Institut d'Art Contemporain, Lyon, France, 2002). At the Bronx Museum he organized a series of exhibitions, including *How to Read* (2005), *Paulo Bruscky: Art is Our Last Hope* (2013), *Martin Wong: Human Instamatic* (in collaboration with Yasmin Ramírez, 2015), *Gordon Matta-Clark: Anarchitect* (in collaboration with Jessamyn Fiore, 2017); and *The Life and Times of Alvin Baltrop* (2019). His essays on concrete poetry and art have been published in several anthologies and catalogs, including *Öyvind Fahlström* (1998), *Architectures of Poetry* (2004), and *The Sound of Poetry/The Poetry of Sound* (2009), *Poetry Goes Visual* (2012). He is the author of *Öyvind Fahlström: The Art of Writing* (2009) and editor (with Odile Cisneros) of *Novas: Selected Writings of Haroldo de Campos* (2007) and *Mary Ellen Solt: Toward a Theory of Concrete Poetry* (2010).

Claudia Calirman is associate professor in the Department of Art and Music at John Jay College of Criminal Justice, New York. Her areas of study are Latin American, modern, and contemporary art. She is the author of *Brazilian Art under Dictatorship: Antonio Manuel, Artur Barrio, and Cildo Meireles* (2012), which analyzes the intersection of politics and the visual arts during the most repressive years of Brazil's military regime from 1968 to 1975. The book received the 2013 Arvey Award by the Association for Latin American Art. Calirman is a recipient of the Arts Writers Grant from Creative Capital/Warhol Foundation and was a Visiting Scholar at the David Rockefeller Center for Latin American Studies at Harvard University. She is a member of the International Association of Art Critics (AICA). Calirman has curated several exhibitions in New York, including *Berna Reale: While You Laugh* (2019); *Basta! Art and Violence in Latin America* (2016); and *Antonio Manuel: I Want to Act, not Represent!* (2011).

Frederico Coelho is a researcher, essayist, and professor of Brazilian literature and performing arts in the Department of Literature at the Pontifícia Universidade Católica do Rio de Janeiro (PUC-Rio). He has an MA in history from Instituto de Filosofia e Ciências Sociais at Universidade Federal do Rio de Janeiro and a PhD in literature from PUC-Rio. He was a researcher for the exhibitions *Tropicália—A Revolution in Brazilian Culture* (2006) and *Hélio Oiticica—To Organize Delirium* (2018). His publications include *Livro ou livro-me: os escritos babilônicos de Hélio Oiticica* (2010), *Eu, brasileiro, confesso minha culpa e meu pecado: cultura marginal no Brasil 1960/1970* (2010), and (with César Oiticica Filho) *Hélio Oiticica: Conglomerado/Newyorkaises* (2013).

Marcos Augusto Gonçalves is a journalist and the editor of *Ilustríssima*, the cultural supplement of *Folha de São Paulo*. He is the author of *1922—A Semana que não Terminou* (2012) and coauthor (with Heloísa Buarque de Holanda) of *Cultura e Partipação nos anos 60* (1983).

José T. Lira is professor at the School of Architecture and Urbanism at the University of São Paulo (FAU-USP). He used to be a research affiliate of the Brazilian National Council of Research (CNPq, 1999–2014) and directed USP's Center for Cultural Preservation (CPC-USP, 2010–2014). His PhD dissertation (FAU-USP, 1997) explores the connections between housing debates, urban culture, and architectural and planning discourses in Recife, Brazil, in the first half of the twentieth century. His post-doctoral research (Tese de Livre Docência, FAU-USP, 2008) focuses on the life and work of Ukrainian avant-garde architect Gregori Warchavchik (1896–1972) in Brazil from the 1920s to the 1950s. He has been a visiting scholar at Columbia University's Graduate School of Architecture, Planning and Preservation (2009) and at the École Nationale Supérieure d'Architecture de Paris—Malaquais (2015), as well as a visiting professor in the Program in Latin American Studies and the School of Architecture at Princeton University (2020). He is the author of

O visível e o invísivel na arquitetura brasileira/The visible and the invisible in Brazilian architecture (2017) and *Warchavchik: Fraturas da vanguarda* (2011); coeditor of *Domesticidade, gênero e cultura material* (2017), *Patrimônio construído da USP: Políticas de proteção, gestão e memória* (2014), *Memória, trabalho e arquitetura* (2013), and *São Paulo: Os estrangeiros e a construção das cidades* (2011); and contributor to numerous books and journals, writing on architectural and planning history and criticism; modernism, architecture, and the city; Brazilian social thinking; housing history; architecture's material production; and ethnicity, gender, and sexuality in architecture and urbanism.

Fernanda Lopes is assistant curator of the Museum of Modern Art in Rio de Janeiro. She received her MA and her PhD in art history and criticism from the School of Fine Arts at Universidade Federal do Rio de Janeiro (UFRJ). She is coeditor (with Aristoteles A. Predebon) of *Francisco Bittencourt: Arte-Dinamite* (2016) as well as author of *Área experimental: lugar, espaço e dimensão do experimental na arte brasileira dos anos 1970* (2012) and *"Éramos o time do Rei"—A Experiência Rex* (2006). Her curating experience includes the Special Room of the Rex Group at the 29th São Paulo Biennial (2010). In 2017 she received the Brazilian Art Critic Association's Maria Eugênia Franco Prize for Best Exhibition Curatorship for the exhibition *In a frenzy—An overview of the Museum of Modern Art of Rio de Janeiro Collection* at the Museu de Arte Moderna do Rio de Janeiro (2016).

Martin Mäntele is lecturer in design history and exhibition theory at the Ulm Polytechnic, Würzburg Polytechnic, and Schwäbisch Gmünd Polytechnic. He is also the director of public relations and education at the Museum Ulm and, since 2013, of the HfG-Archiv, the archive of the former Ulm School of Design (1953–1968). After studying art history and modern German literature at the universities of Tübingen, Newcastle upon Tyne, and Hamburg, he received his MA and PhD in art history from the University of Tübingen. His publications include *Ulmer Modelle—Modelle nach Ulm* (2003), an exhibition catalog published in conjunction with a travelling exhibition celebrating the 50th founding anniversary of the Ulm School of Design.

Simone Homem de Mello is a poet and translator. Her poems are collected in *Périplos* (São Paulo, 2005), *Extravio Marinho* (São Paulo, 2010), and *Terminal, à escrita* (São Paulo, 2015), as well as in anthologies of Brazilian contemporary poetry. She has written libretti for operas, including *Orpheus Kristall* (composed by Manfred Stahnke, Munich, 2002), *Keine Stille außer der des Windes* (composed by Sidney Corbett, Bremen, 2007) and *UBU—Eine musikalische Groteske* (composed by Sidney Corbett, Gelsenkirchen, 2012). She has translated into Portuguese novels by Peter Handke and several modern and contemporary German poets (including Arno Holz, Thomas Kling, Ulf Stolterfoht, and Barbara Köhler). She has also translated Augusto de Campos's poems into German (*Augusto de Campos: Poesie*, 2019). Mello studied German literature at the University of São Paulo and at the University of Cologne. Her PhD thesis in translation studies at the University of Santa Catarina is about the translation of avant-garde poetry. From 2012 to 2014, she coordinated the Centro de Referência Haroldo de Campos (Casa das Rosas, São Paulo). Since 2011 she has directed the Center for Literary Translation Studies at the museum Casa Guilherme de Almeida in São Paulo.

Adele Nelson is an assistant professor in the Department of Art and Art History at the University of Texas at Austin, where she is also associate director of the Center for Latin American Visual Studies (CLAVIS). She received her BA in Portuguese and Brazilian Studies and Art Semiotics from Brown University and her MA and PhD in Art History from the Institute of Fine Arts, New York University. She specializes in twentieth- and twenty-first-century art of Latin America, with a focus on the postwar and contemporary art of Brazil. She is the author of *Jac Leirner in Conversation with Adele Nelson* (Fundación Cisneros, 2011), which was translated into Portuguese by Cosac Naify in 2013. Her articles have been published in *Art Journal* and *ARTMargins* and national and international museum publications, including *Lygia Clark: Painting as an Experimental Field* (2020), *Mário Pedrosa: De la naturaleza afetiva de la forma* (2017), *Hélio Oiticica: To Organize Delirium* (2016), *Mário Pedrosa: Primary Documents* (2015). Nelson is co-organizing, with MacKenzie Stevens, the exhibition *Social Fabric: Art and Activism in Contemporary Brazil* for the Visual Arts Center at the University of Texas at Austin in fall 2021. The project has received the Andy Warhol Foundation for the Visual Arts grant. She also contributed to the catalog and helped to organize the award-winning exhibition *Joan Miró: Painting and Anti-Painting, 1927–1937* (MoMA, 2008). Her current book project, *Forming Abstraction: Art and Institutions in Postwar Brazil*, studies how the practice and theory of abstract art developed in Brazil in the 1940s and 1950s in close relation to new modern art institutions. Her research has been supported by the Fulbright US Scholar Program and the National Endowment for the Humanities.

Eduardo Jorge de Oliveira is assistant professor at the Institute of Romance Studies at the University of Zurich, where he also coordinates the Institute of Brazilian Studies (literature, culture, media). He published several articles on the topic of animals and animality in Brazilian art and literature, concrete poetry, and performance and contemporary literature. His research interests include literature and visual arts; modernities and migration in literature and art, representations of violence, and technics of writing.

Claudia Saldanha is the director of Paço Imperial in Rio de Janeiro, an institution dedicated to contemporary art. She has a PhD degree in visual arts from UERJ and an MFA degree from Pratt Institute, New York, and teaches art history at the Universidade do Estado do Rio de Janeiro (UERJ). She also used to be the director of the Escola de Artes Visuais do Parque Lage (2008–2014), the Division of Theory and Research at the Museum of Contemporary Art, Niterói, Rio de Janeiro (2003–2005), and the Visual Arts Division at RioArte (1993–2005) and organized many notable exhibitions, including: *Alviceleste*, a survey of performance artist Márcia X; *Paulo Roberto Leal—Espaços Articulados*, at Paço Imperial (2015); *Paulo Werneck—Muralista Brasileiro* at the Museu de Arte Moderna de Recife and the Museu de Arte da Pampulha, Belo Horizonte (2014); Pinacoteca do Estado de São Paulo and at Caixa Cultural de Brasília (2011); *Da Matéria Nasce a Forma—Paulo Roberto Leal* at Museum of Contemporary Art, Niterói (2007); *Abrigo Poético—Diálogos com Lygia Clark*, at the Museum of Contemporary Art, Niterói (2006); *Márcia X.*, at Galerie Weisser Elephant, Berlin (2006); *Márcia X. Revista*, at Paço Imperial (2005); *Insertae Sedis: José Rufino*, at Museum of Contemporary Art, Niterói (2005).

Eduardo Sterzi is a writer, critic, curator, and professor of literary theory at Universidade Estadual de Campinas (Unicamp), where he also coordinates the Graduate Program in literary theory and history. His research includes the relations between the Middle Ages and modernity in literature, as well as the *topos* of the waste land in modern and contemporary poetry and the survival and dissolution of myth, as well as the relationship between anthropology, literature, and the arts in Sousândrade, Oswald de Andrade, and Mário de Andrade. He cocurated the traveling exhibition *Variations of the Wild Body: Eduardo Viveiros de Castro, Photographer* (SESC Ipiranga, São Paulo, Brazil, September 2015 to January 2016; Weltkulturenmuseum in Frankfurt, Germany, November 2017; and International Center of Arts José de Guimarães, Portugal, February 2019). He carried out part of his doctoral (2003–2004) and postdoctoral (2009) research at the Università degli Studi di Roma La Sapienza in Italy. He received scholarships from the main research promotion agencies in Brazil (CAPES, CNPq and FAPESP). His publications include *Por que ler Dante* (2008) and *A prova dos nove: alguma poesia moderna e a tarefa da alegria* (2008), *Prosa* (2001), *Aleijão* (2009), *Cavalo sopa martelo* (2011), and *Maus poemas* (2016). He used to be the editor of *Do céu do futuro: cinco ensaios sobre Augusto de Campos*.

Luisa Valle is a doctoral candidate in art history at the Graduate Center, City University of New York (CUNY). Her research focuses on Latin American architecture and its implications for art production from the region, with a special interest in the local, national, and global contexts of modernism. She has published articles on Roberto Burle Marx and the synthesis of the arts, Mary Vieira and concretism, and Thomas Hirschorn's *Gramsci Monument*. She is in the process of finishing her dissertation entitled "The Beehive, the Favela, the Mangrove, and the Castle: Modern Architecture in Rio de Janeiro, 1885–1945." She has received several fellowships—including a CUNY Teaching Fellowship at Hunter College and an Avery Foundation/The Bronx Museum of the Arts Curatorial Fellowship—and has taught art and architectural history at the City College of New York and Hunter College.

INDEX

Page numbers in italics indicate an illustration.

Form and Feeling: The Making of Concretism in Brazil is made possible with major funding from the Andy Warhol Foundation for the Visual Arts, with additional support from the Consulate General of Brazil in New York.

Operations of The Bronx Museum of the Arts are generously supported, in part, with public funds from the City of New York, Mayor Bill de Blasio, New York City Department of Cultural Affairs, Bronx Borough President Ruben Diaz Jr., New York City Council and the Bronx Delegation, and the New York State Council on the Arts with the support of Governor Andrew M. Cuomo and the New York State Legislature. Additional support is provided by the Charina Endowment Fund, Cowles Charitable Trust, Donald A. Pels Charitable Trust, Francena Harrison Foundation, Ford Foundation, Jockey Hollow Foundation, Lambent Foundation Fund of Tides Foundation, Lily Auchincloss Foundation, Marshall Family Foundation, May and Samuel Rudin Family Foundation, New York Yankees Foundation, NYC COVID-19 Response and Impact Fund in The New York Community Trust, Shelley & Donald Rubin Foundation, Rockefeller Brothers Fund: Culpeper Arts & Culture Program, Scherman Foundation, Individuals and Bronx Museum Board of Trustees.

BRONXMUSEUM

The Andy Warhol Foundation for the Visual Arts

CONSULATE GENERAL OF BRAZIL NEW YORK